HIS
FAVORITE
WIFE

HIS
FAVORITE
WIFE

TRAPPED IN POLYGAMY

A true story of violent fanaticism.
SUSAN RAY SCHMIDT

His Favorite Wife–Trapped in Polygamy
by Susan Ray Schmidt
© 2006

First Edition, May 2006
Second Edition, September 2006

Cover photo by Scott McKinney
Book design and typography by Hunt's Graphic Arts
A production of Kassidy Lane Publishing, L.L.C.
Logo design by Suzann Nielsen
www.kassidylane.com

Questions?
Go to susan@hisfavoritewife.com
Printed in China.

ISBN 0-9779730-0-X

Acknowledgments

I wish to extend my heartfelt gratitude to the following people, who in various ways had a hand in the successful completion of this book. First of all, thank you, Pat Kaes, for your initial belief in my story and for your tutorship and patience with my inept efforts when I began this book so many years ago. To my friends and fellow authors, Dean Shapiro and Dean Pettinger, thank you for the amazing faith you displayed in my story and for patiently coaching me in my search for a publisher. To fellow author Cliff Johnson, bless you for your cheerful guidance and for your altruistic assistance in seeing that the publishing of my book became a reality. I couldn't have done it without you.

To my Aunt Susanne Morley, a talented writer and poet, to Connie Woebke and to fellow author, Lowell Gard and his wife Mary Carol, and to my friends Barbara Kelly and Daryl Hunt, words are not adequate thanks for the many hours you selflessly gave in editing the manuscript. God love you all! I'll never forget your goodness to me.

My appreciation goes to the following people for reading *His Favorite Wife* and for cheering me on. First of all, to Darren Belin and his wife, Leslie, for challenging me to blow the dust off the pages sitting so long on the shelf and get the darn thing finished; then for reading the completed manuscript and assuring me it was wonderful. To Eleanore Burkhart, retired English teacher, who after reading several chapters called to assure me I had an innate writing talent. She would have laughed to see my frantic scrambling through the dictionary to look up the word, innate. Thank you, Eleanore, for spurring me on.

Many thanks to my friends Kathy Nielsen, Victoria Ray, Stuart Bearup, Bill Studebaker, Flo Harper, Cindi Schmidt, Kay Wilson, Shirley White, Betty Veeh, Jody Wright, Bob Erickson, Marlene DeWiese, and Lisa Gauger, for giving me rave reviews. But most of all, to my daughter, Melanie, who upon completing chapter 28, dashed out to purchase and send me a beautiful new guitar. I love you, honey.

Thanks to my son, Forrest, a tireless entrepreneur, for his strong faith in the book and his energetic, cheerful assistance in the marketing of it.

Thanks to my new friend Kathy, who loaned me the perfect old pickup for the cover's photo. A mountain of thanks to my long time friend, Scott

McKinney, a gifted photographer, who patiently took shot after shot until he caught the perfect one for the book's cover.

To my daughter, Jeannette; thanks for loving the book and for resembling me enough to be the model for 'Susan' on the jacket. And to my grandchildren, Dakota, Bailey, and Sailor, you were perfect and patient models of the 'children'. Thank you, my darlings! I am so blessed!

Lastly to my husband, Dennis, who for many years put up with my hours in front of the computer, who brought me food and drink night after night, and who selflessly allowed me to tell the story of my "other life." I am the luckiest woman in the world.

Author's Note

I n telling this story, my wish was not to offend, and if I've done so, I extend my deepest apologies. Although I've chosen to no longer live the lifestyle depicted in *His Favorite Wife*, I do understand and in some instances respect the reasons why the fundamentalist Mormon people cling to the practices of early Mormonism.

While the events related here are factual, for brevity's sake and for story flow I've taken the liberty of compiling, on rare occasions, two separate events into one. In a couple of minor instances, I've placed myself as present during an incident when in reality I heard the details from eyewitnesses. My reason for this was to present my readers with a "bird's eye view" of something I deemed important to the story.

The conversations I've recorded are not verbatim, but are as close as my memory allows. I've endeavored to relate the facts as best I can.

Susan Ray Schmidt

"And it shall come to pass that I, the Lord God, will send one mighty and strong, whose mouth shall utter words, eternal words; while his bowels shall be a fountain of truth, to set in order the house of God."

–Doctrine and Covenants
Section 85:7

Fading Footsteps

By Verlan M. LeBaron

You inspire a glow within me that sets my heart aflame
In the lonely hours of darkness, I softly call your name.
In dreams I feel you hold me in your sweet and tender way,
Sweetheart, I am so lonely as your footsteps fade away.

You say that if I love you I will somehow let you go,
If to love you is to lose you and if what you say is so—
I want you to be happy, don't mind the tears I shed,
You're free to go my darling, and forget the vows we said.

In dreams please always hold me in your sweet and tender way,
Awake I am so lonely, as your footsteps fade away,
As your footsteps fade away . . .

Prologue

"Run! Run!" I gasped, pushing at Melanie's back. I clutched James' hand and half-dragged his small body across the uneven ground. At the back of Dad's lot I pulled the barbwire fence apart, shoved the kids through and dropped the bundle I carried over the fence. Then Mona and I climbed through after them. We dashed into the orchard—they wouldn't find us deep in the trees. Mona raced next to me, my baby bouncing up and down in her arms.

Our rushing steps through the frozen underbrush crashed in my ears, and I cringed and darted a quick look behind us. The hazy, early morning silence around Colonia LeBaron seemed ominous. Not even a dog barked. Halfway through the orchard, I found a large tree with a deep ditch bank around it. We spread one blanket and hunkered down under the low, frost-covered branches, then covered up with the heavy quilt.

"What's happening, Mama?"

The terror in my eldest daughter's eyes mirrored my own fear. She was so innocent, so helpless. How could she ever comprehend that her uncle desired to murder us?

Mona's gaze met mine for an instant. With a shudder, she buried her chalk-white face against the baby's blanket-wrapped body and slumped against the tree trunk. I pulled James closer to me and zipped up his coat. My voice quivering, I whispered, "All of you be very, very quiet. We have to stay here for awhile, so let's just get comfortable and take a little rest ... "

Anguished thoughts of the Los Molinos colony, of my husband's families, and the others there—bloody and dying—God, please, let them be okay, just let them be okay, my heart chanted. Please Lord, please! Don't let them be dead or hurt!

I couldn't begin to imagine the terror all those poor people had gone through ... just last night ... while we, here in their sister colony of Colonia LeBaron, had been sleeping snug and warm in our beds. There were so many children in Los Molinos, women and little children ... What would happen to us? Were we truly next, were the Ervilites actually headed here, to our beautiful Chihuahua colony?

1

Thank God I had decided to leave Los Molinos... And, oh! Thank God that Verlan and some of his wives were safe in Nicaragua! Verlan would have been the Ervilite's prime target...

Los Molinos was burned! My house, with its rose-colored windowsills that I'd painted so carefully, was it still standing? Well, it didn't matter. Who of Ervil LeBaron's people had done this dastardly act? Ervil himself wouldn't dirty his hands...

Chapter 1

E stela Stubbs' dark, Mexican features scowled at me from her seat half way down the aisle of our adobe church. I grimaced with frustration, then returned my gaze to the open hymnbook perched on the piano in front of me. While my fingers automatically roamed over the keys, my attention stubbornly remained on the Stubbs couple seated among the small congregation. The woman was so possessive! All I'd done was grin at Lane, Estela's husband, and that was because he'd winked one of those flirtatious, sage-green eyes at me. Estela was sure out to make our romance difficult.

Even though I was only fourteen years old, I envisioned myself possibly becoming Lane's second wife. Once we were married I certainly wouldn't be jealous or possessive. Unlike Estela, I would willingly share my husband with any other wives he might take, as our faith commanded.

I wiggled around on the piano bench and tried to concentrate on the prelude music before me. But suddenly the special, rare comment my mother made coming to church this morning flashed through my mind. I pursed my lips to hide another grin and allowed my mind to wander back ...

Colonia LeBaron, the central gathering place for the members of our church, nestled against the hills at the north end of a cacti-covered desert two hundred miles south of El Paso. It was mid-April 1968, and the Mexican sun felt warm and delicious as my family strolled up the dusty road toward the whitewashed adobe building where we held Sunday services. The colony's dirt roads were lined with cottonwood and black walnut trees. Shiny new leaves sparkled, and the heady aroma from the fresh-cut alfalfa fields wafted toward us. I slowed my steps and looked around, delight and excitement bursting inside me.

The colony's scattered adobe dwellings, with their gardens and barns and water towers, reflected prosperity to me today. The desert valley felt alive and pulsed with color; the hills above us were covered with prickly pear cacti in full, wine-colored bloom. Everything was in readiness for the Lord's Sabbath, made special because of the prophet Joel LeBaron, leader of our church. He had returned after a lengthy absence, and he would speak to his people today. The soft morning air held an attitude of expectancy.

I glanced down at my new Sunday dress and carefully smoothed the pale pink material. Undoubtedly the most beautiful dress I had ever owned, the polished cotton sleeves were puffed and trimmed with white lace. The wide sash accented the smallness of my waist, while a white, lace-trimmed collar adorned the neck and dipped daringly low over the swell of my chest—so low that I had anxiously watched Mama's face, expecting her disapproval. She smiled though, and told me that I looked very pretty. Even now her unusual compliment sang through my mind. "You look lovely today, Susan, you really do. Pretty as a flower."

I skipped a step and grinned, the knowledge heady and powerful. I was pretty as the desert blossoms around me. Of course, any girl would look good in this dress—it was almost brand new. No one would guess that it came from the sack of Salvation Army discards my father had brought from the states. The dress had to be a mistake. Someone at the Salvation Army store had goofed.

I chuckled, delighted at my good fortune, and then glanced at Dad, noting how his short legs stretched wide with each step and how his sharp blue eyes blazed with purpose. Bald, other than a fringe of graying hair circling his head, at fifty-seven Vern Ray was robust and energetic. He clung firmly to his faith and championed our prophet, Joel LeBaron, with every ounce of his vigor.

I was only six when Dad moved my mother and the five youngest of their nine children (the ones still living at home) away from Utah and the traditional Mormon Church. Without a backward glance, Vern Ray's family joined Joel LeBaron's fledgling Church of the Firstborn in a small colony named Colonia LeBaron, in the Mexican State of Chihuahua. We became part of a group of fundamentalist pioneers who, contrary to the mainstream Mormons, weren't afraid to live the teachings of Joseph Smith to their fullness.

Like most of the men of the Church of the Firstborn, Dad had heartily embraced the doctrine of polygamy. My mother was past the childbearing age, but Dad's plural wife, Maria, thirty years younger, had given him four more children. I foresaw more before she was through. Her dusky-colored daughters flocked around her, their black braids and dark eyes in sharp contrast to my mother's blond, blue-eyed family. My older brother Jay sauntered along next to Dad. Fara and Mona, my two younger sisters, walked on either side of Mom. My father's two wives and thirteen children were his greatest joy and his chief triumph. We would be jewels in his crown in heaven.

I noticed the prophet as he walked from his first wife Magdalena's yard. His long, lean frame swayed with the peculiar lumbering gait common to all five LeBaron men—the brothers who had united to be our leaders. Joel's reddish blond hair rebelliously stuck up in the back. His dark green suit hung limp; his thin shoulders bowed with the weight of his claim of being the only true, living prophet of God on Earth. He claimed to be carrying the unparalleled responsibility of readying the world for Christ's Second Coming and we accepted his claims to such divine inspiration.

But as Joel rounded the corner, walked over the cattle guard, and entered the churchyard, I thought that he lacked the majestic, commanding qualities a prophet should possess. He didn't look like the Moses from the movie *The Ten Commandments*. I'd seen it twice, and I was secretly disappointed in the homely appearance of our prophet. He didn't seem like a religious leader, but more like a sunburned, poverty-stricken farmer.

Throughout the colony, people were coming for the meeting, the men in their Sunday suits, the women in long, ankle-length dresses, and the abundant numbers of children scrubbed and polished. I waved at the Leanys, who noisily hurried ahead of us. The two Leany boys just older then me ran ahead like wild goats, and I eyed them with secret contempt. They still acted like small, rowdy children. No wonder the young ladies of the church were attracted to our older men.

Shading my eyes from the bright sun, I dawdled at the crossroads and peered south toward "Stubbsville" where Brother Stubbs had settled with his two large families. My eldest sister Rose Ann had married the eldest Stubbs boy, Harv, who had built her a house close to his father's clan. But it wasn't Rose Ann I'd been anxious to see. Fara, my thirteen-year-old sister had stopped and whispered, "I'll bet I know who you're looking for, but Estela'll be with him today, and she won't let you near him. Poor Sue, it's so sad!"

I made a face, knowing she was right. Lane Stubbs' wife, Estela, was a newcomer to the church, and she still balked against our belief that husbands had the right to date and marry other women, and that as men of the Church of the Firstborn, they were commanded by God to have more than one wife. We believed that plural marriage was one of the most sacred revelations God gave to Joseph Smith. It was a test of our faith and a requirement for our ascent into Celestial Glory, the highest of the three degrees of glory in heaven that our church believed in. Estela didn't understand this.

Although polygamy was practiced among Utah's Latter-day Saint Mormons for more than 50 years, it was made illegal in the late 19th century, and discarded as a pre-condition for Utah becoming a state. But the practice secretly went on, and a number of "fundamentalist Mormon" churches were founded to accommodate those who refused to abandon what they considered the "true faith."

Our Mormon doctrine also taught that we were the literal, spirit-offspring of God, born first in heaven to heavenly Mothers who were the wives of God the Father. In order for our spirits to obtain bodies of flesh, we must be born again, here on earth. Thus, we members of God's True Church needed to save as many as possible of his spirit-children from being born into worldly homes, to parents who didn't live the fullness of the gospel. Therefore, plural marriage not only was a test for the righteous; it also provided a way for each man to create fleshly bodies for large numbers of God's spirit-children. It was the gospel's continuing revelations, from the teachings of God's martyred prophet, Joseph Smith, and from the mouth of the man we believed to be his true successor, Joel LeBaron.

"Susan, dear." My mother interrupted my thoughts. "Take Thelma's hand and watch her for your Mama Maria during church. She's got her hands full with the baby."

Oh, no! I groaned inwardly, my excitement and anticipation about the day's possibilities coming to an abrupt halt. Why did it always have to be me? Angrily, I grabbed my three-year-old half-sister's chubby hand. Her mischievous black eyes twinkled at me, and I groaned aloud.

"Gracias, Susana." Maria smiled her gratitude, then added, "Thelma will be a good girl today, won't you Thelmita?"

Fat chance of that, I thought, yanking Thelma's hand and pulling her into the dark interior of the church. I loved my sisters, but I was weary of being the built-in baby sitter. Soon I would be married and someone else could have the pleasure. Fara was only a year younger than I was and it seemed she should also help. But she was such a scatterbrain, and at fourteen I was the oldest girl at home, so I was expected to baby sit.

Francisca Widmar, my closest friend, was in our usual spot. I scooted down the bench, and lifting Thelma up, I plopped her little behind firmly on the seat between Franny and me. "Now, don't you dare move!" I hissed. Her black eyes, shaped just like my blue ones, looked innocently back at me.

"Oh, great. I see you have the little terror again," Franny muttered. "And I guess I'm supposed to hang onto her while you play the hymns. I guess it won't kill me."

I whispered my thanks and walked towards the piano in my most ladylike fashion, sitting carefully on the edge of the bench, just as Grandma Maud LeBaron, my piano teacher and mother of the five LeBaron brothers, had taught me. I made sure my back was straight and my knees were together; then, arranging the skirt of my new dress to billow perfectly around me, I opened the hymnal and began to play. The people standing around the room visiting in little groups took their seats.

Returning to the present, I glanced up for a moment. On the platform behind the pulpit sat Brother Joel, his legs crossed at the knees, a Bible opened on his lap. He'd been away from Colonia LeBaron for a few months, and his followers were excited to have him home. We looked to him to lead us to heaven.

Next to Joel, and looking tanned and elegant in a white shirt and gray tie sat our church patriarch, Ervil LeBaron. The tallest of the five lanky brothers, he stood six foot five, and every inch of him exhibited self-assurance and an electrifying magnetism. Fascinated, I studied him as the congregation finally stood and began singing the opening hymn.

Ervil's cool, blue-gray eyes roamed the crowd on the hard wooden benches—the very benches my Grandfather Ray had built before his death. His bold glare hesitated, sizing people up and measuring their abilities and their weaknesses. What exactly his job as patriarch consisted of, I wasn't certain, but I did know that he was a master at preaching from the books that our church considered scripture.

These books consisted of the Holy Bible; *The Book of Mormon*, considered by Mormons as the history of a family from Jerusalem who became the very first inhabitants of the Americas; *The Doctrine and Covenants*, a series of God-given revelations to Joseph Smith; and, the *Pearl of Great Price*, more revelations to Joseph Smith. We had other books also, histories of latter-day prophets and presidents, such as the *Discourses of Brigham Young*. One of this leader's most famous teachings was the Word of Wisdom, from which derived the Mormon belief that for health's sake, caffeinated drinks shouldn't be consumed, nor should we partake of pork, smoke, or use liquor. Our church members adhered to these teachings. My own father, however, paid little attention to the Word of Wisdom. He still smoked occasionally, and he and my mother both indulged in their morning coffee habit.

Latter-Day Saint Mormons in Utah considered Brigham Young to be Joseph Smith's true successor, but our Church considered him to be only a great leader, pioneer, and man of God. We believed Joseph Smith's true successor to be Joel, our own beloved prophet.

Ervil's eyes watched me, and I swallowed and looked nervously back at my music. He was a hell and damnation preacher, and everybody here knew he considered his elder brother Joel to be simple man and a weak leader. The adult members of the church observed an ongoing power struggle, over matters that I didn't understand. I had heard Dad, Mom, and Maria discussing the situation many times. Just the sight of Ervil caused me uneasiness.

Next to Ervil and sharing his hymnal stood Verlan LeBaron, the youngest of the five LeBaron brothers. Verlan held the lofty position of President of the church's Twelve Apostles. I hardly knew Verlan. I'd been only eight or nine when he moved his five wives and two dozen kids away from our colony. They'd gone to a Mexican town in the mountains for a few years, then recently on to Los Molinos, our church's brand new sister colony starting somewhere out on the Baja California peninsula.

It was rare to see so many of the LeBaron brothers all in the same place. Usually they were scattered around on missions, or in Baja, or somewhere taking care of the Lord's business. It was a special day indeed for us here in Colonia LeBaron.

After the second hymn I returned to my seat. "Whew," Francisca whispered as she relinquished a squirming Thelma to my care. "She is such a handful! I can't keep her quiet—how do you do it?"

I reached for Thelma's arm and squeezed hard. With my meanest look, I glared into her black pupils. She stared back at me, her will as strong as my own, but finally her eyes watered and she blinked. She relaxed with a sigh and sat in a dejected heap. I shot Franny a triumphant look and settled back for Joel's message. As an up-and-coming young woman of the Church, I really needed to pay attention.

"My dear brothers and sisters," the prophet began, then hesitated as Apostle Hector Spencer translated his words into Spanish. "It's so good to be back among you again," Joel paused and waited for Hector to echo his words. "Although most of my families are in Los Molinos, my heart reminds me Colonia LeBaron is still home." He searched the congregation for his first wife, Magdalena, smiling into her dark eyes. Magdalena's features softened in appreciation at the compliment that her husband, a man with four other wives, had given her in front of the congregation. She looked steadily back at him as he continued. "I'm pleased to tell you that Los Molinos is progressing

8

beautifully. We have two fine adobe buildings up. The largest one we're using for a combination church-schoolhouse, the other one for a tool storage building. Meanwhile our people there are getting by in tents and a few trailers. All ten families are working steadily to erect homes so that the living conditions will be more comfortable. They send their love and prayers to you." Joel cleared his throat and opened his Bible.

"Will you all turn with me to the Book of Revelation..."

I listened to the latter day prophecies, but the talk soon bored me, and I craned my neck for another look at Lane. He and his wife had an aisle seat a few benches back, his straight, longish blond hair in sharp contrast to Estela's raven mane. I grinned at him and he gave me a wink, but before I could turn around, Estela's angry glare caught mine and made me shiver.

I instantly stared at the prophet behind the pulpit, but his long, dry speech could not penetrate my mind. Obviously Estela still refused to willingly sharing Lane. She'd left him and gone home to her parents for a few weeks when he first started paying attention to me. But she'd come back, and if I were to spend any more time with him it would be with the knowledge that Estela was on the warpath. Well, there was plenty of time for her to get used to the idea. I wasn't ready for marriage yet, although I had thoughts of it. A few of the girls my age were already engaged, but I planned to finish school and to have some fun before I settled down to have my family.

"Hey, Sue," Francisca whispered in my ear. "Guess who keeps staring at you? Verlan LeBaron! He's been ogling you for the past two minutes." She smirked, her green eyes shining wickedly. "I wish I could read his mind, don't you? What would an old man like him be thinking?" She boldly looked him up and down.

Startled, I glanced up. Oh, there was no doubt that Brother Verlan's questioning gaze was fastened on my face. A slow, intimate grin softened his lips as I stared back at him, and I hastily glanced away. My cheeks burned. I'd seen that look before, that hungry, devouring look in the eyes of the eldest LeBaron brother, Alma, the church bishop. My sister Rose Ann's husband had also smiled and eyed at me with that suggestive, almost physical familiarity.

As a young woman of the church I had the privilege of selecting my husband. It was my right, as it was the right of all the single girls. Unlike the men, we women only married once, so naturally we got to choose which of the men we wanted to be our spiritual head. I had to make sure I chose a man who was devoted to God and the church, and as the wife of a godly man my place in heaven would be secure. Brother Ervil had preached that just last week.

Ervil followed Joel to the pulpit and opened with his views of the recent assassination of Martin Luther King, Jr. Then he proceeded with a lengthy, windy discourse about people's civil rights. As he spoke his high-sounding words that I didn't recognize, Ervil batted and nabbed at a stray fly that buzzed around his head. Finally catching one in his fist, he squished it with his fingers and tossed it aside.

I stole another glance at Verlan. He wasn't watching me now, so I ignored Ervil and stared at Verlan. Of the five LeBaron brothers, I had always thought he was the best looking. Wide shoulders and a slim waist complemented his long legs. Brown hair feathered from a receding hairline, the slight graying at his temples adding to his appeal. Dreamy lashes rested against his cheeks as he looked at his book. His nose was a bit large, but I decided that it fit the rest of his frame perfectly. He appeared businesslike and prosperous in his brown serge suit and shined loafers.

I tucked my ragged tennis shoes under the bench so they wouldn't show. Good shoes seldom turned up in the sacks of clothes Dad brought us from the states, and I was glad that all Verlan could see of my clothing was my new dress. With my blond hair braided and pinned up, I knew I looked at least sixteen.

What, in reality, did I know of Verlan LeBaron, besides the fact that he had five wives? According to Dad, next to the prophet Joel, Verlan was the most righteous man in the church. Rumor had it that he readily lent a hand to anyone in need. He was honest in his dealings with others, completely self-sacrificing, and his wives supported their husband in every way. As the president of our church's Twelve Apostles, and head of the missions to the world, Verlan LeBaron was a staunch, dedicated man of God.

"How old is Verlan, Franny?" I whispered idly as I observed him. "Do you think he's over forty?"

Francisca considered for a moment, then whispered, "No. Alma's the oldest LeBaron brother here, then the prophet Joel. Then Ervil, and Mom told me Ervil is forty-one. He's older than Floren— and Verlan is the baby. He must be thirty-something. Why?"

"He's gorgeous, don't you think? And so tall. I just love mature men."

Francisca snorted, "Mature? He's not mature, he's *old*. I'll never marry an old man like him! I'm gonna be the first wife to someone my own age. What's the matter with you, Suze, don't you want to have some fun in life?" She glared at me, then whispered into my ear again, "You think you're a live-in babysitter now; just what do you think you would be if you married someone with a hundred kids like Verlan has? I can't believe you're even thinking about him."

Francisca was right—Verlan LeBaron was awfully old, but in heaven it wouldn't make a particle of difference. This life on Earth was just a tiny speck upon the vast screen of eternity, and in eternity, he wouldn't be old. Verlan would be a certain admission to the highest of the three heavens.

A sudden blur to my right was Thelma jumping off the bench. In an instant she scooted past me and escaped down the aisle. I darted after her, lifted her squirming, chunky body, and planted her bottom back on the seat. "You little brat," I hissed in her ear. "You hold still or I'll spank you when church is out!"

She glared at me. "I'll tell Papa if you do," she retorted. She would, too, and I would be the one in trouble. Darling little Thelma was the apple of my father's eye. I sighed and handed her a pen and some paper. "Here, honey, draw me a horse." She eagerly took the paper and began to scribble.

Without even looking, I felt Verlan's attention focused on me again. I glanced up, directly into clear, sparkling, aqua-colored magnets. The beginning of a smile tipped the corners of his mouth, and I couldn't help it, I grinned back at him. My whole body tingled as Thelma, the congregation around me, Lane, Estela, everyone melted into a gauzy fog. Brother Paisano's voice droned on and on in Spanish, but sounded far away and made no sense. All I could see were those calm eyes, surrounded by long, silky lashes, and his smile that suggested more to come. I could hardly breathe, and I felt shaky and hot as I forced myself to look away. I had to get back to reality and stop staring at this near stranger and remember who he was, and his age. I had to think of Lane and how much I liked him. Anyway, I was probably imagining that such an important man was interested in me. My brother Jay always said I had the wildest imagination of anyone he'd ever known.

I glanced across the aisle at Maria, Mom, and Dad. Maria was taking in every word brother Paisano said and furiously nodding her head in agreement. Devoutly religious, Maria often tried to correct my father's view of the scriptures, causing heated arguments between them at home and amusing my unassertive mother. Maria was opinionated and had a fiery temper, but just as Verlan's wives did, she and my mother got along with one another.

Thelma tugged on my arm. "Susie, I have to go to the outhouse," she announced out loud.

"Shh!" I squeezed her arm and glanced quickly around us.

"I have to go ca-ca, come and take me," her high-pitched voice rose with each word.

Francisca snickered. The Jensens, seated in front of us, turned around and stared. "Go on, Susie," Franny whispered merrily. "Take her so she can go ca-ca."

With face flaming, I hauled Thelma down the long aisle, past a widely grinning Lane, and out the door.

"You little loud mouth," I scolded when we were out of earshot. "Why couldn't you whisper to me?"

"I did, but you didn't hear. And I had to go bad."

We raced down the path to the outhouse, and I waited while she went inside. "There's no paper, Susie," she hollered after a moment.

"Shit." I said the bad word out loud as I looked around, hoping to find a scrap of paper in the weeds. Suddenly the outhouse door opened a few inches. Thelma's small brown hand reached out, picked up a smooth rock, and disappeared inside again. That's improvising, I thought, shuddering.

As we hurried back to the church, Thelma suddenly let go of my hand. With a cry of delight, she darted toward a huge robin that busily scratched and pecked at the bank of the irrigation ditch, some twenty feet from the side of the building.

"I want a bird! Oh! I want a bird!" she hollered. In a flurry of color, the robin flew up and landed in the cottonwood tree on the other side of the ditch. Thelma dashed up the bank and stopped just short of the thick mud layering the bottom.

"Thelma, now you behave yourself!" I commanded, glancing at the open side door of the church. "You can't have it, it's wild. Come on, we have to go back to the meeting," I said as I reached for her hand, but she shrugged me away.

"Susie, go get me that bird!" she ordered.

I reached for her again, my anger choking me as I grabbed her dress. The flimsy material ripped away from my fingers when she sidestepped, and before I could grab her, she walked into the ditch. Gluey, gray slime rose up above her ankles.

"Oh, Thelma!" I howled. I reached out as far as I could, my shoes on the very edge of the mud. Still I couldn't reach her. As she struggled to pull her feet free, fear crossed her face. "Get me! Susana, get me!" she wailed, panic showing in her black eyes. "My feet won't come out!"

"Give me your hands," I ordered.

I pulled hard, but the heavy mud sucked at her feet and held fast.

Suddenly the slippery bank gave way and I plunged, ankles and elbows deep, into the ditch.

Thelma wrapped her arms around my neck, her fingers catching in my hair and pulling strands of it down around my shoulders. I yanked her free, her shoes leaving wide black streaks on the pink material of my new dress. I carefully backed out of the ditch, sat Thelma down on the grass, and dropped down next to her.

"I hope Daddy whips you!" I gritted. "I ought'ta blister your butt myself till you can't sit down. Just look at me!" I wiped at the mud on my ankles and arms, then cleaned my fingers on the grass. My shoes were caked and dripping.

"I didn't mean to." Thelma sniffed and dabbed at her eyes. Picking up the hem of her dress, she wiped her nose then rubbed her shoes against the grass. Huge tears slid down her brown cheeks.

The side door of the church grated open, startling me. "Hey, you're needed in here." Dale Leany blinked against the bright sunlight. A smothered giggle suddenly escaped him as his eyes focused on us. "Wow," he drawled, "what happened to you two?"

Without waiting for an answer he ducked back inside.

Panic gripped me as I rose to my feet. It was closing hymn time and I was supposed to play the piano! I gazed down the road toward home, wishing I were safely in my room and away from all these people. I scraped my shoe soles hard against the grass as I pondered what to do. Why didn't they just start singing without the piano? Dale stuck his head back out the door.

"Hey, hurry up! Everybody's waiting for you. *Comprende?*" he growled.

I hesitated at the open doorway, searching the congregation for someone capable of taking my place at the piano. But there was no one in sight, and I could see Anna Mae, the song leader, standing impatiently on the stage. I shoved the loose strands of hair hanging about my face behind my ears, took Thelma's hand and walked into the building. The people standing on either side of us stared as we trudged up the aisle. As we passed Lane and Estela, I held my head high, then shoved Thelma in Maria's direction and walked on to the piano. Anna Mae's wide face broke into a startled grin. Behind her, the men on the stage made an effort at hiding their amused looks as they watched me take my seat.

"Come, Come Ye Saints" was a hymn I knew by heart, but as I pounded out the first chords I hit more wrong notes than right ones. Somehow I managed to get through the song and sit still through the final prayer, but I wanted desperately to cry.

As soon as the final *Amen* was said I sensed movement on the platform. A hasty glance confirmed that Verlan LeBaron, smiling widely, was heading straight for me. I stood up and bolted out the back door of the church.

The sun shone bright and hot as I scurried up the road toward home. My braid had come loose, and I yanked the strands apart so that it cascaded down my back in heavy rippling waves. In a matter of seconds the back of my neck felt wet and sticky. I mopped at my forehead then dabbed angrily at my eyes. How could this have happened, today of all days? Was I cursed? Maybe I was too vain and this was God's way of taking me down a peg. Whatever, Verlan LeBaron by now must consider me an awkward, clumsy little girl. He would never look at me again.

Behind me I could hear the usual noises of church adjourning. Children shouted and grownups called to one another. Engines started—everyone was going home, doubtless to discuss over the dinner table the spectacle Susan Ray had made of herself in church today.

Someone behind me was calling my name. "Wait up!" Lane puffed as he jogged toward me.

Oh, great. I reluctantly slowed my pace and allowed him to catch up. With a quick sweep of his green eyes he surveyed my red nose and slump shoulders.

"Hey! Don't act so shook up," he said briskly, handing me a hanky. "A little mud never hurt nobody. You honestly don't look that bad."

"Oh yes I do," I sniffed as I wiped my nose. "I'm so mad at Thelma I could strangle her. Just look at my new dress!"

He shrugged, grinned, and grabbed my hand. "It'll wash. Come on, I'll buy you a *paleta*."

Ahead of us under a black walnut tree, the little man from the neighboring city of Casas Grandes stood with his ice cream cart. He came every Sunday in good weather and peddled his frozen treats. "*Paletas*," he sang out as we approached. I peered into the cool interior of the white cart and selected my favorite, a lime-flavored Popsicle. Lane chose an ice cream bar, then dropped a peso into the man's brown palm. We sat under the walnut tree on the ditch bank and ate the cold treat. I looked up after a particularly large, cold bite to see the little muscles around Lane's mouth twitching.

"Good, huh?" he said gravely.

"Lane Stubbs, what are you laughing at?" I demanded.

"Oh, nothin'." He licked his ice cream. "Actually, I was admiring that cute pug nose of yours." His smile wrinkled up his cheeks in small furrows as his eyes touched my face, throat, and hair.

"My nose is not pug!" I retorted. His roving looks made me tingle uneasily and caused the blood to rush to my face. I wiped my hands on my muddy skirt and began to rise. "I–I need to get home," I stuttered. "Thanks for trying to cheer me up."

"Wait! I–"

Suddenly behind us a woman's cold voice said, "Lane."

Estela stood over us, her small son on her hip. Mahogany eyes blazed at Lane. Her fists were clenched, and my insides turned icy.

"Estela," Lane murmured as he stood up. His voice sounded nonchalant and totally relaxed. "Susan and I were having a *paleta*. Would you like one?"

"What I would like is for my husband to take us home from church!" Estela's voice was high and unnatural as it followed Lane to the ice cream cart. "We've been waiting for you, and we're sick of waiting! You take us home. And you stay away from her," her glance bristled with hatred.

Lane calmly selected a *paleta*, walked to his wife and handed it to her. "Here," his voice was even, "Eat this and behave yourself. I'm going to walk Susan home, then I'll come back for you and the baby. Now go on."

Estela stared at the Popsicle in her hand. Suddenly she threw it, hitting Lane in the chest. "You eat it!" she shrieked. "Or feed it to your scroungy little girlfriend. Don't bother coming for the baby and me. We won't be there. We'll be at home, and I'll be packing!"

With the baby bouncing on her hip, she dashed back up the road, past my father and mother, Maria and my little sisters as they trailed toward us. They all turned to watch her and Dad shook his head. "Come on, kids, don't stare; it's rude," he cautioned.

My insides shook with guilt and with embarrassment for Lane. What a scene his wife had caused! She had a lot to learn and a lot of accepting to do if she planned to stay in the colony.

"Just go on and take her home, okay?" I whispered. "I'll talk to you later."

"Yeah, I probably should. I'm sorry about all this," he whispered back.

"What was that all about?" Dad asked as my family circled us. He knew, of course. But he wanted to see how Lane was handling the situation.

"My wife's a mite jealous of your daughter here, Vern," Lane grinned apologetically. "I guess she didn't appreciate me buying Susan a *paleta*. Well, we'll see ya later." With a wave of his hand, he strolled after Estela.

Daddy watched him go, then turning to me he wagged his head and whispered, "I could'a warned you this would happen; I seen it coming." He scratched his leg, grinned, and shrugged. "Well, that's what you're in for, honey, when you start flirting with married men. You might as well sharpen up your claws if you plan on chasing that boy. That Estela woman is full of piss and vinegar, and I wouldn't count on her giving you a warm welcome if you're thinking about joining the family." He solemnly shook his head again, his eyes twinkling.

I fumed inside. What made him think I was the one doing the chasing? I wanted to straighten him out and tell him that Lane was pursuing *me*, not the other way around. But I kept my mouth shut.

"Daddy, can we have a *paleta?*" Ema and Thelma danced eagerly in front of us. Soon the whole family, Mom and Maria included, were taking their turn selecting from the little cart.

"How in the world did you and Thelma get all muddy?" Mom asked me as she waited her turn. "Just look at your pretty new dress! Goodness, Susan, can't you be more careful?"

Jay had caught up to us, and he looked at me and snickered. "What, were you kids making mud pies during church?"

I bit back a sharp retort and instead mumbled a quick explanation. But it was drowned out by my father's boisterous laughter. I glared from one member of my family to the other, then turned on my heel and stalked up the road.

As Fara and I hauled the water in from the well, heated it on the stove, then washed the dishes after lunch was over, my thoughts returned to Lane. His roving, intimate glances today had made me uncomfortable. He was getting serious, and I wasn't ready to think seriously about anyone. I enjoyed our flirtation, but because of it he was having big problems at home. He'd made it plain that he was willing to go through the fights with Estela to see me. But he would expect me to seriously consider marriage. Of course, if the end result were a new wife to add to his family, the problems with Estela would be worthwhile for him. But if I was just dating him for the fun of it, I was out of line. You just didn't date a married man for the fun of it, not in Colonia LeBaron. In fairness to both Lane and Estela, I needed to break it off.

Chapter 2

S lamming the door of his old green pickup, Lane Stubbs ambled to the front porch of my parent's five-room adobe house. He appeared tired and discouraged, and he hadn't bothered to clean up before coming to see me. His white shirt and baggy pants were stained with black grease. I was dreading this meeting. Two weeks had gone by since I'd seen him, not since the letter I'd made Franny deliver. I'd written that I didn't want to cause further problems with his wife, so I didn't plan to date him anymore.

"After he read it, he just sat there, all slumped down on his tractor seat," Franny had glared at me accusingly. "Jeez, I hated seeing him like that! I don't think you even liked him all that much; you were just goofing around, and now you've broke his heart."

"Francisca, that's exactly what I'm trying to avoid!" I exploded. "Yes, I liked him, but I'm not ready for a—a marriage commitment, or anything! I'm too young! I don't know how it happened, but somehow this whole thing's gotten out of hand."

"Well, he wants to talk to you," Franny said primly. "He's still got it bad for you, and I hope you've got enough sense to make a clean break." She'd sniffed and walked to the door, saying over her shoulder, "You should've told him in person, instead of being such a chicken and sending him that stupid letter. Can't believe I even agreed to take it."

She was right; I shouldn't have sent it. Now, opening the screen door, I stepped out into the shade of the front porch.

"Hi, Suze," Lane's gruff voice sounded apologetic. "I guess Franny gave you my note."

I nodded, fidgeting.

He pushed long locks of blond hair from his eyes and peered through the screen door behind me to see if anyone was in the living room. Satisfied, he turned back to me. "I hope you're not mad, but I need to talk to you. Can you leave now?"

I nodded, stuck my head inside the house, and hollered, "Mom, I'm going to play practice. Be back around six." I didn't wait for an assent. If she hadn't heard me, she would figure it out.

17

He opened the pickup door and I climbed onto the worn leather seat. I wet my lips nervously, knowing that before me loomed a sticky, uncomfortable situation, and that I had no idea how to handle things.

He backed the old truck around and we putted down the road. I cranked the window down so the breeze blew on my hot face, then I glanced at Lane. He sat stiffly; his mouth stern as he guided the truck down a side road, parked beneath a cottonwood tree, and turned the engine off. Then he slumped over the wheel, his moody green eyes distant and thoughtful.

"I don't know what you think there is to say," I began impatiently, wanting to get this over with.

"Now, Suze, just hold on a minute and let me say what's on my mind." He reached for my hand, and I reluctantly allowed him to rub my palm with the tips of his rough fingers. "I know you're young. Hell, you're a kid, really. But you don't act like a kid, and you sure don't look like a kid."

He swallowed a time or two, then turned in the seat and searched my eyes. "All I've ever wanted in life was to do what's right," he continued soberly. "I want to serve the Lord and raise up a righteous posterity. Maybe I don't show it all the time. Maybe I get sidetracked, but if we can find some laughs and happiness along the way, why, so much the better. Life here is hard enough."

He stared at my fingernails. I sat quiet and miserable, waiting for him to proceed. Suddenly he pulled my hand to his lips and kissed my palm, pressing it against his half-open mouth. The sensation was disturbing in a strange, thrilling way, and I hastily pulled my hand free and tucked it into my lap. "Don't," I snapped.

"Sorry," he mumbled. His face instantly turned crimson, and leaning his head against the window, he watched a cow graze in the rich, green pasture seemingly out of place in the midst of all the cactus and mesquite bushes. "Whose cow is that, do you know?" he muttered suddenly.

I glanced at the Guernsey, startled. "It's the Leany's, I think. Why?"

"They'd better keep an eye on her. She's takin' in that alfalfa pretty fast. If someone's not careful, she'll founder."

I fidgeted. I had to do something to move this situation along. My thoughts raced.

Abruptly he faced me again, his eyes bright with determination. "I realize Estela's the problem, Suze, and I can understand how it's affecting you. But she's getting better with each passing month. She's beginning to accept the gospel; she really is. Deep in her heart she knows it's right. She just needs a little time is all."

I studied my hands, ashamed to see the pleading in his eyes. Estela wasn't the only problem. Franny was correct; I had led him on. Somehow I had to make this right. I had to find the proper words, so that he wouldn't hate me and so that we could still be friends. I wanted to remember all the fun we had shared—the movies, the long talks, and the cavorting at the colony square dances. Not this, this bare glimpse of his heart, when I didn't know how to return the feelings.

"Please don't say anymore," I gulped. "Lane, didn't you understand my note? I don't feel right about this. For one thing, I'm too young..."

He put his hand under my chin and tipped my head up so that I had to look at him. "Don't say that," he groaned. "This is right; I know it is. I know it because I—because I love you. I guess I didn't realize it until I got your letter. Oh, you just don't know—The past two weeks have been hell." Tears filled his eyes. He sniffed them back then wiped them away. "I realize you're young. But you're so strong, and you're grounded in the church. With you behind me, Estela will soon get the picture. Don't get me wrong; I love her, Suze, I do. But I won't let her be a stumbling block when it comes to doing what Joel has taught me is right."

Rough fingers reached for my face again and he forced me to look into his earnest eyes. "We're meant for each other; I just know it," he whispered. "Don't tell me no! You can take all the time you want to think about it."

My throat felt tight and dry. His eyes were so intense they made me physically weak. I slowly nodded, detesting myself for giving in. "Okay, I'll think about it." I pulled away from him and repeated dazedly, "I'll think about it."

He heaved a relieved sigh and dropped his head onto the steering wheel. I sat stiffly, my mind in a whirl. Oh Lord, I thought wildly, why didn't I just tell him the truth? What am I doing! I've never been more sure of anything- I'll never love Lane Stubbs!

Of course, I knew of other girls in the colony who had married men without being in love. The brethren had assured them that the proper feelings would come, if they married a righteous man of the priesthood. But I would never do such a thing. Anger flashed over me, and my thoughts raced back three weeks.

My friend Carmela, a fifteen-year-old Mexican girl, had walked me home from school. She and my brother Jay had been in love for months. I'd been so excited at the thought of Carmela joining our family—but with tears streaming, she'd told me that her stepfather, Alma LeBaron, had forbidden her to see Jay

19

again. "But why?" I had asked, shocked.

"He told me that he's raised me to be the plural wife of a worthy man, not to marry some young kid who hasn't proved himself," she'd sniffed bitterly. "He has someone all picked out for me, too. And he's fifty, if he's a day."

"But what about Jay?" I'd shouted. My brother was just as good, and just as worthy as any old man in the church! I wanted to personally make sure Alma realized it, and I told Carmela so. Didn't love count for anything?

Sighing, I pulled myself back to the present. What about Lane's love for me? Did that count? He was a fine enough man, and I cared about him. But I knew that, unless God or the prophet told me to do otherwise, when I married someone it would be someone I truly loved. Someday Lane would find a plural wife, someone willing to help him build his family properly. Meantime I had to find the courage to tell him no. Soon.

"We had better go," I said abruptly. "We'll be late for practice."

By the time we pulled up in front of the church, Lane seemed back to his old self. He raced me to the door and caught me around the waist just before I opened it. I laughed with him, but even to me my levity sounded hollow and forced.

Three benches filled with colony teenagers were discussing the play for the upcoming church conference. They turned to stare at us as we tiptoed into the coolness of the building. Esther LeBaron Spencer, the only LeBaron sister who was a member of the church, stood behind the pulpit, her play manual open before her. She stopped speaking and waited until we took our seats. She looked hot and uncomfortable in her flowered polyester dress. Her graying hair curled moist around her neck.

She glowered at us. "As I was saying, if you want to have an active part in the play, you will make an effort to be on time at the practices. Now, our operetta this year is called "Welcome to Gay Havana," Esther rattled on and on.

My sister Fara, sitting on a rear bench, raised her eyebrows at me and darted a look at Lane. Franny glared disapproval as she scooted over to make room for us. "What are you doing?" she growled into my ear. "I thought you were breaking up with him!"

"Shh! I'll tell you later." I glanced at Esther. She looked up at us, briefly hesitated, and then continued outlining the play.

Few people in the colony had tried harder than Esther Spencer had to bring a touch of culture to our pioneer-type existence. She had made up her mind years ago, when the church was first started, that the young people of the colony wouldn't be deprived of whatever refinement she could teach them. She organized plays, piano concerts and talent shows for us to participate in, giving us something special to perform during our church's semi-annual conferences, something to show the visiting investigators of the church that just because we lived in Mexico and practiced polygamy, we weren't ignorant or illiterate.

"Let's give the adults something to smile at!" Esther said in conclusion. "And during these hours together in practice, let's have some good, clean fun!"

Lane rolled his eyes, his face a mask of seriousness. Franny suppressed a giggle. Esther was staring pointedly at the left end of the first bench where a girl named Debbie Bateman sat. Fresh from California, Debbie's legs were crossed, giving a full view of her thighs. Her short, tight skirt rode high on her hips. The huge wad of gum in her mouth popped and cracked as she watched Esther. Gossip had it that Debbie's parents had accepted Ervil LeBaron's offer to bring her to the colony, the plan being to get her away from her wild friends in California. And Esther, who took a maternal interest in all of us, was afraid that Debbie's foul mouth and worldly experience would be a bad influence. Debbie was well aware that Esther, as a charter member of the church and a sister of the prophet Joel, considered herself an authority on spiritual matters. So the new girl made a point of annoying her at every opportunity. With Debbie here, I knew that play practices would become interesting, indeed.

Jay and Carmela sat close together on a rear bench, paying little attention to the rest of us. I could sense the strain between them, and Francisca noticed it too. "Are they just going to let that mean old Alma dictate to them?" she whispered. "He's not her real father. How can he order her not to marry Jay?"

I shrugged and sighed. I had enough problems of my own to worry about at the present.

"Do you suppose Esther will tell Alma that they're sitting together?" Franny breathed into my ear.

"Oh, my Lord, I hope not!" I glanced at Esther. Being Alma's sister, she was no doubt aware of the situation. Didn't Jay and Carmela have enough sense to be discreet if they were going to disobey Alma's orders? I would have to talk to Jay when we got home, make him see he was being foolish.

As we walked out into the sunlight, I turned to Debbie and whispered, "Don't let Esther upset you, okay? She's old fashioned and not used to someone from the states."

"Don't worry about it," she said, shrugging. She glanced over at Lane. "So.

You and Lane back to makin' it?"

I stared at her in confusion. Debbie chuckled, her hazel eyes snapping. "Don't look so shocked. It's not like he has V.D. or anything."

"What's V.D.?" I almost hated to ask.

"You don't know what V.D. is?" Debbie shouted. "This place really is the end of the world, isn't it? V.D, dummy, is a disease people get who have lots of sex..."

Esther was suddenly behind us, and she dropped her heavy hand on Debbie's shoulder. "Okay, young woman, you can hold it right there," she snapped. "You're not in California anymore, and we don't talk about such things here in Colonia LeBaron. You're a member of God's true church now, Debbie. You need to remember that." Esther looked her up and down, from her long brown hair and slanted eyes, dark with makeup, to her bare legs and high-heel shoes. "You need someone with a stern hand to take control of you and straighten you out."

Shaking her head, Esther marched past us. Francisca, Debbie, and I stared after her, then Franny glanced at me, her green eyes smoldering.

"That old bag don't know it yet," Debbie muttered, "but she hasn't seen the last of me." She tossed her long brown hair. "Let's go see if anyone is going to Casas to the movies tonight. Sue, is Lane going?"

The "Casas" she was talking about was Casas Grandes, the city forty miles to the north, where most of our people shopped. The small Mexican city boasted of several markets, gas stations, banks, a hospital, and two theaters where mostly American films, captioned in Spanish, were shown. Other than two villages, one on either side of the colony, and another little town twenty miles to the south called Buenaventura, our colony lay surrounded by miles upon miles of desert. Chihuahua City, a bustling metropolis, lay almost four hours to the south. The border towns of Juarez and El Paso were four hours to our northeast.

"What makes you think I know his plans?" I answered Debbie crossly. I glanced back toward the church where Lane and Jay were loitering. I eyed them, wondering what Lane was telling Jay. They finally joined us.

"Let me take you home, Susan," Lane said.

"Hey, Lane," Debbie interrupted before I could answer, "how about taking us to the show tonight? That new movie with Burt Reynolds is playing and we want to see it." Her bright eyes made note of his hesitation as he glanced at me.

"Oh, she'll go with you," she assured him with an airy wave of her hand. "Won't you, honey?"

"Debbie," I snapped. "Lane's going to give me a ride home. We'll discuss it then."

"Okay, fine. Well, let me know." She looked after us as we walked to the pickup. Fleetingly, I felt sorry for Debbie. She seemed so lonely and misplaced. I should be a better friend to her.

We passed Esther turning into her gate, then Lane swung the pickup around the corner. As we bumped over the cattle guard, a lone woman walked down the middle of the tree-lined road ahead of us. She moved to the right and turned to stare as we drove past her, and suddenly I realized it was Estela.

"Lane!" his wife called out, her voice clear and loud through my open window. "Lane, stop!" Suddenly she was running alongside of us and she reached out and grabbed the door handle. "Stop, I said!" she screamed as the door flew open. Panicked, I began to scoot over next to Lane. Estela reached in and grabbed my arm, her eyes blazing. She yanked on me, trying to pull me out of the truck as she ran to keep up with us. Lane held onto my left arm and swore at Estela in Spanish. "Let go of her!" he shouted.

"Stop the truck!" I screamed, but Lane ignored me. The pickup careened down the bumpy road, with Estela half-dragged beside us. She hung onto my arm, her face smeared with tears. "Lane," she sobbed, "don't do this! Please get her out of here."

Suddenly Estela tripped. When she let go of my arm, the open pickup door hit her hard. I whirled and stared out the rear window, watching her roll over and over in the dust along the side of the road. Immediately she sat up, covered her face with her hands, and slouched forward, her shoulders shaking.

Glancing at her crumpled form in his rearview mirror while we moved on down the road, Lane shrugged. "Well, that's too bad," he said evenly. "Maybe it'll teach her a lesson."

I gaped at him, open-mouthed. My stomach lurched. Was this the man I had daydreamed about? What if Estela had been me? Would he have left *me* lying there?

"Stop the truck. Right now," I demanded.

He ignored me for a few seconds, then grudgingly pulled off the side of the road under the trees.

"Go back and see if your wife is hurt," I said coldly as I opened the door.

Determined fingers grabbed my blouse. "Cut it out," Lane snarled. "She's not hurt and she's got to learn. I told her before we ever got married that there would be other women. She knew I would marry again. I'm not going to let her come between us. I love you, and she's just got to accept that."

I yanked my blouse free from his fingers. "Our marrying won't work, Lane." Alarm replaced the anger on his face as I continued. "A marriage between us won't ever work, because *I don't love you*. I should have told you before," I stepped down onto the road.

Feeling his eyes on my back, I hurried away. After a full minute the engine started up. Gears whined and shifted, and when I turned the corner, I glanced behind me. The pickup was idling next to Estela.

All I could think of during evening chores as I milked our two cows and scattered grain in the chicken feeders was Estela, huddled in a heap in the dirt. She loved her husband. She had been a good wife to him, at least as far as I knew. She had given him a beautiful son. How could he treat her that way? Shouldn't he convert her to polygamy instead of forcing it on her? Shouldn't he have helped her to realize the benefits and eternal blessings that plural marriage provided? Shouldn't she have some say about who joined her own family? The whole thing made my head ache and I crawled into bed at twilight, grateful that none of my family had noticed my reticence. Life was so confusing. Lane and Estela filled my thoughts as I drifted off to sleep.

Chapter 3

The snakes crawling all around me were long and black, slimy and horrid. I screamed but the sound caught in my throat. A dense, enveloping fog floated about me. I wanted to run, but I couldn't move. One of the snakes wrapped itself around my ankle and crawled over my bare foot, its scales scratching my skin. I tried to scream again, knowing I was going to die. I could feel myself being sucked into the blackness inside of my mind.

I forced my eyes open. An illusive apparition hovered just over my head. Suddenly I realized that there were several of the ghost-like creatures. Two of them reached down and tried to lift me up, but my body passed right through their arms. I screamed and moaned in terror, their arms reaching for me again and again. "God," I prayed frantically, "Oh, God, don't let them get me."

Out of the thick mists, a human form appeared and hastened to my side. I sensed immediately that he had come to my rescue. Relief overwhelmed me! Strong arms pulled me close. Under my cheek was a rough material. It rubbed against my face and smelled clean and good and I clung to him as we floated away, higher and higher. I looked down. Below us the ghosts were gone, but the snakes crawled and writhed together. Suddenly the man kissed my lips. "Susan," he whispered. Startled, I raised my eyes to his face.

"Susan! Susan, wake up." My mother's voice was calling to me from far away, like an echo. Her hand was firm on my shoulder—shaking me. I tried to open my eyes, but they were too heavy. She shook me again. "Come on, honey, wake up. Wake up."

Her anxious face peered down at me, the tail of her long, gray braid tickling my cheek. I could smell the Noxema on her skin. She had on the flannel nightgown Dad had given her for Christmas. "You about scared me to death," she said. "You must have had a mighty bad dream."

Blinking, I sat up and looked around my lamp-lit bedroom. My mind felt hazy. Out the window between the open curtains, I could see the black sky. Blackness...The nightmare filled with twisting, crawling snakes and satanic power rushed over me and I buried my face against Mom's shoulder and sobbed.

"Honey, everything's okay! You just had a bad dream. It's over now. It's all over."

Her arms felt so safe around me, so real and good. I shook my head again, trying to block out the vision.

"Oh, Mom, it was so awful!" The words tumbled out as she gently rubbed my back. "There were all these huge sna—snakes, and such evil spirits, and they were grabbing at me, and trying to take me to hell. Oh, Mama!" I pulled away from her arms and rubbed my eyes hard.

"Now, now, sweetie, it's over." Her voice sounded tired as she patted me. "Did you eat some of Maria's enchiladas for supper? Sauce so hot it would give anyone nightmares. I didn't eat much of them. Maria saw me scrape my plate into the dog dish, and she felt bad."

In frustration I threw the covers back, stood up, and walked around my bedroom. The cement floor felt cold under my feet. The curtains at the open window billowed in and out. Everything around me was normal, even the long, flickering shadows that the coal oil lamp cast against the wall. But the depth of fear the nightmare had left me with was totally out of the ordinary. Then suddenly I remembered the man.

The scent of him came sharply back into focus. I had smelled that mixture of soap and after-shave before, and somehow the scent clung to me. Impulsively I picked up the skirt of my nightgown and inhaled. Nothing. Just the smell of the yellow bar soap Mom melted to do the wash. It didn't even smell good. I stared at the twinkling stars out the window, so distant in the blackness of the sky. What was happening to me? I felt bereft, so hollow inside.

Mom yawned and stretched. "Come back to bed. Do you want a glass of water?"

I turned from the window and searched her face, desperate for her to understand that this was no ordinary dream. Something significant had happened. I didn't understand it, and my brain whirled with confusion.

"Mama," I slowly walked back and sat down beside her. "You'll probably laugh, but that was the most real dream I've ever had. A man came and saved me from hell. He kissed me."

I could almost see the wheels of her mind turn. She eyed me in grave, thoughtful appraisal. Reaching for my hand, she absently stroked it. "Who was the man?"

I hesitated. Would she think I was crazy? Would she chuckle, as we did behind Maria's back at the long, colorful dreams she related to us almost every morning over breakfast? She would probably shrug it off and tell me to stop eating chili at night.

"Was it Lane?"

"No!" I shuddered. A lightning image of Estela rolling in the dirt flashed through my mind. I shook my head, wishing I had kept my mouth shut. Sometimes I spoke before I thought; it was one of my most irritating habits. I needed to think about this, to make sure of what this was all about before opening a door to something I might regret later.

Sensing my reluctance, Mom quickly said, "Susan, dear, you tell me when you're ready. Only remember, as a woman of the church, you have the right to personal revelation about whom you should marry. I'm sure your sister Rose Ann told you about the dream she had about Harv. But, then again, what you had could just be a plain old bad dream. You're so young, honey. Sometimes I think you're trying to grow up too fast. Believe me, being a grownup isn't all it's cracked up to be. I wish you'd concentrate on enjoying your youth."

She hugged me and started to pick up the lamp, then, thinking better of it, turned the wick down and left it where it was. "You might like the light for awhile," she said gently. "But try to go back to sleep. It'll be milking time soon."

I settled under the covers, laced my fingers behind my head, and stared at the water stains on the plaster ceiling. I tried to concentrate on the dream, but the details had begun to evaporate. Something about snakes and evil spirits, and the horrible feeling that I was headed for hell. Then Verlan LeBaron had rescued me. Was any of this because of what had happened with Lane and Estela? Or was this an honest-to-goodness revelation, the kind the ladies in the church whispered about?

I thought about Rose Ann. A few months ago she'd told me in one of her big-sister talks about the revelation she'd had about Harvard. She had cried in remembrance of it, and told me if I prayed, God would give me a revelation of my own. "It's your right," she'd insisted. "It's such a blessing to know that you've married the man God has picked out to be your husband through eternity. It carries you through the hard times. Believe me, I know. Susan, you need to get on your knees and ask the Lord."

Only I hadn't prayed. Oh, I really believed God answered prayer. He had answered the prophet Joseph Smith's when he prayed in the grove of trees and asked which church was the true Church on the earth. And then there was the wonderful story about our prophet Joel. I heard him tell it one Sunday. The story had given me goose bumps, and from then on I was convinced as never before that Joel was a true prophet of God.

"Before my father, Dayer LeBaron, died," Joel had said, "he laid his hands on my head and bestowed upon me the Mantle of the Priesthood that Joseph

27

Smith held. Joseph Smith had passed the Mantle to my great grandfather in secret, and he passed it down to my father, who gave it to me. Two years later I went to Salt Lake to legally incorporate the church as God had directed me to do. Only I lacked knowledge of organization. So I went up onto a mountain by Salt Lake and asked God for directions. After I prayed for a time, heavenly messengers appeared to me and counseled me."

I vividly remembered Joel's talk that day. I had listened to him carefully, thrilled at his testimony. And from then on I personally believed in his mission. Yes, I believed in answered prayer. But I hadn't felt ready to pray about a husband, and if the truth were told, I didn't feel righteous enough to expect an answer. I thought about some of the other girls, who were so obedient and submissive to the leaders that they trusted them completely to guide their lives and place them in the families where they would do the most good. And then there was I, headstrong and self-pleasing. I wanted to have fun and be happy, and I wanted to marry the most romantic guy I could find. For a daughter of the true church, that was definitely not the proper attitude. Maybe that was why God had sent the dream. He wanted me to wake up and realize how far from being righteous I really was. Maybe I needed to do an evaluation of myself and just see where I really stood on the scale of righteousness.

I shifted uncomfortably on my pillow and forced my mind backward over the highlights of my life. I had been baptized when I was eight, down at the springs, the crystal-clear swimming hole ten miles away, where most of the baptizing was done. I remembered Saul Singleton, a boy a year older than me, telling me that all my sins had been washed down the stream, and I was now clean enough to go to heaven. "But you can't even tell the tiniest little lie now," he'd informed me, "or you'll never make it. You only get to have your sins washed away once, and then you have to pay for your own. And if you never do anything good, you end up in hell. So watch it!"

If that were all true, I was going to have to change my behavior and my attitude. I thought about all the times in Sunday school and church when I had read my novels through the whole meetings, hiding them behind my open Bible. Uncomfortably, I remembered night after night reading until I fell asleep instead of taking time to pray. I thought about my nasty, judgmental attitude where certain people were concerned and how I'd made fun of them to my friends. I had been hateful and disrespectful to my mother lots of times. I must behave myself, take life seriously, buckle down, and do what was expected of me if I wanted to go to heaven, which I did, of course.

28

Little fingers of excitement tickled at my skin as I thought about Verlan LeBaron. That was the part of the dream that was the most vivid. He'd had his arms around me, and he had kissed me, his lips clinging firmly to mine. In my dream I'd wanted to melt into him and hold on forever. I had felt so safe, so wildly happy. Strange how I remembered the feeling so well. How could it be that I could picture this man so clearly when I hardly knew him? Was God letting me know that he was my husband-to-be?

I felt hot and sticky under the covers, and I kicked them back and turned onto my side. So, what now? Was I just supposed to wait around until something happened? What if nothing did? Or what if years went by, with me afraid to go on with my life, afraid to have a boyfriend, to kiss anyone else for fear of being untrue. I couldn't let that happen! I had to have answers.

I sighed with frustration, my mind reeling. There was only one thing I could do unless I was willing to patiently wait and see what happened. I needed to talk to someone about this, someone who knew how to interpret dreams. And there was only one person I trusted to do it. Grandma LeBaron!

Maud LeBaron, who most of the colony kids called "Grandma," was my piano teacher, but she was more than that. She was a wonderful friend, and many an hour had passed with her talking to me about her life, about how God had spoken to her in dreams. She had to be the most righteous woman in the church, especially as she was Verlan's and the Prophet Joel's mother. I would tell Grandma my dream while I was at my piano lesson tomorrow, and she would be able to tell me what it meant.

With that settled, I pulled the covers back up around my shoulders against the chilly morning air and drifted into a restless sleep.

Grandma's house was one of two oven-baked, red brick homes the colony boasted of. Its bright color stood out among the brown adobe houses everyone else had and seemed to me to show stability and wealth. I knocked on the door, my blood racing.

Grandma's delicate, lined face broke into a smile when she swung the door open. Her tiny body was covered in a silky, cornflower-blue dress. As usual, her mousy hair was twisted into a bun and pinned at the nape of her neck, with little escaping tendrils curling softly about her face. The slippers on her feet slid across the tile floor as she gingerly moved on arthritic hips. Grandma always made me feel like a valued guest, as though she especially appreciated the opportunity of giving me piano lessons. I knew she received little, if anything for her efforts, but she enjoyed teaching and considered it her way of serving God. She filled her days by teaching piano to half the kids in the colony.

As I followed her into the comfortable, spacious living room, I could see that she wasn't alone. I immediately recognized Ervil's broad shoulders and massive head. He was seated at the dining room table, just off of the living room.

"Susan, dear," Grandma was saying, her voice crystal clear and melodious as a lark's, "go play 'Gypsy Rondo' for Ervil, while I finish putting this bread in the oven."

Ervil, the church Patriarch and Second Grand Head of Priesthood glanced at me. His mouth was full of something that looked like peach cobbler. He barely waved and turned back to his dessert.

In the years I had lived in the colony, I had rarely been around Ervil. Something about him always made me self-conscious, and I sighed. Why did Grandma always want her students to play for everyone? Ervil was a prestigious, busy man, and I knew he couldn't care less about hearing me play. But I dutifully sat down and ripped off the tune in my best form as Grandma fussed around her giant son. She served him up a second plate of cobbler as he talked steadily to her. I felt as if I were interrupting, so after the tune was over, I stopped.

Immediately Ervil turned to me. "That was nice," his voice was soft for such a big man, his deep-set eyes serious, as he looked me up and down. "Very nice. You do Mother proud."

"Thank you, Brother LeBaron," I murmured, my voice drowned out by his chair scraping against the floor. He stood up, such a huge man beside his frail mother.

Suddenly he coughed and choked and gasped for air as he grabbed a handkerchief out of his pocket. He spit in it and wiped his eyes on a clean corner. Grandma had reached up and was patting his back. "Now Ervil," she reproached him, "see why I insist you wear wool on your chest? Bring me a bunch of your cotton T-shirts and I'll sew woolen patches on for you. You're going to have to start taking care of yourself, or you'll end up back in bed." She was walking him to the front door and talking to him as if he were only ten.

As they reached the entryway someone pounded on the door.

"You ready to go?" a man's voice said when Grandma swung the screen open. I peered out at Dan Jordan, one of the Twelve Apostles. He owned the other red brick home in the colony. He stood on Grandma's threshold, a quizzical smile on his round face while he looked at Ervil. Dan was of medium height, with a perpetual beard shadow, black hair and eyes and a dry, almost sarcastic humor that made the adult Sunday school classes he taught entertaining as well as educational. He was Grandma's grandson by marriage and he leaned down and kissed her cheek.

"Everything all set?" Ervil inquired as, without a backward glance, they moved across the gravel drive. I could see them through the window when they climbed into Dan's waiting pickup.

"Come back soon," Grandma called after them. She stood in the doorway a moment, watching them drive off. When she limped back to me, there was a strained expression in her clear hazel eyes.

"Sometimes, no matter how grownup your kids get, you still feel like they need a good pounding," she declared. Shaking her head, she settled down beside me at the piano and opened my music book.

The mental picture of Grandma trying to pound on Ervil made me giggle. "You're worried about his cold?" I asked.

"Oh, that. And other things..." Her voice drifted off. "No matter. So tell me," she said, "have you practiced much this week?"

Impulsively I reached my arm around Grandma's delicate shoulders and hugged her. She was so sweet and motherly, and it amused me that she was worrying about her grown son. Ervil was a man I subconsciously ranked with the angels, right up there next to Jesus, so perfect and good. And yet his own mother wanted to shake him. It was amazing and almost unbelievable. I considered asking her just what she was talking about, but it was none of my business. "Grandma," I said instead, lightly fingering the keys, "I need to tell to you about something."

"Well, go ahead, dear. What is it?"

I turned and searched her wrinkled face. "I had this strange dream last night," I began. Quickly I told her about the scary blackness around me, the snakes and evil spirits and the feeling that I was going to hell. And then I told her about my quickly uttered prayer, and the appearance of a man. "What does it all mean, Grandma?" I asked in conclusion. "If anyone can tell me, you can."

She looked at me steadily throughout my account. "Do you know who it was?" she repeated my mother's question.

My face reddened, but I managed to look her in the eyes as I squeaked, "Your son, Verlan."

Grandma tried, but she couldn't hide the pleased look that crossed her face. "Are you sure it was him?" The thrill in her voice was unmistakable.

I smiled at her, and suddenly I felt like crying. She approved of me marrying

31

her son. Verlan was a special man, and Grandma knew it. "What does the dream mean, Grandma?" I reminded her.

"Why, honey, there's no doubt in my mind what it means. Our Heavenly Father knows that you're almost of marriageable age, and He loves you and recognizes you as a Daughter of the True Church. I've known there was something special about you since you were a small child, and He knows it, too. He's guiding your life even though you're not aware of it, and He has your spiritual welfare in mind. However, if you fail to follow His guidance, you are an open target for Satan's trap." Grandma gave me a serious, almost brooding look. "I have a feeling Satan is standing by watching you and has big plans to ruin your life. You must always keep the Lord close to you. He knows your potential, and I'm even surer of it since you told me about Verlan being the one in your dream. Verlan is a powerful influence for good in this world, Susan, and he's going to need strong wives to back him in his mission."

"Grandma," I said quickly, "you can't say a word to him about all this. If he's the one God wants me to marry, he will know, too. I would just *die* if he thought I was chasing him! I'll remember what you've told me, and I'll just wait and see what happens. Do you promise?"

She smiled at me and squeezed my hand with her bent, knobby fingers. "You know I won't say anything. Let him chase you! It's good for a man not to be too sure of where he stands with a woman. It makes him appreciate her more. Now," she concluded briskly, pointing at the thick music book, "where were we?"

It was late when I left Grandma's house. The sun had all but dipped behind the blue mountains, causing a rosy orange glow over the colony. A rooster in the distance was crowing as though it was dawn instead of dusk.

I felt elated as I hurried along the streets of the little Mexican pueblo, my home for eight years. God loved me! He wanted me to be the wife of the President of His church. I didn't know Verlan at all, really, but the thought didn't even scare me. In fact, I felt relaxed about my future. I had no doubt that I would fit into his family and learn to love him, just as the brethren had told those other girls would happen to them.

It was all I could do to keep from skipping down the road while I thought about him. I thought about his wives, too. I knew his first three wives, but only slightly. Charlotte, his first wife, was tall, olive-complexioned and serious. Irene, his blond, plump second wife, was Charlotte's half-sister, and was always full of jokes and laughter. Lucy, his third wife, was a cousin to the other two and was quiet and unobtrusive. He had married two Mexican girls since his family had moved to Baja. I didn't know either of them. But I wasn't worried about anything; God had plans for my life! I didn't need to fret about Lane anymore either, and that was a tremendous relief.

Mom, Jay, and the little girls were out in the garden, making use of the last minutes of daylight when I walked by the fence. Fara looked up at me from where she was dropping seeds into the furrow Jay was digging. "Well, Sister Sue. How nice of you to come home," she scowled. "Mom made Mona and me do your dishes, and Jay finally milked your cows because they were about to burst. Any chance you could spare a little of your time to help us out here?"

I glanced at Mom but she didn't say anything; she just kept hoeing. Fara handed me the sack of seed and stalked to the house. Not even her bad temper could touch the elation I felt. The evil of the dream had vanished at Grandma's words, leaving only the wonderful peace of having a place on earth all picked out for me by God Himself. I wasn't worried about the devil. I had been warned, and I was on the lookout.

I knelt and began dropping seed peas into the furrows Jay was making. I was so lost in my daydream about Verlan that I failed at first to notice Jay's agitation.

Chapter 4

Jay and I worked in the garden planting peas until it was almost too dark to see. As we reached the end of the last row, Jay straightened up and, leaning on his hoe, said in a low voice, "Sis, I need to talk to you."

I peered up at him, surprised at the seriousness of his tone. "Well, go ahead. Talk." Standing up, I massaged my lower back.

He glanced pointedly over at Mother and whispered, "Not here. Come on over to my room. I'm just going to put these tools away."

It must be about Carmela, I thought, as I followed him across the street to the little adobe house he had built. Jay had been working in New Mexico with Dad off and on for the past year and had put every dime he earned into the tiny house that sat across the road from our place. He had laid the adobes himself and had pounded every nail and set every window. I knew he had built the house with Carmela in mind. Although he had made a show of accepting Alma's wishes that Carmela marry someone other than him, he didn't fool me. He loved her, and he wasn't the sort of person to give up easily.

The house was filled with shadows and Jay struck a match and lit the lamp. His boyish face beneath his shock of dark brown hair looked pale and serious in the dim light. I could sense his nervousness. "Sit down," he said, motioning toward the unmade bed in the corner.

I settled down on a rumpled mound of covers and leaned my back against the wall. "What's going on?"

He stuck his hands in his pockets, pursed his lips, and rocked on the balls of his feet. Keeping his voice low, he said, "Sis, I need your help. I need to see Carmela."

I nodded, "I figured that's what you wanted to talk about."

His wiry body moved back and forth in front of me, his words coming out in angry bursts. "She sent me a note saying that Alma is having her watched, and she doesn't dare try to meet me anymore. Get this; her own brothers are spying on her for him, watching her every move!" He scowled and shook his head. "It makes me sick. Now Alma's decided that she will marry Hector Spencer. Being as how Hector's over fifty and only has one wife, Alma's afraid he'll lose out on the Celestial Kingdom and godhood. So Carmela's supposed to go to Hector's rescue."

"Okay, and how does Hector feel about all this?" I asked angrily. "Does he want to marry Carmela?"

Jay grimaced. "Oh, I guess he's agreed, though he's dragging his heels a bit."

"Well, what about what Carmela wants?" I snapped. I could feel the blood pounding in my head, and I had lost control of my voice. "And what about you? I suppose your feelings in the matter don't count!"

"Alma reminded me again that the young girls in the church were being raised to be plural wives to the older men. I'm supposed to go out into the world and convert me a wife." Jay's laugh was a tight, unnatural sound. He leaned against the door and looked ready to cry.

"Well!" I yelled suddenly at Jay's bowed head. "What are you gonna do about it? Just sit back and watch both your lives be ruined? Go after her, dammit! Tell that mean old Alma to kiss your you know what!"

Jay tried to give me a look of big brotherly reproach for being so disrespectful about a leader, but he couldn't pull it off. A flash of humor momentarily lit up his eyes. "Here's what I want you to do," he said abruptly. "Go to Carmela's and sneak her over here so I can talk to her. I've got to convince her to elope with me." His blue gaze fastened on mine. "Will you do it?"

"Elope!" I breathed, my eyes widening. "Elope?" No one I knew had ever done such a thing. Alma's face flashed before my eyes, that thin, hard face that was so unlike his brother Verlan's kind and handsome one. "Jay," I said, my voice rising in panic, "Alma would kill you!"

Jay soberly regarded me, "Now, let's not be melodramatic. Sure, he's gonna be mad. I'm counting on that. But at this point I don't have any other choice." He ripped at his fingernail, glanced at it, tore at it with his teeth, then sighed. "I just wish Brother Joel were here. He wouldn't back Alma in this, and he would tell me how best to handle the situation. But he's not, and things with Hector are happening fast. Now, I want you to sneak her over here tonight. Her family won't think anything about you going to see her because they know the two of you are friends. Just act like you've invited her to go for a walk or something, and try to get away without anyone knowing."

"But where will you go? What will you do? Jay, the brethren will ban you from the colony, or cut you off from the church, or something. Alma won't take this lying down. He'll consider it a slap in the face of his authority."

"Suze, just trust me. I've got it all planned out. I'll tell you about it later, after I've talked to Carmela. Just go get her, okay?"

The spirit of adventure grabbed me, and I slowly nodded, my eyes shining. Nothing would make me happier than to have a hand in beating Alma LeBaron at his own underhanded schemes. "Right. I'll leave right now!" I bounded off the bed.

Jay grinned at my enthusiasm and gave me a hug. "I'll cover for you with Mom. Get back as soon as you can."

It was dark enough for me to jog through the streets without anyone noticing. I stayed close to the trees as I ran, so if someone drove by I could duck out of sight. I followed the same route I had taken earlier that day, toward Grandma LeBaron's, then past the dim lights of her house and on toward the big ponds the LeBaron men had dug to store irrigation water.

Surrounded by old willow trees, Carmela's house looked dark and scary. As I scampered up the hedge-lined path at the rear of the house, two big dogs started to bark. They dashed around the corner of the house and leaped toward me, snarling and yapping.

"Here boy, here boy. Down!" I tried to sound commanding and unafraid, but the dogs continued to howl and circle me. *Susan, you idiot,* I told myself, *they're Mexican dogs.* I crooned to them in Spanish, my voice shaking.

The screen door at the back of the house slammed. "Perro! Ven a ca." Carmela's older brother Ernesto ambled toward me, peering at me through the blackness. The dogs trotted to his side, their tails wagging.

"Why, Susana!" He laughed as he recognized me. "What're you doing here this time of night?"

"Hi," I giggled shakily. "Oh, my goodness, am I glad to see you! I forgot about the dogs or I wouldn't have come." I eyed them and moved closer to Ernesto. "I was at Grandma LeBaron's, and I decided since I was so close I'd come and see Carmela. Is she home?"

My voice sounded phony, but Ernesto didn't seem to notice. His smile flashed in the darkness, and in perfect English he answered, "She's doing the dishes. Come on in."

Ernesto was about five foot four, with teasing black eyes, a perfect set of white, even teeth and deep dimples. His smile would melt almost any girl's insides. But I remembered what Jay had told me about Carmela's brothers spying on her, and I was privately seething. Tonight Ernesto's charms annoyed me.

As we entered the dimly-lit kitchen, Carmela looked up in surprise.

"What's going on?" she asked when Ernesto was out of earshot.

In a hurried whisper, I explained. Her lovely face turned grave as she rinsed a glass over and over. "How in the world does he expect me to leave here?" she whispered dejectedly. "Alma's ordered Ernesto and the twin to follow me wherever I go. I can hardly go to the outhouse in peace! It's just not possible." She threw her hands up in the air, splattering dishwater all over the counter.

"Carmela!" I threw a cautious look at the curtained doorway through which Ernesto had disappeared. "Are you going to let Alma force you around? Nobody, but *nobody* would make me give up my true love and marry some old man I couldn't stand. Don't let him do this to you! If you do, you'll pay for it the rest of your life. You love Jay, don't you? Then be willing to take some chances."

She scrubbed a huge pan in silence, her face pale in the poor light. Finally she cast a glance at the doorway behind her and whispered, "What have you got in mind?"

As I hurriedly helped her finish the dishes, we talked and laughed loudly about colony gossip for Ernesto's benefit. When we were through we traipsed past a reading Ernesto and on to Carmela's tiny room. We closed the door, and Carmela leaned against it. "What if they catch us?" she moaned.

"Have you heard about Francisca and Alma D?" I asked loud enough for Ernesto to hear. I motioned fiercely for Carmela to hurry. "They're going out together at least twice a week..."

As I rattled on, Carmela turned up the radio to cover the sound of the bedroom window sliding open. She slipped her legs over the ledge and dashed across the dark yard. Once she was out of the gate, she called softly for the dogs. The two huge mutts padded after her as she raced down the road toward Grandma's.

"Oh, Carmela," I continued my monologue, my heart pounding with fright. "I just don't know what to do about Lane. I like him a lot, but Estela's so horrible..." I rattled on until I was sure Carmela had reached the corner of the road, then leaving the radio on, I followed her out the window and sprinted away from the house. Soon the two of us were jogging through the streets of Colonia LeBaron. The dogs bounded along with us until we reached the last corner; then, Carmela commanded them to go home.

In a matter of minutes we stood panting inside Jay's little house. Jay looked at me over the top of Carmela's head, his blue eyes dark with gratitude. As I left them alone, Carmela was saying, "Oh, Jay, you really built all this for me? What color are we going to paint the kitchen?"

I stood guard in the shadows outside. Across the street I could see Mom's bedroom light, and I wondered if she was worrying about me. Wrapping my arms around my shoulders against the chilly air, I slid down in a huddle at the side of the adobe wall. The grass was sparse and no cushion at all for my bottom. I shifted uncomfortably, wishing Jay and Carmela would hurry and do whatever they were going to do.

I thought about Alma and wondered how he could be so mean. I'd never liked Alma much. He made his kids eat cracked wheat cereal with goat's milk and molasses for breakfast and wouldn't let them eat chocolate cake or fudge, or anything with refined sugar or flour. He wouldn't let his daughter Rosa wear pants, and she had to keep her hair braided. It was strange how different the people in the same family could be. I felt confident that Verlan would never try to run his children's lives. He wasn't forceful and manipulating like Alma. He couldn't possibly be.

It was a good thing that Jay and Carmela were eloping. I didn't know just what my brother had in mind yet, and I wished he would come out and let me know. I was beginning to feel nervous. They were taking too long talking. They needed to decide what they were doing and get on with it.

As the worries plagued my mind, car lights began to make their way down the main road that ran half a block away from me. I held my breath, for fear they would turn down our street. But they went on down the bumpy road toward the western mountains. I relaxed for a moment, then started to worry again. What would I do if Alma came looking for Carmela? Oh, God forbid.

I was beginning to shiver and my legs were cramped. I stood up and began to walk around to warm up. This was ridiculous. Maybe I should go knock on Jay's door and make them hurry.

The sound of a distant engine coming nearer made me dash in panic to the corner of the house. Bright headlights swept down our road and a white pickup turned sharply into Jay's gravel driveway. Alma climbed out and slammed the door shut. In his right hand he held a shotgun. I stood outlined in the bold glare of the headlights, squinting as I stared at him. He walked toward me, his face hard and pale under the lights of the pickup.

"Okay, young lady, where is she?"

His voice sounded absurdly friendly and conversational, and I eyed the shotgun in his hands, its double barrels glistening in the yellow light. I had to answer him, lie like crazy, say Carmela wasn't here, but my tongue and brain were frozen. Tearing my eyes away from the gun, I glanced hastily over my shoulder, praying they had heard him and ran out the back door to safety.

Alma pushed me aside and started around the side of the house. Suddenly I found my voice. "Jay!" I screamed through the stillness. "Alma has a shotgun!"

My heart pounded with every step as I ran after him. "Jay! Look out! Alma has a gun!" I screamed again. I wasn't afraid anymore, and grabbing his arm as he reached for the screen door, I yanked hard. "You leave them alone, you hear me?" I shouted. "Just what do you plan to do? Shoot them? What a mean old bully you are!"

He shook my grip free and shoved me back. I stumbled and fell onto the grass. "You stay out of this!" he roared. "Someone ought to teach you some respect for your elders."

The door to the house swung open. Jay and Carmela filed out and stood gaping at us. Alma eyed them in cold fury; the shotgun held loosely in his hand. Across the street, Mother's bedroom door banged. She hurried toward us, her slippers flapping.

"What in the world is going on here?" she snapped, pulling her robe tighter around her. The shotgun in Alma's hand brought her up short. A look of incredulity crossed her features.

"Alma LeBaron, just what do you think you're doing!" she gasped.

"Mathel, I warned Jay to stay away from my daughter weeks ago," Alma said stiffly. "I meant what I said. I don't want there to be any trouble, and there won't be if he will abide by my wishes. But he'd better take me serious. I have other plans for Carmela." He turned back to Jay, his eyes two dark slits. "If you're looking for trouble, boy, you're headed in the right direction. I won't warn you again. Stay away from my daughter."

Jay's face looked white as marble as Alma grabbed Carmela's arm and pushed her down the sidewalk. She gaped back at Jay before she got in the pickup, her eyes two black circles in her dark face.

I picked myself up from the grass. My knees felt rubbery as I stood next to Mom and Jay and watched the white pickup back out of the driveway.

Mom was the first to speak. Her voice shook, "I don't know how this all came about, but I would like to personally fill that man's butt with bird shot for having the nerve to bring a gun over here, onto our property, and threaten my son with it. How dare he! I wish your father were here! He'd have something to say to that self-righteous . . . "

"Mom," Jay interrupted quietly. "He did warn me. As wrong as he is, at least he warned me in advance. Oh, damn, I don't know what to do. I can't just

39

stand by and watch her marry Hector! I can't believe that's God's will. Alma's wrong! I only wish Joel were here to tell me what to do." He choked, turned away from us, and stumbled into the shadows. He leaned against the house and sobbed.

Mom turned and glared at me. "And just what part did you play in this? Why in the name of heaven are you involved in this stupid fight with Alma?"

"Jay is my brother and Carmela is my friend!" I said fiercely. "That makes me involved. Jay wanted to talk to her and I invited her over, that's all."

"I asked Susan to bring Carmela over here," Jay's voice sounded hollow. "None of this is her fault. I'm sorry, Sis. Did he hurt you?"

I shook my head. "What are you going to do?"

"Leave it alone for now, I guess. I'll think of something. You two go on to bed. Mom, I'm really sorry about this," Jay walked back and put his arms around us. We hugged for a moment, and as I felt the tears on his cheek, a horrible hatred filled my soul like I had never known before. I wanted to yank Alma's thin hair out, tear his eyes out, and scratch his face.

"It'll be okay, Jay," I whispered in his ear. And then Mom and I walked across the street and left him alone in his and Carmela's little dream house.

Chapter 5

The rest of the month swiftly passed, filled with school and church activities, piano lessons and play practices. The early spring leaves on the cottonwood trees had matured to jade colors. Roses and painted daisies were blooming, and summer heat and freedom were just around the corner. The three-room adobe building that served as a school for the colony's elementary and middle school grades was stifling in the desert heat. Our government paid Mexican teachers were as anxious as their gringo students were for the summer break.

Jay went back to New Mexico with Dad to work. I knew it was because he couldn't stand to be in the colony with things the way they were with Alma and Carmela. In school, Carmela was distant and withdrawn. I ached for her.

As for my own life, I harbored the secret of my dream like a hidden treasure deep in my heart. I had finally confided in my mother about it, but other than her and me, no one knew but Grandma LeBaron.

Francisca begged me to tell her what was going on with me. "I know you're not telling me something important," she complained. "I tell you everything. It's not fair." Francisca had fallen in love over the past month with Alma LeBaron's oldest son Alma D. She was crazy about him. Alma D. had been gone for the past six or eight months, working in Las Vegas. He'd come home with fancy new clothes and a brand new red Chrysler sedan. He was taking Franny out every few nights and spending lots of time with her, which made her too busy to have much time for me. So I found myself thrown together more and more with Debbie Bateman.

Debbie was so different from the girls I had grown up with. For the first few months of her life in the colony, she was full of Babylonian ideas about men and life in general. Yet as the weeks passed, it seemed to me she was becoming a bit ashamed of her wild ways and was honestly trying to become one of us. She was wearing less makeup and had stopped wearing her mini skirts. She'd moved in with Ervil's wife, Anna Mae, and seemed to really enjoy being a member of Anna Mae's busy household. At play practices, Esther Spencer had noticed a difference in Debbie too. For the past few weeks she'd gone out of her way to be nice to her and make her feel a part of our group.

Lane had kept pretty much to himself since the day I had told him I didn't love him. He barely nodded to me when we were in the same room. I knew we had lost for good our special friendship. In a way, it made me sad.

Conference was almost upon us, and I was filled with nervous excitement about it. I knew I would get to see Verlan again. I could hardly wait to see what he looked like. Of course, I basically knew. But when I would try to imagine his face before me, I couldn't seem to get it in the right proportions. I would be seeing him through different eyes, now that I planned to marry him someday.

The meetings would take place on a three-day weekend. Six hundred people from all over the Western United States and Mexico would be gathering to Colonia LeBaron to hear the prophet Joel and the other leaders preach and outline their plans for further missionary work. Each evening there would be a social event. Friday night would be thè play, and Saturday night we would have a big square dance. Sunday evening would conclude with the young people's Fireside or spiritual lesson.

My father's sister, Thelma Chynoweth, her husband Bud, and their three unmarried children were coming from Utah. I hadn't seen my Chynoweth relatives since I was a small child. They would be staying at our house, and I was delighted at the thought of getting to know them again. Due to my father's insistent ministry, they had joined the church a couple of years ago, and their oldest daughter, my cousin Lorna, had become Ervil LeBaron's fifth wife shortly after that.

Aunt Thelma, Uncle Bud, and their kids arrived late Thursday night, and Mom and Dad scurried around, carrying lamps back and forth as they bedded everyone down. I could hear the adults visiting until the wee hours of the morning.

The following day dawned full of clouds and rain, and I hurried through my chores outside so I could take a bath and dry my hair before the ten o'clock meeting. While Mom made Wonderberry pancakes in honor of our company, Aunt Thelma bustled around the kitchen, setting the table, straining the milk for me, and talking non-stop.

Aunt Thelma didn't look a thing like my father. She was above average height and had kept a trim, firm figure for being in her fifties. She had perfect skin, laughing blue eyes and exceptional white teeth. Her light brown hair was just beginning to show a little frost. She wore large pearly earrings and carefully tailored clothes. Elegant was the word for Aunt Thelma.

Uncle Bud was a jolly man, and immediately I loved him. When I looked at his face, kindness and goodness barely stayed hidden behind the smirk of a lighthearted tease. I was soon to find out Uncle Bud teased the people he loved until they wanted to pinch him.

"You're going to have to watch this girl, Vern," he mumbled between bites of pancake as he reached over and gently yanked on my carefully pinned up hair. "She's going to steal all those men's hearts at meeting today. How old are you now, Suze? About twenty-three?"

"Now, Bud, don't you start in on her," Aunt Thelma interrupted. "I was the same way when I was her age. We Ray women mature early, and not just in looks. She may only be fourteen, but she could give any eighteen-year-old a run for her money. Couldn't you, Susie?"

I managed a tight smile and excused myself from the table.

Cousin Mark, the boy just older than me, grinned and winked at me as I walked past him, and I fumed. I hated being treated like a child. I was grown up, whether Uncle Bud thought so or not. Hadn't God given me a revelation about whom to marry?

As I walked down the hall to my room, Uncle Bud was keeping it up. "Yep, Vern, you're going to have to oil up the old shotgun because of that little blond."

"Speaking of shotguns," Dad's deep voice boomed down the hall, "we had a little run-in with a shotgun here about a month ago. I tell you, Bud, some of these LeBaron men think they're above the law."

I propped my bedroom door open a bit so I could eavesdrop. Dad went on and on about Alma's visit to Jay and just what he thought about the whole thing. As they talked, I fixed my hair where Uncle Bud had pulled it loose from the French twist. I had on my favorite pink dress, but as I examined myself in the mirror, I pulled it off and changed into the blue and gray dress with the full skirt because Jay had told me it matched my eyes. Also, I was afraid Verlan would recognize my pink one.

Dad's voice carried well down the hall, and suddenly I heard him say, "You know, Bud, those LeBaron men are all so different. But in some things they're like peas in a pod. Take Ervil now; just like Alma, Ervil thinks he can run people's lives."

Dad's voice abruptly dropped in volume. Whatever else he was saying about Ervil LeBaron was being muffled. I hurried to the door and stuck my head out, but the conversation was being carried on in a whisper. I lingered for a moment, but Dad's voice remained too low. Whatever he was discussing now was a secret and it sounded like Dad was unhappy with Ervil again. Bud's oldest daughter was one of Ervil's wives, and what was Dad doing ragging on Ervil to him? I wished I knew more about what was going on.

I closed the door and took one last look in the mirror. Today of all days I wanted to look my best. Staring back at me was a five-foot-five-inch young lady of medium build, with high cheekbones, a clear complexion, and big blue eyes fringed with dark, curly lashes and brown, even brows. Thick, ash-blond hair, pulled up in a mature style, definitely made me look eighteen. My dress was belted snug around my waist, and my bosom pushed hard at the fabric. I might not steal all the men's hearts today, but there was one man's heart that I hoped would at least skip a beat or two. I put just a dab of Mom's perfume behind my ears, picked up my Bible and Book of Mormon and walked into the kitchen.

"Are you guys ready?" I called to Jay and Mark as they combed their hair at the mirror above the wash stand by the back door. They certainly looked ready—a couple of lady-killers, all dolled up in their suits and ties. I whistled my admiration. Mark's hair curled long over his collar and glistened with blond highlights. He'd inherited Aunt Thelma's perfect, white smile and Uncle Bud's hazel eyes, complete with the constant twinkle. He wasn't very tall, but his muscular body sported a golden tan.

Next to Mark, Jay's serious persona seemed especially grave. He looked his best, with his dark brown hair all plastered down and his nicest clothes on, but his dark blue eyes were thoughtful and distant. I ached for him.

"I will certainly feel proud to walk to church with the two best looking guys in town," I declared, smiling brightly.

Jay grinned self-consciously. Taking my books, he tucked them under his arm, then bent his other elbow and held it out to me in a gallant gesture. "Ya don't look too shabby yourself, Sis," he eyed me up and down.

"You kids run along," Mom said from her seat at the breakfast table. "We're just going to finish our last cup of coffee then we'll join you at the church."

"Save us a seat," Aunt Thelma sang merrily after us.

As Mark, Jay and I walked out the door, I hesitated momentarily, looking back at the lovely picture my Uncle Bud and Aunt Thelma made, seated with Mom and Dad, drinking the forbidden coffee in a cozy family group around the table in our kitchen. That memory would come back to fill me with haunting sadness in the years to come—tragic years that changed one of these loving, God-fearing people into an accomplice to murder.

I knew Verlan would sit up on the stage with the rest of the leaders. The thought filled me with a glowing, tingling pride. My future husband was a man of such importance, and the more I thought about it, the more I liked the idea. The prophet Joel, of course, led the church; then came Ervil, the church patriarch, then Verlan's position was next in prominence. The president of the twelve apostles! Marrying me, Susan Ray.

I chose a seat four benches back, not too close to the front but close enough so he would be sure to notice me. I wondered if he had brought any of his wives with him from Baja. I hoped not. I wanted him to have plenty of time to look around.

The church building was full already, people hurrying about, shaking each other's hands, laughing and crying—all the things people do who haven't seen their friends and relatives for months. I sat quietly and watched the goings-on around me, and waited expectantly to see a certain tall man in a business suit walk in. I leaned back on the hard bench and imagined how it would be when Verlan arrived. He would see me sitting here all alone, and he would walk over to me. I would be studiously reading my Book of Mormon, and he would reach for my hand and say, "Well, hello, Susan. I was hoping to see you today." And he would smile at me with that intimate look in his eyes. I knew that look by heart, because I had thought about it for weeks.

The benches were filling up around me. Mom, Dad, and Maria walked in and sat down with Uncle Bud and Aunt Thelma. Mark traipsed in and walked straight to where I was sitting. "Scoot over," he demanded. "I want the aisle seat."

"Too bad. I got here first," I grinned and moved my knees so he could get by. "Where's Jay?"

Mark motioned with his head toward the door. "He said he needed to wait for someone, but I got tired of that hot sun." His hazel eyes shifted around the room as he spoke. "Wow!" he suddenly whispered, "*who's that?*"

Debbie Bateman, shining like a golden angel in her creamy yellow dress, was seated with her parents who'd come from California. She waved to me, her eyes resting fleetingly on Mark. I had always been the kind of person to enjoy playing matchmaker, and I recognized a perfect opportunity. Debbie didn't hesitate when I motioned for her to join us.

"Hi!" she said as she approached our bench, her smile flashing flirtatiously at Mark. He slid over to make room for her to sit between us, and in a matter of moments the two of them were completely ignoring me. I continued my search of the crowded room. Esther Spencer was fighting her way down the middle aisle with Grandma LeBaron leaning on her arm. Grandma's fine hair had been done up into fancy curls, with strands of silver gleaming among the soft brown. Her silky maroon dress rustled as her feet slipped across the concrete floor.

Noticing me, she hesitated, her eyes sharp as a teenager's. "Susan! My, don't you look nice!" She threw me a conspiring smile, as if she knew I had taken special care with my appearance today, and why. I blushed a little as I touched her knobby fingers.

Several of the brethren came in together and took their seats on the stage. Still there was no sign of Verlan. I'd wanted to ask Grandma about him, but not with Esther so close to her. I looked to the back of the building, expecting that at any moment he would be coming in.

Joel blocked the doorway. He was talking to someone hidden behind him. I twisted, trying to see if it was Verlan, but when the Prophet finally started up the aisle, I realized the man following him was Jay.

As my brother dropped onto the bench directly behind us, I turned around and anxiously studied his face. His expression was unreadable, his eyes trained on the stage and the men preparing to open the meeting. I couldn't help but wonder what his little visit with the Prophet had been about. Carmela? I hoped so! If so, what had Joel's response been, and how could I stand to wait until after meeting to find out?

Esther was at the piano beginning the prelude so people would settle down. A sinking feeling was forming in the pit of my stomach. Oh, what if Verlan hadn't come at all! Maybe I had waited all this time, and he wasn't even going to show up. If that were the case, it could be another six months, until next conference, before I would see him again. Suddenly I wanted to cry.

Bishop Alma LeBaron stood up on the stage and walked to the pulpit, and a hush settled down around the crowded building. He called the meeting to order, announced the opening hymn, and asked a Mexican member to open the meeting with prayer. A rush of anger replaced my disappointment as I watched Alma. How could he act so good and humble today, when he'd been so hard and heartless the last time I saw him?

As Brother Castro stepped to the pulpit and bowed his head, the back door by the stage opened with a grating sound. Verlan stepped through the doorway. He glanced quickly around, noticing everyone's bowed heads. Hesitating at the side of the stage, he clasped his hands together in a hurried effort at reverence. Brother Castro grinned at him, cleared his throat, and prayed.

I wanted to laugh out loud. He had come! He was here! With pounding heart I stared at him all through the prayer, reveling at how very tall and distinguished-looking he was. My body burned hot and then turned icy with excitement.

Once the prayer was over Verlan stepped onto the stage and sat down on the bench by the Prophet. Grinning widely, he leaned over and shook hands with all the men, then he settled back and looked over the crowded building. He nodded and smiled at several people as his eyes quickly roved around. I stared at him with bated breath as he looked in my direction, waiting for our eyes to meet in joyful recognition. But he looked right past me, down to the last bench and back again. He didn't even hesitate as his eyes swept over me. I waited and watched him for an hour, but he ignored my desperate stare. The meeting droned on forever and I didn't even try to pay attention. I sank lower in the seat, suddenly wishing I could just disappear. All I wanted was to go home and lock myself in my room. How could I have set myself up for such a plunge? What a silly girl I was, to imagine a stupid nightmare with a pleasant ending was guidance from God!

Oh, if only he would just look at me! Maybe he figured five wives were enough, and he wasn't interested in marrying anyone else. Maybe his wives had laid down the law with him and told him they wouldn't accept him marrying another woman. When it came right down to it, five wives were a lot for a man to have. Certainly nothing to be ashamed of if he decided to stop there.

I glanced over the men on the stage and was suddenly conscious of Brother Ervil's eyes straying in my direction. What was *he* staring at? I watched him for a few minutes and soon realized it wasn't me he was looking at, but Debbie, seated next to me. She and Mark had been whispering back and forth and looking into each other's eyes in a telltale way that anyone could recognize as mutual attraction. Ervil seemed fidgety and concerned as he watched them. What's the matter with him, I wondered, doesn't he like Mark? Maybe he feels responsible for Debbie because she's staying at Anna Mae's, and he's being protective. Surely he's not like Alma and wants Debbie to marry an old man!

It reminded me of Carmela, and I looked over to where she was seated next to her mother. Her face was turned away from me, but as I watched her she cast a furtive glance at Jay. Soon she looked at him again, obviously trying to catch his eye, but he wouldn't look at her. Maybe he'd finally given up hope and was trying to let Carmela know. I pondered the situation again, but today my own uncertainty and sense of rejection smothered my anger.

What had ever made me think that someone like Verlan LeBaron could secretly admire me? He probably only remembered an awkward young girl covered in mud. The embarrassment of that day so many weeks ago flooded over me again.

The second the meeting was over; I dashed out of the building. Verlan hadn't spared me so much as a glance, and to watch him visiting with everyone but me, as would probably happen, was more than I could bear.

As I helped Mom and Aunt Thelma prepare lunch, Mom said, "Susan, you're going to have to take your turn staying with Maria's kids this afternoon. You won't mind, will you?"

I instantly agreed. Of all days to stay at home, this was the perfect day. I wouldn't have to see Verlan again and feel the agony of his disinterest.

That evening as I got ready for the play we were to put on, I heard a knock on my bedroom door. "Come in," I yelled, my mouth held funny as I applied heavy pink lipstick in front of the mirror. Jay walked in, all dressed up in his costume, and lounged against the wall as he watched me primp. "That stuff looks awful on you. Why do you smear it on like that?" he shuddered.

I glared at him in the mirror. "If you came in here to gripe at me, then you can just go back out again. I have to wear this for the play, remember?"

He abruptly moved closer to me. "Suze, I need you to get a message to Carmela for me tonight," he whispered.

I whirled and stared at him. "Did you talk to Brother Joel? What did he say?"

Jay avoided my question. "Just tell her to be behind the back hedge at her house tomorrow night at ten. Tell her to be ready."

His face looked strained in the dim light that filtered through the window. I knew this was the most difficult decision he had ever made. He was planning to run away with Carmela, and he knew just what the implications would be. He would lose his fellowship in the church at the very least, and possibly his membership. He might not be allowed to return to the colony.

"What about Alma?" I said abruptly. "What are you going to do if he catches you? He said he wouldn't warn you again. Aren't you afraid?"

"He was just trying to look tough the night he showed up here. He would no more use that gun on me . . . " Jay's eyes softened. "I love her, Suze. He's got to realize that some people are just meant for one another. I've tried to tell him but he won't listen, and I can't think of any other way."

"Where will you go? What will you do once you're married?" I thought of his house across the road and of his big plans to bring his bride to live in it with him.

"I have it all worked out, but I don't want you to know anything about it. Alma will probably question you, and I don't want you to have to lie for me. I'll let you know where we've gone as soon as I can. Okay?"

"I'll tell her tonight," I promised.

Jay kissed my cheek and hugged me hard. "You're a good kid, Sis," he whispered.

The play, as Esther had assured us, was a "grand success." Our audience deafened us with applause and whistles. Their faces were a white blur to me from up on the stage where I stood with the other girls and sang harmony to 'Welcome to Gay Havana.' I tried to find Verlan's face in the crowd, but my searching almost made me forget my lines, so I gave up and paid attention to my part.

I had the perfect opportunity to speak with Carmela while we were changing out of our costumes after the play ended. There were other girls around us, but I made sure I was next to her, and I whispered Jay's message. Her fine, black eyes widened and locked with mine, and her full lips pursed in anxiety. She slowly nodded her head to let me know she would be waiting for him.

"I'll be praying for you," I whispered.

As I walked toward home with the rest of my family, the moon was low and orange on the eastern horizon. Eerie light shone softly where the trees didn't make shadows. Dad carried little Thelma as she slept and Uncle Bud held my baby brother, Ariel, tucked snugly against his chest.

Maria gabbed in broken English to Aunt Thelma and Mom about the "wonderful play," causing them to laugh merrily at her efforts. My thoughts were heavy and troubled as I trailed behind the others. Nothing was going right. If Jay got hurt, or worse, I would be partly responsible. I had encouraged him about Carmela from the start. I liked her as much as any girl I knew and

49

wanted her in our family, but suddenly I was feeling scared. What if Jay was wrong about Alma not being serious in his threat? The thought was too horrible. I remembered the moonlight gleaming on his shotgun barrel and the timbre of his voice when he told me that someone should teach me to have respect for my elders. I shuddered. He might even come after me as an accomplice. I had never, in all my years in the church, heard of anything more awful than this.

The following day, Saturday, was a repeat of the previous day, with meetings and preaching. There was a two-hour stop for lunch, then the preaching lasted until six. Verlan paid no attention to me and I had given up hope that he would.

There was a mad scramble at home to get chores and supper completed in time for the big dance. It was the highlight of the whole weekend for the young people, and I tried to be excited about it.

"What's for supper, Mathel?" Dad boomed as he walked into the kitchen with a brimming milk bucket.

"Chili beans, and they're hot ones. Fara, call everyone for the blessing so we can eat." Mom dropped a hot pad onto the table and lifted a huge kettle onto it, then turned to my aunt, noting her attempts to slice bread with our dull old knife. "Thelma, are you sure you're up to going to that shindig tonight?" she asked.

"Why, I most certainly am! I wouldn't miss it for the world." Aunt Thelma two-stepped around the kitchen, holding the knife in one hand and a plate of sliced bread in the other, a silly smile on her face. Then she plopped the bread down on the table and said, "God's neat; let's eat."

My stomach was turning in knots through the meal. Jay kept his attention on his bowl, and I marveled as he spooned beans into his mouth as though he hadn't a care in the world. I sighed, wondering how someone who planned to elope and leave the home of his childhood this very night could act so nonchalant. What would Mom and Dad say if they knew? But they couldn't know. Dad would probably get a kick out of it, but Mom would be frantic.

I adored my brother and would miss him terribly, and now that I really thought about it, seventeen was awfully young for a man to marry and make his way in the world with a wife to support. Oh, everything was such a mess! This was the worst conference of my life.

Chapter 6

As my family and I strolled up the starlit road to the dance, we could hear the tinkling sounds of piano music long before the building could be seen. The music was mixed in with the low tones of my Dad and Aunt discussing someone's sermon from this morning's meeting.

The night air felt soft and cool against my neck after the day's heat. Quiet as a shadow, Jay walked beside me, and I wanted to reach out and touch him. It was eight o'clock, only two hours before Carmela was to meet him. I wondered how he planned to leave the colony, and as I glanced at his pale face, I wanted to hug him and to beg him not to carry out his plan. But I couldn't do that. He had his mind made up, and I felt he was justified. Heaven alone knew what the night would bring.

Two caballeros on dark horses galloped past us in a wild, furious race, the hoofbeats pounding in rhythm to my heart. Cars were parked for a block on either side of the road as we crossed the cattle guard by the church. The churchyard was packed with Mexicans from around the valley that had gathered to peer into the huge windows and watch the festivities. Their dark faces turned to stare at us as we made our way up the sidewalk.

The benches in the big meeting room had been removed, leaving room for the dancers to rest. Someone had hung gay-colored serapes and Mexican sombreros on the plastered, white-painted walls. Red and blue streamers were woven together and hung in wild array from the ceiling. The cement floor was sprinkled with baby powder for easier gliding. The small electric generator was purring, and two naked light bulbs glared on either end of the big room, casting shadows along the walls. Younger people milled in the center of the room, talking in small groups.

As we walked in, Gaye, one of the Prophet Joel's wives, was seated at the piano pounding out 'Turkey in the Straw' in an effort to get people onto the dance floor. My gaze automatically swept the building. Verlan was on the far side, leaning against the wall, talking animatedly to his brother Ervil. The grin on his face made my heart ache, because I wished he were smiling at me. I forced my eyes away from him and quickly looked among the crowd. Debbie, in a flowing, crimson gown, her chestnut hair bouncing around her shoulders, motioned for me to join her on the bench under the window. Her eyes were sparkling with excitement.

"Oh, Susan, Mark is so gorgeous!" she whispered in my ear the moment I sat down. "I think I'm in love. Why haven't you told me about him?"

I chuckled. "He is cute, isn't he? I haven't seen him for years. I hardly knew him before now. He likes you, too, by the way."

"Do you really think so?" she sounded anxious.

"I know so," I grinned. "He's definitely interested, so relax and enjoy it."

Soon one of the brethren called the dance to order and said a quick prayer. Immediately the piano music started up again and people began to choose their partners for the Virginia Reel. As one of my classmates whirled me around, I searched the crowds for Jay, but he had disappeared. I tensed, wondering about him.

The dance ended. I excused myself and moved from the floor. As the piano player began the next tune, Mark strolled toward Debbie and me, and with a courtly bow extended his hand.

"Who, me?" I joked, determined to put my anxiety aside and have some fun. I looked quickly at Debbie to see her reaction.

"Go on," she laughed and pushed me.

My cousin swung me onto the floor for a fast and furious square dance. Lane Stubbs' younger brother, Kimball, was the caller. His high-pitched voice rose above the music: "Swing your partner 'neath your arm, and all line up for a doe-si-doe! Swing the gal on your left, then the lady on your right. Swing her all around, all around you go . . . "

Laughing breathlessly, I almost forgot about Jay until I was swung next to Carmela. She was dancing with her brother, Ernesto. Her dark brown skin had a yellow tinge to it, and gray circles stood out beneath her eyes. She smiled gently at me before Ernesto whisked her away.

For the next hour I scarcely had time to catch my breath. Several gentlemen, young and old, swept me around the floor. As I danced, I kept a nervous eye on Alma, and noted Carmela's dark hair among the other dancers. Jay hadn't reappeared, and I fretted about his whereabouts. I assumed that he had decided to stay away, hoping that Alma wouldn't connect him to Carmela's disappearance.

The prophet Joel, dressed in his business suit, gallantly waltzed my mom across the floor, and as I watched, he winked at his own mother, Grandma LeBaron, who was dancing with young Elias Paisano. She ignored Joel's teasing gesture of derision for her partner. With her head held high, she allowed Elias to lead her around the room. Half way through the waltz, the other dancers cleared the floor for Grandma and her partner. Elias' black eyes never left her face as he guided her across the floor. Grandma's hair was piled high like a tiara, and in spite of her bad hip, she waltzed with stately bearing, as if the young boy was a prince. Their audience clapped with noisy appreciation as the last strains of the waltz sounded.

The floor was soon crowded again. As I glanced around, I caught Alma's nod of approval at his son Alma D., as Francisca swayed in the young man's arms. I turned my face away. Amazing how it was acceptable for Alma's young, single son to choose the church-grown girl of his choice, but not for my brother to do so.

Mark and Debbie had danced every dance together since his first one with me. At least they were enjoying themselves. I grinned at them as my partner swung me near. Suddenly Mark's eyes widened in surprise. Ervil had appeared at his elbow. Abrupt and commanding, he yanked Debbie away, leaving Mark alone on the dance floor. My cousin looked around self-consciously, then moved to a bench and sat down. Well! Our patriarch certainly was taking his role as Debbie's protector seriously. It had been downright rude, the way he had cut in. I sniffed in distaste. Alma wasn't the only LeBaron who had behavior problems.

As soon as the dance was over, I casually made my way to the bench where Carmela was seated and eased down beside her. She was talking to her mother in Spanish. "I'm feeling so sick!" she was saying. "I can't stand to sit here any longer. I'm going to get Ernesto to take me home."

"What's the matter with you?" Flora asked sharply, "is it that headache again?"

"Si. It must be all this noise." Carmela really did look sick as she covered her ears with her hands. Flora motioned for Ernesto and asked him to take Carmela home. He grudgingly agreed but complained about missing the dance. Carmela didn't even glance at me as they walked away.

I looked hastily around for Alma, to see if he had noticed Carmela's departure. But there he was, already stalking toward the door. Oh, *no!* I thought in panic, what should I do? There has to be something...! I wanted to scream at him to leave her alone, and I bounded off the bench and raced toward him.

Just as he reached the door, the prophet Joel stood up. "Where you going, Alma?" he called out. "Don't be leaving; we've got a meeting starting right now, back in that small room down the hall. Did you forget?" Alma hesitated

53

at the doorway. Reluctantly he turned and followed Joel.

"Oh, praise the Lord!" I breathed. I dropped onto the bench by the door, my legs shaking and weak as hot wax. Did Joel know? Or was it just luck and God on Jay and Carmela's side? I closed my eyes and leaned my head against the wall, feeling drained with the stress of the last two days. Now, if Carmela could just ditch Ernesto somewhere . . .

"Young lady, are you too tired to dance with me?" a musical voice asked. Opening my eyes, I looked into Verlan LeBaron's grinning face. His huge hand was outstretched for mine. I stared at him, tongue-tied. I swallowed and tried to say something, but the words wouldn't come. My mouth was dry as chalk.

He was dressed in a navy suit, with a striped tie pinned neatly into place. His blue eyes twinkled at me, and I remembered them from my dream. In a daze, I reached for his hand. It was warm and firm as he led me onto the dance floor. His arm slipped around my waist and he grinned down at me as we swayed to the music. The sweet, spicy scent of his after-shave washed over me. I trembled, overcome with emotion. I recognized the scent from my dream.

White teeth flashed in his tanned face. "You're all grown up, aren't you? Seems like the last time I looked at you, you were just a tiny little thing with a long blond ponytail. My, how time flies."

I wanted to say something to him, anything, so he wouldn't think I was a total idiot. But the words refused to come. What I had been waiting for had finally happened and it left me speechless. My dream had been real! I no longer doubted it. Only the formalities remained, but I didn't question that they would happen. True, this was only a dance, but it was the beginning of a marriage, whether Verlan LeBaron realized it or not. I closed my eyes and swayed in my future husband's arms, too moved inside to hear the music. I was glad the lighting was poor so Verlan couldn't see the tears on my cheeks.

When the dance ended he escorted me to my seat, squeezed my hand as he released it, and smiled into my eyes. I didn't remember sitting down. I didn't remember anything about the rest of the social. Jay and Carmela's elopement seemed far away. Verlan LeBaron's eyes were the color of a tropical sea.

After the closing prayer and the people around me were leaving the building, after Mom motioned for me to join the rest of the family for the walk home, I felt the daze of unreality gripping me. The moon floated like a yellow balloon in the clear night sky. The family was silent—tired after the long day and exuberant activity. I lagged behind, lost in my thoughts. My mind felt drained and exhausted. So many things had happened in such a short time. Had it only been an hour since Jay and Carmela's departure?

Dad slowed his steps to match mine and put his arm around me. I leaned my head on his shoulder, glad for the support. My legs felt so weak. We had lagged quite far behind the others, and suddenly Dad cleared his throat. "Well, Sis," he said softly, "I guess I might as well tell you now. Verlan LeBaron asked me tonight if he could court you. What do you think about that?"

I stopped and turned to stare at him. His face, usually so jovial, was serious beneath the brightness of the moon. I felt no real surprise at his words, only a radiant, liquid warmth seeping over me like melted butter. My dazed mind began a slow, monotonous chant...*He wants to marry you. He really wants to marry you.*

I started slowly down the road, with Dad falling into step with me. Finally he could stand it no longer. "Well? What do you think? It's up to you, you know. If you don't want him hanging around, just say the word, and I'll..."

"Daddy," I interrupted, "I want to have him hang around. I mean, I want him to court me. But I would like to tell him myself if it would be all right with you."

"I kind of figured you'd say that," he chuckled. "Okay, I'll tell him tomorrow that you want to see him. But just so you know, I warned him that if you said yes, there was to be none of that kissy stuff going on. You are only fourteen, and I told him so. He was surprised."

"I'll be fifteen in October," I reminded him.

We walked into our yard and stood for a moment on the front porch. I gathered that Dad wanted to say more to me, but he shrugged it off and hugged me instead. With a wave of his hand, he sauntered around the house to spend the night at Maria's.

I fell into bed, drained by the emotional upheavals of the day. But my mind refused to clear. I examined the fact that Verlan's request to court me was giving substance to my dream. It was amazing. My thoughts lingered on the soft look in my father's eyes as he told me of Verlan's interest. I relaxed into the warm feelings that coursed through me as I thought of Verlan. Verlan, the man I would marry.

Suddenly, thoughts of Jay and Carmela invaded my mind. I tossed restlessly, listening to the sounds of the crickets outside my window. Their incessant clicking was like seconds on a clock marking off minutes until Alma discovered that his step-daughter was gone. I wondered where they were—if they had gotten safely away.

I fought sleep. Snuggling against my pillow, I rested my tired eyes for just a moment. It seemed as if I had barely closed them when someone was shaking me. Instant fear gripped me.

"Susan, you've got to wake up!" my mother's voice sounded frightened.

Chapter 7

Alma LeBaron paced back and forth like a wild man on the sky-blue linoleum of our living room. As I hesitated in the shadows of the hallway and peered out at him, I felt like my heart had swollen into my throat and was choking me. "You've got to get a grip," I whispered to myself as I shivered in terror. "There's not one thing he can do to you. Jay and Carmela are long gone and out of his reach. His being here proves that." My stomach felt queasy and my hands were shaking, but I clutched my robe and stepped into the lamplight.

Against the wall in the shadows, Mom, Dad, and Maria waited. As I walked into the center of the room, four pairs of eyes glued themselves on me. Alma stopped his furious pacing in the middle of a stride, his penetrating blue gaze coated in ice.

"Susan Ray," he barked, "I don't want you to even attempt to deny knowledge of why I'm here. You've been in cahoots with that brother of yours from the start. You helped him make away with my daughter, and you, young lady, are going to tell me right now where they've gone."

His voice resounded like a physical slap and I winced. My lips felt stiff as I tried to make them form words. "I don't know where they've gone. Jay wouldn't tell me because he knew you would try to make me tell you . . . "

"Alma," Dad interrupted, "why are you so bound and determined to break those kids up? The way you've been acting, you'd think my son was a criminal! He's a good boy who loves Carmela. He's been raised in the church. He's a member of the priesthood. He loves the gospel and plans to live a godly life. As long as your daughter is happy with him, why should you meddle?"

Alma whirled on Dad. "Vern, I happen to care about my girl's future! I'm the only father she's ever known, and I think I know what's best for her! She's strong-willed and needs a mature man to be her spiritual head, not some punk kid who doesn't even show a beard shadow yet. We have the church to think of, and the Kingdom of God and its growth and strength to consider."

By now they were toe to toe, Alma's height towering over my father's short body. "The man who wants to marry her needs a plural wife for his own spiritual growth," Alma's voice had taken on the tones of a sermon. "You know it's no easy task for a married man to convert and marry a woman from the outside. The girls who are raised in the church must be saved for plural wives. Your boy can go out in the world and convert himself a girl to marry. Now, he's not having my daughter, and if it's too late by the time I find her, I will bring that son of yours up on Mann Act charges."

Alma whirled on me again, his eyes grim and determined. "If you know where they've gone, you'd better speak now, or plan to see your brother in jail."

"Okay, hold it right there." Dad's voice was abrupt, his indignant blue eyes flashing. "Susan says she doesn't know where those kids went, so stop trying to browbeat her. If you want my opinion, there's some so-called laws and ordinances taking place in this church that are about as Christian as Communism. I don't know who exactly is responsible for coming up with this garbage you're spouting about, but I've a strong feeling Joel has nothing to do with it. Now, I've heard all I want to hear about this. Just for the record, I'm proud of my boy! You sell him short. I'm glad he had the guts to stand up to you, Alma. You *forced* him to elope with Carmela! They would have waited if you hadn't tried to make her marry Hector." Dad paused for breath, then continued, his voice lowering, "Now, it's late and I'm tired. You go ahead and rant on about this if it makes you feel better, but do it somewhere other than my living room." Reaching out for the front door, he swung it wide. "Goodnight, Alma," he said gently.

Mom and Maria sidled over to my father and stood next to him, strong and silent in their support like soldiers behind their captain. Alma stared at the three of them in helpless rage. He started to speak, reconsidered, and stormed past them. When he reached the porch, he looked back. "You haven't heard the last of this," he bristled.

As Dad closed the door I collapsed in a heap in the rocking chair. I wanted to scream and sob my fear and anger, but my strength was gone and I sat in numb silence, waiting for my parents' wrath. But I had misjudged them. Maria walked over to me and lightly stroked my hair. "*Pobrecita*," she said softly, her brown eyes full of tears. "You carried the burden of this fear for your brother all alone, yes? That Alma! He's like a Hitler!" She clucked her tongue and shook her head in sadness.

"Susan, how long have you known about this?" My mother's voice shook.

"Since yesterday. Jay didn't want you all to know. He didn't want to worry you."

"Well," Dad sighed, "there's no use stewing over it. What's done is done. Those kids won't be coming back to the colony for awhile, I can tell you that. I don't know how serious Alma was about sending the law after Jay, but just in case, he'd better stay out of his way. Carmela is under age."

"It will all work out!" Maria said firmly in Spanish. "It will blow over soon. Come on, Vern. Let's go back to bed."

Dad leaned down and kissed my hair. "You kids!" he muttered. He gave my mother a pat and trailed Maria out the door.

Mom wandered around the kitchen, her eyes deep caverns in her pale face. Suddenly she glanced at me, as if noticing for the first time that I was still here. "Go to bed, girl," she said quietly. "Let's not worry any more about this. Like Maria said, it'll all work out."

As I made my way through the dark hall past Aunt Thelma's and Uncle Bud's door, past Fara and Mona's room, I wondered how they had slept through the yelling that had occurred. I crawled into bed and lay still for a long time, staring into the darkness. Finally, the ice that had formed on my insides melted and fell in giant drops on my pillow. Why did things seem so confusing? Almost everyone considered Alma a godly, righteous man. After all, he was the Bishop of God's true church, a church that would encompass the whole world one of these days. But was he right in this present issue? Would God agree with Alma's reasoning? In my heart, I couldn't feel that He would.

I tossed and turned, my body alternating from freezing to dripping with sweat. When sleep finally came, it was restless and filled with nightmares.

Uncle Bud's and Aunt Thelma's usual banter was lacking the next morning. Jay's disappearance had caused a dark gloom to settle over the household. Fara's and Ramona's eyes grew huge with shock when they heard about it. "Isn't he ever coming back?" Mona's voice quivered, as her round chin trembled.

"Of course he is," Mom said quickly. "Just as soon as he can. You have a new sister now, Mona. When Jay comes back, he'll bring Carmela home with him."

The news quickly spread. It was Sunday, the last day of conference, and people huddled together to discuss the elopement. As I hurried in the door for the afternoon meeting, one of the colony busybodies was saying, "…didn't surprise me in the least. Hector planned to marry her, you know, the poor man."

Throughout the afternoon, Verlan grinned and winked at me several times. He seemed so carefree and happy, as if he understood the uneasiness I was experiencing and wanted to cheer me up. It did make me feel better. As the day passed, the excitement of being courted returned, and it almost replaced the empty, gnawing feeling inside me.

Directly after the meeting Verlan excused himself from the men gathered up on the stage and made his way towards me. "I understand you will have time to talk to me tonight?" he said in a low tone. His eyes were warm, his smile intimate.

I felt so shy and tongue-tied, just like an awkward child. "I would like that," I said, hesitantly smiling back at him.

"Are you going to the young people's Fireside Social at my mother's tonight?"

I nodded again, and he said, "Real fine, then. I'll be there, waiting for you. I'll be in the back bedroom when it's over, so just come find me, okay?" He flashed his lopsided grin and went back to the huddle of men.

Tonight. Could I wait until then? I didn't think I could. Before I walked out the door I looked back at him. Tonight seemed an eternity away.

After dinner was over, Mark walked with me to Grandma LeBaron's. One of the Apostles would be speaking tonight, followed by refreshments and games. The Chynoweths were planning to leave shortly afterward to return to Utah. As we hurried along in the twilight, Mark glanced over at me several times, his sharp hazel eyes noting my nervousness. "You're not still worrying about Jay, are you?" he chided. "If you are, don't. He and Carmela are probably hidden away in some motel room in Chihuahua City right now, calling room service for supper. I'm betting they'll be back here within a year. Jay just needs to prove to all these old duffers that he can take care of a wife, and then Alma will welcome 'em home with open arms. So stop your fidgeting, Susie. You're not his mother," Mark poked me in the ribs.

I smiled at his efforts, but Jay wasn't the one on my mind. My meeting with Verlan loomed before me, and I was excited, yet so scared!

It was past ten o'clock when the noisy teenagers in Grandma's living room began leaving. I walked outside with Debbie. Her family had arrived to tell her goodbye, and they were loading into their station wagon, preparing to head for the border.

"Debbie, sweetheart," her mom was saying as she hugged her oldest child, then dabbed the tears away from her rouged cheeks, "You'd better write more often from now on; promise me you'll take care of yourself. Honey, I miss you so much, and I worry about leaving you down here."

"Now, Mother, I'm a big girl." Debbie threw an exasperated look at Mark, who was hovering close.

I wandered back into the kitchen where Grandma was washing up the Koolaid glasses. Absently I glanced at her hardwood cabinets with the white tile counter tops and the stainless steel sink with running tap water. A huge refrigerator stood in the corner. Creamy Spanish tile covered the floor. A big table against one wall held freshly made bread that smelled delicious. It looked so modern and comfortable, a palace in comparison to our home, where we hauled well water and kept jars of milk and other perishables in pans of cold water.

Grandma wiped her hands on her apron. "That was a nice crowd that showed up tonight, wasn't it? It's so good to see young folks enjoying themselves. I can't believe conference is over already, can you? It just went by in a flash."

"Grandma, which room is Verlan in?" My face flamed. I peeked at her out of the corner of my eye, then busied myself putting away dishes.

Her smile lit up the dim kitchen. "Does this mean what I think it does? Has he said something to you?"

"Yes. Well, sort of." I glanced at her shyly. "He asked my dad last night if he could court me."

"Well! Now isn't that something, after your dream and all! He asked me about you yesterday morning. He thinks you're awfully pretty, you know."

Warmth and delight tingled through me, clear to my toes. "Did he really say that?"

"Well now... not in those exact words. He said you'd certainly grown up. But I know my son. I could see that gleam in his eyes."

Disappointment wiped the grin from my lips. It wasn't the same thing at all. "Grandma," I reminded her after a moment, "which room is he in?"

"Oh, yes... Honey, it's the far one on the right, down the hall. Just knock on the door, and make yourself at home. I'll see that no one bothers you." She grinned at me like a conspirator.

I stood in front of the bedroom door several moments before I had the nerve to knock. What was the man on the other side of this door really like? I had no personal knowledge of him. I only knew of Verlan through other people who spoke highly of him. I liked his appearance, and I loved the way his eyes twinkled at me. His smile was charming and full of humor, but what was he really like? I knocked. The door opened, and his warm grin welcomed me.

"There you are!" his voice rang out. "I was about to go looking for you. Come on in."

I quickly took in the furnishings of the bedroom—the bed with its beautiful tied quilt, an opened Book of Mormon face down on it, an old fashioned white bureau with a hand crocheted runner covering its top, the cream-colored tile floor, softened with a bright braided rug. The homey, comfortable atmosphere somehow helped with the awkwardness of this meeting.

"I appreciate your willingness to see me," Verlan was saying as I walked to the center of the room and turned to face him. He leaned against the wall and bending one knee, rested his foot on the edge of the bedstead. Crisp beige jeans hugged his hips. A turquoise western shirt that exactly matched his eyes was open at the neck, revealing dark, curling hair on his chest. He rested his folded arms on his knees, leaned forward, and cleared his throat.

"I'm sure your father told you that I would dearly love an opportunity to get to know you better," his magnificent eyes touched me, warm and friendly.

I nodded, shaking with nervousness. Somehow I managed to say, "Yes, he did, and I would like that very much. But will your wives be okay with this?"

He looked taken aback. "Well, they understand that I'm highly in favor of plural marriage, and they've accepted that way of life. I don't want you to worry in the slightest about them." He suddenly grinned, "I want you to think about me, not about them. This is the beginning of a relationship between you and me, okay? Let's just concentrate on getting to know each other. I know it'll be difficult, with me away from town, but I'll write to you real often."

In one long step he was standing beside me, looking down into my eyes. That now familiar scent of him washed over me in gentle waves. "Do you think you could drop me a line, once in a while? I'd sure love it. For every letter you write, I'll write two to you, okay?"

"Okay," I echoed. My heart pounded at his nearness. He was just a few inches away, and I fought the urge to put my arms around his waist and bury my cheek against his chest. What was the matter with me! I didn't even know this man, but the knowledge that he was going away and I wouldn't see him again for months suddenly made me blink back tears.

Verlan reached into his pocket, pulled a business card out of his wallet, and handed it to me. "That has my address on it." He took a deep breath, the raggedness of it causing me to tremble. "Would it be all right if I walk you home?"

I nodded and took a step back, turning so that he couldn't see my face. "I do need to go now," I mumbled. "It's late, and I have school in the morning."

We tiptoed through the silent hallway, left the house, and crossed Grandma's front yard. The full moon glowed in the dark sky, making the potholes in the road ahead of us appear as shadowy pits. Verlan's body radiated warmth as I walked by his side for the first time. He made no move to touch me or to hold my hand. How different he was from Lane, who had never missed an opportunity to touch me or kiss me.

"I understand your brother Jay eloped with Alma's daughter last night," he said, breaking the silence. "I'll bet you've been shook up about that."

I swiftly glanced at him, wondering what he was getting at. "Jay and Carmela love each other, and Alma was trying to marry her off to someone else," I said hotly. "I don't blame them in the least. I absolutely disagree with forced marriages."

"I do too, and I want you to know that right now," Verlan interrupted. "Just for the record, I told Alma that in my opinion he was way out of line. The Lord gave the gift of love between a man and woman for a purpose, and it's not to be taken lightly. Jay's a good man, and I told Alma so." In the moonlight I could see a smile crease his face. "What's this I was told about you helping in the elopement? Did you really do that?"

I blinked my eyes and trudged along in silence. What was he going to do, bawl me out? "Verlan," I primly declared, "I love my brother and I would do anything for him. I'm sorry that Alma's mad at me, but I'd do it again tomorrow if I had to. I hate to say this ... and I hope you won't think I'm terrible, but I really don't like your brother Alma much."

Our feet crunched gravel in unison, the sound loud as I awaited his response to my arrogant announcement. Suddenly he chuckled. "Well, don't let anyone say you haven't got any guts." He looked down at me, his voice warm with admiration. "Yep, you've certainly grown up to be a lovely young lady, and in such a hurry. Seems to me the last time I saw you, you had fallen in the ditch."

Oh, Lord! Instantly I could feel my face burning and I groaned aloud, stuttering with embarrassment. "I—I was afraid you remembered that. It—it wasn't my fault. You see, my little sister was ... "

His loud laugh rang out in the stillness. "You don't need to explain," he broke in, "I'm just teasing you a little bit. I'm sorry. I knew it was something like that. Do you know, I never realized how a girl could shine, even covered in muck. You looked absolutely beautiful."

We stopped moving, and I realized we were at the front gate of my home. As Verlan said those last words, his voice lost the tormenting quality. His shadowy features appeared grave and sincere, and suddenly his finger lightly traced my jaw from neck to chin. His hand was trembling.

I searched his face. I wouldn't see this man of my dream again for many months. Our new friendship was being severed before it had barely begun. Why did he have to live so far away? How could I stand it until I saw him again?

"Susan, it is what you want—for us to become better aquainted, isn't it?"

Uneasiness electrified me, and suddenly I was shaking with alarm. What ... why had he said it like that, as though the idea was mine? What was he implying? A horrifying thought invaded my mind. Grandma told him about my dream! Oh God, surely she wouldn't have! I *told* her I wanted whatever happened to be his idea! That he might know about it and think I was "after" him. . . . Oh, please, God, I thought, *please*, don't let him know!

He was studying me, waiting for me to say something. Finally I nodded, my head bent. I stepped back, away from his nearness.

"I'll write you real soon, okay?" His voice was gentle. "Take good care of yourself." He picked up my hand and kissed it, hard. Then abruptly he released it and waited for me to walk up the path to the door.

I turned and waved once I reached the porch. "I'll write back to you," I called after him.

He sauntered away into the night.

Chapter 8

The summer months swept the Mexican desert into a heat wave that turned the fields and gardens of the colony an ugly brown. The seasonal rains, though hovering in heavy gray mist over the distant western mountains, stubbornly refused to make their appearance and relieve the parched terrain. The weeks of school vacation slipped away, the days and nights hot and uncomfortable.

Lazy days and fun were only wishful thinking for me. The chores of summer kept me occupied. With Dad and Jay gone, Mother relied on my help. The garden, a valuable source of my family's food supply, needed constant care. Our windmill slowly pumped precious water into a giant tank, and my mother and I irrigated until big blisters formed on our palms, blisters that later became hard calluses. The thirsty land sucked up the water, only to be dry and cracked again in a matter of hours.

The duties my mother, sisters and I performed seemed endless. We had two cows, three hundred chickens, several fruit trees and a huge garden, a demanding chore for anyone. Water required hand pumping and hauling for the animals, kitchen use, and laundry. The motor for the old Maytag Dad had hauled across the border had finally quit, leaving us with an old-fashioned plunger and a glass scrub board. There were peaches, peas, corn, and beans for canning, and later there would be pineapple, apples, and pears. On the weekends when Dad came home, he would haul the cleaned and boxed eggs we had to Casas Grandes for selling. We crawled into bed each night exhausted.

Two weeks after Jay and Carmela eloped we received a letter saying they were living in New Mexico. Jay had found a new job there, doing the electrical work Dad had trained him for. He wrote that they were happy and getting along fine. Dad was working only thirty miles away and drove to see them often. His frequent trips home always brought more news of Jay and Carmela.

I missed Jay, his sweetness and comradeship, also his help with the chores. His little house across the street remained empty, and I longed for the day he and his new wife would return.

Alma continued to be furious regarding their elopement. He perceived it as a personal affront to his church position and his role as a stepfather. He pointedly ignored me as he drove his pickup and tended to his farms and animals. It appeared to me that he spun his tires extra hard when passing me. He vehemently proclaimed to all his resolution to maintain Jay's disfellowship status for many, penalty-paying years. I secretly despised him.

True to his word, Verlan's letters came with faithful regularity. Full of poetic phrases and guarded suggestions of love, the letters were the joy of my existence. He told of new converts, and missions to different states with brethren, and of his job as a house painter in Las Vegas. He revealed little of himself or his families. The first letter was signed, "Sincerely, Verlan." The next one, "With love," and on the third letter he had written across the bottom in his firm hand, "I love and miss you, Darling." I nearly cried with happiness, and eagerly anticipated his weekly correspondence.

One week the expected letter failed to arrive at Jensen's store. Earl Jensen's plural wife, Maudie, was the post-mistress there, and the small store contained limited groceries. My feet wore a trench on the dusty road each day I checked the mail in vain. The note that Verlan finally sent seemed distant and cold. He had been busy, his families needed him, he hoped I was well. He closed with a dash of the pen saying, "Stay in touch, Verlan." The perfunctory tones pricked my heart like a dull needle, and that night I cried myself to sleep.

Who was I kidding, anyway, I bullied myself. How could I expect romance and constant attention from a busy and important man like Verlan? Again, I wondered if Grandma had told him of my dream. If so, he undoubtedly felt obligated to court me. Several times during my piano lessons I wanted to ask her about it, but I just couldn't say the words aloud. Whenever I looked into her honest eyes, I felt ashamed that the thought had entered my mind, and I had to wonder if I was worthy of her friendship. Still, the worry continued to haunt me.

School restarted the end of August. But this year, rather than sending our high school youth to a neighboring town and a Mexican, state-run institution, our leaders had voted to keep us in the colony and have us taught by members of the church. Every adult who was remotely qualified was called upon to teach a class. Quickly our days were filled with lessons. My mother taught English and literature in our kitchen and living room, with sixteen students crowding the two tables.

One of these school days in early September, Debbie took me aside. "Susan," she whispered, "this morning before I left Anna Mae's, Ervil told me to let you know he wants to see you. He said to have you go over there after school today."

"Huh?" I sucked my breath sharply. "Why does he want to see *me?*"

She shrugged. "Beats me. You screwed up lately?"

Apprehension prickled me. What in the world could Ervil LeBaron want with me? I barely knew him. He seemed so distant at church, and too important to waste his time with me. During the eight years I'd been in Mexico, he had hardly spoken to me. But then, he was the Second Grand Head of Priesthood of God's Church, and I was only a fourteen-year-old kid. Was he planning to reprimand me for helping Jay and Carmela when they eloped? That must be it. He wanted to warn me that I was messing with regulations.

After math class, I dutifully walked to Anna Mae's. I'd just hold my head high and let him rant. Then it would be over with.

I timidly knocked on the door of the rock house. "Come in," Anna Mae's musical voice called. She stood at the sink peeling potatoes. Her hefty body was covered in a moss green, baggy muumuu. Her long, carrot-colored hair was pulled away from her face with a rubber band and cascaded down her back like fiery lava. Her face and arms were covered with freckles. Her brown eyes also contained flecks. "Well, looky who's here!" Her bubbly laughter filled the kitchen. "My goodness, Susan Ray, it's been ages since you came to my house! What can I do for you?"

Her friendliness didn't ease my apprehension. "I understand Brother Ervil wanted to see me about something. Is he here?" I hoped he wasn't, and I'd turn around and leave.

"Oh, yes," Anna Mae dashed my hopes. "He's in there." She inclined her head toward a door that led off the living room. "He's actually in bed with pneumonia, but he's not all that sick. Just go on in."

As I opened the door into Patriarch Ervil LeBaron's bedroom, my nostrils were assailed by a variety of odors—Vicks, damp wool, and stale urine being the most distinguishable. I wrinkled my nose. A sheet hung over the window, leaving the room shrouded in semidarkness. I blinked my eyes, unaccustomed to the gloom, and peered at the bed. Dark, cavernous eyes stared at me from the pale face that lay on the white pillows. A huge hand listlessly motioned to me.

"Come on in," Ervil's voice rasped.

With a thumping heart, I walked to the armchair he was pointing to. What could he want that was important enough to send for me, as sick as he was? I wiggled back into the chair and looked at him.

He was staring at me, his deep-set eyes ringed with dark smudges. His huge body was covered to the neck with a homemade quilt, his feet hanging six inches past the bottom of the mattress. I remembered Grandma warning him to take care of himself. Well, he must have ignored her. He really did look sick.

He coughed and grabbed the roll of toilet paper near his side, spit phlegm, wiped his mouth, and wearily tossed the tissue into the overflowing trash can at the side of his bed. Then, dropping his massive head onto the pillows, he turned his attention to me.

"I want to thank you for taking the time to see me today. I apologize for this..." He waved his hand in a feeble sweep around the room. "I haven't felt well enough to care about anything except sleep. I guess I look pretty bad, huh?" He sniffed and coughed again. "Oh well, I'm getting better."

He smiled at me, and suddenly I noticed that his eyes glowed with a strange, unearthly light, like a cat's eyes in the dark. I involuntarily shivered. It's the fever that makes them shine like that, I assured myself.

I looked at the cramped, cluttered room. Clothes hung from a chair. A makeshift closet with a bedspread draped in front erupted clothing onto the floor. Under the bed I could see the edge of a porcelain chamber pot. The nightstand held medicine bottles and a fruit jar half full of water, a dead fly floating in it. I squirmed and swallowed hard. "Debbie said you wanted to see me," I squeaked, tearing my eyes away from the fly.

"Yes. I've had you on my mind lately, and I felt we should talk awhile." Ervil struggled up on his pillows, his glowing eyes assessing me. "How old are you now, Susan?"

The question startled me. What did my age have to do with anything? "I'll be fifteen next month."

"Aha." He nodded and stared at me some more. "You do realize that fifteen is considered a marriageable age in our church." It was a statement, not a question, and his glassy eyes searched my face. "Do you have anyone in mind?"

I could feel the blood rush to my cheeks. Well! So this was what he wanted to see me about! I wasn't aware that the colony girls were expected to discuss their marriage plans with the Patriarch, or any of the leaders for that matter! Someone should have warned me. The last thing I wanted to do was inform this man that I was being courted by his brother, especially now, when I was feeling so unsure of Verlan. Only yesterday I had received another letter from him, another curt, businesslike note that had left me stunned and confused.

"I understand you're planning to marry Verlan, is that right?" Ervil questioned in a calm, raspy voice.

My eyes widened in amazement. How... Who had told him? It had to be... It had to be Verlan. Anger ripped through me. He was busy broadcasting our courtship as if it were all settled. How dare he take me for granted!

I leaned back in the armchair and closed my eyes. Hurt boiled in me until I had to squeeze back the tears. I had a little pride. I planned to marry for love, not because I would fit nicely into someone's family. I wanted someone to adore me and want me for *me*. I wasn't just another female—just another womb to bear some man's offspring! If this was the way Verlan thought of me, then he could just think again. Furious, I turned my head and stared at the door, away from Ervil's insulting gaze.

The huge, smelly man in the bed choked and spit again, then settled weakly back onto his pillows. "Well?" His voice was almost tender. "You are contemplating marriage?"

Haughty defiance replaced my fear of him. Lifting my chin, I swept my eyes back to his pale face. "Brother Ervil," I said in my most prim voice, "you are a very busy man, and right now a very sick one. I appreciate your interest, but I haven't decided as yet about my future. I have plenty of time ahead of me. When I *do* decide, I'll let you know, if you like." I stood up, my shoulders back, shaking inside at my bravery. I was definitely Vern Ray's daughter.

Ervil clutched the bedstead, and with effort pulled himself into a sitting position. He motioned me nearer to him. I hesitated. He reached toward me, his fingers wrapping around my arm in a vise-like grip. I found myself being pulled down onto the bed—seated closer to this man than I had ever been in my life. I stared at him in stunned surprise.

"Do you realize the task we have before us as God's chosen people?" Ervil's voice rasped stern and commanding, his eyes intense, his breath nauseating. "We're just a handful of people, young lady, yet we've been given the responsibility of taking God's word to the world before it's too late! *No other people on this earth* are qualified for such an enormous undertaking, just us men, here, around you. God has asked us to sacrifice our own lives, in a manner of speaking. Life in this mission field is a battlefield, and Verlan and I and our other men are God's soldiers, set apart to do His bidding. What better thing could we possibly do with our lives," he demanded, "than give them in service to the King!"

I stared into his stormy eyes, unnerved by his earnestness. I had always known of these things he was saying. But never had I been told them in such a direct way. With every breath, this man offered his life as a living sacrifice.

Even sick as he was his devotion and wholehearted loyalty to the cause he championed was remarkable. I watched him in awe, and I suddenly understood why so many of the people of the church were almost hypnotized by him. He was on fire for the Lord. No wonder his eyes glowed.

His voice had risen through the short speech, climaxing at the end. Now it dropped, the tones taking on a pleading note. "Where do you women fit into all of this? Well, I'll tell you." He released my arm, then glanced at me, his gray eyes soft and beautiful.

"Susan, you women play a gigantic part in God's Kingdom," he declared. "Your support and loyalty to our men is what keeps us strong and able to carry on with the work set before us. We couldn't possibly do it without you. You are the real strength! Let any man try to say that without the support of his wives he can function in the Kingdom as God has commanded him...and I will show you a man who is a damn liar." Ervil vehemently shook his head. "It can't be done. A man is only a miserable failure without good, believing women at his side. Ask me. I know."

He wiped at his forehead, his face a grayish mass. I stared at him, too moved to comment. With his bright gaze fastened on my face, he spoke on, his voice raising to vibrant tremors, then dropping to whispers. The depth of feeling Ervil stirred within me transfixed me, and I began to see his vision of the church and my part in the order.

"You've been raised in the colony," he continued quietly. "You have a responsibility. You're not like most of the girls your age. You may be rather young, but you're mature. Tell me, what better thing could you possibly do with your young years than to be a blessing to a worthy man of God? Leave the silly, romantic notions to the girls of the world. Be willing to place yourself in the service of the only Living God! You will be greatly rewarded for it."

He dropped onto the pillows and closed his eyes. I stood, so touched by his words and manner I couldn't speak. I looked at him, so drawn and pale. Surely he was a great man of God! His righteousness was supremely evident and I wondered how my father had thought otherwise about him. I walked to the door in a spirit of reverence. The dim, dingy room had taken on the aura of a great cathedral, a place where only a holy hush would do.

Ervil's voice broke the spell. "I'd like to see you tomorrow afternoon, same time. If anyone should question what you're doing with me, just tell them I'm giving you endowments," he turned his face away, exhausted.

As I left Anna Mae's house, the clouds, which had delayed their coming for so long, finally whipped themselves into huge thunderheads. The late afternoon sky was dark and foreboding. The wind tore at my hair and blouse as I walked the dirt road, past Wakeham's chicken coop, past the church house, and on toward home. Ahead, a tumbleweed rolled across the road and lodged against the barbed wire fence. I hurried, leaning into the wind, bent on reaching shelter before the full force of the rain hit.

My mind and body felt numb from being in Ervil's presence and from his soul-searching words. He was right. I had needed his sermon in the worst way to get me back on the right track. I had been so self-centered! I had totally ignored my responsibility to give God my life in service. I had worried about petty things, like love and romance, and a man's attention, when I should have been thinking of how best I could serve God, how best I could build up His Church. I shook my head in ashamed exasperation at how foolish and weak-minded I was. Ervil had called me mature! I chuckled in self-derision as I pushed my way against the strong blasts of wind. If he only knew. I was glad he didn't. I was going to change, and offer myself as a soldier in God's army. I would line myself up shoulder to shoulder with people like Ervil, and gladly serve the Lord.

The rain came softly, then in a deluge. The pelting sheets of water plastered my hair against my face and thin blouse. It was past milking time as I dashed through the kitchen door. I stopped on the porch only long enough to scrape the mud off my shoes.

"There you are!" my mother's voice snapped at me from the dinner table. "Where have you been? I've been worried sick about you with that storm outside."

My sisters were sipping at steaming bowls of soup. Mona looked up at me and giggled. "Holy Moly, you look like a drowned rat. You been at Franny's?"

That sounded good. "Um hum..." Mom would have many questions if she thought for a moment that I had spent the afternoon with Ervil LeBaron. I wouldn't know how to explain. "I'd better go milk," I said quickly, and grabbed my raincoat and two milk pails. Fara gave me a knowing glance, a look that said, "Sure, you've been at Franny's". But she kept her mouth shut.

"Miss Susan," Mom began, "I get so tired of you ignoring the rules around here! You know I have asked you so many times to come straight home after school..."

I slammed the screen door, and as I sloshed through the mud puddles toward the barn, I could hear my mother's scolding voice, droning on as if I was still there.

The rain was hammering down in torrents, and I shivered. I was soaked underneath the raincoat, and I wondered why I had worn it. Our two cows were standing as far under the overhang of the barn as they could, their hides steaming with the rain. Cleo moved toward me when I opened the gate as if to say, "Well, where have *you* been?" I guided her to her stall, forked hay into the manger, and started an even splat-splat into the milk bucket. The rain, pounding down on the tin roof of the barn, had a hollow and lonesome sound. I tucked my head under the flap in Cleo's hind leg, and, to the rhythm of the squirting milk, I sang, "We Thank Thee, O God, for a Prophet, to guide us in these latter days. . . . " Ervil wasn't a prophet, exactly, but he was the next best thing. What an extraordinary, godly man!

I adjusted the one-legged milk stool more firmly beneath me. It had sunk in the mud nearly to the seat. Mud stuck to my fingers, and as I wiped it off on Cleo's steaming hide, my mind spun with the events of the afternoon. I thought about the things that Ervil had told me concerning marriage. I tried to picture Verlan's face, and I wondered again if he wanted to marry me, or if he felt it was his duty. Was I being oversensitive about his letters? Probably. He had talked several times about love and called me "darling." I had my dream. It would all work out.

The following day, when school was out, I raced through the rain to Anna Mae's. I wondered why Ervil wanted to see me again. What more did he want to say to me? I turned into the gate and walked up the path to the rock house. Two small boys were staring at me through the window. They had red hair like their mother's and big, solemn brown eyes.

"Ervil was hoping you'd come again today," Anna Mae beamed at me. Go right on in, and here, take this lamp with you. That storm has made it almost dark as night in there."

Aromas of fresh, hot bread surrounded me. Anna Mae's muumuu, the same she had worn yesterday, was splotched with flour and oil. I smiled at her, admiring her warmth and kindness. There was no doubt she was one of the "soldiers" Ervil had spoken of.

I carried the lamp past the two staring boys and softly rapped on Ervil's bedroom door. He was looking better! As I moved the Mason jar of water—no fly in it today—and the cough syrup on the nightstand for the lamp, I looked at him and grinned. His hair was neatly combed, and he was clean-shaven. A fresh white shirt was buttoned to his neck and he was propped on his pillows in a sitting position. He appeared ready for company. As he reached out to shake my hand in greeting, I caught the distinct smell of toothpaste and a hint of after-shave lotion! I smiled inwardly. Was this for my benefit?

"Sit down, sit down!" he offered heartily.

I removed my raincoat and glanced around, noticing the armchair I had used yesterday was absent. Ervil obligingly moved his feet. I could feel the color stain my cheeks as I perched on the end of the bed. This was so cozy. It was almost intimate. A few days ago I couldn't have imagined sharing a bed with Ervil LeBaron, regardless of the innocent circumstances.

Then began a lengthy discourse, the subject of which took me totally by surprise. "Did anyone ever tell you I was a star basketball player in high school?" Ervil opened the conversation. "All of us boys played, but I was the best."

I stared at him, initially taken aback, and then fascinated as he spoke. He carried on of his previous athletic talents, how Mesa College in Arizona had offered him a scholarship and how he had begged his father, Alma LeBaron, Senior, to further his schooling and his sports. His father refused to allow him college entrance. His help was needed in Mexico, on the ranch caring for the goats.

"At the time," Ervil said reminiscently, his gaze sad and faraway, "I thought he was the meanest and most narrow-minded person I'd ever known. I didn't understand how he could insist his own son pass up a basketball scholarship to be buried on a little ranch out in the middle of nowhere. But now," he sighed, "now that I'm older, and Joel has been given the Mantle and needs my help to run this church, I realize how wise my dad really was to get me out of the United States when he did. If he hadn't—who knows, as young and innocent as I was, where I would have ended up. God was guiding him," he concluded. "My father knew there was a mission in store for me."

Although I knew little about basketball or scholarships, Ervil's manner was so touching and humble that I found myself immediately drawn to him. Although he had bragged about his ability in sports, his obvious willingness to follow God's lead impressed me, and again I sat in awe of him.

He was watching for my reaction to his story. He appeared satisfied as his eyes roved over my face. "Susan," he said quietly after a moment, "God wants me to give you a message."

As the weight of his words slowly sank, my breathing labored. I stared at him, wide-eyed. I could feel the blood drain from my face. Dear Lord! A message from *God–to me?*

"What do you mean?" I gasped.

"God wants you to know that He would be extremely pleased if you married me," he said evenly, his gray eyes never leaving mine.

I slowly exhaled. My hands were clammy, and I wanted to run, to fly, anywhere, away from this stifling room and this strange, charismatic man who claimed God talked to him. I glanced at him and then looked away. What was I supposed to say? What could I say?

Suddenly I thought about my dream. I had been given my own personal revelation, my own guidance about the man I would marry. It had nothing to do with Ervil. Something was wrong here; something didn't make sense. Yes, I decided; I had to tell of my dream.

Shakily I said, "Brother Ervil, I don't mean to make light of what you just said. I don't want you to think that I discount your word, but you must know that I had a dream a few months ago. A special dream. It was about a man— the man I would marry. That man wasn't you. I believe that the dream was a revelation from God. Since then, I've planned to marry this man."

If he was disturbed by what I said, he didn't show it. "Who, Verlan?"

I hesitated for only a moment. "Verlan," I echoed.

Ervil calmly nodded his head. "Verlan's a good man. I don't mean to steer you away from him. But you must realize that dreams can come from two sources. Know what I mean? Many people have found themselves in deep trouble from relying too heavily on dreams."

He fell silent, and I was speechless. The seconds passed. I shifted on the bed and glanced longingly at the door. Noises from the living area of the house— kids chattering and Anna Mae's high-pitched voice answering them seemed louder than before. I could feel Ervil's eyes studying me. He cleared his throat, his voice gentle. "God told me personally that He would like you in my family. There's no mistake about this, Susan. I know he wouldn't give you a dream about someone else and then tell me to ask you to marry me. I'm sure you can see that. So, what should we trust, your dream or direct word from God? You tell me."

My body, as I listened to Ervil denounce my dream, shook with shame and uncertainty. I slumped and dropped my face into my hands. Verlan. Was it all just a figment of my imagination? Just a common nightmare? All this time I had thought God considered me worthy and had chosen to personally direct me. Was it my imagination? Perhaps Verlan knew and had been trying to tactfully end his courtship. I wanted to die.

Ervil's voice cut into my heavy thoughts. "Will you just think about what I've said?" he asked softly. "You don't have to give me an answer right now. Just say you'll give it some serious thought."

I tried to speak, but my tongue refused to form the words. So I nodded, my listless fingers tracing the pattern on the quilt.

"Good girl!" he beamed. Sitting upright, he grabbed my shoulders, pulled me across the bed, pushed me onto his pillow, and began kissing me hungrily, his mouth open and probing. I was so surprised I didn't have time to protest. He was grinning down at me, his arm under my neck, when the bedroom door opened.

Kristina, Ervil's youngest and prettiest wife, came in. She abruptly stopped as she saw us, her hazel eyes growing wide with shock. "What is going on in here?!" she choked.

She stood adhered to the floor, hands on her hips as she stared at her husband, holding me tightly against him as he lay in his bed. I leaped out of Ervil's grasp and straightened my skirt. Never had I felt so embarrassed or flustered. Oh, God! What was Kris thinking! Surely she didn't think that...

"Susan, will you excuse us for a minute?" Ervil said smoothly. "Go on out and talk to Anna Mae, would you?"

"Please do!" Kristina's voice was icy, as she looked me up and down. "I can hardly wait to hear what you have to say, Ervil."

My face flamed with shame and indignation as I stumbled past Kris. I wanted to go home! I wanted to go home and never come back, to lock myself in my room and scream and scream. How could Ervil have put me in that position? What kind of a man would just grab me and kiss me like that? And then Kristina... Oh, what must she think?

I closed the door and wiped at the hot tears filling my eyes. "Get control of yourself!" I breathed, as I moved blindly across the living room.

I had forgotten my raincoat in Ervil's room. I didn't care. The cool rain felt good on my hot face. I moved swiftly down the muddy road until I rounded the corner, then I slowed my pace to fit my anguished, heart-wrenching mood.

"Oh, Lord," I sobbed aloud, the drizzle running into my eyes and mouth, "I don't know what's right anymore. Am I supposed to trust that guy? Is he truly Your servant, and does he speak for You? I don't know what to believe. I thought You were guiding me! Oh, God, I thought You were guiding me," my shoulders shook as I stumbled down the road.

"Susan! Susan, wait!" Behind me, a voice called through the rain. I turned and peered through the downpour. Kris was swathed in yellow rain-gear, with a hood over her shiny brown hair. Her lovely face, as she neared me, had a tentative smile. "You forgot your raincoat," she said, holding it out to me.

"Oh, Kris," I began, wanting desperately for her to understand, "I don't know what to say..."

"No," she interrupted, her voice gentle, "you don't have to say a word. Ervil told me what happened. I just didn't realize... It was a shock, is all... But I want you to know I'm thrilled! Oh, Susan, I mean it. Really I do. *We need you in our family.*" Her eyes shone with seriousness and with just a trace of tears in the corners. She wrapped her arms around me, hugging me tight. Her voice broke as she whispered in my ear, "Welcome, Susan, welcome into our family."

Chapter 9

Days after Ervil having told me of his visit with God, I sat in the kitchen with Mom, a huge tub of freshly picked green beans between us. We were snapping the ends, readying them for the pressure cooker. Suddenly, the back door flew open and Maria stomped in. Her round face was a picture of fury. Black eyes blazed as she pulled out a kitchen chair and dropped into it.

"Ay, Mathel," she stormed in broken English, "You will not believe what I just hear! I just come from my papa's house and he say they are going to be forcing us to keep the Civil Law. Can you believe it?"

"What?" Mom eyed Maria, alarmed.

"Yes! Is the truth. I tell you, that's what the men are saying, they are soon putting people to death or other punishments, like common criminals, right here in Colonia LeBaron," Maria nodded vehemently and chewed on a raw green bean.

"What in heaven's name are you talking about? They can't do that! Even if they wanted to bring the Civil Law of Moses back, the laws of the land wouldn't allow it." Mom's voice sounded wary.

"I know, that is what I was saying to Papa," Maria snapped, "that even if there were bad ones among us, *adulteros* and thieves, you know, don't our leaders see they would have the *gobierno* all mad over them? It's that *maldito* Ervil and Dan Jordan, I just know it. It's another of Ervil's *planes estupidos*."

I stared at Maria in shock. I sort of knew what she was speaking of, but I hadn't really grasped the full meaning of it until now. Were they actually thinking of putting to *death* the people who broke the Ten Commandments, or the Civil Law of God, as we called it? Oh, no. As usual, Maria was getting things twisted. It would never happen. There wasn't a criminal of that nature among us. True, Dan Jordan's Sunday school lessons every week had been about the Civil Law. And he had spoken in church yesterday on the same subject. Why did Maria think Ervil had anything to do with it? Ervil hadn't been to church for weeks, because of illness. I recalled Dan's speech in detail as I listened to Maria. Suddenly it was making sense.

"Now, calm down," Mom tried to soothe her. "I'm sure the men don't plan on literally carrying out the punishments; they're just trying to explain to us what life was like back in the days of Moses. Maybe one day in the distant future some of those ways will be put into practice again. But I'm sure Joel would never try to take the law into his own hands. They're only trying to teach us the positive side of the Ten Commandments—you know, encourage us to put the Lord first and keep the Sabbath Day Holy. They would never try to put anyone to death; don't be silly! The government wouldn't allow it." Mom shook her head vehemently as she shoved beans into a quart jar.

"No, no, I'm not saying Joel!" Maria fairly shouted. "I'm saying *Ervil*. He's the one, and Joel knows nothing! Joel's over there in Baja and has no idea what Ervil's up to. Oh, I wish Vern was here." Maria pinched her nose and looked ready to cry.

I kept silent and busy with the green beans, but my mind was in a whirl. Was this what the Church was coming to— actual enforcement of the Ten Commandments, as the Bible referred to the Twenty-first chapter of Exodus— "An eye for an eye and a tooth for a tooth?" That's what Dan had elaborated on yesterday. The thought sent chills down my spine. I needed to learn more about this before seeing Ervil again or answering him as to marriage. If he was in favor of enforcing the death penalty here in the colony, I wanted to know.

It had been four days since I last saw Ervil. Debbie had mentioned in Sunday school that he'd moved camp and was now staying with Kris. Although I was dreading it, it was time I visited.

The following afternoon, after school I bolstered my courage and hurried across the northern part of the colony to Kristina's. Her home was colorfully furnished, clean and neat, and I glanced around in appreciation. Our home was so bare and shabby in comparison. I definitely planned to have a nice place like this when I got married.

"I'm so glad you finally came!" Kris whispered. "Please know that you're always welcome here. I'm keeping my fingers crossed that you'll join our family soon— Anna Mae and I both are. I'll just leave you and Ervil alone." She smiled brightly as she left me at her bedroom door. Her acceptance of me, especially after the shock of seeing me in Ervil's arms last week, was remarkable. He certainly had Kris convinced to accept whatever he did without question. I marveled at her strength and her trust in him.

Ervil was fully dressed and sitting on the edge of the bed with a church pamphlet in his hand. "Hey, young lady! I've been thinking about you." His bluish-gray eyes lit up, the strength of his personality overpowering as he motioned for me to sit by him.

"So, what's going on? Umm, let me guess. You've thought things over and have decided to marry me."

I threw him a faint smile as I seated myself. He certainly wasn't wasting any words today. He wanted an answer, and now. "No, I haven't had enough time to make a decision," I said quickly. "I have been hearing some things, and I want to know if they're true."

"Shoot," he grinned. He looked huge and ruggedly masculine as he sat beside me. His white shirt accented his broad shoulders, and I couldn't help but look appreciatively at him. Now that he wasn't sick, he looked positively handsome. But I needed to keep my mind on my business. Taking a shaky breath, I plunged ahead.

"Well, first of all, I'll admit I don't know a lot about church doctrine, but I do know that the talk going around about the enforcement of the Civil Law is sort of scaring me. Is that really going to happen? Are you pushing for the death penalty to be enforced among church members?"

He leaned back against the bedpost and cupped his knee in his hands, then calmly asked, "Why should that scare you? The only people who would be affected by it would be those who broke the commandments. You're not planning to do that, are you?" His question sounded playful.

I shook my head, frowning.

"I didn't think so. Look at it this way—won't it be wonderful to be able to leave your house unlocked and know that no one will be stealing from you? We're going to have to start thinking in those terms before you know it. We won't always be a small, neighborly church. Once the law is enforced, all people who join us will take it seriously. They won't be tempted to commit a crime if they know they will have to pay the penalty." Ervil's voice had risen slightly, his thin lips twisting into a sneer, and then he seemed to recall himself. His voice lowered again to almost a whisper.

"Don't you see, we're talking about God's law, not mine. All the way through the Old Testament people abided by that law. Why should we question it? When is a better time to begin the practice of it than now, while we're still a small gathering? We're His chosen people and we shouldn't have to be governed by heathen outsiders. Crime has got to stop throughout the world before Jesus can come again, and it needs to start with us."

I searched his face as he talked, and I found myself agreeing with his logic. I hadn't thought about it that way. When he explained, it made sense. Ervil was wise and farseeing, and I was a fool to question his judgment.

"Don't let all that worry you," he dismissed the subject with a wave of his hand. "It'll be ages before we come up to that standard. Ignorant people are just making a big deal out of it. They're not using their heads or reading the Scriptures." His voice was filled with contempt, his eyes hard. Then they softened as he smiled at me.

With a sweep of his arm he pulled me onto his lap. "Now," he said, grinning, "let's talk about something important, like us. How about coming over for a Pinochle game tonight? Just you and me, Anna Mae and Kris. Sound like fun?"

For the next few nights, the Pinochle games at Kris' house became the highlight of my existance. With averted eyes I told my mother that Kris was the one who had invited me. Ervil had insisted that I not tell my parents about him yet. He was completely well now, and he and his wives always made me feel like a part of the family. We had a great time, and I felt very grown up and important. Kris made popcorn and fudge and other goodies, and every night was a party.

Ervil had ceased to pressure me for an answer to his proposal. He seemed content to wait and let me acquaint myself. I was beginning to feel very comfortable in his presence. He had hugged and kissed me several times, and it no longer seemed so distasteful.

"I'd rather you not tell your folks anything about what's going on," he stressed again one afternoon when we were alone. "I'm not saying you don't have wonderful parents, Susan; your Dad's a brilliant man, and a born organizer. I'd make him a bishop if he'd quit smoking. For some reason your Mom and Dad act like they don't necessarily like me, and we wouldn't want to upset the apple cart at this point. So let's just keep things between us."

I had reluctantly agreed. My parents didn't understand Ervil at all, and if they were to learn about us, they would immediately halt everything.

I finally wrote to Verlan, breaking off our courtship. Ervil had insisted I do so, and I knew it was inevitable. Verlan had to be told before he returned for fall conference, believing that we were still courting. I closed my mind to the image of his face and grimly scribbled off a quick, terse note. I was sorry for leading him on, I wrote, but I had given a lot of thought to marrying him and decided it wasn't the right thing for me. I wished him well, and signed off, "Sincerely, Susan." He'll probably be relieved, I thought sadly. I dropped it in the mailbox.

One Saturday afternoon as I hurried toward Anna Mae's, I encountered

Debbie. I'd seen little of her since Ervil had asked me to marry him. She still lived with Anna Mae, but she spent most of her time at Franny's. As we walked, she opened a subject that immediately filled me with consternation.

"Oh, Susan, I'm so excited!" she whispered, her upturned hazel eyes snapping. "Ervil told me he was courting another girl too, but I had no idea that it was you! Oh, this is going to be so much fun! Can you imagine the riot we'll have, with both of us married to the same guy? We, my dear, are going to have a total blast!"

I gave Debbie a startled glance. A knot had instantly formed in my throat, and it was getting bigger and bigger with her every word. Ervil was courting Debbie, too, and he hadn't even bothered to tell me? Oh, I thought, grimly, this is too much! It was unheard of for a man to court two girls at the same time.

I looked away from Debbie's happy face and fought to compose myself. How could Ervil do this? Why hadn't he warned me? And why did I feel so angry about it? I was the one who had been raised in the church. I was the one who had such high ideals about polygamy and living in harmony. Was I just jealous? Debbie was a new convert, still saddled with Babylonian ideas, and yet she was thrilled about sharing a fiancee with me, and later, a husband. She was obviously strong and selfless like Anna Mae and Kris, and I, on the other hand, was weak and being childish.

"What about Mark?" I asked, my voice cracking. "I thought you were crazy about him."

Debbie chewed on a corner of her lip. Shrugging, she said, "Mark is just a kid, Susan. He's got fun and games on his mind, not serving the Lord. It will take him *years* to grow up. Ervil thinks that...Oh, never mind. He's your cousin. Far be it from me to say anything negative about him."

What was she talking about? Mark was a wonderful young man! What had Ervil said about him? I stomped along at her side in stony silence.

She was impervious to my withdrawn mood and continued babbling. "You know, as much as Ervil will be gone, with all his other wives and church business and stuff, we should tell him we'd like to live together in the same house! That way we can be company for each other. Bitchin' idea, don't you think?"

"I guess you're right," I muttered.

"We can fix up some old place and have a garden and grow some real cool flowers. It will be so neat, like playing house only this will be the real thing!" Debbie giggled, her eyes dancing. "You're on your way over there now, aren't you? Why don't you talk to him about it?"

In spite of my muddled thoughts I smiled at her enthusiasm. "Okay," I agreed.

It took me a few minutes to get my temper under control before I dared enter Ervil's room. I sat on the couch at Anna Mae's and played with her children, while remembering Ervil's face when he relayed his revelation to me. I was destined to become his wife. Why was I fighting it? I needed to be happy about Debbie and not mind sharing my future husband with another new wife. I concentrated on all the reasons I should be pleased. Debbie was a lot of fun. She was a good person and I would be lucky to have her for a sister-wife. We would both be a blessing to Ervil's family, and I needed to stop mistrusting his every move. With these thoughts firmly in mind, I finally tapped on Ervil's bedroom door.

"There you are!" His eyes were bright with animation and he jumped up and wrapped his arms around me. "Has Debbie talked to you? What do you think?" He kissed the top of my head and then looked down into my face. His eyes searched mine.

"Wait a minute," he said slowly. "You don't look too thrilled. And I thought you would be, because you and Debbie are friends."

"Yes, we're friends," I snapped, "But why couldn't *you* have talked to me about this? You know, warned me? Prepared me? I didn't have a clue until today, but she knew about me! Why didn't you just tell me yourself instead of having her do it?" I pulled away from his arms and sat wearily on the bed.

"I didn't realize you'd take it so hard," he said gently. "She wanted to be the one to tell you."

"She thought you'd be as glad about her as she is about you." He paused, his voice taking on a businesslike tone, "I may as well tell you now, I'm also courting Teresa Rios, you know, Brother Rios' daughter, the one who lives in the mountains."

I closed my eyes and leaned back onto the pillow. I could feel the gauzy tangle of unreality creep into my brain. This couldn't be happening. I was having another nightmare. This whole day seemed like a bad dream, and I would awaken, and laugh at the crazy things one's mind comes up with while sleeping.

When I opened my eyes, Ervil was still watching me. "I'd like for you and Debbie to marry me at the same time, in the same ceremony," he continued firmly. "It's never been done in the church before, and I'd like to be the first one to do it. We'll have a double wedding." He stopped, his long fingers

82

smoothing the thinning strands of hair at the top of his head back into place. "Debbie's a little older than you, so I'll take her on a honeymoon first. Then when we get back she can tell you all about it, so you'll realize there's nothing about sex to dread or fret about. Then it will be your turn, and we'll go some place real nice. How does that sound? Does that make you feel better?"

Someone pounded on the bedroom door. Ervil grabbed the handle and swung it open. I was sitting too close to the wall to see who was in the doorway, but I immediately recognized Dan Jordan's nasal voice. "Well, Chief," he drawled, "I'm afraid we've got problems. Some idiot called Joel long distance and told him what's going on, and from what I can gather, he's . . ."

Ervil's head motioned toward me, and Dan peered around the corner of the closet. "Oh, sorry. I thought you were alone."

"I have a meeting right now, Suze," Ervil said abruptly. "I'll see you later. We'll finish this conversation later, okay?"

Dan's black eyes avoided me as I stood up and hurried past him. He had always made me uncomfortable and I didn't like the tone he used when he spoke of the Prophet. Suddenly Grandma LeBaron's face flashed before me, that day at her house, when she said that Dan and Ervil were "up to something."

I left Anna Mae's in turmoil. Images of Debbie and me in matching wedding dresses, standing on either side of Ervil, flitted before me. I imagined Teresa Rios' dark, Indian features—for a moment clear—then fading before me like a mirage. I couldn't concentrate. Oh, I definitely wanted to serve the Lord. I wanted to earn my blessings and do what was right. But now I didn't have that illusive answer as to what was right or wrong.

What could be such a big secret that Ervil had quieted Dan? Because I was in the room? Oh, I wished Jay were home—or Verlan! Fall conference was only a week away—Verlan would be coming. How I wished I could just talk to him! He would help me straighten out this mess I was drowning in. I had no doubt that Verlan cared enough to guide me, even if I didn't marry him.

The next day at school I pulled Debbie aside from the other girls as we walked to a class. "I have to know something," I whispered. "How do you really feel about you know who? I mean, do you love him?"

Her eyes locked with mine, her expression unreadable. I waited for her answer with growing impatience. "Well?" I finally demanded.

Squeezing her eyes tightly for a moment, she vehemently shook her head. "No! I do not love him. Sometimes I can't *stand* the man. He's so damn smooth and—so sarcastic. He doesn't wear any deodorant, have you noticed?

There are times he makes me so mad."

She stopped, swallowed, and visibly squared her shoulders. Her chin came up and she started walking again. "The thing I keep reminding myself of is that he's the Patriarch of God's true church. He's promised me that I'll begin to love him. So I just have to trust him and be patient."

She shrugged and switched her books to the other arm. "He's a strange guy in lots of ways. But he has his redeeming qualities, and I just love Anna Mae and Kris. And now there is going to be you! Oh, Sue, it'll be okay! Everything'll work out just fine. In time we'll both learn to love him, and we'll be happy. You'll see." She gave me a brilliant smile. Her hair glinted with golden highlights in the sunshine, then faded to chestnut as she ducked into the darkness of the school building.

That afternoon, as I walked home I said a silent, desperate prayer. "Dear Lord, please help me to have more faith. Help Debbie and me to learn to love Ervil. Help me to believe in him and take away all these stupid doubts I'm feeling." I wanted to believe in him. Maybe the devil was playing with my brain, and I was being too judgmental. Maybe God used a man like Ervil, a man who got on people's nerves, to strengthen others' faith. What had he done that had me so upset? Was it the secrecy he demanded? Was that so wrong? I wasn't sure anymore. Maybe I was looking for a convenient means of escape from a situation that seemed too much for me to deal with.

My mind was like a feather, blown back and forth by the slightest stirring of the breeze. At times I was self-confident, and at times I was totally confused.

Conference was scheduled to begin on Friday. On Wednesday, Ervil sent for me. I fidgeted as I waited in Anna Mae's living room until Dan Jordan left him. Dan again! Was it his eyes? His voice? He was an Apostle in the Church and dang it! I should trust him.

Ervil was very direct as soon as the door was closed. "I have something I'd like you to do," he said calmly. "I've thought this through, and I've decided it would be best." He sat me on the bed and took my hand, his fingers lightly rubbing across my palm. Eyes the color of new nails bored into mine, capturing my gaze.

"How would you feel about becoming sealed to me?" his voice was curt.

"Sealed?" I asked cautiously. "What do you mean?"

Ervil tried to be patient. "You know, as in married in heaven. For all eternity. You do understand that once a couple becomes sealed, God honors that union *forever*. So once you're sealed to me, and I'm given my crown of godhood in heaven, you'll be one of my goddesses. We'll have an eternal family together, Susan! We'll populate our own worlds. Imagine all the little spirits we will become parents to!"

Ervil waved his hand, "But that's a ways in the future. For now, I want you to be sealed to me to help settle your mind. Later, after you're a little older, we would be married again. For time, which means while we're here on the earth. That's when we would start living together as man and wife in a physical sense of the word. Understand what I mean?"

I tried to comprehend it, but I was slow. "So, we would be married in heaven, but not here on earth," I stated, frowning. Something didn't seem right. "I still don't get it. What's wrong with just waiting until the time is right and getting married, once and for all, then?"

"I just think you need to get used to belonging to me before we consummate the marriage." He smiled and began to relax—confidant that I would do as he asked. "Once it's done it will help to settle your mind. Would that be so bad, being sealed to me? Knowing that you are my wife, forever?" His question was playful, his fingers lightly brushing up and down my thigh.

I stared at his huge hands. There were as many complex sides to Ervil as a prism. Married in heaven, but not on earth. What a strange thought. Debbie had Ervil pegged. He was definitely strange. And scary.

"I would want you to promise me one thing, though," he said firmly. "I want you to *swear* to me that you'll tell no one about this. No one, not even your parents. The only ones who are to know are you and me, and Dan Jordan, who'll perform the sealing ceremony. It's no one else's business. I can have him come over, and we'll take care of it this evening."

A strange shiver raced through me. *I was to tell no one, and he wanted to do it now. Why? WHY?* One by one, the intricate pieces of Ervil's scheming game settled into place and were glaring at me. I understood. Yes, I was beginning to see.

"Wait just a minute," I said slowly. I pulled away from him and stood up, my body taut. Chills were galloping up and down my spine. I faced him, my head level with his as he sat on the bed.

"You want me to marry you without the consent of my parents?" My voice was flat, my fists clenched. Mom and Dad's faces flashed before me, their trusting eyes full of faith in their leaders... faith in this man. My parents were wonderful, upstanding people, who had given their lives to this church. They had sacrificed everything for their beliefs. The deception that Ervil was suggesting rang as false and unchristian as anything I could imagine. I felt an alarming anger, one that left me hot, then cold. The aura of spirituality that Ervil carried with him cracked and crumbled. I knew clearly that he wanted me tied to him before anyone had a chance to dissuade me. Only a conniving, self-indulgent man, a man who used the name of the Lord for self-fulfillment, one who would crush anyone to accomplish his purposes, would do this. My awe of him completely evaporated, replaced by a raw, shocking contempt. How could I have revered this despicable person?

"Your parents don't necessarily like me. You know that," Ervil was saying smoothly. "There will be plenty of time to tell them about our marriage later." He waved their importance off with a flick of his fingers. "I'll handle them. Don't you worry about it."

Wide eyed, I stared at him, aware for the first time of the callousness and deceit etched into each line of his face. Suddenly I felt an urge to spit on the floor. There was a horrid, sour taste in my mouth.

"No!" I said abruptly. "Absolutely not." I whirled and stalked to the door, then turned back to face him. "My parents will be very interested to hear all about this little plan of yours." I yanked on the doorknob. "So will Verlan," I whispered over my shoulder.

Ervil leaped off the bed. In a flash he grabbed my arm, squeezing until it hurt. "Susan, now wait a minute..." his voice was threatening. "You don't understand. Don't be a fool, Susan. You don't want to cause trouble..."

"Let me go!" I shouted, pulling free and running past a surprised Anna Mae. I flew out the door of the rock house as though pursued by evil, out into the twilight, where the air was pure.

Dad was due in from the States at any time. All through the night I had stewed over how to tell him about Ervil, but the more I thought about it, the more I knew it was a mistake to say anything. Dad would be furious. He would ground me to my room for my part of the deception, and I couldn't bear the thought. I wasn't sure just what he would do about Ervil, but I didn't want Dad to confront the man. There had been something in Ervil's eyes yesterday that frightened me.

How I wished I could talk to my mother about all this! But I knew that her nerves would never handle it. She would take to her bed and be ill for a week.

Through the morning Mom was occupied with scrubbing and polishing everything in the house, cooking up pies and cakes for the conference guests, and sending me on one errand after another. I was accustomed to doing the outdoor chores and was little help in the house, but Mom found plenty to keep me busy. She didn't seem to notice my agitation.

I had to see Debbie, to talk to her before it was too late and she did something stupid, and I finally convinced Mom to let me leave the rest of my chores until later. As I ran through the shortcut to Anna Mae's, I breathed a prayer that Ervil wouldn't be there.

If Anna Mae knew what had happened between Ervil and me she gave no sign. She was her usual, bubbly self. She informed me that the Bateman's had arrived and Debbie had gone somewhere with them. I hurried through the streets, looking for their station wagon, finally spotting the dusty new car parked in front of Franny's house at the Southern end of the colony. The whole Bateman group was seated in the Widmar's living room. Franny watched with unveiled interest as I hurried to Debbie's side.

"I have to talk to you," I whispered. "It's important. Can you get away?"

"Uh, sure, I guess. I'll ask Dad for the car keys," she whispered back.

Soon we were bumping down the pot-holed road. I took a shaky breath and plunged in. "Deb, I just need you to know that I'm not going to marry Ervil. I've decided that for sure."

"Why on earth not?" she gasped. "I thought it was all decided! Oh, Susan, don't tell me this! What happened?"

I stared out the window, a lump in my throat. Somehow I had to make her see what Ervil was really like. "Did he tell you he had a revelation that you were to marry him?" I asked abruptly.

The car swerved off the road, and Debbie braked to a sudden stop. Dust boiled around the car. She whirled in the seat, instantly defensive. "Yes, he did. He was very certain about it. Why?" Her eyes widened as she stared at me. "Oh, come on!" she groaned, "Don't tell me you don't believe in revelation?"

"I'm not saying that. I do believe that God guides people if they'll let Him, but doesn't it strike you odd that Ervil claimed to each of us that he had a revelation to marry us? I'll bet he had one about Teresa Rios, too. Now, isn't that convenient? I'll bet she doesn't love him, either! The only reason we've agreed to marry him is because he says he's had a revelation about us." I shook my head. "I've thought about this a lot, and I think it's bullshit. He's practically forcing us to marry him! We either marry him, or say we think he's lying. Do you see the spot he puts us in? He's the Patriarch and..."

"That's exactly right!" Debbie shouted. "What do you expect me to do? Ervil's a powerful man and is being guided by the Lord! I can hardly believe you have the nerve to question him! So we're not madly in love with him. So what? I care more about my spiritual welfare than about passion and romance, and you should, too. My hell, Susan, grow up!" Debbie's eyes flashed with scorn.

I sat in silence, biting my nails. Her spiel sounded just like Ervil. What could I say to her? Desperately, I wanted her to see what I had seen in Ervil, but how could I open her eyes? She was just as impressed with him as I had been. Whatever I said was hitting against a solid wall. He had her completely.

"Okay," I said, "Just tell me this. Has he sworn you to secrecy about your relationship with him? Do your parents know?"

She darted a quick look at me. "He asked me not to talk about it," her voice sounded hollow.

I watched her, noting the dark smudges beneath her eyes. She reached for the ignition switch, started the car, and just as suddenly turned the engine off again. As she dropped her head against the steering wheel, sympathy rushed through me.

"Deb, what right does Ervil have to demand you keep this from your parents?"

"He has his reasons. He knows what he's doing."

"Promise me you'll tell them! This is not right! Besides, they're going to find out anyway. You may as well tell them now."

Debbie shook her head, her long brown hair hiding her face. "I can't. I just can't," she wailed. "Susan, please don't back out on me! This all seemed so much easier to handle with you marrying him too. We were going to live together, remember? We were going to be best friends and sister-wives! I don't think I can stand it if you aren't with me."

"Tell him you won't marry him then! It's your choice. It's your life."

"I can't," she faltered. "You don't understand."

"Why can't you?" I hollered. "You don't even *like* him! Do you honestly think God would make you marry someone you don't like? Oh—I don't know how to tell you what I'm feeling, Debbie, but something about Ervil scares me."

"It's just that you don't know him as I do. He gets so . . ." Her hazel eyes were full, and she swallowed hard. "Please say you'll change your mind," she whispered.

I shook my head as the tears flowed down her cheeks. With nothing more to say, I leaned back against the blue vinyl car seat and closed my eyes in dismay. I pictured Ervil's face, the thin lips, the wide, lined brow jutting out over his eyes—eyes that could look so friendly at times, and yet become so hard and scornful like cold, gray cement.

"Okay, well, do what you think is right," I managed a little, apologetic smile. "I've got to get home."

Throughout the rest of the day I feverishly cleaned house at my mother's side as I tried to forget the turmoil my mind was in. Debbie's last words to me as she dropped me off in front of my house had been, "Please, please reconsider, Sue. Don't let me down; I need you; Ervil needs you." I shook my head as I walked into the house. She sounded just like Kris.

In the late afternoon Dad arrived, and soon after that Aunt Thelma and Uncle Bud pulled up in front of the house in their new pickup and camper. Mark, Duane, and Rena piled out of the camper and raced each other across the back yard to the outhouse.

"What do you think, Vern?" Uncle Bud asked as he led us around the vehicle and had us step into the tiny interior of the camper. "We plan on taking this with us when we move to Los Molinos in a month or two. We'll use it for a kitchen until our house is built. Pretty nice, huh?"

"So, you really are leaving Utah! I'm proud of you, Bud," Dad declared. "It's a big step, selling out and moving away from the states, especially moving to Los Molinos. I guess that place is about as primitive as you can find, worse than Colonia LeBaron was nine years ago. Mathel thought this was bad. Didn't you, honey?"

Mom nodded grimly, "It takes a lot of faith. My family in Salt Lake practically disowned us, thought we had lost our marbles when we announced we had joined Joel and were moving to Colonia LeBaron. They still think we're lunatics."

"Well, Bud and I know this is what the Lord wants us to do, so we just do it. It doesn't matter what anyone thinks," Aunt Thelma said.

"Hey, Sue," Mark eagerly pulled me aside. "Is Debbie still here? I've been going nuts worrying about her. She stopped writing a couple of months ago. Just stopped... What's going on with her?"

I sighed and kicked at a rock in the path. I didn't want to be the one to tell him, but I didn't want Debbie to go through it, either.

"Debbie's pretty involved with someone else, Mark," I said quietly. "I have a feeling you better forget about her."

He slowly nodded, his jaw clenched. "I figured as much. Some old man's got his claws into her, hasn't he? Who is it?"

"She'd better tell you herself."

"Why?" he snapped. "Does everything in this church have to be a secret? Did you know that when my sister Lorna married Ervil, her own family didn't know anything about it for *months*? If the people around here are so convinced that polygamy is the right way to live, then why not be open about it? All this sneaking around! It would be funny if it weren't so sickening."

"Mark!" I gasped. "You just don't understand. Sometimes there's a reason for secrecy. There are other people's feelings to consider. You just don't understand."

He leaned against the fence post and eyed me with disgust. "Boy, oh boy. They've sure got you brainwashed, haven't they? I suppose you plan on jumping in with both feet, marrying some old fart and having a dozen kids, too. What an idiot."

I stared at him, aghast. What had happened to him? The last time he was here he seemed so accepting of the church doctrine. His Utah friends must have talked to him and convinced him that the church was wrong. No wonder my aunt and uncle were both in such a hurry to move away from the states.

"We all have to do what we think is right," I snapped back. Then I reached out and squeezed his arm. "I'm sorry. I can understand how you feel. This is all new to you. Just give it some time, okay?"

"I'm going to find her," he turned on his heel and stalked across the yard. I watched his retreating figure until he rounded the corner, hoping against hope that he would be successful in talking some sense into Debbie.

Maybe I was being melodramatic, but when I thought of Ervil a tremor crept over me. A bad, bad thing was happening in our church; something sneaky and underhanded and evil. I didn't understand how it could be this way. Ervil was right next to the prophet Joel in command of the church. Nevertheless, I hadn't a single doubt that his actions were anything but godly, and they should be reported to someone. Yet, who was I to do it? Should I keep quiet about it just because Ervil scared me? Or should I... But, who...?

Deep inside me a sudden, wild desire to see Verlan sprang to life. Oh, if only I could see him! I was desperate to share my fears, to tell him what had happened, and to have his reassurance that things were under control. And, thank God! Tonight Verlan would be arriving for conference. I had to see him!

Throughout the evening my plan was forming. It was past eleven before the household settled down. Ramona, who was sharing my bed, was sleeping soundly, and I lay down by her until I was sure all the lights in the house were out. I was going to have to sneak away; Mom would never agree to let me go see Verlan this time of night. She would want me to explain, and I couldn't.

I quietly got up and donned a pair of Levis and a dark blouse. I took an old baseball cap from the closet, twisted my hair up, and shoved it beneath the cap. As I opened my bedroom door, I could see the flickering light of a lamp in the kitchen. Oh, hell! I thought. Someone's still up. I tiptoed up the hall and peered around the cupboard. Mom sat at the kitchen table with a book opened in front of her, stirring a steaming cup of tea. I felt like stamping my foot, I was so angry. The wooden floor in the living room creaked too much; I would never manage to sneak past her. I tiptoed back to my room. I would have to wait. I could see the stars from the window, flickering and twinkling in the blackness, marking the minutes until I would see Verlan.

What would he think of me going to see him so late in the night? Well, he would just have to understand. This was too much for me to deal with alone. I had to talk to someone, give the problem to someone else. My stomach churned. Ervil's face haunted me. The minutes ticked by as I watched the light beneath my door.

Suddenly I sat up. "You dummy!" I said aloud. I rushed to the window and shoved at the wood slider. We had painted the frames earlier, and the paint had sealed the window closed. It wouldn't budge. I tried the other window, shoving my palms against the wood. Slowly the sash gave about an inch. I felt around in the darkness for something to pry with, but could only find a Coke bottle. I stuck the small end in the opening and used it as a wedge. The old wood creaked upward until I could get my arms, then my back under it. I struggled until it was open wide enough to allow me to wiggle through. The sandy flower-bed cushioned my fall.

I brushed the dirt from my clothes and skirted around the house, my heart racing at my daring. Giving a wide berth to Uncle Bud's camper parked in front, I sped up the deserted road and on past Spencer's barking dogs. Some of the houses still had light shining through the windows, and I hoped Grandma LeBaron's would be one of them. I wouldn't allow myself to think what I would do if everyone was in bed. I was probably acting foolishly. Verlan might not even be there yet.

Grandma's red brick house loomed ahead in the blackness without a flicker of light at the windows. I walked into the yard, dismayed. I was too late. Everyone was asleep, and I had come for nothing. A pickup with a camper shell on it was parked in the yard, and I peered closely at it. It had California plates. It could be Verlan's.

I crept to the house and leaned against the rough brick, wishing I had the nerve to awaken Grandma. She wouldn't ask any questions, she'd just wake Verlan. Did I dare?

A faint noise from the small window above my head caught my attention. Looking up, I could see a thin line of light along the outer edge of the heavy drapes. "Oh, hallelujah," I breathed.

I tapped on the pane, hoping the person on the other side was either Grandma or Verlan. I tapped again. After a minute the front door opened; Grandma peered out at me, clutching her robe around her with one hand and holding a lamp in the other. "Why, Susan, dear!" she exclaimed. "How nice! Do come in." She let go of her robe, took my arm, and ushered me into her home.

"Oh, Grandma, I . . . I shouldn't have come so late," I stammered. "I should have waited until tomorrow, I . . . "

"Now, now. You are welcome here anytime. You know that. Honey, something's wrong. What is it?" She set down the lamp and turned to me, her eyes filled with concern. Her soft, silver-brown hair was in a long braid down her back. Her tiny frame swam in the huge robe that she clung to.

"I–I just need to see Verlan. Is he here?"

"Why, no, he hasn't shown up yet." She picked up the lamp. "But come see who I have in here!"

I followed her, protesting. I didn't want to see anyone else–just Verlan. He wasn't here, and I needed to go home before I was missed.

Grandma tapped lightly on a bedroom door. A woman's voice called for us to come in. Standing in the middle of the room in only her bra and panties, was Verlan's second wife, Irene. I recognized her immediately, and wanted to turn and run. I didn't know if Verlan had told her about me. For all I knew, she might be furious and even hate me. Sudden visions of Estela popped into my mind. I felt awkward and embarrassed as I stood in the doorway while Grandma charged confidently into the room. She turned and motioned for me to follow her.

"Irene, dear," Grandma beamed, "look who I have here! She wanted to see Verlan, but you'll have to do. Come in, child," she motioned to me again.

Oh, Grandma! I thought as I stumbled out of the shadows. Irene watched me as I self-consciously removed my baseball cap. My hair fell around my face, and I pushed it out of my eyes. "Hi," I mumbled.

"Well, hello." Irene grabbed her nightgown and slid it over her head. She turned her back and removed her bra from her enormous bosom, wiggling the nightie down over her hips. Then she turned, and without hesitation, walked to me. Her ample arms enfolded me in a hug.

"I'll just leave the two of you alone to visit," Grandma said smugly. She nodded her head at us and grinned as she left the room.

I wanted to shake Grandma. Either she knew Irene well, and knew she would be nice, or she had a mischievous sense of humor and enjoyed fireworks. I stood uncertainly, staring at Verlan's second wife. I didn't know what to say. I frantically wished I knew her better. Had Verlan told her about me?

"Why don't you sit down, Susan?" she invited.

She sounded friendly. I remembered her from when I was small. She'd taken care of Fara and me right after we had moved to Mexico, when Mom was in the hospital giving birth to Ramona.

"Irene," I haltingly began as I sat down on the bed, "I'm really sorry about this. I had no idea that you were here, and Grandma didn't tell me. I just needed to talk to Verlan for a minute, and it wouldn't wait. I hope you're not mad."

She plopped down next to me on the bed. "Now, why would I be mad?" Suddenly she chuckled, "Hey! I don't know what Verlan told you, but I was thrilled when he said he was courting you. I mean that, so stop feeling bad about being here, okay? I'm glad you came! Verlan will be, too."

Irene's eyes were an intense blue. She was a pretty woman, with a boisterous, fun-loving personality. I relaxed, and suddenly I was glad I was here. Irene wanted to be my friend, and I needed a friend.

"I wasn't planning to come to conference," Irene was saying, "but Joel had room to bring me, and I got ready at the last minute. Verlan doesn't even know I'm here. Boy, will he get a hot surprise when he crawls into bed!" She chuckled again, and sat silently for a moment, then cleared her throat. "It's none of my business, but why did you break up with Verlan? When he read me your letter, he cried. He loves you, Susan. He was so upset. Want to talk about it?"

Her voice was concerned and was offering relief from my burden. My shoulders sagged. I buried my face in my hands, rubbed my tired eyes, and tried to clear my thoughts. I suddenly felt the need to hide my face on Irene's broad shoulder and sob my confusion.

Instead, I proceeded to tell Irene about Ervil. The words came slowly at first, then tumbled over each other as I told her of his claiming revelation about me, about my visits to him, and about the secrecy involved. I told her about Debbie and Teresa Rios. I was reliving the past six weeks—the initial excitement at the thought of serving the Lord, the hurt and the confusion, and finally the mistrust. As I drew the story to a conclusion I was talking through tears, and unmindfully wiping them on the bed sheet.

Irene said very little as she listened to the story. She waited until I reached the part about Ervil wanting me to be secretly sealed to him. At that point she could contain herself no longer. "I can't believe the *gall* of that man!" she raved as she jumped up. She began to walk the floor in furious strides, her nightgown clinging to her full figure. "In the first place, he has no business claiming a revelation about you or any other woman. You, as a woman of the church, have the right to expect your own, personal revelation, directly from God about whom you should marry. It's your life, and it's your choice, and I don't care if Ervil claims to be the King of Sheba, he had no right to try and manipulate you." She dropped back on the bed and rearranged her pillow against the headboard. She continued to rave and rant. Her short, auburn hair and ruddy complexion emphasized the anger in her blue eyes. They snapped with fire.

"I have a little story to tell you, one that will perhaps show you what a conniving manipulator he is." She stopped for a moment, staring at her nails, gathering her ammunition. "You don't know about Anna Mae, do you? About how she came to marry Ervil?"

I shook my head, frowning.

"I didn't think so," Irene sniffed. "You know that when Anna Mae first joined the church she was married to Nephi Marston. They had four children.

Well, anyway, Nephi left the colony to go back to the states to work. He was gone for a month, and when he returned, he pulled up in front of his and Anna Mae's house, loaded his arms up with the things he'd brought for his family, and walked in the door, all excited about being home. He put down his packages and leaned over to kiss his wife. And, what do you think she tells him? "Nephi, I can't kiss you," she says. "I married Ervil while you were gone."

"Can you imagine that!" Irene snapped. "He had no idea. Ervil didn't even wait for a divorce. When Joel found out about it, he wept. He asked Ervil how he could do such a thing, and Ervil said that because of his position in the Church, he didn't feel obligated to wait the customary six months. That's just for people who have sex on their minds, Ervil told Joel. "Well, Joel contemplated taking Ervil's authority away. But he figured that he'd learned his lesson and would clean up his act. Boy, was Joel wrong!"

My insides were churning, and my head felt heavy. I lay down on the bed, Ervil's face swimming in front of me. More than anger and betrayal, I felt sadness and hurt. How could the Patriarch of our Church do these things? Grandma LeBaron's son! A brother to the Prophet Joel? I couldn't comprehend it.

Irene's voice dropped to a low, tired tone, her eyes looked haunted. So caught up in my own problems, I had failed to see how this whole thing would affect anyone else.

She gnawed at her lip, then said, "I'm breaking a confidence to tell you this, but I think under the circumstances, it's justified." She hesitated again, then glanced over at me. "I found out a little while ago from Ruth Bateman that Debbie is already sealed to Ervil. Susan, she has been for the past two months."

I gasped, "Oh, no! Oh, Irene, you've got to be kidding." But even as I said it, I knew it was true. The trapped look in Debbie's eyes earlier today flooded back into my mind. She had been beyond convincing, and Ervil had sworn her to secrecy. She was miserable about it, but knew it was too late. "Oh, no," I groaned, bursting into tears.

"She doesn't love him," Irene said. "She can hardly stand him, but he convinced her that she would go to hell if she didn't marry him. And he promised her she would learn to love him. I feel so sorry for her, Susan. Her mom and dad are furious. They're ready to string Ervil up by the balls. Why do you think he's in such an all-fired hurry to get *you* sealed to him? Because he wants it settled before Verlan can show up and throw a monkey wrench into his plans, that's why. He's a low-life ass! I can't imagine Joel putting up with him any longer."

I blushed at Irene's language. She was the wife of the President of the Twelve Apostles, and it shocked me, but I admired her for it; she certainly wasn't stuffy.

Irene pulled the covers back from the bed and crawled under. She had started to wind down, and I stood up, thinking I should leave. "Susan," she yawned, her sleepy voice stopping me, "Maybe you still feel marrying Ervil is the right thing to do. If so, go for it! But let it be your decision, not Ervil's, or Verlan's for that matter. Whoever you marry, make sure you love the guy. If you don't, you'll never be able to put up with this way of life."

I put on my hat and left the dark house, running through the quiet streets of Colonia LeBaron. For the first time in weeks, my mind was wonderfully free of that horrible confusion. I didn't begin to understand Ervil or what the Church would do about him, I only knew that I was no longer under his spell.

I pushed to the back of my mind the look that crossed his face when I refused to be sealed to him. I'm free of that man, I reminded myself. And Irene had said Verlan still loved me . . .

Chapter 11

I t was customary for the brethren to hold priesthood meeting early on the opening morning of conference. This was a traditional, men's get-together to discuss church issues and to talk over the theme of the upcoming meetings. I knew Verlan would be there and I also knew there would be a recess before the general session began. My plan was to find him and talk to him during that recess.

After I dressed, I stood in my bedroom and surveyed myself in the mirror. A crisp, freshly ironed white blouse lent me a mature and business-like appearance. My blue and red plaid skirt still looked fairly new, and this morning Aunt Thelma had presented me with a new pair of nylons. My legs looked great, but as I glanced at my feet, I groaned with frustration. My big toes were plainly in view through the holes in my shoes.

A few days ago Dad had brought us another bag of goods from the thrift store in the states, but the two pairs of shoes in the bag had fit Fara, and were ugly. My fifteenth birthday was three days ago, and Mom had assured me that before conference, she would take me to Casas and buy me a brand new pair of shoes. Such a purchase was an unheard of luxury in the Ray family. Time had slipped away, and I was still stuck with my dingy old tennis shoes. They would never do. I would have to go to Franny's and ask her to loan me a pair.

As I hurried across the colony, once again in the direction of Grandma LeBaron's, I wondered why I allowed myself to be so forward. "You could just wait and hope Verlan comes looking for you, you know," I muttered to myself. "That's much more ladylike. If Mom knew what you were doing she'd ground you for a month." Well, I couldn't wait. I had to see if what Irene told me last night was true. I had to see if Verlan loved me.

I wondered if it was difficult for Irene to say. Did it bother her much to know that her husband loved other women? I believed in plural marriage, but I realized that it would bother *me* more than a little bit, but that was the sacrifice we had to make.

A peach orchard separated Grandma's house from the Widmar's attractive, white clapboard house. As I hurried through Franny's gate, I thought, "This will be just perfect. From here I can see Verlan when he comes down the road from the church."

Francisca was getting dressed as her mother ushered me into her bedroom. Her honey-blond hair was held out of her way in a ponytail on the top of her head. Her large body was scantily covered in a white silk slip. As soon as the door was closed, I asked about the shoes.

"Sure you can borrow a pair, but they'll probably be too big." Franny frowned as she dug through her closet. "These are the tightest on me; try these on."

The white pumps were huge on me. "Here," she giggled, handing me tissue paper. "Stuff 'em. They'll work. They're better than those rags you have on." I blushed with embarrassment. Francisca had never known what it was to do without.

"Why did you get ready so early?" her green eyes were alert with interest. "Church doesn't start for over an hour. Are you doing the music?"

"No, Esther is. I have someone to see." I turned my back, hoping she wouldn't ask who.

"Who?" she demanded.

"Verlan," I mumbled, knowing she would preach.

Settling back against the headboard, she crossed her legs, cupped her hands under her chin, and studied me. "You really like him, don't you? I thought you said you broke up with him."

"Yeah, I did, but . . ." my voice trailed off.

She shook her head and sighed. "I'll never understand you, my friend. It's like you're just begging for a miserable life. Do you realize what being married to him would be like? Pure hell." She shuddered. "He's old enough to be your father; doesn't that matter to you? He's practically bald, for heaven's sake. He has all those wives . . . You'll get lost in the crowd."

"He's not bald!" I said defensively. "He's just a bit thin on top. I think he's handsome, and he's so nice, Franny! Besides, even if you marry Alma D. you won't be the only one for long. You'll have to put up with him chasing other girls and getting married again and again. Verlan has five wives already, so he's got to be about ready to call it quits—which would mean that I'd be his last. I'd rather be the last than the first, any day."

That silenced her. Looking pensive, she pulled her dress on, then moved to the mirror and finished putting on her makeup. "There!" She gave her eyelashes a final sweep of mascara. "Let's go get a cup of cocoa."

We took the steaming mugs onto the porch. As I sipped, I walked to the edge of the grass and scanned the road toward the church, then searched the plowed field between the road and Grandma's back yard. Nothing. I sat down on the swing by Franny. My heart was beginning to thump, my insides were fluttering, and my hands were sweaty. Would Verlan be happy to see me? Would he want to court me?

I closed my eyes. After my long visit with Irene last night, I'd gotten little sleep. My eyes were burning and my head was starting to ache, and Franny was gossiping nonstop about trivial nonsense until I was ready to scream. I needed time to think, and I wished I'd just stayed home! Chances were that Verlan wouldn't go to Grandma's after the meeting—what had possessed me to come looking for him? I should have been ladylike and waited . . . I set my empty mug down and wished I hadn't drunk the cocoa. I could taste the bad breath.

"What's going on with Debbie and you?" Franny finally asked. "She won't talk to me, and she's been acting so strange. Something's bothering her, and she refuses to say what. The two of you have been so chummy, I know you know. Don't you?"

I nodded. "I wish I could tell you, but I can't. You'll find out soon enough. You're going to be sick, though. No . . ." I shook my head as Franny began to plead with me, "I can't tell, I promised. She'll tell you real soon. There's no use in her hiding it any longer."

Franny gasped. "Oh, no! She's pregnant! Is that it?"

I stared at her, shocked. "No! It's nothing like that, Franny. At least I don't think so . . ."

Over the top of Franny's head, in the field behind Grandma's house, I saw movement. My heart began to pound, making it hard to breathe. It was Verlan. With my eyes glued on his form, I said, "Franny, I have to go now." I stepped off the porch.

"Susan," Franny's voice was low, "Do you love that old man?"

I moved on down the little path through the peach trees, to the fence that separated Francisca's yard from Grandma's. "I guess I have my answer," she called after me. Without looking back, I waved to her.

Like a giraffe, Verlan's long legs covered ground at an incredible speed, his head and shoulders leading the rest of his body. I hesitated at the gate, savoring his every movement. Blood roared in my ears, my breathing was shallow.

Suddenly he glanced over at me. Stopping abruptly, he stared at me across the plowed field. Even though a good distance separated us, our eyes locked. I searched his features, looking for a sign of feeling or emotion. As I recognized my own fear of rejection mirrored in his face, all the doubts, the confusion, and the strain bottled inside for the past six weeks, sprang to the surface. I wept with relief. Raw, unrestrained emotion hit me with such force that I could scarcely stand, and I grasped at the fence for support.

The brilliant colors of autumn swayed through my tears, the morning air soft and sweetly scented by Widmar's fresh cut alfalfa behind me. Somewhere close by a chicken clucked. The world around me shone brilliant, a bounteous gift from God, faultlessly framing the most intense, overpowering revelation of my life. I loved Verlan LeBaron.

Through a blur I could see him motion to me. Resuming his giraffe-like gait, he walked into Grandma's back yard. He stopped under the water tower, and turning, waited for me.

My legs were shaking as I drew nearer to him. His eyes searched my face, tried to read what the tears meant. Suddenly his tense shoulders relaxed, and he opened his arms to me. Without a word, I stumbled into them. His familiar scent enveloped me, and I buried my wet cheeks on his chest. He rocked me and kissed the top of my hair, then slid his hands up to cup my face. Tipping my head up so he could see my eyes, he planted a soft kiss on the end of my nose.

"You're so thin!" I croaked. My arms tightened around his waist.

He hesitated, searching my face. "I've been worried about you," he said simply.

I knew it was true. His face was pale and the lines around his mouth deeper than I remembered. Love for me practically leaped from his eyes, and suddenly I felt so ashamed. This man in my arms was the one God had shown me was to be mine. He'd given me my own personal revelation, and I had cast it aside. I'd allowed myself to be swayed by a self-serving manipulator, who used God's name to get what he wanted. Anger and hurt confounded me as I thought of Ervil's treachery, and I hid my face against Verlan's chest. My shoulders shook with grief.

"Hey! Don't cry like that, sweetheart," Verlan pleaded. He led me to the back steps and sat me down, his arm around my shoulders. "We're going to get through this, somehow."

He gazed into the field, his voice filled with pain as he said, "Irene told me about Ervil. Susan, I can't tell you how sorry I am, or how grieved and disgusted I feel. My own brother! It's hard to believe. Oh," he sighed, "He's pulled this before on other men, but I guess I thought he was above stealing his own brother's girl. Goes to show you how wrong a man can be, doesn't it?"

He wiped the tears from my face with a huge thumb. "We need to talk, don't we?" He said softly. "See if there's any way we can straighten this mess out."

I nodded and buried my face in my palms. How could I admit to him how I'd fallen so easily into Ervil's trap? How did you explain to someone what a scoundrel his brother was, and what an idiot you were?

Verlan's eyes darkened with anxiety. "Honey, Ervil's a power-hungry man. I know better than anyone does what kind of influence he's capable of wielding over other human beings. I don't know where it all will lead, or just what sort of scheme he has up his sleeve...I haven't trusted him for months, and now, with this last trick, I've lost all respect for him." He shook his head, his mouth a hard line. "Joel's going to have to deal with him, and he just can't put it off any longer." He looked at me, and then looked away, squeezing my fingers nervously.

"What?" I asked, searching his face. "What else were you going to say?"

His eyes suddenly seemed black with grief. "Susan, even if Ervil made you swear not to tell anyone, you have got to tell me! I have to know. Did he have you sealed to him, too? Did he convince you to . . . "

"No!" I snapped. "I wouldn't do it. He wanted me to, but I wouldn't." I stared, shocked, at Verlan. "Is that what you thought? Didn't Irene tell you about our conversation? I would've told her if I was sealed to Ervil. I wouldn't even be here with you, if that were the case. Do you mean all this time you thought I was sealed to him?"

Comprehension and joy slowly changed Verlan's wild countenance. He grabbed me and hugged me. "Then, do I still have a chance?" he shouted. "Oh, honey, you're no pushover, are you? I thought I was too late! Say I still have a chance with you!"

He pulled me to my feet at the edge of Grandma's porch. His hands were trembling as he held mine, his aqua-colored eyes dark with emotion. The strain of betrayal had left his face, and his rugged features were softened as he looked down at me. With shaking voice, he said, "I love you, Susan. I have since the day I saw you sitting there in church six months ago. I knew you were supposed to be mine; I just knew. Oh, honey, are you gonna be mine? Are you gonna marry me? Will you marry me?"

I wanted to be a challenge. I wanted to make him beg me, plead for my love. But I couldn't hide my joy and relief. I couldn't answer him, tell him with dignity that I would be honored to be his wife. I sobbed and clung to him, and he knew.

"Susan . . ." he whispered my name. He bent his face down, his blue eyes closing as he pressed his mouth down hard against mine. Suddenly, with an impact that left my senses reeling, my dream of months ago flooded over me. Verlan—his blue eyes—his hard kiss. He had come to me, held me in his arms—whispered my name—rescued me from evil and terror—rescued me from . . . Ervil!

The knowledge rushed through me and I gasped, wide eyed at the revelation. Ervil LeBaron? It couldn't be. Verlan's own brother, Ervil . . . the evil, grasping spirits in my dream? It couldn't be true. No. It just couldn't be true. It couldn't be, but even as I battled against the conviction, I knew it was.

Chapter 12

T he hours, filled with meetings, dragged by. I sat with Fara and Mona in the back of the church building and tried to be inconspicuous. I was hoping Kris and Anna Mae would stay away from me, and I prayed that Ervil wouldn't corner and pressure me.

Before Verlan left Grandma's this morning, he'd assured me that he would "handle" Ervil. The look in his eyes as he said it had left me cold. I didn't want to know how he would handle him. I couldn't imagine the two of them slugging it out—it wouldn't exactly be their style. But something dreadful was going to happen.

I watched the LeBaron men, sitting side by side on the stage behind the pulpit. To all appearances they seemed united. But I knew inside, two of them seethed at each other. Ervil was seated slightly apart from Verlan and Joel. His legs were crossed, and there was stiffness about him, his eyes stoic and unreadable. Verlan was stern-faced. As I looked from Verlan to Ervil, the family resemblance was evident—the large bone structure, the deep-set eyes and receding hairline. I hated that there was tension between them, and though I knew I was part of it, I was certain I wasn't the only reason.

As soon as the meeting was out, I fled home. I couldn't bear waiting to see if anything happened between the brothers. I just wanted it over. I wanted Ervil to know for certain that I wouldn't marry him. After the connection between him and my dream, the thought of anything between the two of us made me ill.

It was after the evening's talent show before I spoke with Verlan again. I'd started toward the back rooms of the church, my arms filled with the stage drapes to fold and put away. Standing in the darkness of the hallway, Verlan held Irene in his arms. He was pleading with her about something, I could tell by the tone in his voice. She was crying, and my heart ached with sudden guilt. Was he letting her know about us, and she was falling apart? I stopped short, and they both saw me at the same time. Irene dabbed at her eyes and managed a shaky smile.

"There you are!" Verlan exclaimed, forcing cheerfulness. "I was just coming to look for you. I wanted to walk you home."

I blushed in the semidarkness. Oh, how I wished I knew what Irene was crying about! I didn't want her to weep because of me. I liked her so much, and she had been good to me. I wanted her to be my friend. I hoped we would be close. I didn't want her to feel pain because Verlan was marrying me. Oh, God, couldn't a plural marriage happen without causing pain?

Suddenly I wanted to cry. I wanted to run away and spare Irene the heartache she was feeling. Verlan was her husband! How could she not be aching inside?

"No, no, I'll just go," I croaked, stumbling backward. "Fara is still here, waiting for me. I'll go home with her."

Irene moved to me and grabbed my hand. "It's all right, you know," she said softly. "I want Verlan to take you home. I mean that." She gave me a little hug. "You are going to be a wonderful addition to our family, Susan, and I couldn't be happier. You will be a beautiful jewel in Verlan's crown. Don't mind my tears, okay? They're not because of you." She sniffed and tried to smile again. I didn't believe her for a minute, but I admired her intensely for trying to ease my discomfort.

"You really don't mind?" I whispered.

Verlan took the drapes out of my arms. "Here, Irene. Put these curtains away, will you. I'm going to take this girl home." He leaned over and gave her a quick kiss, took my arm, and hurried me out the back door of the church.

We walked, hand in hand down the dark, deserted road. I wished Verlan would say something. Even more than with Estela and Lane, I felt the depth of hurting and heartache that polygamy caused. I sensed although Verlan wasn't saying anything, he felt Irene's torment as much as if it were his own.

"I had it out with Ervil this evening," he said abruptly. "You won't have to worry about him any more."

I tensed and glanced at him. "What happened?" I asked.

"It was all I could do to keep from knocking his teeth in, if you want to know the truth," he said dryly. "I'm not given to physical violence, but today, well, I have never come so close. You should have heard him try to oil his way out of the corner he was in. He had one excuse after another. He said you misunderstood his intentions and that you were the one who initiated the relationship between the two of you. That kind of garbage. He apologized, said he didn't realize I was courting you."

"Your brother is a liar," I snapped.

Verlan visibly winced. "Oh, he has his weaknesses. His biggest problem is he thinks he's above the law. But... his help as a missionary has been invaluable to the church," Verlan's voice trailed. "I talked to Joel about it all . . . " I held my breath, waiting for him to continue. "He thinks we need to be patient with him."

Verlan drew me to a stop beneath a huge cottonwood tree and we sat down on the ditch bank. I shivered in the cool night air. Off in the distance, some *caballeros* were singing a mournful, Mexican love song. I tried to make out the words, but the singers were too far away.

Verlan picked up a twig and started snapping it into pieces. "So?" His voice sounded loud in the quiet of the night. "What would you think about us getting married on Sunday?"

"*This* Sunday?" I gasped.

"I know it's soon. But I can't come back here again for some time, and I can't abide the thought of leaving you, Susan. Besides, Joel's here to perform the ceremony, and all our friends are already here because of conference. What better time for a celebration like a wedding?" His voice was becoming more enthusiastic with each word.

"But, I don't even have a wedding dress! Or anything! I can't possibly get everything ready in two days! I would need to see about a wedding cake, and . . . "

"Sweetheart, what'da' ya' say let's don't go overboard. I'm sure you'll find something nice to wear," he squeezed my shoulder. "As for a cake and all that, you just leave that to me. Don't even worry about it. Okay?"

I groaned and shut my eyes tight. So much for my dreams of a beautiful, fancy wedding. I reluctantly nodded my head. For Verlan, I was willing.

He pulled me to my feet, and putting his arm around me, we continued toward home. "What do you think your mom and dad will say?" he questioned. Before I could answer, he continued, "I pray they say yes, because I can hardly wait until you're really mine."

He kissed the top of my head. "Do you know something? That day in church last April, the day I fell in love with you, you looked like an angel sitting on that bench, smiling at me. I told myself that if there was any way on God's green earth, I was going to make you mine. You can't imagine the hell I went through after I got your last letter saying you were through with me. I wanted to drop everything then and run to you. But it just wasn't possible, especially with conference so close."

He kicked a stone out of the way and stalked along for a few paces. "If I'd had any idea what and who was behind it all, I'd have been here anyway, in a flash."

We stopped at the gate in front of my house, and Verlan leaned against the adobe wall. "There's one thing I want to hear before asking your folks for you," his voice was low. "Can you tell me that you love me?"

My heart was in my throat. I'd thought about this many times, envisioning how I would say those words to him. I wanted to sound mature and romantic, my words ringing in his ears with conviction. And now the time had come. He stood waiting. I looked up at him, into his eyes that glistened in the starlight. "I love you," I squeaked. I was mortified. I'd sounded like a scared chicken. But Verlan didn't seem to notice. He grabbed me, squeezed me, and when he was through kissing me my face burned from his whiskers; my lips felt bruised.

We knocked on Mom's bedroom door. Her sleep-drugged voice told us that Dad was at Maria's. We ran around the house like two kids, giggling with excitement as we pounded on Maria's door. As we waited, the moon came out from behind a cloud and I could see Verlan's face clearly. He looked relaxed and happy and it thrilled me to think that I was the cause of his happiness. I was marrying a great, godly man. I was so lucky.

Dad finally came outside, buckling up his britches. He was barefoot and stepping gingerly. "Okay. I'm here. What's up?" he demanded.

I could detect shakiness in Verlan's voice. "Vern, we've decided we'd like to get married, and I came to ask your permission for Susan. What do you think?"

There was silence for a moment. "Well!" Dad finally grumped, scratching the top of his bald head, "I think you could have picked a better time to ask an old man than in the middle of the night. When do you propose to do all this?"

"How does Sunday night sound?"

I expected my father to shout his disapproval, but he only stared at Verlan, taken aback. Then he chuckled, "My, my. Aren't we in a hurry! Verlan, do you realize that she barely turned fifteen a week ago? Don't you think you're rushing things just a little?"

Now that I had decided to be married in two days, I couldn't bear the thought of putting it off. "But, Dad," I began, "I'm as old as . . ."

Verlan interrupted me. "I would take good care of her, Vern. She's young in years, but she's mighty wise, in more ways than you know. She's ready to make a marriage commitment. I love her, Vern."

"Well," Dad paused, "If it was anyone but you . . . Well, let's go see what her mother has to say. Let me get my shoes."

Soon we were standing in a little group in our living room. Dad presented the question to my mother, and she quietly said, "If it was anyone but you, Verlan, I wouldn't even consider it. But something tells me that you are the right man for Susan. You may as well go ahead."

Verlan kissed me in front of Mom and Dad. He pumped my father's hand and kissed Mom on the cheek. "You won't be sorry," he assured them. Then, with a wave of the hand, he was gone.

I shivered with excitement as I got ready for bed. I thought about waking Fara up and telling her, but I decided to wait until tomorrow. I felt such a mixture of emotions, now that it was settled. I was thrilled and scared. How would Verlan's family accept me? It was going to be a shock to his wives, except for Irene. What would I do if some of them were angry? Where would I live? I hadn't thought to ask Verlan these questions. I wasn't even sure about how many children he had. Somewhere around twenty-five, I thought.

Slowly it dawned that I was placing my entire future into the hands of a man that I scarcely knew. It was practically said and done! It took a lot of faith and trust in an individual to do what I was doing. But then, Verlan LeBaron wasn't just anyone.

Verlan had made arrangements to have the wedding in brother and sister Wakeham's living room. The ceremony was set for nine o'clock. It was almost time for my wedding, and I sat in Wakeham's bedroom in the middle of the bed. The beautiful, lace-wedding gown that had belonged to Esther Spencer's daughter, Doris, was puffed up around me like billowy clouds. Francisca's white pumps, the toes stuffed with tissue, stuck out in front of me.

The minutes passed as I fidgeted alone in the bedroom. Doris, who had gleefully insisted that, since she had loaned me the dress, she should be the one to help me, had left me to see what was keeping Verlan and the men. It was after nine, and the men, who were in still another meeting, were running late. Verlan, my sweet Verlan, was late for our wedding.

I scooted to the edge of the bed and gingerly stood, then walked to the bathroom, so I could have a look at myself without being under Doris' scrutinizing gaze. I peered at my face by the lamp light and wished that I had my mascara. Doris had taken it with her, along with my makeup bag. "You want to look young and innocent when you walk down that aisle," she insisted. "Not like a made up woman of the world. Uncle Verlan will like you better just the way you are, believe me."

I had resentfully placed my makeup bag into her outstretched palm. My eyes looked huge and ringed by dark circles. I pinched my pale cheeks, hoping for a miracle. It was no use, I looked horrid.

I opened the bedroom door a crack. People were milling around the kitchen, waiting impatiently for the wedding to begin. Aunt Thelma was trying to calm my father down.

"If that man doesn't show up within ten minutes, I'm calling this wedding off!" he was threatening.

I closed the door and went back to sit on the bed. Actually, I was glad the men were late. It gave me some time to be alone. This had all happened so fast that my head was still reeling. Today was October 27th, 1968. So much had happened in the six days since I'd turned fifteen. Was it only three days ago that Ervil had planned to have me sealed to him? I shuddered. Well, Verlan was taking me to Baja, and I wouldn't have to see much of Ervil.

I thought about leaving Colonia LeBaron. I loved this place and the people who lived here. They were all like my own family. I knew all their sorrows and joys. I knew the name of every child, and when every new baby was due. I hadn't realized it before, but I really loved Colonia LeBaron. And now, the name LeBaron would be mine. Susan LeBaron. It sounded elegant.

I thought about leaving my mother, and felt a rush of emptiness. I realized how little I had appreciated her in the past. In the last year I had convinced myself that I was ready for a home of my own, where nobody could tell me what to do. Now, I wasn't sure at all.

Tears surfaced. How I wished Jay were here! I had never contemplated Jay missing my wedding. I had missed his, and he was missing mine.

Suddenly there was a knock on the bedroom door. Dad peeked in. He was decked out in his sky-blue suit and tie. "Well, young lady," he growled, trying to hide the emotion in his voice, "I hope you're ready. The groom has finally showed up. Forty minutes late to his own wedding! But then, he's a LeBaron, so we're supposed to put up with it."

He walked into the bedroom and helped me from the bed. "Said they couldn't get out of their meeting any sooner." He continued, disgusted, "If they'd all stop their arguing and get to the point, it'd help. Well, it don't make any difference, I guess. They're here now, and mighty anxious to get the show on the road."

Dad fussed with my train, and then took my arm. "You ready? Then, give your daddy a kiss."

He marched me out of the bedroom and down the long aisle formed by people standing on either side of the room. I tried to make him walk slowly like I had seen in movies, but he was in a hurry to have it over with. We fairly flew past the admiring crowd, Franny's shoes slipping up and down on my ankles with each step.

Certain faces stood out in the crowd of people. I could see Grandma LeBaron, a pleased smile on her face as she looked at me. Then Debbie's solemn features caught my attention. She darted a glance at Ervil, who was staring at me over the top of Anna Mae's head. I lifted my chin and looked straight ahead as we swept past.

Irene, appearing calm and serene, stood next to Verlan in front of the fireplace. She took my hand from Dad's arm, squeezed it, and placed it in Verlan's. He grinned at me as together we turned to face the prophet Joel.

Without further ado, Joel opened his manual and the ceremony commenced. As he read the words of the sealing ceremony, his voice rose and fell with emotion. When he paused to wait for Verlan and me to recite our vows, his eyes glistened with pride. The words of the sealing escaped me, but a feeling of reverence, a bounding holiness, enveloped me. I spoke the words with firm resolve as Verlan looked down into my face, and I shivered with the magnitude of the vow I was speaking. Joel was sealing us to one another in marriage for eternity. Forever and ever, throughout the worlds to come, I would be Verlan's wife.

The crowd pressed around us. Out of the corner of my eye I could see Aunt Thelma's face, a contented smile on her lips. Mom stood next to her, somber and pale, and a sudden flash of remorse clouded my happiness. How would she ever manage with both Jay and me gone? I hadn't thought of that until this very moment.

After the ceremony, Verlan kissed me, and the guests hugged me. I was passed around the room, while everyone talked, and wished me happiness. Suddenly I was face to face with Ervil.

I steeled as he bent over and kissed me on the cheek. "Susan Ray," his voice was a husky whisper against my ear, "a man in my position doesn't receive false revelations." Straightening up, he smiled good-naturedly and said out loud, "Best wishes. Verlan is a good man."

I stared, electrified by his whispered words and sickened by his duplicity. The threat pounded in my brain. What was he trying to say to me?

Instantly, Grandma was at my side, her thin arm protective around me. "Susan, honey, Verlan's going to take good care of you." Her voice was reassuring as she maneuvered me toward the kitchen. "I'm glad you're feeling better, Ervil dear," she said over her shoulder, not even glancing at him as we left him staring after us.

"You are the most beautiful bride!" Grandma continued softly to me.

"Thank you, Grandma."

"Now, now," she squeezed my hand. "You should call me Mother, like the other girls do. I'm so pleased to have you married to my Verlan."

"Can I get in on this party?" Irene interrupted. "Oh, Susan, what a lovely bride you are," she kissed me on the cheek.

"Thank you," I murmured, wondering how she truly felt. Was she honestly as glad about me as she appeared?

As Irene rattled on, I sent a swift glance in Ervil's direction. Aunt Thelma and Uncle Bud were huddled near him. Ervil had his arm slung loosely around Bud's shoulder, and they all burst into laughter at something Ervil said. It suddenly concerned me to see Ervil patronizing my relatives.

I searched for Verlan. Men surrounded him in a corner of the dining room, and they were slapping him on the back and talking all at once. He noticed me and threw his hand in the air in an exaggerated wave. I smiled and moved in his direction.

Kristina and Anna Mae approached me. Flinging her arms about my neck, Kris wailed, "Oh, I can't tell you how disappointed we are that you married Verlan instead of Ervil, Sue! I'm sick about it! I could hardly come to your wedding."

Anna Mae yanked Kris away from me. "Now, don't you mind her, Susan, she doesn't mean it. You just be happy!" She smiled brightly, the gold flecks in her eyes sparkling. I squeezed her hand. Ervil had some wonderful wives. I quickly moved away from them. When I looked for Verlan again, he'd disappeared.

On the dining room table was a huge sheet cake with pastel green frosting, and a crystal bowl of strawberry punch. I guessed this to be Verlan's idea of a wedding reception. I took a slice of cake and looked around the room, wanting us to feed each other, as I had seen at other weddings. I moved among the guests out in the lantern lit yard, looking for a tall man in a dark suit. There was not a tall man among them.

Wait a minute, I thought slowly. Where's Joel? And the other men? None of them were in sight.

"Mark," I called as he walked outside, "Have you seen Verlan and Joel?"

He slung his arm around my shoulders. "Sweet little Cuz, they all just left. I think they went back to finish their meeting."

110

"No!" I whispered, aghast. "Oh, Mark, you're teasing me!"

Brother Jensen's third wife, Lawreve, hurried across the yard toward me. "Susan," she avoided my eyes, "Verlan asked me to tell you that he's sorry, but he had to go back to a meeting. He wants me to help you get your things, and take you to my house to wait for him. That's where the meeting's being held. You can rest there until it's over. I'll be just a few minutes."

I nodded, thanked her, and moved away. Lawreve was feeling sorry for me, I could tell. Instant anger flared inside me. Why couldn't Verlan have told me himself! Well, Suze, I thought grimly, this is just an example of what's to come, being married to an important man.

I wandered around for awhile among the guests and thanked them for coming to my wedding. No one seemed shocked by the disappearance of the groom. Mom and Dad soon left, taking Fara and Ramona home to bed. "I'll be there in a while to get my things," I called after them.

Soon the last of the guests left. I put an apron over my wedding dress and helped wash saucers and glasses. "You don't have to do that!" Sister Wakeham protested.

"No, I want to, really," I assured her. I needed something to keep my hands busy, to fill the time so I wouldn't feel so much like I'd been abandoned.

"Ready to go?" Lawreve was finally at my side. She drove me to my parents' house for my bags, and so that I could tell my family goodbye. I ran into my bedroom and changed out of the borrowed wedding dress, putting on a pair of jeans and my old shoes. I kissed Ramona's soft cheek, and she wrapped her sleepy arms around my neck. "I love you, little sister." Homesickness rushed over me, and I wept.

Fara's gray eyes were full of assurance. "You are going to be fine, Sue. Stop your crying. You are going to have a blast!" She hugged me and kissed my cheek.

I set my suitcase down on the front porch and tapped on my parents' bedroom door. "Come in, honey," Mom called.

"Oh, Mama," I sobbed, burying my face against her neck.

"There, there, you are going to be fine," she echoed Fara's words as she patted my back.

"Here, little girl," Dad said, handing me my wedding present. It was a ten dollar bill, American, crisp and green. "This is to buy you a new pair of shoes. We can't have our girl going off on her honeymoon without decent shoes." I hugged him good bye and tucked the money into my suitcase. It was more money than I had ever had before.

The Jensen's home was a mansion compared to most of the homes in the Colony. Lawreve and I tiptoed across the tiled floors, past the sunken living room with its closed doors. Behind the doors I could hear the murmur of men's voices. I paused, hoping to hear Verlan, but Lawreve turned and motioned me to follow her. We walked down stairs, and she set my suitcase down in a cool, basement bedroom.

"You might as well get comfortable," she advised. "Put your pajamas on, and go to bed. I know those men. That meeting won't be over until the wee hours. Get some rest. It's been a big day for you, and tomorrow will be another one."

Turning the lamp down low, she gave me a quick hug, and left.

Wide awake, I wandered around the bedroom. My wedding night was certainly turning out differently than I had thought it would. But I *had* expected to spend it with my husband.

After an hour, I tiptoed up the stairs and stood in the wide hallway outside the heavy living room doors. I could hear angry voices, but they were too muffled to comprehend. As I strained to catch the words, I heard Ervil's raise above the others. Were the men taking Ervil to task about Debbie? Unable to identify their words, I crept back to the bedroom and lay down on the bed still clothed. I pulled a blanket over me and snuggled under it to wait for Verlan.

I wondered what the men would do about Ervil. The memory of his whisper rang in my ears. "A man in my position doesn't have false revelations." Well, Verlan and I were married now, and Ervil's so-called revelation was indeed false. Yet his taunting words haunted my thoughts. What was he trying to say?

Chapter 13

"Susan, it's time to go," Verlan shook me. "Put on your shoes, honey. I'll get your bags." I struggled to awaken, trying to place where I was. Verlan was hurrying out the door, his arms full. Suddenly I remembered. I was married! Verlan and I were married and we were going on our honeymoon.

As I sat up and reached for my shoes, I looked around me. The window above my head revealed a piece of black sky through the edge of the curtain. The lamp on the dresser still burned low, the chimney smudged with soot, which told me that several hours had passed since Lawreve had left me here. Just as she'd warned, the men's meeting had lasted until almost morning. I picked up my jacket, blew out the lamp, and followed Verlan through the quiet Jensen home.

Parked in the driveway with its lights on and its engine running sat Dan Jordan's green Volkswagon bug. Verlan moved to the front of the car and handed him my suitcase. My heart sank. Verlan had mentioned we would be traveling to Chihuahua City with someone, but I'd had no idea that it would be Dan Jordan. What a lousy way to start a honeymoon!

Now Susan, be nice, I thought. He's probably a fine enough guy in spite of those shifty black eyes. Just because he hangs around with Ervil is no reason for you to dislike him. He's an Apostle of the Church, just like Verlan. Don't be so quick to judge people.

Dan's wife, Sharon, scooted up to let me into the back seat. Sharon was Esther and Floyd Spencer's daughter, and she had her father's thin birdlike features. She was heavy with pregnancy and looked miserable as she turned to greet me.

"It's a terrible time of the morning to start a long trip, isn't it? You look worn out." She clucked her tongue as she peered at me in the dim light. "Didn't you sleep while the men were in their meeting?"

"Yes, some. But I was too excited to rest really well." I wiggled on the hard seat. "I hope we won't be crowding you too much."

"Now, don't you worry about me!" She moved up again to let Verlan in next to me. "I'm just glad to have a chance to spend some time with Uncle Verlan. It's been ages since we've had a chance to visit, hasn't it, Uncle?"

"It certainly has!" Verlan's voice sounded hearty, and not a bit tired. "Since you were just a little thing. And now Dan's got you all saddled down. Four kids, right?"

"And one on the way." Sharon said brightly. "Mother's keeping the kids for me until the baby is born."

As Dan backed the car out of the driveway, Verlan wrapped his arms around me. "Susan, honey, I'm so sorry about tonight." he whispered, his lips against my cheek. "That meeting was important, or I would never have left you. Forgive me?"

"Of course," I murmured, anticipating the rest of our honeymoon. The stars twinkled above our heads as we bumped over the cattle guard at the front entrance to the colony. As we climbed onto the highway, I looked back through the Volkswagon window at the town of my childhood. All I could see of Colonia LeBaron was a dark group of trees and a thin, gray ribbon, which was the main road that ran past the church house. I followed the ribbon with my eyes, to the end of the colony and back again, but the darkness hid my family's place from my view. I stared for a minute, imagining the ramshackle adobe where my mom and dad, Fara and Ramona slept. I hadn't even told my cows goodbye. I swallowed the lump in my throat and turned back around, settling into the seat. Verlan's hand held tightly onto mine.

The little car quickly gained momentum and soon we were flying down the highway and passing every vehicle on the road. I could tell the reckless speed made Verlan nervous. He peered over Sharon's head as he watched every move Dan made. His tense fingers gripped mine. After a while he began to relax.

Once the winking lights of Buenaventura were far behind us, Dan turned slightly in the seat and drawled, "Well, Verlan, I don't know about you, but I'm not too thrilled about the decisions that were made tonight. You didn't say much. How do you feel about the stand Joel has taken against Ervil?"

I pricked my ears and watched Verlan. "You know very well how I feel," he replied promptly. "As a Church, we have no right whatever to try to force people into anything. Ervil's way off base. Joel was right to put his foot down with him. He should have done so long ago, in my opinion, but he was hoping Ervil would come to his senses on his own. He's way too pushy, and people won't stand for it. If he keeps it up, he'll run off our members! There is a Civil Government to handle criminals; we don't have to worry about it. We should be concerning ourselves with men's souls, with teaching them the law of love— not with trying to push our weight around on a civil level."

So, Ervil had lied when he told me that he wasn't planning to start an immediate enforcement of the Civil Law! I knew why now. He had been afraid it would scare me away.

"You're saying that we should continue to let the law of the land handle our people?" Dan's nasal voice interrupted my thoughts. "Come on, Verlan! God's people who break His Law should be tried and punished by the leaders of His Church. That's the way it was back in the days of Moses and all through the Old Testament, and that's the way it should be now. Why can't you and Joel and the others see that?"

Verlan's tone turned abrupt. "Let's not discuss this. We're not going to agree; besides, it isn't a subject to talk about in front of women. I'm on my honeymoon, remember? All I want to think about is this sweet girl in my arms."

Verlan nestled his head in my neck. His whiskers had grown during the night, and they burned. I settled back again and tried to ignore the tension in the car. As Sharon picked up the conversation, talking about family news and other small matters, I hugged my new husband, stroked his hair, and tried to get used to the thought that I was married. Soon he dropped his head onto my shoulder and began to snore. I lay my head back and drifted into a sound sleep.

The sun was coming up when I awoke. I could see the outskirts of Chihuahua City. Tingling with excitement, I looked around. The city appeared dingy and forlorn in the predawn light, with garbage and old rusty cars lining the highway. A plastered adobe wall ran for miles along the road, the name of the president of Mexico painted on in bright red and green. A group of people walked along the highway, making their way into the city for the day's trading. The man in the group led a burro with its pack stacked high and held the hand of a barefoot boy. The two women were wrapped in shawls, the younger one holding a baby. The other woman carried a huge, earthen jug on her head. She wasn't holding on to it, and I turned in the seat as we passed, marveling at her perfect sense of balance.

We drove on through the streets of Chihuahua, leaving the poverty stricken section with its adobe shacks and lean-tos, behind. Dan maneuvered the car into a nice residential area and pulled into the driveway of a cream-colored, brick home. Wearily, we piled out of the cramped car.

Verlan's long legs had been scrunched the entire, three-hour trip, and he stretched and groaned, "I don't know about the rest of you, but I'm ready for a nice, soft bed."

Dan had to eat and run to work, so Sharon bustled around the homey kitchen, cooking potatoes and eggs. In spite of my growing dislike of Dan, I felt sorry for him. He had been up all night, for the meeting and then the long drive. I was so tired I could barely keep my eyes open, and I wondered how he could go to work.

After breakfast, Verlan pushed back his chair. "Sharon, where do you want Susan and me to rest?" he questioned. His eyes looked strained and bloodshot, his face pale with weariness.

My heart pounded at his question, the blood rushing to my cheeks. "Oh," I said quickly, "I'm not ready to go to sleep yet. I'm going to help Sharon clean up the kitchen. You go ahead. I'll take a nap later." He didn't argue. He followed Sharon to a bedroom down the hall, and in a matter of minutes I could hear him snoring.

"What are the plans for your honeymoon?" Sharon asked as she pushed a broom across the floor. She looked exhausted, and I decided that when the dishes were done, I would nap, so she would feel free to rest.

"I haven't had a chance to ask Verlan yet. We got married so quickly, and we've hardly seen each other in the last two days. I'll just have to wait and see what he has in mind." I dried the last pan, then turned to her. "Would it be all right if we go downtown later on? I need to buy some shoes." I lifted my foot so she could see the holes in the toes of my sneakers.

She grinned. "Looks like you could use a new pair. Sure we can. Now, I'm going to bed! Are you ready to relax for awhile?"

She waddled off to her room, and I lay on the couch. I couldn't bring myself to enter the bedroom and lie with Verlan. The thought was all too new and scary. I tried to imagine lying next to him—what it would be like, and I shivered with nervousness. For him, it would be no big deal. He had slept with a variety of women for years, with five wives before me. I remembered Irene's joking words a few nights ago at Grandma's, when she told me that Verlan would get a "hot surprise" when he got into bed that night. A hot surprise! She'd sounded as if she enjoyed the thought. It worried me a lot. Verlan was used to hot surprises, and I knew almost nothing about sex. It had all been shielded from me at home. Mom was very prim and old fashioned and the subject had never been discussed.

I remembered one time when my curiosity about the male anatomy had gotten the best of me. Shaking with shame, I'd peeked through the curtain that hung in front of Jay's bedroom door, knowing he was taking a bath, and dying to get just a glimpse of what a naked man looked like. I had to know, I told myself, so I could put my curiosity to rest. What I saw on the other side of the curtain was my dear, innocent brother, kneeling at his bedside in prayer. I could have cried, I felt so evil, and I thought the Lord had planned it that way to teach me a lesson. I shifted uncomfortably on Sharon's couch. Soon I would have my answer.

It was three in the afternoon when I awoke. Bright afternoon sunlight streamed through Sharon's living room window, and Verlan was leaning over me. "Why are you sleeping out here?" he demanded. "You should have come into the bedroom. I don't bite."

Maybe not, I thought as he hugged me, but you snore. And heaven only knows what else you do. I smiled into his eyes.

Sharon came out of the bathroom, braiding her long hair. She looked rested, her dark blue eyes sparkling in her thin face. "Do you want to go get your shoes now, Susan?" she asked.

I shyly looked at Verlan. "Do you mind? Dad gave me the money."

"Let's go," he said promptly.

We drove to downtown Chihuahua and wandered down the crowded street until we came to a shoe store. I tried to appear calm and indifferent, but I was quivering with excitement. In the fifteen years of my life, this would be the second pair of brand new shoes I ever had. I remembered the first pair. It was right before we moved to Mexico, when I was six and just starting first grade in Arizona. My father had taken me, bouncing with excitement, to buy me my first pair of new shoes. "We can't have our girl starting school without new shoes," he had said.

I'd stared in awe at all the beautiful shoes, my attention focusing on a pair of black patent leather ones with bows on the toes. Gleefully I had pointed them out to Dad. "Those are the ones I want," I had shrieked. Dad paid no attention to me. After careful deliberation, he picked up a pair of boy's two-tone oxfords, bent them at the toe, examined the stitching, and then motioned for me to sit down. Horrified, I had watched as he tried them on me. "There," he'd smugly said as he waved my protests away, "those ought to last you for a while." I wore those shoes to school in shame. They were ugly, boys shoes, and all the prissy girls at school had teased me. This time, I promised myself, I was having a pair of pretty shoes. I was a married woman with my own money, and I deserved to have something nice.

We walked into the store, its huge windows displaying the latest shoe fashions for the entire family. A gentleman in a suit and tie hastened to be of assistance. "Si, Senores, what can I help you with?" He respectfully bobbed his head.

117

I hesitated momentarily. Buying shoes was new to me, and I wasn't sure how to proceed. I opened my mouth to tell the man that I wanted a pair of black, patent leather shoes, with bows on the toes, shoes that shined like his hair.

"Here, Senor, the young lady would like to try these on," Verlan commanded. In his hands he held a pair of shoes, and he gave them to the man. With a quick jerk of his head, Verlan motioned for me to sit down.

Openmouthed, I stared at him, the blood pounding in my ears. Surely he wasn't planning to choose my shoes! Verlan's blue-green eyes never wavered as he stared back at me.

"Sit down, Darling," he said gently, "let the man try them on you."

I stood frozen and humiliated, with three pair of eyes watching as they waited for me to obey. I wanted to scream in protest, inform Verlan that I was a grown woman, and that I would choose my own shoes. But the words wouldn't come. They choked in my throat as I stared at my new husband, the man who only hours before, in a long and solemn ceremony, I had sworn before God to obey.

Shuddering with the effort, I forced my muscles into action. I sank into the leather seat. Oh, Lord, I silently, desperately prayed as the little man knelt in front of me. Don't let them fit.

He gingerly removed my tattered tennis shoes, holding them carefully away from his body with the tips of his fingers. He replaced my old shoes with Verlan's selection— a pair made of brown leather, with square toes and sturdy heels, ideal for mountain climbing. The shoes slipped perfectly onto my feet and the salesman laced them up tight. He pinched the toe to check for fit, then triumphantly nodded as he stood up and grinned at Verlan. "Si, si! Son Perfectos. Son Perfectos!"

My vision blurred and my head throbbed as I stared at the ugly shoes. I hated them! I despised myself too, for not having the nerve to say anything, but marriage was all too new to me, and I didn't know what my rights were.

Verlan was watching me, a contemplative look on his handsome face. "Go ahead and walk in them," he said impatiently.

Dutifully I obeyed. Words of rebellion were in my head but choked out of utterance. I felt stifled and out of control of the situation. How did a bride argue with her groom, when he was twenty-three years older than her, and the President of the Twelve Apostles? Verlan stuck out his hand. I put my ten-dollar bill into his palm and watched without a word as he paid for the shoes, pocketed the change, then ushered Sharon and me out of the store.

"Real fine, then!" he said happily. "Those ought to last awhile!" Where had

I heard those words before? I plodded along next to him, too mad to see.

Sharon's eyes met mine as we climbed back into the car. *Why did you let him do that?* she silently questioned me.

Verlan seemed oblivious to my withdrawn mood. As we drove through the streets of Chihuahua, he talked to Sharon, asking her about the historical landmarks of the city. She drove past a huge market place that was under tents, where the smell of fried Mexican food permeated the air. I brooded in the back seat of the Volkswagon. Was I being childish and silly to feel so upset? Maybe Verlan made all the decisions for his wives. I wondered if he selected their shoes, also, or if he thought that I was so young and inexperienced that I needed someone to choose for me. Well, I would have to put a stop to it in the future.

Sharon pulled up next to a little stand along the road and purchased zucchini squash and tomatoes. "Let's go home and make supper," she said.

Dan was on the couch, gently snoring, as we walked into the house. We tiptoed past him and on into the kitchen. "Poor baby," Sharon crooned, looking at him from the kitchen doorway. "He won't be much company tonight."

Good, I thought. I had dreaded the possibility of another doctrinal discussion between Dan and Verlan. It made me uneasy, and I knew Verlan wanted no part of it. I wondered how long he planned for us to stay here, and I hoped tonight only. I wanted time alone with my husband— time to get better acquainted before we arrived in Baja where the rest of his family was. I'd thought constantly of the shoe incident, and was convinced that it was nothing more than a misunderstanding. Verlan was wonderful, thoughtful and loving, and I needed more patience. I wanted to recapture the closeness between us, the feeling of companionship that we had experienced before the wedding. I needed to behave as a wife behaved, and then he would surely stop treating me as a child.

Sharon made a delicious dish with the zucchini and tomatoes, and she cooked steaks that were pounded thin and breaded. She called them 'Milanesa'. We squeezed lime juice over the top of the meat, and the dish tasted exotic and delicious.

Dan joined us at the table, his eyes swollen from lack of sleep. With his mouth full, he began as I knew he would, to talk doctrine. "Verlan," he mumbled through the food, "I want to show you a place I found in the D&C that backs up Ervil's position on the Civil Law. I don't think you've really studied on this before, Brother, and I'd like to help you to understand. Maybe there's hope still, that we leaders of the Church can see eye to eye."

The "D&C" Dan was talking about was *The Doctrine and Covenants*, the book of revelations from God to Joseph Smith. I glanced at Verlan, and could feel him tense. He chewed, then swallowed and answered, "I'm willing to listen, but it'll to take a lot to convince me."

"Well, for your sake I'm going to try," Dan said wryly.

I glared at him. Boy, didn't he think he was something! Verlan made no comment, and I admired him for not losing his patience. If he were speaking to me, I would have wanted to smack his insolent face.

After the meal, the men retired to the living room. As Sharon and I did the dishes, I could hear Dan's nasal voice as he read aloud. I tried to ignore the sound, and I wondered how long this impromptu meeting would continue. As the time for my delayed wedding night drew near, I hoped the meeting would linger. I was scared.

"Susan," Sharon said suddenly. "If there's anything I can do for you, or any questions you have, I'd be glad to help you. Feel free to ask, okay?" She was smiling at me, and I nodded, my face flaming.

All too soon, Verlan called to me. "I'm going to get ready for bed. I'll be waiting for you, honey."

I fidgeted nervously. Dan grinned at me as he walked into the bathroom. "Just make yourself at home, Susan," he drawled. Take a bath, or whatever. Take your time."

I glared at his back. He was so smug! I sat alone on the couch for a few minutes, searching for the courage to face my wedding night. Finally I walked into the bedroom.

Verlan was in bed with the covers pulled up to his chin. He winked at me as I grabbed my suitcase. "I'll be right back," I muttered.

Sharon was in the bathroom combing her hair. I joined her, set my suitcase down, and closed the door. She glanced at me in the mirror, then turned to me questioningly. "Everything okay?"

"I do have something to ask you," I whispered.

"Go ahead, honey. Don't be afraid to ask."

I looked down at the floor. My face burned as I asked, "Do you think I should wear my bra to bed?"

Her effort at hiding a grin failed. "If you do, it won't stay on very long."

I nodded and felt miserable. She consoled me with a gentle pat on the shoulder. "It'll be okay. Just relax and enjoy it." She patted me again, kissed my cheek, and left the bathroom.

I stared after her for a minute, then locked the door and undressed. As I showered I thought about Aunt Thelma. At home on the day of my wedding, she'd pulled a pale pink negligee out of her suitcase. Holding it in front of her, she'd danced around the bedroom, singing, "Boy, won't ol' Verlan love this!" She'd handed it to me with a sweep and a curtsy, and I couldn't bring myself to tell her that I wouldn't wear something like that. My dilemma was, I didn't have a real nightgown. There had been no time to think about it in the two busy days before the wedding, and now I found myself in a quandary. Should I wear the sheer nightie, or a tee shirt and panties? In desperation, I searched my suitcase, hoping for a miracle, a nice, long flannel nightgown. I groaned as I slipped Aunt Thelma's nightie on and looked in the mirror. My full breasts, the nipples appearing dark and round, were plainly in view through the filmy, pink material. No! I told myself in panic, this won't do! What would Verlan think? I removed the frothy, wisp of nothing, put my bra back on, and pulled my red tee shirt on. It reached my waist, leaving my white panties and pale legs uncovered. I can't have him see me like this, I thought grimly. I yanked the nightie on, over the tee shirt. Why, oh, why hadn't I anticipated and prepared? I didn't even have a robe.

The lights in the hallway were off and Dan and Sharon's bedroom door was closed. I tiptoed to our bedroom and stood outside the door. My heart pounded alarmingly as I tried to convince myself that I could do this.

My hand shook as I opened the door a fraction, reached, and flipped off the light switch. Then I ran swiftly and threw myself onto the bed, diving under the covers. I did it quickly, and it occurred to me that I was in bed with a man for the very first time.

"Hey! Wait a minute," Verlan chuckled. "You didn't even let me see your nightgown!" He reached over in the darkness and shoved at me, trying to push me off the bed. When I wouldn't budge, he crawled over me and turned the light back on.

"No, Verlan, no!" I shouted in panic. "I don't want you to see it! Please don't look!"

"Shh, shh!" He darted a hasty look toward the door. "Keep your voice down, Dan and Sharon will hear you!" He eyed me in exasperation, and then flipped the light switch back off. "It's all right for me to see you, now, Sweetie. You're my wife, remember?" He crawled back over me and got under the covers.

As Verlan had stood in the light, it shocked me to see that his body was covered, to the wrist and ankle, in long white garments, the type that

Mormons wore who had been through the temple ceremonies. They wore the garments as a symbol of purity, and as a covenant with God. Why Verlan wore the garments of another Church, didn't make sense, but I couldn't worry about it now. I would have to ask about this later, when I knew him better. He looked strange, with black tufts of hair poking through the three sets of strings that tied the top of it together. A pair of white briefs, over the cotton leggings, covered his hips. I felt the urge to giggle. My wedding night attire couldn't look stranger than my bridegroom's did.

I trembled as I stared at the dark ceiling and waited for Verlan's hands to touch me. I was as far over on my side of the bed as I could be. I knew I was being childish. I loved him, and I was his wife. I shouldn't be afraid. But I was afraid, and I jumped when he reached for me. He casually ran his hand up and down my back. The material of Aunt Thelma's nightie was smooth and thin over the top of my tee shirt, and Verlan's hand stopped abruptly.

"What are you wearing this thing for?" He demanded, pulling out on my bra strap.

"I always wear it to bed."

"Humph," he growled. "You should take it off. It cuts off the circulation during the night. What's this thing?" He was yanking on the sleeve of the tee shirt. I ignored him and turned away from him. The silence between us grew, and as the minutes passed, I wondered if he was asleep. Then out of the stillness, he whispered, "Can I?"

The uncertainty in his voice amazed me. Verlan, timid and hesitant? This important man, with five wives, was as nervous about our wedding night as I was! He seemed at a loss as to proceeding. My fear of him lessened considerably, and I began to feel in control of the situation.

"Can you what?" I whispered back.

"You know."

"No, I don't. Can you what?"

Verlan sat up in bed, his voice filled with whispered alarm. "You don't? Susan, don't you know?"

Immediately my heart went out to him. I couldn't bear the uncertainty in his voice. "Yes, Verlan, I know," I patted his arm in reassurance.

In one movement, covers were tossed aside, my panties were removed, and Verlan's garment-clad body settled on me. His hard, dry kiss stifled the silent screams that arose as burning agony tore through me. My invaded body trembled with pain and shock, and my hair became damp with the tears that ran from my eyes.

It seemed an eternity; in reality, however, only a few minutes had passed. Verlan had moved to his side of the bed. He fumbled for my panties, kissed my cheek as he thrust them into my hand, wrapped his arms around me, and mumbled words of endearment. In moments he began to snore.

After a few seconds, I moved from his tight grasp. Tiptoeing out, I dashed for the bathroom. Still shaking and swallowing sobs, I sat on the toilet and heard the droplets of blood and other matter reaching the water below. Dear God! My paralyzed mind screamed for release. Had this raw, disgusting union been it? Was this the beautiful act my sister Rose Ann had smilingly, smugly told me of? It was horrid.

I sat huddled and insensate until my quivering legs began to cramp with cold, then I gingerly moved to the sink, cleaned myself, and tiptoed to our room. I crawled in next to Verlan's sleeping form and pulled the covers up. Wide-eyed in the darkness, my private parts still burning and numb, my brain mulled over what had happened.

I had expected gentle kissing and shy fondling, rosy happiness and breathtaking exhilaration, and a dizzying, bonding rapture. How could I have been so misled? What had I done wrong?

Surely there was more! Verlan was such a warm, caring man. It had to be me. I was an ignorant child, and I'd led him to believe I was mature and ready for womanhood.

Well, it was over! The worst was behind me and there was no turning back. I was married and I had to make the best of it, and I would. I would show Verlan a warm and willing wife, and together we would build a satisfying relationship. Next time would be better. It had to be.

Chapter 14

Verlan seemed happy to be leaving Chihuahua City and as anxious as I was to leave Dan far behind. "I've had enough of his nonsense," Verlan whispered to me. "Let's get a start on our honeymoon. We need to be alone."

Sharon took us to the train station where we waved goodbye and boarded a train bound for the resort town of Mazatlan. From there, Verlan told me we would go by bus up the Sonora coast. First to Hermosillo, then on around the top of the peninsula, through Mexicali, and on to Tijuana.

I sat by Verlan on the train's unpadded wooden bench and snuggled against him. Forcing away thoughts of the previous night, I determinedly nestled my hand in his and grinned up at him. We're finally going to get to know one another, I thought. We will visit, and laugh, and feel comfortable with personal questions. We will simply erase last night and begin anew. So long as we can be friends and sweethearts, I can handle the other thing.

After the train was underway Verlan squeezed my fingers and quietly said, "Susan, sweetheart, we are going to have to be a bit discreet. You see, these people traveling with us won't understand if they see us like this all cuddled together. They'll figure you're too young to be my wife, so you must be my girlfriend. See what I mean? We wouldn't want to give the wrong impression, would we? We're supposed to be an example to the world. We better let them think you're my daughter. Don't you agree?"

Wordless, I withdrew my hand, moved to the opposite seat, and stared out the window. Hurt and resentment bubbled inside me. We were married, weren't we? What did I care what other people thought! Did their opinions count with Verlan more than mine? Verlan lounged on his bench, looked around, then opened his *Book of Mormon* and immediately became engrossed. He made no move to soothe my wounded feelings or speak, except once when he said, "Honey, I hope you don't mind my taking the time to read for awhile. I've needed time to catch up on my reading for ages so I would have an idea about how to handle certain Church problems. You understand, don't you?"

He didn't wait for my response. Instead he dropped his eyes to the book and turned the page.

Throughout the day as he read and napped, I concentrated on controlling my anger and confusion. I determined to make the most of my trip. I'd traveled little enough, and seen few places, and the eleven-hour train ride was breathtakingly beautiful. The train ran through mountain passes and along rivers and sheer ledges. The hillsides were a gorgeous array of fall colors, with brightly plumed birds, and small furry animals darting among the underbrush. Occasionally the train chugged through gorges so deep I felt claustrophobic before we finally reached the top.

We arrived in Mazatlan after dark and took a taxi to a motel where we settled in for the night. In spite of my clumsy efforts at conversation during dinner, and although I tried acting romantic once we were in our room, our intimate time together was again painful and bewildering. The night proved to be miserable and sleepless for me.

Why, I wondered as I lay next to Verlan's snoring form, was he so abrupt? Was it because he considered sex for procreation purposes only and not an act of love? While I was certain Verlan desired me, it just didn't compare to the intense love and need I felt for him. Why couldn't he treat me with gentleness? He must be afraid that behaving the least bit sensual was displeasing to God. Oh, I had so much to learn about him! Even conversation had become a struggle.

At breakfast the next morning I quickly agreed that we should forget the sightseeing in Mazatlan and leave immediately for Ensenada.

By mid-morning a taxi dropped us off at the bus station. Shifting my suitcase to my other hand, I looked around for a place to sit, while Verlan bought our bus tickets. I spied a vacant spot on a bench next to an old Mexican gentleman and, picking up my bag, I lugged my things to the bench. The old man obligingly scooted over and moved his suitcase to make more room.

"Gracias, Senor," I murmured as I sat beside him. Scrunching up his lined old face, he gave me a toothless smile and winked his faded brown eyes. He looked jolly and happy and seemed like a sweet old man. I wanted to put my head on his shoulder and tell him my troubles.

I looked in Verlan's direction as he stood in line for our bus tickets, and I sighed again. Within me burned the desire to be a good wife. How could I accomplish this? What was lacking in our relationship? I realized he had lots to think about, the problem of Dan and Ervil, the Church work, other wives, and children to care for. At this point I was truly grateful that we had decided to cut our honeymoon short. I couldn't take any more strain, as I had for the past three days.

He hurried toward me waving the tickets triumphantly. "Okay, it's all set and the bus is ready to pull out. Let's go."

I smiled and said goodbye to the old man and followed Verlan to the bus. The huge bus was different from the old wrecks I had ridden in Chihuahua. It was shiny and new with gray tinted windows and it glistened like silver in the bright sunshine.

Strutting in front of the bus was our little Mexican driver. Dressed in a starched gray uniform with a matching chauffeur's cap, his crisp black hair curled jauntily over his collar. A handlebar mustache drooped around full lips. He rattled off Spanish in a commanding voice as he directed the loading of our luggage. "No-no, Chico! Do it right, do it right! Watch how you handle people's belongings!" he shouted. The young boy doing the work cast resentful glances at him and continued to toss luggage into the compartment.

When all was loaded, the driver skipped up the bus steps and settled into his seat, then motioned for his passengers to board. I walked up the steps and held out my ticket. But instead of taking it from my hand, the man leaned his arms on the steering wheel, lazily allowing his gaze to travel from my new shoes to the tip of my head and then down again. The look was impudent and suggestive, and I haughtily dropped my ticket on the floor and stepped past him.

Cocky little rooster! I looked over my shoulder, expecting to see an angry glare in my husband's eyes. But he was oblivious to the driver's lustful leers. He scanned the loft above us for a spot to stow my overnight bag. "Would you mind if I sat by the window?" he asked. "I'll have better light to read by."

Why wasn't I surprised? I settled in my aisle seat and glared at the *Book of Mormon*, which Verlan has hastened to pull from his jacket pocket. I wanted to swipe it from his hands and toss it out the window. How could he be so insensitive? How could he not care if other men came on to me? Didn't I matter as much as his old book?

Making certain boxes and bags were stowed properly, the driver hustled down the aisle. He grinned at me, and I almost laughed. His two front teeth were capped in silver, and gleamed like the mirrored sunglasses perched upon his thin nose. Like a brazen, silver robot in his starched gray uniform, he swaggered to his seat and backed the bus from its berth. Suddenly we were barreling through the streets of Mazatlan, swaying around corners and darting through traffic. Verlan's book crashed to the floor and slid down the aisle, gliding over the slick metal surface, and into the swinging, open door of the rest room. A smug feeling of satisfaction passed through me. His book was

126

exactly where it belonged during our honeymoon.

"He's worse than Tijuana taxicab drivers, and they're the worst I've ever seen!" Verlan gritted out as he clung to the back of the seat in front of him. He motioned to the front of the bus where a long rosary hanging over the rear view mirror swayed. On the wall nearby was an oval miniature of the Mother Mary. "Now we know why he has his Saints and beads hanging around. He's counting on them to save us all! We'll be lucky to get to Hermosillo in one piece."

Soon we were on the highway. Verlan scooted past me to retrieve his book, and I glanced around, my gaze stopping on the rearview mirror up front. Staring at me from the mirror were the driver's black eyes. He'd removed his glasses and arranged the mirror so that he could watch me. I hastily looked away.

Verlan climbed over my legs and settled into the plush maroon seat with a sigh. "At least it's not wet," he scowled, examining his book. "It's a wonder, too, the shape that restroom is in." He opened it, found his place, pushed the button to recline his seat, and was once again preoccupied.

I looked at him. His expressive eyes followed the lines on the page, fascinated. The wind from the open window had blown his hair on his forehead, and he appeared young and handsome. I wanted to touch him, but I knew he would frown. He'd been very strict about any show of affection in public. I didn't begin to understand why. It was our time alone before the rest of the family could have a claim on him. We couldn't act like sweethearts or even like a couple because the strangers around us might not understand. I wished I had the nerve to tell him how lonely and unhappy, how hurt I felt at his various forms of neglect. I'd even practiced the words. I'd run through them in my mind repeatedly. Verlan, I would say softly, I want with all my heart to please you. I want to make you happy. But I want you to pay attention to me. Can't you please put your book away and let's just talk together as man and wife? As friends? But the words would catch every time I tried. My throbbing pulse would slowly return to normal, and I would wipe my wet palms in cowardly despair. I just couldn't do it.

My gaze roamed the bus in misery as our time alone ticked away. There were those flirting black eyes in the mirror again, bold and voracious as they swept over me. Suddenly the prominent eyebrows raised twice in suggestion, the full lips pursed, and the conceited man blew me a kiss. I gasped in repulsion. I wished I had a wedding ring! I would flaunt it in "Mr. Hot Shot's" face. Of course, with the kind of person he seemed to be, it probably wouldn't matter. Men of the world were so wicked.

Verlan turned a page and cleared his throat. I looked at my left hand and tried to imagine what it would look like with a wedding ring. Verlan had told me he would buy one soon. I wondered if it would make me feel any more married.

We finally careened into Hermosillo, screeching and swaying into the enormous bus station. Hermosillo, the capital of Sonora, was our first big city on the sixteen-hour trip to Ensenada. It was nearly midnight, and once we exited the bus, Verlan stretched his legs, arched his back, then walked to the ticket window and conversed with the agent. "Well, come on," he said in a discouraged voice as he walked back to me. "We may as well go get something to eat. The first bus heading to Mexicali doesn't leave until 4:00 A.M. I'm hungry. Let's find a taco."

I trotted obediently after him. The dark street was deserted, and Verlan's long strides made it difficult for me to keep his pace. My pride, my understanding of male chivalry, and mostly, my romantic ideas of love—were being shattered. As the frustrating, last days of my honeymoon were nearing, I thought of Verlan's wives and children who would be expecting a radiant bride. I would need to conceal my hurt feelings and my confusion. I had made my own bed, as my dad would say. I couldn't have them see a whimpering, homesick little girl. I hoped with time, things would improve. Meanwhile, I would have his children to become reacquainted with. Verlan would be away most of the time, and presently, the thought was a relief.

The taco shop was quaint. The smells of fried corn tortillas and fresh, spicy salsa reminded me of my favorite little restaurant back home, and a wave of homesickness overcame me. Verlan led me to a table and ordered tacos. Feeling numb, I ate in silence. He hadn't bothered to ask me what I wanted for supper. Instead he ordered for me as if I were a child! Yes, I was only fifteen, but he had thought me old enough to wed, hadn't he? Surely I was old enough to be respected. He had selected my shoes and my food. I had to find the courage to stop it. He needed to understand that I had my personal opinions and preferences, and a perfectly good brain. I had to get the courage to tell him.

Verlan swallowed the last of his food and cleared his throat. "By the way," he said, "I called Charlotte from the bus station. She'll pick us up at the Tijuana bus stop. She's taking an extra day off from school so that she can take us right on down to Ensenada. I did tell you, didn't I, that she lives in San Diego and teaches pre-school? She drives home to Ensenada every weekend to see her kids. Lucy's taking care of both hers and Charlotte's right now. It's quite a handful for Lucy—you can imagine. Fourteen kids under one roof. I'm sure she would appreciate any help you can give her."

As he said this, I remembered Franny's words. "You'll be stuck tending all the other wives' kids, Susan," she had said. "A free baby sitter." It sounded as though Franny was right.

As we hastened back up the street, I thought of Charlotte. I knew she was Verlan's first wife, and I remembered her from my childhood, when I'd played with four of Verlan's children. Three of them were Charlotte's. I felt ill at ease at the thought of meeting her again. I'd learned through the years that Verlan's first wife had a profound influence over him. How would she react to me? Would she be as warm and welcoming as Irene had been? Charlotte had obviously accepted Verlan's four other wives—surely she would do the same for me. She must be a firm believer in the principle of polygamy, especially being married to the President of the Twelve.

Taking a determined breath, I boldly took hold of Verlan's arm. I knew I was being rebellious, but I had to begin somewhere showing him I had a mind of my own. My heart pounded as I waited for him to unwind my fingers. To my surprise, Verlan tucked my hand beneath his arm and covered it with his. He slowed his stride to mine and grinned at me in the darkness. Suddenly stopping, he pulled me into his arms and kissed me, gently, then passionately, as he had at Grandma's prior to our marriage. The hurt and rejection I had felt over the past two days crumbled. The stored up tears released and coursed their way down my cheeks. I was glad it was dark so he couldn't see my face. I couldn't understand his change, but he had, and that's what mattered.

We entered the bus station, which smelled of stale urine and tobacco. The worst odors were emitting from the restroom, and Verlan led me to an empty corner at the opposite end of the station, past tired travelers, who lounged on the hard benches with their boxes and bags piled near them. He sat close to me on the bench, his legs stretched in front of him.

Exhausted, he leaned back against the wall. I snuggled my head against his shoulder, and again he made no move to protest. He was so warm, and his shoulder was like a soft pillow. I drifted into a peaceful slumber.

In the midst of the night, the announcement came for boarding our bus. I sank onto the soft seat, and before we were out of the city I was asleep again, my head resting on Verlan's chest.

It was daylight when I opened my eyes. Verlan was shaking me. "Susan, we're here. Come on. Get your things."

The passengers were retrieving suitcases from the loft above. One of the gentlemen that had sat behind us was standing in front of me, blocking me from the aisle. His rancid body odor was over-powering. It brought sharply to mind my own appearance having slept in my clothes all night. And Charlotte was meeting the bus! I frantically searched my purse for my mirror and comb and quickly combed my hair. Then I rubbed at the red lines creased into the side of my face from where it had rested on the seat.

"Are you coming?" Verlan stuck his head back inside the bus doorway and motioned for me to join him. I sighed with frustration. I didn't want Charlotte to see me this way, but it was too late to do anything about it. I walked down the bus steps, trying to smooth out my wrinkled blouse and Levi's. The bright morning sun shone in my eyes as I stepped down onto the pavement. I blinked, momentarily blinded.

Verlan grabbed my arm to steady me and said, "Susan, you remember Charlotte."

She stood before me in the shade of the bus depot. Her brown eyes looked right through me as she said, "Hello. How are you?" in a voice so cold it reminded me of a Utah winter. I mumbled a "Hello," and looked her up and down. Charlotte wore a pea-green polyester dress that reached the middle of her calves and a pair of shoes that looked suspiciously like the new ones Verlan had selected for me. She stood rigidly as Verlan leaned to kiss her, and turned her face so that his lips landed on her cheek. Deliberately turning her back to us, she busied herself searching her purse for her car keys.

We loaded our bags into the trunk of a gold-colored Chevelle and Verlan hastened to open the door for us. Charlotte quickly scooted past me and slid onto the front seat beside Verlan. Involuntarily, my fists clenched. Wasn't this my honeymoon?

"So!" Verlan said gaily, "How's everything been going? Everybody well? Kids all okay?"

"Everyone's just fine, thank you, Verlan," Charlotte snapped. Verlan looked at me over the top of her head and winked.

As we reached the main thoroughfare, I immediately saw why he'd said what he had about Tijuana traffic. Cars were cutting in and out, dodging around each other, and giving the impression of complete chaos. Verlan skillfully maneuvered the car around a stalled truck, then turned south onto the road toward Ensenada.

"Has Joel shown up from Chihuahua yet?" he smoothly continued his questions to Charlotte. "Have you heard from the guys in Vegas? They were supposed to call about that huge paint job we bid on. I wonder if we got it."

Charlotte answered his questions in monosyllables. She sat stiffly between Verlan and me, and I found myself feeling sorry for her. I knew his marrying me had taken her by surprise—a totally unpleasant surprise. You need to say something to her, I told myself. Try to break the ice. Taking a deep breath, I hesitantly said, "Verlan and I had a lovely honeymoon, Charlotte. The Mazatlan train ride was just beautiful. We've had a wonderful time." When she didn't answer, I glanced at Verlan. He was scowling at me, so I muttered, "And conference was real nice, too."

She made no comment, and I gave up trying to make conversation. Verlan took over the job, asking Charlotte about her schoolwork and other activities she was involved in. Then he told her the details of conference. I eagerly looked out the window at the scenery, letting Verlan's words float past me until he abruptly said, "Charlotte, I can't begin to tell you how sick I feel about what's going on with Dan and Ervil. You should have heard the song and dance Dan gave me in Chihuahua the other day about Ervil's position over the Church. He informed me that Ervil holds full authority, that he has the power to remove Joel from the presidency. And that he plans to do it if Joel doesn't begin to see things his way in regard to the Civil Law. I laughed in his face, Charlotte—I couldn't help it! And now Ervil's talking of forcing people to go to church so they can learn about the Civil Law. Then they won't have any excuse if they break it." Verlan glanced in the rearview mirror and tightened his grip on the wheel.

Charlotte stared at Verlan. "But that would do away with people's religious freedom! Doesn't he see that?"

"I guess not," Verlan said dryly. "Even if he does, at this point it wouldn't matter to him. In one of the meetings, Ervil made no bones about his position. Joel had to leave for a few minutes, and while he was gone, Ervil stated to the rest of us that he knows as surely as God lives that his program is the only one that will establish God's kingdom. He said he's aware that there are men in high positions who disagree, and it would either be them, or him! Unbelievable! I tremble to think what he means by that."

Charlotte snorted. "Ervil doesn't have the guts to carry out his threats." She looked over at Verlan when he didn't answer. "You're not worried about it, are you?"

Verlan shook his head, but I could tell by his eyes that he wasn't saying how he really felt. The conversation between them filled me with alarm. Verlan hadn't talked to me about any of these things! It was all new information to me. Ervil had said either them or him? He meant Joel and Verlan, of course. Either they had to go—or he would go. Either way, the church was in for upheaval. I closed my eyes, trying to block my feelings of unease. Then I stared out the car window at the Ensenada coastline. The beauty of it seemed unreal after the subtle horror of Verlan's words.

Mesmerized, I watched the rolling ocean waves, breaking into frothy foam against the shore. The sea was new and intoxicating, its crashing roar sweeping me into a trance with its power. Looking over the immense, breathtaking body of water, I realized what an insignificant part I played in God's universe. Even in my new family, my dubious role was absorbed amidst the problems in the church, the wives and the children who had a claim to my husband. At least Verlan talked to Charlotte. He told her what was going on in his world. I wondered if he would ever feel free to talk to me about the things that worried him.

His voice had become a blur as I watched the sea. Suddenly his speech returned into sharp focus as he told Charlotte of Ervil's secret marriage to Debbie. The new, fearful emotions that I was experiencing ached in my chest and throat. Verlan's words about Ervil had filled us all with a sense of impending disaster.

The freeway followed the sea for hours, and finally signs told us we were coming into Ensenada. My senses told me we were entering a city that smelled like spoiled fish. The smell became worse as we made our way to where Verlan's family lived, in a small suburb seven miles from the city.

Several little shanties lined the dusty, unpaved streets of the suburb and were haphazardly situated between the nicer adobe homes. The hamlet appeared dirty and trashy. Rusted barbed wire fences fell onto weed-covered yards. I was shocked this was the romantic Ensenada I had heard so much about, where Verlan had chosen to raise his children. This—was to be my new home?

We drove past a smelly winery with a corrugated tin tower set off to the side. Verlan turned the corner and pulled the car into a big barbed wire enclosed yard that was littered with trash and spindly weeds. Dust boiled around us in soft swirls as Verlan braked to a stop, then it settled on the car in a fine layer of gray powder.

132

Chapter 15

Sprawled in front of me was a one level, purplish brown clapboard house. Out the front door poured streams of children yelling, "Daddy, Daddy!" kicking up the dust as they ran toward us. Verlan was out of the car in a flash and hugging children. Sliding out, I stepped aside for Charlotte to get to her children. I watched the reunion self-consciously, anxious for it to be over so Verlan could introduce me.

The door of the big house opened and Lucy, Verlan's third wife, came onto the porch. She hesitated momentarily as she wiped her hands on her apron. I remembered Lucy from my childhood and I had fallen from her mulberry tree in Colonia LeBaron. She'd rescued me, carried me to the house, and patched up my scraped knees and elbows. Her kindness had left a warm, pleasant memory, and I knew she would welcome me.

As expected, there was a welcoming smile on her face. Then she walked into Verlan's arms and hugged him tight. He rocked back and forth with her, and it reminded me of how he had done with me that day in the field outside of Grandma LeBaron's, the day he asked me to marry him. I quickly looked away.

Verlan released Lucy and walked around the car. He squeezed and kissed me in front of everyone. "Welcome home, Susan," he cried happily. Turning to the waiting family he said, "Lucy, children, this is Susan. She's part of our family now and I want you to make her feel welcome. Susan, do you remember Lucy?"

Lucy stepped forward and wrapped her thin arms around me. Her gentle, light-blue eyes were moist as she looked into mine. "Welcome into the family, Susan. We're glad to have you." Her voice was sincere. My! I thought, what a difference between her and Charlotte.

From out of the crowd of children appeared a tall, very good looking young man. "Remember me?" Verlan Jr. grinned. "We used to compete against each other in spelling bees, back in Colonia LeBaron. Remember?" He scratched his head, "Let me see, was it seven—or was it eight years ago?"

One by one the children came and hugged me. "Hello, Aunt Susan," several of them shyly said. They seemed determined to make me feel welcome, and I laughed with relief. After Charlotte's coolness, I'd feared the others' attitudes. Aunt Susan! The title thrilled me.

We trudged into the living room and I sat on the couch. The smaller children crowded around and stared at me. One of the younger boys couldn't take his solemn, blue eyes off me. "You're pretty," he announced suddenly.

"Thank you," I laughed, embarrassed. I impulsively leaned and kissed his wind-burned cheek. "What's your name?" I asked.

"Byron. And I'm five." His serious eyes never left mine as he added, "I'm glad my dad married you."

With an audible sound of exasperation, Charlotte stalked from the room. An uncomfortable silence descended as the rest of the family stared after her. I watched her retreating back with dismay.

Verlan whispered apologetically, "Don't worry about her. She'll come around."

He chatted with Lucy and the children for a while, and then excused himself to visit Beverly, his fourth wife. She hadn't arrived to welcome us with the family and I guessed that she, too, would have to "come around." Beverly lived with her baby daughter in a tiny, one-room house behind the main house. I vaguely remembered her from years ago in Colonia LeBaron. She was a Mexican girl, a daughter of one of the first "Lamanite" members of the Church. We called the Mexican people "Lamanites" because of a man named Laman, a prominent figure in the *Book of Mormon*. According to Joseph Smith, Laman's family was originally from Israel and they traveled by boat to the American continent around 600 B.C. The story told that God cursed Laman with a dark skin because of his sins, and we believed that the American Indians who populated both North and Central America were descendants of this man.

I wanted no tension with my new sister-wives. It was expected of us to love one another and to maintain harmony in our husband's home, but from Charlotte's cool reception, I wondered if all of Verlan's wives supported polygamy.

Charlotte's two oldest girls, Rhea and Laura, pulled me up off the couch. "Come on, Aunt Susan. Want to see your trailer?" Rhea asked.

Rhea was only a year younger than me. I giggled and answered, "You're not planning to call me Aunt Susan, too, are you? Just call me Susan, okay?"

"Okay," she agreed.

We walked through the enormous dining room where they proudly showed me the dining bar that Verlan had built. The bar was attached to all the surrounding walls. "This is so there's room for all of us to eat at once," Laura explained. Grinning, she added, "That takes quite a bit of table space."

134

Both girls were tall and large-boned, with brown hair and eyes. They resembled their mother except that their faces were friendly while Charlotte's was not. We strolled outside, past a cement slab that held an old Maytag wringer washing machine, and two huge tubs. We walked past the outhouse to a small, white and turquoise colored trailer. It contained a bed with a heavy, homemade quilt for a bedspread, a small couch, a built-in nightstand and dresser, a tiny table and chairs, and a closet. My suitcase and over-night bag were on the bed. I looked around and tried to envision that this was my new home, at least presently. Surely before long Verlan would provide me a nice little house.

Kicking the dust from their shoes, Rhea and Laura crowded in behind me and sat at the table. They watched with unveiled interest as I unpacked, and placed my things in the dresser. "This is going to be so much fun, having you married to Daddy!" Rhea giggled. "We don't have many friends our age to do things with around here. All our school friends live too far away, so we get bored."

"Yeah," Laura chimed in. "Do you play jacks?"

Before I could answer, the door opened and Verlan appeared. His eyes were sparkling with happiness, and he leaned over and gave each of the girls a smacking kiss, then pulled me near him on the bed. Leaning his back against the wall, he wrapped his arms around me and sighed with contentment.

"Do you girls have any idea how lucky and blessed I feel having a beautiful new wife to add to our family?" He grinned. "God is so good to me. I don't know what I've ever done to deserve her, but she's going to be such a blessing to us. I just know it." He hugged me and kissed my cheek.

Embarrassed, I looked at the girls. They grinned, exchanged glances, and then turned their attentions to the floor. Verlan was sure giving me a reputation to uphold. How did he expect me to be a blessing to his family? What was I supposed to do?

Verlan released me and continued visiting with the girls. He teased them and made them laugh. It was obvious they adored him. Enviously, I watched their easy, close relationship. No strain. No tension. I wanted so much to have that, so much that my heart ached. I remembered too, how easily he had conversed with Charlotte.

Soon one of the boys pounded on the door. "Aunt Lucy said to come to supper!" he yelled in a high-pitched tone. We traipsed into the dining room amidst the clamor of fourteen children and two women. The children were all seated at the bar, their backs to the center of the room. In the midst of the room was a dining room table, set for four. Verlan and I seated ourselves at the adult table with Charlotte and Lucy, while the girls sat at the bar. Verlan said a long blessing, thanking the Lord for his goodness, and for giving him such a lovely family. He prayed for the Church and for Joel. His voice was resonant and sincere, and I swallowed my emotions.

Fried potatoes, mashed beans, and green salad began to disappear, along with the thick slices of homemade, wheat bread. Throughout the meal the children kept up a lively chatter. Lucy and Charlotte spoon-fed their babies, who gooed and cried and added to the din, which made it hard for the adults to converse. I covertly watched Verlan's wives. Charlotte remained withdrawn, and heeded only her dinner and the baby on her lap. Even without makeup, she was an attractive woman. She wore her long brown hair in a severe French twist, which detracted from her appeal. Her best features were her wistful brown eyes and long dark lashes. I knew I was partly at fault for her melancholy attitude. I presumed she was also concerned regarding the problems within the Church.

I glanced at Lucy who, like Charlotte, was Verlan's age. But unlike Charlotte, Lucy seemed relaxed and happy as she joked with Verlan. She was thin and angular with a large nose and blue eyes framed by pale lashes. Her mousy brown hair was thin and short. The gentle, giving ways of a selfless spirit shone from her eyes. It was obvious she deeply loved Verlan and wanted his happiness.

Before we had finished the meal, Rhea and Laura began clearing the dishes and the leftovers. I watched them and marveled at their efficiency. As they heated the huge kettle of water for the dishes, they swept the cement floors and scrubbed the dining bar and table. They needed no instructions and they worked quickly.

Soon, Verlan's huge family drifted to the living room, with some of us sitting on the floor and piano bench. The room buzzed with conversation and laughter. How would it be, I wondered, if his twelve other children and three absent wives were also here? I glanced about the living room and tried to convince myself that I belonged here. The room was plain, the furnishings threadbare. The sofas were a faded plum color. A tattered oval rug covered the cement floor. The cotton drapes at the windows were magenta colored with white orchids throughout the material. In one corner of the room on a small bed, Lucy's flaxen-haired toddler amazingly slept through the din.

Verlan sat beside me as children crowded for a seat on either side of us.

Verlan looked around with obvious pleasure as he squeezed my hand. I glanced at him and smiled nervously.

"Lucy, go to the piano and play us some songs," Verlan said enthusiastically. "We could use some singing." Soon we were all crowding around Lucy as she played hymns. Charlotte stood beside me, and I glanced at her as we sang. Her eyes briefly met mine. For the first time since Verlan and I had joined her in Tijuana, she gave me a tight little smile. Involuntarily, my eyes teared. The tension eased some, and I fervently thanked the Lord for the tiny show of acceptance.

Insisting it was still our honeymoon, Verlan spent the night with me in the small trailer. Guilt gnawed at me, as I lay in his arms, aware of his three wives nearby who must undoubtedly be wishing he was with them rather than me. I shifted positions on the hard mattress and pulled the covers higher on my body. I could understand why the bulky quilts were on the bed. The ocean air lent a teeth-chattering, damp cold that filtered through the loose-fitting windows and had me shivering under the heavy blankets. I was glad for Verlan's warm body.

As I lay listening to his snoring, I had lots to ponder. A whole new family! So many children! I wondered at Verlan's memory of their identities. They seemed well mannered, sweet, and anxious for my friendship. Lucy had accepted me, and Charlotte was beginning to. There was still Beverly, whose absence spoke volumes. Verlan hadn't insisted I meet her in a timely manner, which led me to believe she was upset at his taking another wife. Living so close, we would surely meet soon. If we were planning to serve the Lord, we would need to compromise.

At the first sign of daylight, Verlan arose from bed. In his garments, he shivered as he dressed. I snuggled under the quilts, wishing he were still holding me. Reaching my hand to him, I silently begged him to stay. His mirrored reflection grinned as he combed his hair. "So, you're beginning to like having me around, hey? What happened to the scared girl who I had to chase to make love to a few days ago?"

"She'd rather be scared than cold," I retorted. I pulled my icy hand back under the covers. "Where are you going?"

"I thought I'd have breakfast with Beverly, maybe see if I can make her feel better. Then later on today I'll head on down to Los Molinos and spend a day or two with Ester and Irene. Joel should be down there by then. I need to have a meeting with him while I'm here in Baja."

He faced me, his hand on the doorknob. "See if you can get to know your sister-wives a little better while I'm gone. Lucy's a fine woman, and really glad you're ours." He hesitated a moment, then said, "Don't worry about Charlotte, Susan. She'll be a bit cool to you for a while, but she'll get used to the idea." He winked at me and left the trailer. I could hear the squeaky hinges of the old outhouse as he went in for his morning visit.

The people in the two houses around me were beginning to stir. As I forced myself out of the warm bed, I wondered if I would ever acclimate to the cold, damp air. It was so different from my nice warm home in Colonia LeBaron.

It seemed awkward entering the big house alone. There were so many people, all new, all family now. I couldn't remember the children's names as they approached and shyly said, "Good morning, Aunt Susan."

The children's schooling was in Ensenada, and as they prepared themselves, they were in various stages of undress. One was looking for his socks and shoes, and one of Charlotte's brown-haired little girls needed her dress buttoned in the back. I bent, buttoned, and tied her sash. All the little girls had long braided hair, which needed re-combing. Someone handed me a brush and comb, and I began brushing and braiding.

Breakfast was a bowl of coarsely ground wheat mush with milk and honey, and a slice of bread. I had to gag mine, and I wondered how the children could eat with such relish. Oh, yuk! Is this going to be my new diet? I said to myself, beginning to feel sick as I tried another bite. It certainly wasn't Mom's pancakes, maple syrup, and bacon. As I swallowed a dry piece of bread, a new thought occurred. Verlan can't afford better food than this! With so many wives and children, he has to provide inexpensive foods! I had never thought about money where Verlan was concerned. I'd assumed he must have plenty, or he wouldn't have such a large family, adding even more wives. The Bible referred to a man taking another wife, and it said not to "Diminish the first wife's raiment and apparel, and duty of marriage"—whatever that meant. Surely Verlan wouldn't go against the Bible. Maybe he was a health nut and wanted his children to eat healthy grains and vegetables, and that was why there hadn't been any meat on the table last night.

Lucy tore around, organizing the children. When they were finally off and trudging through the early morning fog to the bus stop, we both sighed with relief. Four pre-schoolers remained at home—three little girls and the little boy, Byron, who had told me I was pretty. As Lucy hurried toward her bedroom to dress, I looked around, wondering what I should do next.

Lucy's flaxen-haired toddler was wandering about, dragging an empty baby bottle. A wet diaper sagged between her legs. Her little bare feet were blue with cold. "Come here, Little One," I crooned. She raised her arms; I lifted her, found a diaper, and proceeded to make her more comfortable.

I was changing the baby when Verlan breezed into the living room. "Looks like you've found something to keep you busy," he said, grinning. Reaching down, he tweaked the little girl's bare foot. I smiled at his handsome face and puckered my lips for a kiss. But he turned away and sauntered into the kitchen. "Charlotte, Charlotte, where are you?" he called.

After a moment, they strolled past me and entered Charlotte's bedroom. Before the door closed I saw Verlan's arm slide around Charlotte's waist. He pulled her close, nuzzled his face against her neck, and closed the door tight. I heard the lock snap into place.

Suddenly I was annoyed. I felt an unpleasant stirring inside that made me want to throw things and stomp my feet. What did Verlan want with Charlotte? What were they doing in the bedroom? I sat stiffly, holding his little girl, my throat constricted, making swallowing difficult. The minutes ticked as I stared at the locked door, and I wanted to go kick it.

He's married to her, you little ninny, I reminded myself. He was married to her long before you came along. It doesn't matter what they're doing—it's none of your business. I stared at the door for awhile longer, then I stood and placed Lucy's little girl down on her thin legs. She toddled into the kitchen, and I followed her, allowing myself one last, agonizing look at Charlotte's bedroom door.

I dashed blindly past the baby, through the dining room, and out into the sunlight, my heart pounding so loud I almost missed Lucy's call to me. Her voice sounded maddeningly normal. "Susan, do you have anything you want to put in the wash?" She was standing at the old Maytag, filling the tubs with the hose. I nodded, not trusting my voice, and climbed into the trailer for my dirty clothes. It took a few minutes of fishing around to find what I wanted. I fought to control my anger. I had never felt so unnerved, so uncontrollably angry. I had been raised in the Church, prepared all my life for polygamy. Yet here I was, crying. Jealous! So jealous my hands were shaking, and I wanted to physically tear into Charlotte. I wanted to slap Verlan for touching her. His hands belonged to me . . .

I closed my eyes as I tried to erase the scene, burying my face in the armload of laundry I held. I dried my eyes on a sock and swallowed the rest of my tears.

I was being so silly! He wasn't just mine and I'd have to get used to it, just as Charlotte had to get used to all the other wives—just as she was getting used to me. Plural marriage wasn't easy, but that's the way the Lord planned it. He had given us the opportunity to overcome our petty, childish jealousies, an opportunity that other people in the world didn't have. We would grow in selflessness and love for our fellow man—or woman, as the case was here. We would be the conquerors. We would get the prize, the Celestial Kingdom!

I retrieved the clothes I had dropped on the bed, threw my shoulders back, and left my trailer. "Can I help you do the wash, Lucy?" I spoke evenly. There wasn't a hint of tears. I had overcome my first trial as the wife of a polygamist, and I held my head high. I had won out over the devil.

Chapter 16

The wind blew dust swirls around my feet as I surveyed the mountain of dirty clothes piled on the cement slab. Denims were mixed with towels and sheets, socks and dresses—enough clothes for an army, and Lucy expected me to sort this into compatible batches.

"Oh, hell!" I groaned under my breath. "I don't even know where to start." Why hadn't Mom made me do this? Why hadn't she insisted I learn something useful besides how to milk a cow? One thing for sure. I refused to let the other wives discover that I knew little about housework. After the way Verlan had bragged about me, the humiliation would be too great. I could just picture the disdainful glances from Charlotte. And I could imagine Verlan's disappointment, knowing his new wife was untrained in the art of homemaking. He would probably instruct one of his daughters to teach me, and I would never live it down. Taking a determined breath, I knelt by the mountain of dirty clothes.

Common sense, Susan, just use your head. Darks with darks, whites with whites. Put all the towels together. By elimination, I made piles, leaving the two-tone colors and nicer clothing for last. I stared at the remaining heap of clothes and prayed for a means of escape.

Lucy picked up a batch of sheets and put them into the washer. She poured in powdered soap, then returned to the dirty diapers she was rinsing. Relief flooded over me. At least the sheets were okay. I was on the right track.

"Susan," Verlan's loud voice rang out behind me. "Got a minute?"

I dropped the red and white blouse I was debating about and thankfully ran for the house. Lucy wouldn't discover my secret! I'd have to be more cautious about offers of help in the future. And I would have to learn fast.

Verlan wrapped his arm around my waist and pulled me toward my trailer. "I'm going to spend a few minutes with Lucy, then I'm leaving for Los Molinos. I've decided to take Beverly with me. You'll be okay, won't you? You'll find enough to keep you busy?" As we walked past Lucy, I threw a guilty glance at her. She was kneeling by the pile of clothes I had left, busily sorting away. She didn't even look up.

Verlan helped me up the high step into my little trailer and, after the door was closed, he kissed me hungrily. His cheeks were smooth and soft, and they smelled faintly of Old Spice. I held onto him and squeezed my eyes hard, blocking the thought that he would be spending the day with Beverly, the wife who didn't even want to meet me.

The feeling that I was a stranger in Verlan's home swept over me again. I was being deserted—left in the midst of people I barely knew! Panic gripped me, and I had to bite my words to keep from begging Verlan not to go. I buried my face in his chest and blinked back tears.

Susan, you're a grown woman now, I reminded myself. You're living God's Holy Commandment, and you are married to an Apostle in His Church. Stop acting like a baby. Verlan's not just yours, remember? I looked at him and forced a smile.

"That's my girl!" he said proudly. Planting a quick kiss on my lips, he left for Lucy's, and I sat forlornly on my bed. Loneliness and homesickness washed over me in harsh, drowning waves. I pulled the faded blue curtain from the window and stared out at Charlotte, who was hanging clothes on the line. The wind whipped her full skirt up around her hips. Strands of hair had escaped her bun and were flying about her head. As the wind flapped the wet sheets into her face, she raised her apron and wiped her eyes. I wondered if it was just water from the sheets, or, if like me, she was also feeling abandoned and alone.

Why wasn't I happy? I had a wonderful new family. I was living as the Lord wanted me to. I needed to make myself useful and serve Verlan's family as Lucy did. Lucy seemed to be content with our way of life. She acted cheerful and selfless, even though she had spent little time with Verlan since our arrival.

Through the window, I saw the door of Beverly's house fly open. A short Mexican lady, with raven hair to her hips, preceded Verlan outside. She carried an overnight bag and her purse. Verlan held a blanket-wrapped baby tightly against his chest. They hurried past my trailer and on to the car. I had to change windows to see Verlan open the car door for Beverly. He handed the baby to her, then moved to his side of the gold Chevelle and backed from the driveway. Clouds of dust spiraled behind as the car sped down the dirt road and turned the corner. I stared at the empty road until tears blinded me. Dropping onto the bed and burying my face in the pillow, I sobbed until I could scarcely breathe.

Why, oh why had I gotten myself into this situation? I wanted my mother! Never had I felt so homesick. I wasn't ready to be dumped in with my husband's other wives and left to fend for myself! How could he do it to me?

Sometime later I snuggled under the blankets. The wind caused the trailer to shake, and it whistled through the little hole in the window. I could hear the clothes on the line whipping and flapping, and the sky looked ominous. Verlan and Beverly would be driving through this storm.

I closed my eyes and shivered under the heavy blankets. As I drifted to sleep, images of a beautiful girl with coal-black hair filled my dream—her long tresses blew softly into Verlan's face as he chased her, caught her, passionately kissed her...

In the furthermost recesses of my subconscious, I heard a soft, repetitious sound. It became louder and louder, and I suddenly awoke. Someone was knocking. "Who is it?" I called through a sleep-drugged haze.

"Susan, it's Rhea. Can I come in?" The door opened to reveal a cloudless blue sky behind Rhea's head. I had slept through the storm, and the children were home from school. Suddenly things didn't seem so bad.

I climbed from the covers and slipped on my new shoes. As I rubbed my eyes, Rhea started to laugh. "Your face is all swollen!" she exclaimed. She moved closer and inspected me, dismay replacing her mirth. "Oh, Susan! You've been crying, haven't you?"

I glanced into the mirror on the closet door. My eyes were buried inside swollen puffs of flesh, and I groaned, dropping my face into my hands. I couldn't let Rhea know how unhappy and lonely I felt! She'd think I was a big baby.

Suddenly a soft arm found its way around my neck. She pulled my head onto her shoulder and patted my back. "It must be tough marrying a man who takes off practically the minute he gets you home," she said quietly. "I'll bet you feel pretty bad, huh? Well, I think you're brave marrying someone with so many wives."

I sat straight and stared into her brown eyes. "You think I'm brave?" Could there be someone in Verlan's family that understood the turmoil?

"I really do," Rhea was saying. "I think you're really brave. I know I couldn't stand to leave my mama and brothers and sisters, and go off across the country to live like you have. I don't blame you for crying."

I looked into my new friend's eyes and smiled. She was sensitive, and mature, almost motherly in her attitude toward me. She straightened and briskly announced, "I'm going to go get you a cold rag for your eyes, then you're coming out and playing marbles with me and Laura. I'll be back in a minute." She threw me a smile and ran out the door.

It had been ages since I'd played marbles, and it sounded like fun. I brushed my hair, washed my face, and followed Rhea outside to the back of the storage shed where Laura was waiting for us. She dug into her pockets and picked out marbles by the handful.

"Okay, here are your marbles," she said importantly. "How we play, see, is the starter throws one against the shed wall and it bounces off like this. Then the next person tries to bounce theirs up close to it. If you can get within a palm's width away, you win the marble. Got it?"

"Sounds easy," I grinned, throwing a marble. It bounced into the dirt, and Laura promptly won it with one of her marbles. Soon there were crowds of Verlan's children around us, cheering us on.

"That's the way, Aunt Susan, you got it!" one of the big boys yelled as I won one of my marbles back from Rhea. Laura concentrated hard and won my nicest cat-eye, snickering as I groaned. I threw a steely and danced with excitement as it landed an inch away from a beauty of Rhea's. "I got it," I crowed. I admired the red cat-eye and dropped it into my pile being held by one of the little girls in her skirt.

The late afternoon passed swiftly as the kids argued and yelled, fighting over whose turn it was. It was my turn, and I bent to retrieve a badly thrown marble. As I straightened up, I noticed movement at the corner of the shed.

Charlotte stood watching us, her hands at her hips. She glared directly at me, her face filled with disdain. Abruptly she turned and stalked toward the house, shaking her head as she walked, and I just knew she was muttering, "Oh, Lord, what will he drag home next?"

I stared after her. Then, glancing down, I realized I was covered with dust. Powdery dirt coated my arms, and my new shoes, and my pants were streaked black where I had wiped my hands. My face felt flushed, and I could tell that my hair was matted. Groaning, I closed my eyes. How long had she been watching me?

"Aunt Susan, come on. It's your turn, Aunt Susan. Aunt Susan!" The children were shouting at me, but somehow the game had lost its charm. The real world of wives and responsibility had crashed in on me with Charlotte's icy stare. I handed my marbles to one of the little girls. "I'm tired. You kids play," I muttered.

Amid cries of disappointment, I walked to the house. Rhea and Laura stared after me, and I knew they wondered as to my lost interest in the game.

I heated water for a bath, then poured the huge kettle into the tub and went to the kitchen sink for a bucket of cold water. Although the sewer pipes in

Verlan's house were connected, there was no running water in the bathroom. I removed my clothing and slipped into the big porcelain tub.

Having a real bathtub to bathe in instead of a tin washtub was a definite step up in the world. Of course, this really wasn't my house—it was my husband's house. But wasn't what was his also mine? I relaxed as I leisurely soaked, and felt like a rich woman. My mother had never had it this good, at least, not since joining the Church. I ran my fingers along the sides of the tub and wiggled my bottom against the smooth porcelain. I could stretch my legs, the tub was so lengthy. There was no doubt about it—married life wasn't going to be the exciting, romantic adventure I had expected as the wife of a leader. There were drawbacks, especially in the sister-wife department. I was going to have to learn about household chores. Oh, I could wash dishes and sweep the floor, as long as no one expected an outstanding job of it. Why hadn't my mother taught and prepared me before allowing the marriage?

Yes, there would be drawbacks, but there were also definite advantages, like this tub, and my own little bedroom, and someday a home of my own. I wouldn't have to answer to anyone, not even Verlan, because he would be gone. Las Vegas was far away, and he had told me he could only return every two weeks. I would miss him dreadfully, but I would learn to manage.

Outside the bathroom door, the family called to each other as they readied for supper. Lucy's baby, Norine, was wailing while another child pounded on the piano. The commotion was nerve-racking, and I reluctantly left the tub and dressed. I was anticipating my quiet trailer and a good book.

Lucy visited with me throughout supper, asking me questions about church members in Colonia LeBaron. "I miss the good ol' colony so much at times," she said wistfully. "There's no one to associate with or hold Sunday meetings with here. Everyone lives too far away. I even envy Irene down in Los Molinos. She and her kids might be living in a tent at the moment, but at least she's got friends around her."

"A tent? Lucy, you're joking," I scoffed.

"It's true. Verlan has men in the process of building her a house, but for the last two months she and the kids have camped out in a tent. Some of Joel's families are doing the same thing. It won't be long, though, until they have some houses ready. It's good for them, makes them tough."

I thought about that awhile as I ate my vegetable soup and the ever-popular unbuttered wheat bread. I would rather not be tough, I decided. I was glad Verlan hadn't moved me to Los Molinos. I wasn't the pioneer type. I wanted to serve the Lord and earn my blessings, but not in a tent.

Charlotte completely ignored me. She sat primly at the end of the table in her somber-colored dress, her hair pulled tightly against her scalp in a demure little bun. Toward the end of the meal, she turned to Lucy and asked, "Do you know anything about Ervil moving Lorna here to Ensenada? Some of the members in San Diego were talking about it. Is it true?"

"Lorna!" I broke in. "Charlotte, that's my cousin! Is she really moving here?"

Charlotte glared at me, then pointedly turned to Lucy again. "Lucy, is it true?" she said evenly.

It was a blatant snub. I frowned, pushed my chair back, and stood. She wouldn't even speak to me! What had I done that was so bad?

I felt Lucy's eyes on me as I walked into the kitchen. "I haven't heard anything," she answered Charlotte. "I hope it's true. It will be nice to have someone else from the church living so close."

The rest of the conversation was lost in the whirl of my thoughts. Lorna, Aunt Thelma's daughter, was moving to Ensenada. The thought thrilled me!

I helped the girls with the dishes when supper was finished, hoping to prove to Charlotte that I did have some mature qualities. It didn't seem to change her mind though. She stalked about the house with a sour grimace on her face and wouldn't even glance in my direction.

Don't let her get to you, Suze, I thought grimly. She's just not being Christian. When no one was looking, I stuck my tongue out at her stiff back. I was so glad she would only be around on weekends. She was probably mean to the poor little kids she taught at school.

My bedroom looked cozy and warm in the lamplight. I read the mystery novel Rhea had loaned me until my eyes wouldn't stay open, then I piled on an extra blanket and snuggled down. As I drifted off, I wondered which of his three wives in Los Molinos Verlan was sleeping with tonight. I wondered also if Ervil would really be moving Lorna close to us.

After breakfast was over the next morning, I stayed in the kitchen and visited with Laura while she mixed up the Saturday batch of bread. I marveled to see her casually dumping in salt, flour, sugar, and activated yeast. She was only thirteen years old, and yet she knew how to do things that I knew nothing about. Here I was, married, two full years older than Laura, and dumb as could be. I watched her movements closely as we visited, taking mental notes of everything she added to the huge pan of whole-wheat flour and what the amounts were. She kneaded the dough for a few minutes, then covered the pan with a clean cloth and set it on the stove where the pilot light would keep it warm.

If I planned to make myself useful and help Lucy with the children and the work as Verlan expected, I needed to know how first. This is the ticket, Susan, I told myself confidently; just keep your eyes open. You'll learn.

I kept watch through the morning for the dough to rise, and when Laura came back in the kitchen and washed her hands, I was right at her elbow. From the cupboard, she pulled a dozen large apple juice cans. Each of them had one end removed. She greased the insides then made the dough into grapefruit sized mounds and dropped them into the juice cans. "This way all the loaves will fit into the oven at one time, because we can stand them up on one end," she explained. "That's why we use juice cans instead of regular loaf pans."

When the dough had risen to an inch from the top, Laura placed them into the hot oven. An hour later a wonderful aroma filled the house, and Laura pulled a dozen golden brown loaves from the juice cans. She sliced the crusty end from one and spread it with honey, handing me a perfectly round slice of delicious, hot bread. It was wonderful! I eyed my new stepdaughter with respect.

After lunch, I walked to my quiet trailer. I felt a growing disillusionment as I lay down. Watching Laura had made me realize my own inadequacies. I didn't know how to cook. I couldn't do the laundry or housework as Verlan's girls could. Sex was a major disappointment. And I felt unhappy about being left behind when Verlan had to go somewhere. I hadn't really complained—at least, not verbally. But inside, I resented it because Verlan had so quickly dumped me off. I couldn't imagine becoming accustomed to this way of life. If this was serving the Lord, why didn't I feel excited and good about it? Where was the joy? A sense of drudgery enveloped me.

Chapter 17

I t was evening time when Verlan and Beverly returned from Los Molinos. It had been a long and boring Sunday. I was alone in the living room when I saw Charlotte's car pull into the yard.

I felt like shouting for joy as I jumped from the piano bench, ran out the door, and straight into Verlan's arms.

"Hi, Angel!" he grinned, almost thrown off balance as I grabbed him around the neck. "Land sakes, you act like you missed me." He held me away from him and devoured my face with his twinkling eyes. "Did you?"

"Yes, I missed you! But I had fun. The girls are so nice, and I like Lucy, and—"

My breathless sentence was cut short when I saw Beverly's cold eyes, glaring at me over the blanketed baby in her arms. Her short body marched hastily by us. Embarrassed, I let go of Verlan. I had forgotten all about Beverly when I flung myself at him. I would have to be more discreet in the future.

"Beverly! Beverly, wait just a minute!" Verlan called to her, but she made no move to turn around. He seemed annoyed as he watched her retreating back. "Come on, it's time she spoke to you." He grabbed my arm and pulled me along with him.

I wanted to protest, to tell him that I would rather wait until she was ready to meet me. But on the other hand, I wanted to get the meeting over, so I trotted after him. Beverly yanked her door open and went inside, with Verlan and me right behind. We waited in the kitchen while she put the baby in the crib, then she turned to us. Her face was set.

"Beverly," Verlan chided, "Susan has been here for two days now. Don't you think it's time you said hello to her?"

Pain crept into her brown eyes and pulled at the muscles around her mouth "Verlan, she married you, not me," she said in a hollow voice. "I didn't have anything to do with this. I didn't even know about it." She turned her back to us again and began changing the baby's diaper, her long black hair hiding her face like a protective shield.

I gulped and looked at Verlan, and he winked to reassure me. "Susan's going to be living close to you from now on," he quietly told Beverly. "She's part of our family now. You girls may as well be friends, don't you think?"

Her head dropped further over the crib in an effort to distance us. Her hands shook as she pinned the diaper. The silence in the room was heavy and embarrassing.

"It's nice to meet you, Beverly," I said quickly. Then I backed out the door and hurried to my trailer. She was hurting badly, and sympathy overwhelmed me. She was lonely—much more so than I. I sensed her heartache more than I had with Verlan's other wives. Perhaps it was because she was young and relatively new to the family. The other women had been Verlan's wives for many years, and had several children to fill the void in their lives because of their husband's busy lifestyle. Whatever the reason, I determined to make Beverly my friend. I could see the kindness in her face in spite of the cool exterior she had shown. She and I would become friends!

It was late when Verlan stopped by my trailer. "I'll be staying with Lucy tonight, sweetheart," his voice was warm and reassuring. "And before daylight Charlotte and I will leave for San Diego. I'll be going on to Vegas, to go back to work. I may as well say goodbye now, so I don't have to wake you in the morning."

His face looked pale in the lamplight, his eyes dark and shadowy as he watched me. "Leaving you here is one of the hardest things I've ever had to do." He stroked my cheek, his anxious eyes taking in my every feature. "You will be okay, won't you, while I'm gone?"

I wanted to shout, tell him it wasn't fair that he leave me again for two more weeks. I wanted to cry and insist that I wouldn't be okay, that he couldn't go without me. But even as I thought the words I remembered Beverly's haunted eyes.

"I'm not the only one you're leaving, remember?" I tried to sound brave and mature. "If the other wives can handle it, I can. Don't worry about me, Verlan."

He hugged me tightly, then ruffled my hair. "See what you can do to help Lucy while I'm gone. And, honey, Beverly could really use some company. Be nice to her, okay?"

After he left, I lay propped on my pillows and stubbornly tried to read. I needed to erase the image of him snuggling with Lucy only yards away. But I couldn't do it. Exasperated, I threw the book on the table and released the hot tears. I had been exposed to polygamy most of my life. Mom, Dad and Maria had lived it right under my nose. Mom hadn't seemed to suffer. If she resented Dad's marriage to Maria, I hadn't seen it. Why hadn't I realized how difficult it would be?

And yet, I knew why—I hadn't been in love before. I had never desperately loved and needed someone only to have him leave me for the arms of another wife. I wanted Verlan! I ached for the feeling of companionship that we had known before our wedding. I longed to see his eyes twinkling, to hear the music of his laughter. I closed my eyes to the mental picture of Lucy cuddled in his arms. I would have to accept it. It was God's will, and I had voluntarily given myself to plural marriage. It would undoubtedly become easier as time passed.

The morning sun was high in the sky when I awoke. I arose and opened the curtain so I could see into the yard by the big house. It looked empty and forlorn without Charlotte's car. I dressed, braided my hair, applied a bit of makeup, and walked outside into the bright sunshine.

"Good morning!" Lucy called gaily. Once again she stood by the old Maytag, filling the tubs with the hose. "There's some wheat mush on the stove; go help yourself. I've got to do wash today. If you feel like it, I could use your help, but please don't feel obligated. Make yourself at home, and do whatever you like."

As she smiled at me, her plain face was transformed into near beauty. I realized why Verlan was attracted to her. "Lucy," I managed a grin, "I'm the new one here, and I'd like to help, but I'm as green as can be. You'll have to tell me what needs done. Feel free to boss me around, okay?"

She took me at my word. I hung clothes, washed dishes, bathed the little girls, and helped prepare lunch. As I worked, I watched for Beverly. But she remained out of sight, and I found myself wondering if she was home.

As I hung more clothes, I looked at Lucy, hesitated, then asked, "Is Beverly nice to you? I mean, does she talk to you, or does she stay alone all the time?"

She fed a pair of jeans into the wringer, then glanced at me. "Beverly's as warm and friendly a girl as you'd ever want to meet. She's just going through a hard time right now. She needs Verlan to spend more time with her, and he doesn't have the time." Vigorously scrubbing a sock between her fists, she continued, "It would do her a world of good if you would make a point of being friendly to her. She stays alone too much, Susan. She broods. Verlan's marrying you has been hard on her."

"What do you suppose she'd do if I went to see her? Do you think she'd let me in?"

Lucy flashed her warm smile. "You don't know till you try."

It was late in the afternoon before I got the nerve. I stood outside her door, my hands shaking. "You're doing the right thing," I reassured myself as I knocked. It was a while before the door swung open. Beverly held the baby as she looked out at me. Her eyes registered no surprise.

"Do you mind if I come in?" I stammered.

"What do you want?" her voice was cold. She shifted the baby to her other hip, making no move to allow me entry. I hadn't realized she would be so cold. I faltered, searching for words. "I—I was hoping you would invite me to supper," I said lamely.

She studied me, her eyes hooded with dislike. Then she snapped, "Now, why would I do that? You think you can marry Verlan and move here, and everyone will treat you like royalty, right? Well, not me. Now, if you will excuse me, I need to feed my baby." She closed the door in my face.

Dizzy with shock, I stared at the closed door. Then I backed away and ran to my trailer. I sat heavily down at the tiny table and stared at my shaking hands. She hates me! I thought. She hates me as bad as Estela hated me, and I'm going to have to accept it. Mexican women are just that way—they're not cut out to share their husbands. And yet, she married Verlan knowing he has other wives.

I knew I shouldn't take her rejection personally. She would be just as furious about any other woman Verlan married. I should be satisfied that Lucy was good to me, and that Irene wanted me in the family.

What was it Irene had said to me that night in the church hallway at Colonia LeBaron? "You will be a beautiful jewel in Verlan's crown," she had said. She was talking about the crown he would receive from God when he got to heaven. According to Joseph Smith's teachings, Verlan would then become a god too, and his wives would become goddesses. I couldn't even imagine it—jewels in Verlan's crown. Hopefully by then Beverly and I would both feel more secure, and we would get along with each other. From the way she was behaving, I doubted it would be any sooner than that.

The days of the week seemed to drag, and I was feeling homesick. The children were gone to school every day and had scads of homework when they got home. Sometimes in the evenings Verlan Jr. and I played chess, and the other children and I played checkers, jacks, or marbles. Lucy didn't mind when I played games with the children. She often joined us, but only to watch.

Late Friday night Charlotte drove into the yard in the gold Chevelle. Her children hugged her hungrily, and Laura wept on her mother's shoulder. "Mama, I can't stand it, I miss you so much," she sobbed. "I don't want to stay with Aunt Lucy any more. I want to go to San Diego with you. Mama, don't leave me again."

Charlotte wiped her eyes, then dabbed at Laura's. "Honey, we have to do what's best for the family. You know that. Come on. Dry your eyes like a good girl. You'll make the other kids cry too."

She barely glanced at me as she ushered her children inside. I stood on the porch, alone in the darkness. I hadn't realized the loneliness Charlotte's children felt without their mother. They hadn't said anything and I had just assumed that they were used to it. But Laura's outburst had proven otherwise.

Why was Charlotte working instead of staying home with her children? What was the purpose? If she wanted to work, why didn't she keep the kids with her in San Diego? I sighed as I headed toward my tiny trailer. There was so much I didn't understand— so much I had to learn. When Verlan returned, I would have many questions for him. As I thought of him, I fought back my own tears. I wished he could be here, and I wished that I could wrap my arms around my own mother as I had seen Rhea and Laura do with theirs. Loneliness was beginning to haunt me.

I lit my lamp, sat on the bed, and gazed at the honey-colored walls. It wasn't the time to go into the big house, with Charlotte home. She would resent it, and I was in no mood to be snubbed again. I picked up a novel and restlessly leafed through. I had brought it from home, a favorite that I had read twice before. As the book opened to the front cover, I recognized Jay's scrawled signature across the top. Jay! It had been months since I had seen him. I ran my fingers over his name. Then I lay back and laced my fingers under my head, thinking of my loved ones at home. Our family ties were strong, even with my three brothers and sister in Utah, whom I seldom saw. Occasionally they came to Mexico to visit. It was hard on us when they left, but they didn't believe in the Church, and they had their own lives to live. There was something irreplaceable about real family, people who shared your blood. No matter how depressed you were, or how bad your circumstances, you could rely on family to share your burden and ease your pain. Verlan's family was my family now, but it just wasn't the same. I felt like an outsider. I didn't feel free to join in with the rest of them, especially now with Charlotte home.

It was too early to retire and I was too restless to read. What, I wondered, was God's purpose for my being here? My husband was hundreds of miles away. Lucy needed my help, it was true, but I felt like a hired girl instead of a family member. Beverly certainly didn't want me here, Charlotte couldn't stand me, and the children were so busy they seldom had any spare time. So much for my being a blessing here. What a joke. Had it only been two weeks since my wedding day? It seemed like much longer, and already I wished I were back in Colonia LeBaron.

The trailer felt chilly, and I blew out the lamp and climbed under the covers fully dressed. I lay in the darkness for hours before I finally slept.

Late the next afternoon I helped Lucy and Charlotte cut quilt blocks. We sat in front of the big picture windows in the living room. I was the first to see the old, black Ford sedan turn the corner by the winery. The car sped to our driveway and turned into the yard.

"Who's that?" I asked curiously. Charlotte and Lucy crowded around me, peering out the window at the battered car. My fingers suddenly froze on the drapes as Ervil climbed out, straightening his huge body upright. Panic gripped me, and I fought the wild urge to dash out the back door and hide inside my trailer. Somehow I forced myself to remain calm as he hurried to open the passenger door. A thin, dark headed woman, with blue eyes and a smile like Uncle Bud's, stepped out.

."It's Ervil and Lorna!" Lucy crowed. "It must be true! He must be moving her here, close to us. Praise the Lord!" She rushed to the door, and in spite of my apprehension, I followed her outside. Lorna, right here in Ensenada! I would have real family close by!

"Hello, everyone!" Lorna grinned as we rushed at her. "Hi, Suze! My goodness, it's been years, hasn't it!"

We embraced, and then I stepped back so Lucy could get a hug. "Lorna, is it true?" Lucy questioned eagerly. "Are you moving here from San Diego?"

"Sure enough! To a little adobe house that's right around the corner, about six blocks from here, isn't it, Ervil?"

Ervil nodded. He was standing back, watching the reunion between the women, a pleased smile on lips. I was thrilled about Lorna being here, but I hoped Ervil would make himself scarce once she was settled. The memory of his whispered threat rushed over me again. He spared me only a glance, and I began to relax. After all, he was Verlan's brother. By now surely he'd accepted the fact that I was his brother's wife.

"Mama, can we get out?" a little boy whined.

"Yes, Andrew." Lorna opened the back door and a striking little boy, along with an equally lovely little girl stepped from the car. They looked like children out of a fashion magazine, they were so beautiful and well dressed. Their hair was platinum blond, and they had huge aquamarine eyes, satin skin, and perfectly formed noses and mouths. They looked to be about five and three years old.

"Lorna!" I involuntarily exclaimed, "they're beautiful!"

"Thank you. Andrew, Tarsa, this is your cousin, Susan. Can you say hi?"

Little Andrew glared at me, and Tarsa hid her face on her mother's legs. "They're shy," Lorna grinned, unabashed.

Charlotte had finally come outside. She stood on the porch, torn between the duty of hospitality, and her new distrust and repugnance toward Ervil. She stiffly extended her hand to shake his, then nodded to Lorna and reluctantly said, "Come on in."

"I don't suppose Verlan's here," Ervil stated. He settled down on the couch and sat Tarsa on his knee.

The contempt in Charlotte's brown eyes clearly showed. "No, Ervil—too bad. He'll feel terrible to have missed you." She arched her eyebrows and pointedly added, "He's working, you know."

Her sarcasm was dismissed with a wave of Ervil's hand. "I'm sure I'll bump into him soon. We have much to talk about, he and I. Much to iron out."

Lorna and I glanced at each other. There was no mistaking the sparring tone in both Charlotte's and Ervil's voices. I gulped and lowered my eyes. How could I have missed Ervil's overbearing attitude while he was courting me? How could I have thought he was righteous, and how could Lorna stand him?

I had a new respect for Charlotte, though. She wasn't afraid to show her anger and mistrust to Ervil or to let him know that she was against his policies and that she totally supported Verlan. Charlotte had spunk.

"I'm sure you all must be hungry," Lucy said as she jumped off the couch to break the tension in the room. "Come on into the kitchen, everyone, and I'll dish you up a bowl of beans. Come on, kids." She hurried into the kitchen and Charlotte, Lorna, and I followed her.

"I hope you don't mind beans," Lucy was saying, "That's all I have cooked. There's some bread, and I think I have a bit of salad left from lunch."

"Beans are fine," Lorna assured her. At the smell of food, the other children traipsed in from the back rooms where they had been playing a noisy game of Monopoly. They served themselves a bowl of beans and joined Lorna's children at the bar. Their clamor was deafening.

"Ervil, you want a bowl?" Lucy called into the living room.

"That would be fine," he called back.

"Here, Susan, take this to Ervil." Lucy handed me a plate with a bowl of beans and two slices of bread. "He can eat in the living room where it's quiet."

I hesitated, my insides gripped with nervousness. But Lucy had turned and walked into the dining room, her hands full of sliced bread. Susan, I sternly asked myself, are you planning to avoid Ervil for the rest of your life? Charlotte wouldn't. I carried the plate into the living room.

Ervil wore his usual garb—a long sleeved, white shirt and black pants. As I handed him the plate, I forced myself to glance at his face for an instant. I didn't want to appear afraid to look at him. Just one swift glance, then I turned back toward the kitchen.

"Wait!" he commanded. He grabbed my wrist with his free hand. Startled, I looked into his eyes. They glowed with that same, unearthly light that I remembered from Anna Mae's bedroom.

"You'd better listen," his voice was low and threatening. "The Lord's mighty sick and tired of girls who ignore Him to gratify their own sexual desires—who marry for love...love that's based on the lusts of the eyes—and of the flesh. That's what you've done, and the Lord won't tolerate it. Hear me? You've blatantly ignored the guidance of the Lord, and you'll have to answer for it."

The magnetic power of his eyes and personality grappled with my will as I tried to yank free of his grasp. His lips twisted contemptuously, "So, you thought you would..." His eyes flickered toward the kitchen and his whisper trailed off. He released my arm.

Behind me, Charlotte's voice sliced through the tension in the room. "Susan! Lucy needs your help."

On rubbery legs, I dashed past her. Oh, God in heaven... I shuddered as I leaned against the stove. Ervil's furious because I married Verlan! That light in his eyes makes him look possessed! What does he want with me?

Charlotte was close behind. She looked me up and down, then whispered, "What was that about? What's going on between you and Ervil?"

I searched her face. Should I tell her? Would she understand, and perhaps advise me what to do? As I hesitated, she coldly whispered, "You should stay away from him! You're married now, remember? I suggest you stay away from his families, too. Do you understand?" Her eyes held mine, insisting that I respect her wishes.

"I intend to stay away from him!" I hissed. I turned my back and began to clear up the dining bar. Obviously she believed I was flirting with Ervil! And she was telling me to stay away from Lorna. Well, that I wouldn't do. Lorna was my cousin, and I needed someone.

Our guests stayed only a few more minutes. They needed to unpack Lorna's belongings and were anxious to get started. "Come see me soon, okay, Susan? We have some catching up to do!" Lorna called as they exited the house. I waved at her, swallowed the lump in my throat, and went to find Charlotte.

She was still in the kitchen. With mixed feelings, I watched her as she washed up the bean kettle. I needed to say something—to explain. I moved up next to her and began to wipe the counter as I searched for words. Clearing my throat, I began. "Charlotte, I would like to tell you what happened earlier with Ervil. There are things you don't understand. He grabbed me and started—sort of preaching at me, and I didn't know what to do or what to say—"

"Well, maybe in the future you'll have enough sense to know who to stay away from," she snapped. Hanging up the dishtowel, she marched from the room.

I blinked my eyes in shock. She acted as though I had sought Ervil out! As though I had gone out of my way to provoke his threat! She was treating me like an empty-headed little trollop. I slammed the dishrag into the sink, stormed across the living room, and out the front door. Hesitating at the gate, I set off toward the winery. I needed to get away. I needed to breathe. I walked rapidly around the corner and up the road toward the highway, past the run-down shacks that lined the road on each side. People stared as I stalked by, unmindful of the village around me.

Why did Charlotte have to act so high and mighty? She wasn't even giving me a chance. She hadn't spoken a decent word to me since my arrival, and I strongly suspected she had no intention of ever doing so. It was obvious that she considered herself Verlan's only real wife. She probably thought of the rest of us as mere concubines. Just because she was the first and legal wife didn't give her any more rights than the rest of us! Mrs. LeBaron, indeed! She evidently thought she could order me around. She'd practically commanded that I stay away from Lorna. Well, I would just show her! She wasn't my boss, and I would do whatever I wanted.

Suddenly Ervil's threatening words filtered through my anger. What had he meant by saying I would have to answer for marrying Verlan? Was he telling me that he thought I would go to hell? Well, he could think what he wanted. I was married to Verlan now and no matter how Ervil disapproved, there was nothing he could do to me.

I stopped by the highway and walked to the little grocery store. I wished I had some money. A cold Coke sounded wonderful, but I had no money. Not a single peso.

I rested in the shade of the store, ignoring the men that lounged in front, who were leering at me. After a while I began to feel silly standing there alone, so I retraced my steps the mile back to the winery.

I was halfway home when the gold Chevelle pulled up next to me. Charlotte leaned across the seat and opened the passenger door. "Get in," she said quietly.

I hesitated, wondering if she planned to apologize or if she had more cutting remarks. I got into the car.

Her face was set, her eyes glued to the road as we bumped along. Sitting stiffly, I waited for her to speak. Finally as we turned the corner, she glanced at me. "Verlan wouldn't want you wandering around town alone," she said. "If you want to take a walk in the future, be sure to take one of the big boys with you." She pulled the car into the yard and braked to a stop. Without another word she walked to the house, leaving me sitting in the car, alone in the evening twilight.

I reclined against the seat and stared after her. I felt so empty and alone. Why had she bothered to come after me? Did she feel it was her duty to Verlan to see that I was safe? That had to be it. She felt it was her duty.

Lucy's baby, Norine, was wandering about the yard, dragging her bottle behind her. She looked lost and unhappy, cold and neglected. I left the car and went to her. As I picked her up, she wrapped her arms around my neck, snuggling her cold little body tighter against me. "Aunt Susan," she lisped.

I took Norine into the big house, to the boys' shadow-filled bedroom, and sat down with her on my lap. As I rocked her, she watched me with her enormous blue eyes. She seemed to say, "I'm your friend, Aunt Susan, I care about you. You belong here." I hugged her, wiping my tears on her tiny shoulder.

The bedroom door was partially open; enough that, when Lucy and Charlotte entered the dining room, I could see them outlined in front of the lamp light. Charlotte held her purse, and she pulled some bills from it and handed them to Lucy.

"This is going to have to last you girls," she was saying. "Give ten to Beverly, and go ahead and send Irene and Ester forty dollars. Brother Castro is supposed to be coming through on his way to Los Molinos on Monday; have him take it to them."

Lucy nodded, squeezed Charlotte's arm, and dropped the money into her skirt pocket. As they walked away, Charlotte said, "My next check will be larger. There should be enough extra to have your tooth fixed, and to fill the spare butane tank. Tell Beverly to make her money stretch..."

They had left the dining room, but I could hear Charlotte's voice droning in the kitchen as she left more instructions with Lucy. I couldn't make out any more words, but I had seen enough. I knew the answer to one of the questions I had planned to ask Verlan—the reason why Charlotte was working. The answer stunned me. She was working in San Diego to support Verlan's families.

Chapter 18

As the first month of my new life slowly passed, I buried Ervil's threat, and became engrossed in the daily chores of Lucy's household. I had become adept at making bread and sorting clothes—tasks that were continual with fourteen children and two adults to care for. Lucy and I worked well together, but our visiting had dropped to a minimum. We had little in common other than the chores and Verlan.

Beverly continued to avoid me, pointedly staying out of my way. I bumped into her at the outhouse and at the washing machine periodically, and attempted conversation, but it was futile. She remained cool and withdrawn. Seldom did she even come to Sunday school, which was held in the living room, with Charlotte teaching the class. I wondered how she could stand the confinement of her tiny house day after day.

I was beginning to know each of the fourteen children who lived in the big house, and enjoyed their different personalities. They were bright and loving and some of the little girls took turns spending the night with me. The younger children had accepted me without question, turning to me as quickly as they did to Lucy to resolve their spats.

Verlan Jr., Charlotte's oldest son, was quick-witted and intelligent. His studies at school were of paramount importance to him. He readily accepted me as his father's wife, ignoring the fact that he was a year older than I was. He loaned me books and let me listen to his Marty Robbins albums. Rhea and Laura treated me like a special friend, and they helped with my loneliness. Verlan had returned twice from Las Vegas to see us, spending a day or two each time. He also traveled on down the peninsula to Los Molinos to spend a day with Irene and Ester.

Having Verlan home was wonderful. He spent a quiet, intimate night with me, and it seemed like a second honeymoon, but much more pleasant. He told me repeatedly how much he missed me and hated being away. He had dreams of all six of his families being together in Los Molinos and of having his own business so he could stay home with us. One day, he promised, his dream would become a reality.

The time Verlan had with us was all too short. I tried to be brave each time he left, but the sobs continued for hours. Then I would dry my swollen eyes, go into the big house, and find some chore in an effort to fill my hollowness.

Verlan and Charlotte came for Thanksgiving, bringing us a turkey and all the trimmings, and we had a great feast. It was wonderful to eat something other than beans, rice, wheat, and green vegetables.

Beverly joined us for dinner. As usual, she ignored me. She sat at the other end of the table, quickly ate, and then grabbed her baby and retreated to her house. I knew it was because of me that she remained so reticent, and I felt bad. But I didn't know how to change the situation.

Charlotte continued her coolness. She spent her time with her children, reading and talking with them. It was clear to me that living away from them was the hardest of her trials. Although I felt no personal closeness to her, I felt bad for them all. I wondered why she was the financial support of the family instead of Verlan. I knew he was earning money and I wondered where the money went. But I didn't feel comfortable asking about it.

Several times as the weeks passed I found myself wishing that I had a bit of spending money, something for the few necessities, or to purchase a Coke or some other small pleasure. I considered asking Verlan if he could occasionally give me a little cash, but I couldn't bring myself to ask him. It was plain that the finances in the family were tight, and I suspected that if he had the money to give, he would. Neither he nor Charlotte ever offered, so I bit back the words and managed to do without. Surely, I thought, he will realize that I have needs, and soon will offer me an allowance.

Totally disregarding Charlotte's advice, twice I walked the six blocks across the small suburb of Ensenada to see Lorna. The first time, she eagerly welcomed me, but stepped back self-consciously as I walked through the door and into her adobe. I couldn't help staring with dismay at the weather worn shack. The walls of the two rooms were rough adobe. Above, a cheese-cloth ceiling sagged, stained brown where the rain had leaked through the roof. The floor was bare cement, broken and cracked in several places. The kitchen cupboards were warped, unpainted boards tacked together. A hot plate on one end of the rickety table served as a stove. Dim light filtered through the old plastic that was tacked up to the one window in the room. At the opposite end of the room was a ratty looking couch and a wooden rocking chair.

I entered the bedroom. In the far corner stood a beautiful bedroom set, the bed neatly made up with a colorful Spanish quilt. On the cement floor to the left of the bedroom door, Lorna's children were asleep on a twin mattress.

With building fury, I looked around the impoverished little house. Lorna wasn't used to living like this—she was used to the luxuries of San Diego! How could Ervil dump her and her beautiful children in a place like this?

Lorna was watching, waiting for my reaction. "It's not fancy," she managed to grin, "but I plan to fix it up. Next time Ervil comes to see me, I want to have this place looking good. It has possibilities, don't you think?"

I tried to smile at her enthusiasm as we went back into the kitchen. I wanted to ask Lorna why she put up with this, living like ghetto paupers, but I didn't know her well enough to voice my opinion. I gazed out the open door, keeping my eyes averted. The yard around the house was packed dirt, swept and water-sprinkled to keep the dust to a minimum. A chicken wandered past the door. I could see an old outhouse at the corner of the bare lot. A neighbor woman from the lot next to Lorna's was walking toward it.

"Lorna!" I exclaimed, "That old woman is using your outhouse!"

"Oh, it's okay. Actually, the cranny belongs to her family," Lorna explained. "They said we could share it with them." She took my arm and steered me to the kitchen table, then put water on the hotplate for tea. As she moved about, I noticed her slightly bulged abdomen. She looked to be about five months pregnant.

"When Ervil comes he's going to have an outhouse made for us. And he's going to get someone to fix the roof." She chuckled, "You remember that storm we had a few days ago? Rain poured through the roof! I had every pot and pan I own scattered around to catch the water. I had to run back and forth to keep them emptied. Andrew helped me."

I leaned back in the chair, my anger subsiding as I marveled at her cheerfulness. She acted as though she enjoyed living in squalor, in a town where she knew practically no one, two kids and pregnant. I shook my head in admiration. Lorna could teach me a few things about keeping a positive attitude regardless of the circumstances. She obviously adored Ervil and was willing to overlook his shortcomings.

I wondered if Ervil had told her about his courtship of me. I shuddered. It was a miracle that it wasn't me living here. If Ervil had apprised her of me, she didn't mention it.

"Lorna, why are you living here instead of in Los Molinos or Colonia LeBaron?" I finally asked.

She shrugged and pursed her lips, her voice light, "Ervil's always traveling back and forth between San Diego and Los Molinos, and he wants a place halfway in between where he can rest. He has plans to start a business in Los

Molinos soon and will need to take care of the paperwork for it here in Ensenada." Her hazel-blue eyes suddenly snapped defensively, "I offered to live here, Susan. He didn't ask me to."

I stared into my cup and quickly changed the subject. We visited for an hour, catching up on each other's lives. As Lorna talked, I was amazed at her selflessness, and by her faith in Ervil. She firmly believed he was a godly man, and she lived for the meager time he afforded her.

As the sun began to lower over the ocean, I reluctantly walked home. Lorna was nothing short of an inspiration, I decided, and I determined that I would go often, in Ervil's absence, to see her. It was absolutely beyond me how Lorna could love him, but she did. For her sake, I prayed as I walked that Ervil would become the husband and the man that his families and the church needed.

I was soon to find out that Verlan's home in Ensenada served as a halfway house for many of the Church members who lived in Los Molinos. Most of the men who had settled in Los Molinos worked in the San Diego area and made the seven-hour trip on the weekends to see their families. Since Ensenada was about halfway, many of them stopped here to rest, eat, or visit. Often the men had family members with them. Occasionally they arrived in the middle of the night, and Lucy bedded people down throughout the house.

One night in late November the Prophet Joel pulled into the yard in his pickup and camper. The roar of his engine woke me, and I peeked out the window. At first I thought he was Verlan when I saw his lanky form climb from the pickup, and my heart began racing with excitement. But as he walked in front of the truck, I could tell by the headlights that it was Joel. Two of his six wives were with him, Jeannine and Kathy, who lived in Los Molinos.

They knocked on the front door of the big house, and had no sooner entered, than another car parked behind Joel's pickup. The woman driver followed the others inside.

I dressed, and entered the side door of the house. Lucy was heating up the leftovers from supper, and she threw me a warm smile. "Hi! Will you help me get this food ready? Joel and some of his family are here. Slice that bread, would you?"

I could hear voices in the living room, and suddenly the young woman I had seen in the second car entered the kitchen. She smiled and said, "Hi, Susan. Remember me?"

"Lillie!" I shrieked, dropping the bread knife. "Lillie LeBaron! Boy, have you changed!"

"You have, too," her laughter rang. "It's been five or six years, hasn't it?"

Lillie was a stepdaughter to the prophet Joel. She was Jeannine's oldest daughter from her prior marriage, and she'd lived in Colonia LeBaron years ago. We'd been fast friends when we were small. I hugged her, then held her away from me and looked her over. She was my height, but slender as a willow. Beautiful, dark blue eyes with curly black lashes dominated her face. Dimples dipped into her cheeks on either side of smiling lips. Softly curled brown hair puffed around her shoulders. Clinging seductively to her slight frame was a tailored, dark blue pantsuit, beneath which peeked the toes of black patent leather shoes. Her appearance was the epitome of perfection. The long drive from San Diego hadn't even wrinkled her clothes.

She stared back at me, smiling, taking in my disheveled attire. Suddenly I felt dowdy and tomboyish in my faded jeans. I reached up and self-consciously smoothed my hair, wishing I had taken the time to put on fresh, feminine clothes.

"So, you're a married woman, huh?" she chuckled. "How do you like it? Talk to me! I want to hear all about it."

I turned and began to slice bread as I filled Lillie in on my wedding details. Her mother, Jeannine, came into the kitchen to say hello and sat at the table to join us. Soon the Prophet Joel and his younger wife, Kathy, wandered in and pulled up chairs. In minutes we were all comfortably visiting. Lucy set bowls of soup on, and our visitors began eating their midnight supper.

Seldom, other than in Church meetings, had I the opportunity to be around Joel. He sat with a kitchen chair turned backward between his Levi-clad legs. Resting his arms on its back, he held his soup bowl in his hands. The sleeves of his plaid shirt were rolled to his elbows, showing spots of black grease between the golden hair on his forearms. Strands of thin, red-gold hair hung over his broad forehead, and he tiredly wiped them into place. His homely face appeared tired, his deep-set eyes circled with smudges.

"Lucy, I didn't think that old truck was going to make it," he mumbled between bites. "I'll take it into Ensenada in the morning. See if I can get Jose over at Venzon's to have a look at it."

He turned to Jeannine. "You girls might as well ride on down to Los Molinos with Lillie, don't you think? There's no sense in you having to sit around tomorrow, waiting on the truck. If it's the alternator it will take most of the day."

"Now, darling, I will just wait with you," Jeannine said firmly. "Kathy can go on down with Lillie if she wants, but I'm staying with you."

Joel looked at his younger, blond and pregnant, wife. "Honey, what do you want to do?"

Kathy smiled at Joel and squeezed his knee. "I'll wait too," she grinned. "Jeannine's not having you to herself."

"Whatever," Jeannine seemed unruffled as she shrugged her shoulders. "We may as well stick together. Lillie, I don't like the thought of you driving all that way alone. Why don't you stay too and caravan with us once the pickup's fixed?"

Lillie considered. "I only have five days of vacation left. I would rather go on down, in a way. But, then, it would give Susan and me a chance to get to know one another again."

"Yes! Do stay, Lillie!" I exclaimed. "We could do something fun."

"Okay, I'll stay," she grinned.

"Bring your things out to my trailer," I suggested. "The bed's not real comfortable, but the company's great." I giggled and moved to the door. "Goodnight, everyone."

As Lillie stood to follow me, Joel eyed us both. "You know," he drawled, "I had a feeling you two would become friends again."

I stared at him, surprised. Joel–thinking about me? When? What had made him think of Lillie and me renewing our old friendship? That was weird . . .

"It's going to be great having you here, Susan," Lillie was saying as we walked to my trailer. "I go to Los Molinos pretty often to see Mom and the kids, and I always stop here at Lucy's. What do you want to do tomorrow?"

"Oh, I don't know. What's there to do around here?"

"We could go downtown and go shopping! Ensenada is so much fun. We could go out to eat and to an early movie. What do you think?"

I lit the lamp in the trailer before answering her. "Maybe we better just stay here," I said quietly. "We could stay here and talk, or . . ."

"Talk!" she scoffed. "Talk? We'll talk tonight. Let's do something fun tomorrow! We don't want to stay around here, with a town like Ensenada so close! Let's go to a movie."

I sat and slowly removed my shoes, lowering my eyes so Lillie couldn't see my embarrassment.

"I'm paying your way, so you don't have to worry about the money," she said lightly.

"Oh, no!" I stammered, "Now, Lillie, I'm not taking money from you, so forget it." She was smart and sensitive, and my insides cringed with shame at not being in the position to carry my own weight.

"Susan Ray, I'm paying your way!" she insisted. "We'll have a blast. I've got a good job and lots of money, so don't worry about it. Shopping, then dinner and a movie?"

"Uh, okay," I agreed faintly.

We visited for hours. Lillie told me about her job in San Diego at a print shop, and about a gorgeous fellow worker she had a crush on. "He's so neat," she sighed. "It's too bad he's a gentile. He's really pretty wild; he even drinks beer. He asked me out once, but I was afraid to go. I was afraid he would try something. You know how immoral men of the world are."

I agreed. Of course, I didn't personally know, but I had heard plenty. We talked on and on and it was early morning before we slept.

We rested until noon, then dressed in our fanciest clothes and left for downtown Ensenada. Pointing out the tourist attractions, Lillie confidently drove through the narrow, crowded streets. Finally parking along the main tourist drag, she announced, "This is where we want to look around."

She looked chic and sophisticated in her yellow pantsuit. As we meandered in and out of the little shops I could tell that the native men, who lounged around against the buildings, admired her. I admired her, too. She had her own car, an exciting job, and lots of money to spend. She was free and happy, and more and more as the day passed, I envied her.

We stopped at a seaside restaurant and ordered shrimp. It was my first time trying shrimp, and I was surprised at how delicious they were. Then we drove to the theater and both cried through *Romeo and Juliette*.

The town was bathed in twilight shadows as we hurried toward the car. "Oh, heck." Lillie groaned, "I hope Daddy's not mad. I didn't realize the show would be so long! They're probably all waiting at Lucy's for me, so we can drive down to Los Molinos tonight."

"Does Joel get mad at you?" I queried. I couldn't imagine the Prophet losing his temper! He seemed much too spiritual and in control.

Lillie grinned and threw me a sidelong glance. "He's human, you know," she said. "He doesn't really get mad, but you can tell."

"Does he seem like your real dad?" I asked presently.

Lillie stopped for a traffic light, then glanced at me again. "I love him as much as though he were my real dad. I respect him more than any man I know. I feel so blessed, Susan. More than you can imagine, to be raised by him. He's so good to me and he treats me like he does his other kids." She shrugged. "I wish he was my real father, but it doesn't matter. He is, in every way that counts."

We drove on, and after a lengthy, thoughtful silence, Lillie said, "You know, it's going to be tough for me to find a husband. I won't settle for just anyone, after having Daddy's example around. Whoever I marry will have to be as dedicated to the Lord as he is. I couldn't stand for my husband to be less."

I glanced at Lillie. She looked soft and lovely under the neon lights. She was so sure of herself and so wise. She liked to have fun, yet she was spiritually strong and knew what she wanted in life. I felt lucky to have her for a friend.

I leaned back and thought over the events of the past two days. Life as a married woman, from now on, wouldn't be so lonely. I had two new friends to spend time with—Lorna and Lillie. I hated to see Lillie and the others leave. She assured me that she would stop again on her way back to San Diego.

It was the middle of December before we heard from Verlan again. He sent each of his wives a letter, hand delivered by Charlotte. They had all been sent to her address in San Diego, all placed together in a big Manila envelope. It was hard for us to get our mail through the postal service, as it required a trip to the post office in Ensenada, and we didn't have a car. As Charlotte sorted through the letters and handed mine to me, her face was impassive.

"Dear One," my letter read, "I hope you won't feel too bad, but I can't go down to see you this time. Ervil's here and tomorrow he and I plan to go on a two-week mission to Utah. He's making an effort to get along with Joel and me, and I feel it's important to spend some time with him. Please understand. I will see you at Christmas. Don't ever doubt my love for you, sweetheart. I miss you more than you know."

The day before Christmas Verlan arrived, the car loaded with Christmas goodies for the children. As usual, the whole household ran outside to greet him and he hugged and kissed everyone in turn.

"My, it's good to be home!" he shouted, tossing baby Norine up into the air then handing her to Lucy. "Now don't any one of you look in the car. Laura, I mean it! Close that door. All of you go on back into the house and give me a chance to hide this stuff. Lucy, you and Charlotte stay, and grab those bags. Take them into your bedroom Lucy, and lock the door. You kids, go on, now."

Verlan herded the group of reluctant children into the house, chuckling as they begged him to give them just a peek. Then Verlan turned to the wives and waving said, "I'm going to go and see Beverly for a few minutes."

He sauntered into the back yard. I watched him go, thrilled that he was home but aching because I knew that he would leave again. Besides, I had spent the last night with him, when he was home a month ago. Unless he stayed for four full days, I wouldn't get a night with him again.

I stood back and watched as Charlotte and Lucy obediently filled their arms with bulging paper bags. They carted them into the house, laughing together. I envied their easy relationship, and I wondered why Charlotte was so accepting of Lucy. She seemed to enjoy Lucy's company, and yet she still hardly said a word to me.

After the children were in bed, Verlan, Charlotte, Lucy and I prepared their Christmas sacks. My job was to write a child's name in large letters at the top of the paper sack, then hand the sack to Charlotte, who put oranges, apples, and a bit of candy in it. Then Verlan would place a toy or a game, whatever he had picked out for the child, in the top of the sack. Lucy took the sack from Verlan and tied a ribbon around the top, then hid it back in her bedroom, to be brought out in the morning.

It was a different sort of Christmas than I had ever seen. We waited until breakfast was over Christmas morning, then Verlan placed all the sacks on the dining room table. The kids lined up, smallest to biggest, and Verlan handed each one his/her sack, soundly kissing each cheek. The other wives and I waited, with Beverly among us, and watched Verlan play Santa Claus. After the last sack had been handed out, Verlan ran to Lucy's bedroom. He emerged after a moment with four more sacks. "These are for you girls," he grinned. "I know it's not much, but I wanted you to have something. Merry Christmas, loved ones." He handed each wife a paper bag, kissing us in turn.

I held mine for a moment without opening it. This had been the strangest Christmas of my life. We hadn't gotten a tree or decorated the house, nothing but these sacks. But everyone seemed thrilled and happy, the kids squealing over their toy and candy.

I watched as Lucy eagerly opened her extra large sack, a broad grin creasing her features. "Well, I'm happy with my gift, thank you, Verlan." She pulled a huge, blue kettle from the sack, big enough to make soup for an army. With a sly grin on her face, she looked at Verlan. "You remembered," she crowed.

Standing next to me, Charlotte opened her sack, glanced inside and smiled. "Thank you, Verlan," she said as she closed the top again. She didn't even allow me a peek, and I frowned. She was always so secretive and superior!

Beverly was next in line. She took her sack, smiled as Verlan kissed her, and walked out the door to her house. Well! I thought, dismayed. She's being just as secretive as Charlotte!

I didn't care who saw mine. I pulled the ribbon from my sack and glanced inside, then retrieved a plastic-covered white blanket with huge pink roses. Beneath the blanket Verlan had placed apples, oranges, and Christmas candy.

"I hope you like it," Verlan grinned. "I wanted to give you something useful."

"Thank you, Verlan," I echoed the others. I tore the plastic off the blanket and ran my hand over the fluffy material. At least it wasn't a kettle, like Lucy's. I would have preferred perfume or a new nightgown, but at least he hadn't forgotten me.

Lucy, Charlotte and I made a turkey dinner, with potatoes, gravy, and salad. There were pies and a soda pop for dessert. After the meal we gathered in the living room, where Verlan told us the story of Christmas. The children's eyes were glued to their father's face as he related the details of Jesus' birth.

"Soon, kids—soon He will come again. It will be during your Uncle Joel's lifetime, so you all will be here. You need to live your lives worthy of receiving Him. You are some of the most blessed of God's children—born under the Covenant. My constant prayer is that you will conduct your lives as such. You are my pride and joy, and I thank God for every one of you."

After Verlan's talk, we played games until bedtime. Then Verlan walked me to my trailer to say good night, followed me inside and waited while I lit the lamp. "Sweetheart, I want to give you your other gift now," he said, reaching into his pocket. "It's not a Christmas gift, exactly, but it's high time you had one of these." He opened a tiny black box and removed a wide, gold ring from the silk lining. Lifting my hand, he kissed it, then slid the ring on my finger.

"Oh!" I gasped, my eyes widening. I held my hand out to admire the ring, then throwing my arms around Verlan's neck, I covered his face with quick, smacking kisses. "Oh, I love it," I said breathlessly.

He pulled back a bit, an amused expression flitting over his face. Suddenly he chuckled. "You are charming, do you know that?" Slipping his arms around my waist, he whispered against my hair. "I adore you, my little charm. Thank you for marrying me."

I melted against him, squeezing back happy tears. He was so good, and I was so lucky to be his wife. I was really beginning to feel married, at last.

Chapter 19

"Oh, Lord, not again. Not again!" I groaned as I threw back the heavy quilts and bolted toward the door of my trailer. I dashed, shivering, through the darkness, the damp Baja earth sticking to the soles of my bare feet. The old hinges of the outhouse squeaked as I opened the door and leaned over the two-holer, vomiting in the direction of the biggest hole. Trembling, I leaned against the wall as I waited for the nausea to subside. Then I grabbed a handful of tissue paper and wiped the seat off. Turning around in the cramped quarters, I sat down, too weak and unsure of my stomach to dare leave the tiny, wooden hut.

It had to be Lucy's chili beans, I concluded. Chili beans always made me sick. My stomach churned as I waited, and I gently massaged it, my whole body shaking in the damp air. Finally I took hold of the door and pulled myself up, stumbling through the black night to the tap outside Beverly's house. The water was icy cold, and my teeth chattered as I scrubbed my hands and rinsed my mouth. I needed to lie down. I needed to get warm. Nausea swept through me again in threatening waves. I whirled in the darkness to run in the direction of the outhouse, but as I took the first step, a bush near Beverly's front door caught my bare feet. I stumbled, falling heavily against a bench at the side of the cement step. On the bench, Beverly had left a metal baby bathtub. The bench and tub fell against the step, clanging loudly in the still night air. I landed on top of the bench, my knees hitting hard against the wooden edge.

"Oh, hellfire!" I moaned. I cried out again with the pain, my cry suddenly drowned as I retched.

"Who's out there!" Beverly's high-pitched voice demanded. She peered at me from behind the screen door; her body swathed in a long white nightgown. "What are you doing?" she gasped. She pushed at the screen, but the bench, the tub, and my sprawled body blocked it. Moaning, I rolled off the cement, careful to stay away from the mess I had left. Beverly pushed again, and the bench and tub grated toward me. "What happened? What are you doing?" she demanded as she helped me up.

"I'm—I'm sick," I mumbled. Shivering uncontrollably, I said, "Would you mind if I waited until morning to clean up the mess?"

"Don't be silly," she snapped. "You're too sick to worry about it. Go on back to bed and I'll clean it up."

"No, Beverly, really," I insisted. "I'll come early and take care of it."

"Whatever," she snapped again. "Go to bed."

I hurriedly rinsed my hands and mouth again and crept back to my trailer. I climbed under the covers, shaking with the cold. My knees throbbed and, reaching down, I gingerly touched them. Sticky, broken skin met my fingers, but I was too tired and cold to care. My head pounded, and I closed my eyes, praying for sleep. How I wished my mother were here. She would bring me aspirin and pamper me and I would feel warm and loved...

I forced myself out of bed at first light, my stomach still queasy as I bundled up against the Pacific winter air. Cold drafts filtered through the thin walls and windows of the trailer, and again I desperately wished there were some kind of heat. There was little wood in Baja for a fire, and we couldn't afford gas or electric heat, so everyone in the family wore sweaters and coats, even indoors. No one else complained, so I wore my warmest clothes and kept silent.

Fog floated through the air as I stepped outside. Beverly's house looked hazy, illusive. I hurried to her front step, examining the ground. Puzzled, I investigated, but there was no sign of the puddle of vomit I had left. The bench had been replaced, and the tub hung neatly from a nail at the side of the house. I stood hesitantly, looking at Beverly's closed door. She was certainly a hard one to figure out. She made no secret of her resentment, yet she had thoughtfully cleaned up after me. I shook my head as I walked toward the big house, wondering what I could do to express my gratitude.

Lucy hovered over the stove in the kitchen as I entered. She wore an old brown sweater over her bathrobe in an effort to stay warm in the clammy house. Her new, blue kettle was on the stove for oatmeal.

"Hi!" Lucy said, smiling as she lit a match and stuck it toward a burner. "You're up early."

I gasped with nausea at the smell of burned sulfur and the odor of raw butane. I sank into a kitchen chair, my legs weak. "Lucy," I moaned, "Oh Lucy, I'm afraid I'm sick."

She hurried to me, her hand gentle as she felt my forehead. "What is it? How do you feel bad?"

"Maybe I've caught the flu," I choked as I lay my head on the table. The kitchen seemed to spin around me, and I closed my eyes, fighting the urge to retch.

Lucy's hand was warm on my shoulder. She stood quietly by my side for a moment, then gently asked, "When was your last period?"

I frowned and looked up at her, startled at the question. "Oh, I don't know, it was a long time ago . . ." My words trailed off as the meaning of Lucy's suggestion hit me. I could feel my face blanch. The room reeled as my stunned mind tried to comprehend. "No," I gasped. "You don't think that . . . that I might be pregnant?"

She chewed on her lip, fighting a grin. "It's a possibility, don't you think?"

I dropped my head back onto the table, tightly closing my eyes. In vain, my mind searched for my last menstrual date. But one day had run into another— one week so like the next. It had been before Christmas. Possibly the week before. Now it was the end of January . . .

Dazed, I stared over at Lucy, who had returned to the boiling water. She calmly stirred in oats with a huge spoon. Her features appeared unruffled and serene. She looked up at me, her eyes twinkling. "Well, what do you think?"

I gulped. I could feel the color flood my face as I mumbled, "It's been at least six weeks. I just can't believe it. It's so soon—I've hardly seen Verlan—"

Lucy chuckled. "It only takes once, you know." She shook her head, chuckling again. "Irene swears that all Verlan has to do is send her a letter, and she's pregnant. I have a feeling you're like her. Another 'Fertile Myrtle'."

I blushed and hid my face in my hands, my stomach churning. I could hear the children stirring in the back of the house as they readied for school. I sat, lost in thought until Lucy placed a bowl of oatmeal in front of me. "Why don't you eat," she said kindly. "It might make you feel better."

As I looked at the gray-colored mass, I gagged and stood, the room spinning maddeningly around me. "I can't," I choked. "I couldn't possibly. I'm going outside into the fresh air."

Lucy's face was sympathetic as I stumbled toward the door. I hesitated in the living room, then returned to the kitchen. "Lucy," I swallowed, "please don't tell Verlan. I want to tell him myself."

"I won't say a word to anyone," she assured me.

I stopped at my trailer for a heavier coat, then set off across the small suburb toward Lorna's. I had to talk to someone, and no matter how good Lucy was about it, it was hard to discuss my pregnancy with her. My pregnancy . . . I shook my head as I hurried through the fog. I felt stunned. Why hadn't I expected it? Why was I so surprised? The thought of becoming pregnant hadn't occurred. I searched my heart, trying to decide if I was happy about it—a baby of my own, a tiny, helpless baby, who would depend on me for care. I battled with my emotions. One moment I was elated, and at the next I was filled with despair and an overwhelming fear.

Verlan, of course, would be thrilled. Verlan adored his children. I would be giving him another child, another jewel to add to his heavenly crown. When I told him, he would hug me and grin and tell me what a blessing I was. He would be so proud.

How glad I was that Lorna was close! She would help me deal with this, I knew, and would help me put away my fears and see only the positive side. That's how Lorna was.

A smile creased my face as I thought of her. I had been to see her often, and without fail she had bolstered my sagging spirit, helping me to see that I was indeed serving the Lord, that my life wasn't being wasted. Lorna was always cheerful. She'd scoffed when I finally got up the nerve to ask her how she could stand to live in such poverty. "How can you call the wealth of two precious children and a wonderful husband, poverty?" she'd asked. With a wave of her hand at her surroundings she'd added, "It won't always be like this. Sometimes we have to sacrifice material possessions for things of greater value. We have to earn our blessings, Suze, and I'm grateful for the chance to earn mine. You need to look beyond what the eye can see and concentrate on your heavenly throne."

As I entered Lorna's yard, her little Andrew stood by the front door, throwing scraps to a couple of chickens. "Hi, Andrew," I smiled. "What's your mom doing?"

He gave me his usual scowl, threw a crust of bread to a chicken and mumbled, "She's grinding wheat in the back yard."

I walked around the house, wondering why Andrew always seemed so defiant. He had the looks and bearing of a prince, yet the intelligence that glowed in his eyes was almost hidden behind a festering anger. He was much too young to be so intense.

Lorna's head was bent as she struggled over the grinder that was fastened to a board against the house. Her face was red with the effort of forcing the handle around. Her body was heavy with pregnancy, and she suddenly stopped, gasped for air, and clutched her abdomen.

"Lorna!" I shouted as I hurried to her. "You shouldn't be doing this, for heaven's sake! Here, give it to me!"

"Hi," she panted. Relinquishing the handle to me, she stepped back. "I'm almost finished." She mopped her forehead.

Finely ground wheat filled a cake pan under the wheel, with a gallon jar of whole wheat sitting on the bench beside it. I poured more wheat into the grinder and forced the handle around. Within minutes perspiration lined my brow, and my back and shoulders began to ache with the strain. Lorna removed the cake pan filled with flour and emptied it into a plastic container, then replaced it under the wheel. Soon it was full again. "There, that's enough," she finally said. "Let's go inside."

"I don't want you grinding any more wheat," I said firmly. "It's too much for you. I'll ask Verlan Jr. to come over and grind up a bunch. He'll be glad to do it."

Lorna set the flour on the table, then slumped into a chair. Her face looked drawn, and her eyes were red around the iris. She inhaled a ragged breath and intently examined her hands. I stared; never had I seen her looking so depressed. I sat in the chair beside her and took her hand. Her knuckles were rough under my fingers, her hands cold. "What's the matter?" I asked softly as I searched her face.

Her eyes strayed over to Tarsa. The little girl was playing with a toy. She sat on a heap of clean, unfolded laundry, and as I noticed the laundry, I also realized that Lorna's usually immaculate little house was completely littered. Dirty dishes were heaped in a dishpan and on the countertop. The table in front of me was covered with bread crumbs and spots of honey. Toys and shoes were scattered.

Lorna sighed and leaned back in the chair. She slowly shook her head. "I'm not good company today, I'm afraid." Her eyes filled with tears. She blinked rapidly to withhold them, then gave in and let them fall. "You see, I'm just not as strong as I should be. I'm weak, and lacking in the faith. I'm letting little things bother me."

"Lorna LeBaron, that's a lot of nonsense you're spouting!" I said firmly. "You always amaze me with how strong you are! You're so selfless. You are one of the most righteous women I know and a true example for me. Shoot, everyone feels blue now and then. Now, tell me what's bothering you."

Lorna reached out her arms to Tarsa, and the beautiful child climbed into her mother's lap. "Just look at my baby's face," Lorna sobbed, her thumb rubbing the little girl's cheek. "Look at the way this weather's ruined her complexion. Look at her little hands, how rough they are! They look like orphan's hands... I've kept lotion on her, but it doesn't do any good... Andrew is even worse. They were so beautiful when we moved here, and now look at them!" My distraught cousin hid her face in Tarsa's platinum hair.

I listened, trying to understand how she could cheerfully endure such poverty, and a husband who left her alone in a strange town for weeks on end, and then crumble because of chapped skin. There had to be more to her wretched state of mind than what she'd told me. Perhaps she'd only acted content and cheerful before for my benefit, and no longer had the strength to hide her misery.

"When will Ervil be here?" I asked.

Lorna eyed me over the top of Tarsa's head, then raised the little girl's chin so she could look in her eyes. "Tarsa," Lorna sniffed, her voice even as she spoke, "Go on outside for a few minutes, will you? I need to talk to Susan alone for a minute. Okay?" The child obediently left the room.

As Lorna looked at me the tears once again welled in her eyes. "Ervil's not coming," she wailed. "At least, not till after the baby's born. I got a letter yesterday . . ." Her shoulders shook.

I inhaled deeply. So, now it was coming out. Lorna, for weeks, had talked excitedly about the baby's birth, because Ervil was coming to be with her. She'd planned her life around Ervil's return. "It's going to be so great!" she'd glowed as she talked. "Ervil wasn't able to be with me when I had Andrew or Tarsa. He plans to spend at least two weeks with me. I need to get new curtains made, and glass in the windows before he comes, so it won't seem so dark in here." She'd chattered on and on about her plans, and now he was letting her down. She was going to be alone again when his baby was born.

"Why?" I shouted, bristling with anger. "What's he doing this time that's more important than his promise to you?"

I jumped up and began to pace, rage at Ervil causing me to lose control. "It's not fair!" I whirled on Lorna. "It's unforgivable for him to do this to you, and you know it. Boy, how I wish he was here so I could give him a piece of my mind!"

I stopped and searched Lorna's face. She sat pale and quiet; slowly wiping crumbs off the table and letting them fall onto the floor. "It's not that big a deal," she finally sighed. "He'd be here if he could. It's just that I was so looking forward to it. I'll be okay."

She glanced at me, her eyes puffy. "I'm going to write to Mom and see if she can come down to be with me. It'll be a bad time for her to leave home, but I think she'll come. They're packing right now, getting ready to move to Los Molinos. Their house in Utah finally sold, did I tell you? They have to be out in a month." Lorna gave me a tight smile. "I should be thrilled right now, instead of so down. Just think, Susan, in one month, Mom, Dad and the kids will be living in Los Molinos, only four hours away! Isn't that fantastic?"

I put my arms around my cousin and patted her arm. "It's wonderful!" I exclaimed. "I'm not just happy for you, I'm happy for me, too. I can't wait to spend some time with Aunt Thelma and Uncle Bud. And Mark, Lorna dear, is a total babe. I pity the poor girls who live in Los Molinos."

She sniffed, then grinned—a real, genuine act of mirth, and I laughed out loud with relief. She was going to be all right; she was strong; she would make it.

"Lorna," I hesitated, then I smiled wide, little thrills running down my spine as I whispered, "I have a secret. I'm going to have a baby, too."

It was late in the afternoon before I got home, and within minutes, I wanted to shout with happiness. Lucy had handed me a letter from Jay, and my eyes quickly scanned the page. He was coming! He would be here, in Ensenada, in a week! Oh, Glory!

"A general priesthood meeting, to be held in Ensenada, was called by the Prophet Joel," his scrawled writing said, "and he sent me a personal invitation, saying he wants me to be there. I think he plans to reinstate me into the fellowship of the church and restore my priesthood. I'll be there with bells on. Can you put me up?"

I closed my eyes and smiled in anticipation. How could I stand to wait for a whole week? I wondered if he would bring Carmela.

Verlan was also coming to the meeting, which would be held in a rented building in town. Charlotte had delivered his message in her usual curt manner. "Verlan phoned me from Las Vegas, said he couldn't get away now. He'll be here next weekend, when the men hold their meeting; he asked me to tell you all; he sends his love."

I had hurried to my trailer to hide my tears. After waiting for two weeks to tell him about my pregnancy, now I would have to keep on waiting. No one knew but Lucy and Lorna. I had toyed with the idea of telling Rhea and Laura but had decided against it. I didn't want Verlan to accidentally hear about it from anyone but me.

I had it all planned how I would tell him. We would be alone in my trailer, and the mood would be just right. I would tell him about the baby, and the shock on his face would turn to joy. He would grab me and hug me, his hand going to my tummy, "Our child," he would whisper. "Yours and mine. We're a family now, my charm."

I wiped the tears away as I thought about it. It was going to be so wonderful when I finally got to tell him. Just one more week.

The vehicles started filling the yard on Friday night. Joel and his wife, Gaye, were the first to arrive. "Lucy," Joel said, "If you have room, we'd like to stay with you. If you don't we'll get a motel downtown."

"Don't be silly, we'll make the room," Lucy smiled. "The boys will let you have their room, and they can sleep on the living room floor." She trotted off to tell the boys.

Within minutes, Brother Castro and Brother Zarate arrived. "Think Lucy maybe can put us up?" Brother Castro asked Joel anxiously. "If she doesn't have the room, maybe we could sleep in the back of your truck."

"Nonsense!" Joel said. "Lucy said the boys' room is available; you men can sleep there."

"That sounds better than your pickup," Brother Zarate laughed, rubbing his hands together.

"Joel," I heard Gaye furiously whisper as Brother Castro left the living room. "That was to be our bedroom . . . "

"Shh," he whispered, "We can sleep in the truck. Come on."

"Wait, Joel," I interrupted. "You and Gaye can have my trailer. I can sleep in the big house with the girls."

He grinned and patted my shoulder. "That big brother of yours is coming tonight. You'll need to put him up. We have a bed all made in the back of the truck, and it's romantic under the stars." He winked at Gaye.

She stared at Joel and shook her head. A smile tugged at her lips. "Well, I hope you plan on cuddling real close to me, darling, so we don't freeze to death while we admire all those stars."

I watched, amused, as Brother Zarate and Brother Castro happily carried their bags into the boys' room. Lucy stopped short, looking confused, then shrugged as Joel motioned her to silence.

Soon the living room was wall to wall blankets, pillows, and boys. Once they had all settled down, I left. I wondered what time Jay would arrive.

It was the wee hours of the morning before he tapped on my trailer window. "Oh, JAY!" I kissed his cheek over and over, my tears running freely as I held on to him. "It's so darn good to see you, I don't even know how to act," I croaked. "I've been so lonesome, and I'm so, so glad you came."

He held me back from him, peering at my face under the poor light. "Are you all right, Sis? Everyone treating you okay?"

"Oh, yes, it's not that. It's just that Verlan is gone most of the time, and I get so lonely. I miss having family around. I've missed you so much, and I miss Mom and Dad . . . " I choked again and hid my face against his chest.

"Hey!" he said softly, "Cheer up, would you? You'd think somebody had died."

I grabbed a tissue and blew my nose. "I'm sorry. I just haven't felt well for awhile. It's good to see you."

As I turned up the lamp, Jay looked at me. "What do you mean? Are you sick?"

I nodded and grinned. "Morning sick. Morning, noon and night, sick."

Jay whistled, his eyes twinkling. "Now, ain't that something? So is Carmela."

"You're kidding!" I squealed. "Oh, Jay, We're both going to be parents!" I shook my head with the enormity of it. Jay solemnly shook my hand. "Congratulations, Sis. I'll bet Verlan's happy."

"I haven't told him yet. He's been gone . . . I can hardly wait for him to get here, so I can tell him."

Soon Jay was snuggled in, on my tiny couch, gently snoring away. We visited over breakfast the next morning, then Jay borrowed my trailer so he could take a spit-bath. I went into the big house to help prepare food for the guests.

It was noon before Verlan and Charlotte arrived. I badly wanted to take Verlan aside so I could tell him about the baby, but there were too many people, all demanding his attention. Lucy, Charlotte, and I were constantly running to fill the many plates.

By early afternoon the yard was empty of vehicles. All of the men were at the meeting in town. I watched the clock impatiently, hoping that it wouldn't last too late. It was my night with Verlan, and tonight was going to be special.

Car after car arrived right after dusk. As the men shuffled into the house, Lucy and I served them food. I glanced out the living room window whenever I had a spare moment. Soon Jay and Brother Leany trudged through the door. "Come get some food, you guys," I called to them.

"Don't worry about us, Suze," Jay said as he entered the kitchen. "Theron and I stopped with some of the other guys to get a taco in Ensenada. Verlan and Lillie showed up there, too. So I don't think you need to fix anymore food."

"Verlan and Lillie?" I said blankly.

"Yeah, you know, Joel's step-daughter. Lillie. They came in just as we were leaving. Lillie sure has grown up pretty, don't you think?"

I could feel the color leave my face. Verlan and Lillie? Together?

Don't be silly, I thought quickly. That's absurd and you know it. Lillie is Verlan's niece, at least by marriage. Just because he takes her to supper doesn't mean anything. But it was strange. Especially since he hadn't taken me to supper since our honeymoon. And, why was he eating in town, without me, on my night?

Jay and I visited in my trailer until past ten, catching up. I told him how sweet Lucy had been, and about the girls being my friends. And I told him about Lorna and her situation. I also told him how we had to catch the bus into town for groceries because we had no transportation unless Verlan or Charlotte was home, and, how the last time Verlan was here, we'd all gone to the beach and had a great time. And I said how sad it was to me to be living only three miles away from the ocean and so rarely see it. I didn't tell him about Beverly, or how she still didn't speak to me, or how infrequently we all saw Verlan.

Jay told me that the family at home was well. Our sister Rose Ann had given birth to another boy. Carmela was living in the colony at last, in the little house Jay had built across from Mom and Dad's. He also told me that Ervil and Dan were in Colonia LeBaron, openly criticizing Joel and his teachings to anyone who would listen. "I don't know what is going to come of it all," Jay sighed. "Ervil's absence here, from this general priesthood gathering, tells me that he refuses to back Joel anymore. I hear that he's succeeded in recruiting some of our church members to his way of thinking. Has Verlan said anything about it?"

I shook my head. "Verlan doesn't talk about church business in front of me very much. I guess he thinks it's not something for the women to worry about. Who has Ervil swayed to his side?"

Jay hesitated. "I don't want to say anything until I'm sure, but I have a feeling that if things don't change soon, there is going to be a real split in the church."

I looked at him, stunned. "You mean, Ervil might start his own church, apart from Joel's?"

"It's heading in that direction, Sis."

I leaned back, shocked and dismayed, and the conversation lagged. Soon Jay excused himself to go to Lucy's to sleep. After he left, I mulled over what he'd told me about Ervil. It was so crazy! I couldn't imagine any of our members choosing to follow Ervil instead of Joel except for, of course, Dan Jordan. The whole thing was unbelievable. I would ask Verlan about it tonight.

I peered out the window. It was almost eleven, and Verlan's car was still missing from the yard. The meeting was long over, the other men who were staying with us were settled into various corners of Lucy's house, and yet

Verlan was still not home. Worry and uncertainty knotted my insides as I got ready for bed and blew out the lamp. The trailer was chilly, and I tossed under the covers, shivering. Nausea added to my discomfort.

Suddenly the lights of a car moved across the curtain at the side of my bed and came to stop only yards away from my trailer. It had to be Verlan. I felt a mixture of relief and annoyance, and waited expectantly for him to swing my door open. I waited and waited. Maybe he'd gone into the big house to tell his wives goodnight, or to Beverly's. Sitting up in bed, I pulled the curtain back and peered out. No lights were on in the big house. The only light at all, was coming from a single bulb over the front porch, plus a small sliver of moon. As I dropped the curtain, a movement inside Verlan's car caught my attention. Startled, I pulled the curtain back again.

The porch light was dim, but it was enough to catch the reflection of Verlan's broad forehead. He sat behind the steering wheel, and cuddled next to him, so close that the two bodies almost looked like one, was Lillie's slender form.

I dropped the curtain as though it were on fire, and scooted away from the window, wide-eyed with shock and too stunned to mentally process what I'd seen.

Surely I was imagining things. I blinked rapidly, my stomach churning dangerously as I sat stiff and tense in the middle of my bed. I was losing my mind. Verlan, cuddled up to Lillie, his own brother's step-daughter? No, it couldn't be real. I was really losing my mind.

I stared at the curtain. The window and what was behind it seemed to tug at me, compelling me to look again. I crawled to the side of the bed, and with shaking fingers, I carefully pulled the faded material back. I stared at the tight huddle behind the steering wheel, and physically shook as I dropped the curtain back into place.

I pulled the covers back and dove under them, huddling in a rigid ball beneath the heavy blankets. This couldn't be happening. Verlan wouldn't be doing this to me; he loved me. Surely he wouldn't be courting another girl when he had hardly seen me in the four months since we'd been married. Yet I knew my eyes did not deceive me.

My body trembled under the covers as I fought nausea and hysteria. Soon Verlan would be coming in, expecting me to receive him in loving arms. Well, he was in for a disappointment in that area. Jumping up, I bolted the door.

Time passed slowly. Twice more, I peeked out the window, only to see the same sight, in the same position as before. Finally I could stand it no longer.

I had to get up and go outside, go relieve the churning in my stomach. I put a coat over my nightgown and slipped my shoes on, carefully opened the door and raced toward the privy. I yanked on the door of the outhouse, surprised that the door held. I yanked again, harder, desperate to get inside. Suddenly from behind the door, Beverly's muffled voice said, "It's busy."

"Oh, sorry," I stammered. I glanced quickly around the dark yard, searching for a place to vomit in peace without Verlan and Lillie, on the other side of my trailer, seeing me. I dashed away from the outhouse, and ducked under the clothesline, holding my hand over my mouth as I ran. I reached the weeds past the clothesline just in time.

When the worst of it was over I leaned against the wooden pole, my legs trembling. Fatigue and illness, coupled with the trauma of Verlan and Lillie's betrayal left me stunned and weak. I felt detached from myself, unable to cope with the hurt that drove deep into my soul. I held onto the pole, sobbing brokenly.

"Susan, are you all right?" Beverly softly asked behind me.

Swallowing back my sobs, I clutched the pole and turned my face away from her.

Suddenly she reached out and touched me. Just for a moment her hand lingered, warm and soft, on my arm. Then she let it drop to her side.

Surprised, I glanced at her. Her features were unreadable in the darkness, but her voice was filled with emotion as she said, "I know what you're going through, Susana. I understand how hard it is. Please don't cry. Please don't cry..."

Chapter 20

Beverly's short figure retreated into the shadows of the yard. I leaned against the damp clothesline pole and stared after her, hearing a soft grating as she closed her door.

"...I understand how hard it is..." she had said. I was certain she'd seen Verlan with Lillie and felt the same shock and distress as I had felt. She'd known that I was crying, but surprisingly, I felt no embarrassment. Beverly understood my pain, and for the first time, I understood her resentment.

I stole back to the trailer, conscious of Verlan's car. I didn't want him or Lillie to see me and to think I was spying on them. Locking the door, I went to bed. My initial anger at Verlan had left me with a dull ache, and a mute questioning of his actions. Had his courtship of Lillie been lengthy... or was today the beginning? I knew the answer. As cozy as they appeared, their relationship wasn't something new. Past experience reminded me that Verlan didn't behave that way, not until he knew a girl well... which meant when Lillie and I had gone to the movie, she'd been hiding their relationship.

I tried to be reasonable. Hey, dummy, I reminded myself, you knew there was a possibility you wouldn't be Verlan's last wife. But I'd seen very little of him in four months—four and a half months, to be exact. I sat up and began counting. I had spent only seven nights with Verlan since our marriage, and four had been the nights of our honeymoon.

I smiled wryly, realizing Verlan's other wives must also feel neglected. Irene and Ester, in Los Molinos, rarely saw him. I wondered if his desire for Lillie was a righteous one or if he was letting the lust of the flesh be his guide. Surely this was rushing into another relationship by anybody's standards.

I lay down again and pulled the quilts higher. It had been more than an hour since Verlan's arrival. How much longer would he stay with Lillie? I wrestled with my pillow, punching it, as I tried to become comfortable. My body and mind slowly relaxed.

Sometime later, a loud pounding startled me. My eyes opened as Verlan's voice called, "Susan, open up."

Immediately awake, I lay still. Instant fury engulfed me. So! I raged to myself. He has finally told that simpering girl goodnight. He's tired now, so it's my turn. Stiff and sullen, I waited as Verlan knocked repeatedly.

181

"Susan, open this door!" he suddenly bellowed. The trailer shook as he angrily yanked on the door handle. "I know you can hear me. Stop being silly and let me in."

So I was being silly! I grimly enjoyed Verlan's ranting, and I let a full minute pass before I turned the lock. He yanked the door open and stormed in, his heavy frame causing the trailer to sway. "What do you mean by locking me out?" he snapped. "You knew I would be coming to spend the night with you." By the dim light coming through the window, I could see his body silhouetted against the curtain. He ripped his shirt open with obvious annoyance.

In the four and a half months since I had become his wife, I hadn't spoken an angry word to Verlan. The words had been there, but I had bitten them back. Now they flew out of my mouth, sarcastic and insolent. "Yes, Verlan. You're absolutely right! I knew you would be coming to spend the night with me. I knew it was my night. My night—what a joke! You have just spent half my night hugging up to Lillie LeBaron!" I flounced on the bed, glaring at him through the darkness. "Oh, I saw you. All snuggled up to that skinny little . . . "

"Susan LeBaron, you hold it right there," he roared. "What I do with Lillie is none of your business." He stared at me, his eyes gleaming in the darkness. Suddenly his voice dropped, taking on a tone of disbelief. "You know, I can hardly believe that my sweet Susan is talking this way. You've never shown me disrespect before! What has gotten into you that you would start now?" As he stood in front of me in his long, white garments, I could sense the puzzled expression on his face.

Suddenly I laughed—a hysterical, weak, female sound. I wanted to scream and cry, but I laughed because his words were so sincere, so innocent of any wrong doing on his part. He honestly couldn't understand my problem, why I was so mad and hurt. As he stepped toward the bed, I quickly scooted over, far against the wall. He climbed in next to me and tiredly lay his head down. I cringed as he reached out and absently patted my leg.

"It's been a long, wearing day, and I've got an early Priesthood meeting in the morning," he yawned. "It's good to see you, Susan."

"Right," I growled. Additional words of hurt and rejection were battling to be voiced. They raced through my mind, thoughts fighting for precedence. So, he didn't think his courtship of Lillie was any of my business, huh? Now wasn't that something, when I would be forced into sharing my husband with her, and be stuck living around her for the rest of my life! I took a ragged breath and opened my mouth to say the sentence, just like that. The words were well chosen, perfect. He would have to chew on that one.

From next to me, a sudden, gentle snore erupted from Verlan's nose, followed by a louder, deeper sound escaping from his mouth.

"Hell and damn!" I said aloud. Amazed, I rolled over in bed to peer at his sleeping form in the darkness. Totally exasperated, I snapped my mouth closed and swallowed back the flood of angry words that coursed through my mind.

Boy, wasn't Verlan LeBaron something! He hadn't been in bed two minutes and already he was asleep. Lillie had worn him out, and now he had no time for me. I fought the urge to yank the pillow from under his head as tears slid down my face, wetting my hair and pillow. I'm too late, I thought disconsolately. I didn't say anything soon enough, and I didn't tell him about the baby. But what does it matter? He doesn't deserve to know.

I barely stirred as Verlan got out of bed the next morning. Keeping my eyes closed, I ignored his movements as he dressed. Soon he left the trailer and I snuggled deeper under the covers. The first rays of sunlight made my temples throb so I quickly closed my eyes. Tired from the emotional stress of the last hours, I drifted back to sleep.

Later when someone tapped on my trailer door, I struggled to awaken. Wrapping a blanket around my shoulders, I opened the door and sleepily peered into the sunlight. Beverly stood before the trailer, a tentative smile on her lips as she looked up at me. "Susana," she said quietly, "Would you have breakfast with me this morning?"

"Are you . . . are you sure you want me to?" I stuttered, pulling the blanket tighter around me.

She looked down at her feet, shifting uncomfortably. "Yes, I do. It's not much what I have made, just huevos rancheros, but I would like to have you share them with me. Yes?"

Warmth and gladness rushed through me, and I wanted to hug her. "I would be happy to," I grinned, pushing the hair out of my eyes. "I'll get dressed and be there in a few minutes."

Stunned at the change in her attitude, I quickly dressed. What had come over her? She was actually reaching out to me, offering me her friendship! It seemed that all Verlan's wives could rely on was each other. To survive the loneliness, we needed to stick together.

Beverly's table was set for two, with a vase of plastic flowers in the center. She pulled out a chair and I sat down, wondering what to say as she bustled around the kitchen. She served Spanish-style eggs and rice, then poured a hot, mahogany-colored brew that I didn't recognize into a coffee cup. I sensed her nervousness as she sat and looked at me across the table.

"Susana," her eyes were a fluid, gentle brown, "I want to apologize for the way I have treated you. It was wrong of me. I want us to be friends, if you're willing."

Suddenly I realized I had been holding my breath. I exhaled, closing my eyes to hide the relief, the guilt, and the turmoil in my heart. Now I understood the feelings Beverly had harbored against me. I opened my eyes again and reached for my cup. I took a sip of the hot liquid before I answered. "I'm the one who should apologize. I didn't realize what you were going through until—" I stopped, searching for words.

Beverly's tone was gentle, "I know. It's hard." She stared at her plate, mixing her eggs and rice together. "I saw Verlan with Lillie last night..." She shrugged and sighed. "I'm more used to it now, I guess. It's all new to you. It's different, somehow, with the wives who are already married to him. It's not so hard to accept them. It's the new ones he chases and marries that about kill you."

Beverly suddenly looked up. Tears had filled her brown eyes, and they threatened to re-open my own wounds. I nodded, swallowed hard, fought to gain control of my emotions, and took another sip of the brew in the cup. "This is good," I said, changing the subject. "What is it?"

She dabbed at her cheeks and tried to smile. "Mom and Dad used to let me drink coffee, back when I was at home. Verlan won't let me drink it any more, so I pretend this is coffee. It's just oven-browned grains that I've ground together and boiled. It's not exactly coffee, but..."

"But it's hot and relaxing," I finished her sentence. I suddenly felt at ease. The tension was completely gone. Beverly fussed as we ate, refilling my cup, and chatting away as though there had never been a problem between us. The food was delicious, and my stomach felt almost normal. I ate greedily.

The moment the baby stirred in the crib, Beverly jumped up and brought her to the table. I smiled, holding my arms out, and Beverly said, "Go see Aunt Susan, Lorraine." She put the blanket-wrapped little girl in my lap, and the baby looked up at me with her huge, curious, brown eyes.

"Aren't you a pretty one," I crooned. "She's seven months, right?"

"Almost nine months," Beverly corrected. "She's so much fun. She's walking around holding onto the furniture now, but she doesn't dare let go and try it on her own. See her new teeth? It's not much fun nursing her, I'll tell you, now that she has them."

I stuck my finger in Lorraine's mouth, felt the tiny teeth, and grinned. "She bites you, huh?"

"Boy, does she bite! I'm going to have to quit breast-feeding soon. I'm hanging on as long as I can, because I'm not ready to get pregnant. One baby is enough in this little house."

I nodded, and wondered if I would still be living in the trailer when I had my baby. And I wondered if Beverly had guessed that I was pregnant and had opened the subject, hoping I would confide in her. I quickly decided against it. As mad as I was at Verlan I still wanted him to know before anyone else.

"Beverly, did you know about Lillie before last night?"

The muscles around her mouth stiffened. "Not exactly," she shook her head. "But I wasn't surprised. Irene told me that a year or so ago Verlan took Lillie out a couple of times, up in Las Vegas. Nothing ever came of it, and I thought that was the end of the courtship. I guess I was wrong."

"Didn't he talk to you about her, tell you he was courting her?"

Beverly shook her head again and started clearing up the table. "He didn't tell me about you, either. The first I knew about you was when Irene came back from Colonia LeBaron, right after you and Verlan were married. She told us all then—it was a shock."

My face flamed. "I'm so sorry. I didn't realize . . ."

"It's not your fault!" she snapped. "That's just the way Verlan is. He told me that he hadn't wanted to worry me about you—until there was actually something to worry me about." Beverly glanced at me as she wiped the table with a wet rag. Then in a scornful tone of voice, she added, "If you haven't already figured it out, I may as well warn you. As Verlan's wife, you have no say whatever in what he does or who he marries. You just have to hang on and like it or lump it."

I stood up, walked to the dishpan, and automatically started washing the dishes. The tight feeling of strangled emotions had begun to tear at my chest again. I furiously scrubbed at dried egg on a plate.

Beverly's voice interrupted my runaway thoughts. "I've upset you, haven't I? I'm sorry, Susan, I shouldn't have said that. It's really not so bad. At least we have a roof over our heads and food to eat. No one ever said plural marriage would be easy."

I handed her a clean plate, and muttered, "At least, no woman ever did." During the silence that lapsed, bitter and angry thoughts warred inside me. "It's not fair!" I suddenly blurted out. "We women have feelings and needs, too—just like men do. But we give up our rights once we become a wife to one of the brethren. How is it fair that a man gets to have so much freedom, and yet a woman of the church has no rights at all? Does God love His sons so much more than His daughters? Is that it?"

Beverly was silent. When she turned to me, our gazes locked. "I don't know, Susana. I think He must," she said soberly.

I gaped at her. I hadn't really meant the words—I had only been venting my anger. Did she really believe it, about God being partial to the men?

As I thanked Beverly for the meal and turned to leave, I threw an appreciative glance over her tidy little home. My roving eyes suddenly stopped as they saw the new, white blanket, covered in big pink roses, displayed on her bed. As my startled brain recognized it, I almost gasped aloud. The blood rushed to my head. It was just like the one Verlan gave me for Christmas! I quickly clamped my mouth shut and turned away from the insulting sight.

So, I thought contemptuously as I marched toward Lucy's. Verlan couldn't even pick out something original, something just for me! More than likely every one of his wives except Lucy, who got the kettle, has a blanket just like mine! And I was gullible enough to think he chose it especially for me. Perhaps the blankets had been cheaper by the dozen. Oh, what's the difference, anyway, I thought. What does it matter? Lillie really missed out by not marrying Verlan before Christmas. She, too, would have been the proud, new owner of a pink and white blanket.

I pushed open the dining room door and walked into the kitchen. Lucy, Charlotte and the older children were busily engaged in various chores throughout the house. "Good morning, everyone!" I called out with a cheerfulness I didn't feel. "Are any of the men back from the meeting yet?"

Lucy glanced up at me from the table, where she and Laura were sorting beans. "I'm expecting them any time," she said. "Verlan asked me to have food ready by ten. I think the whole Priesthood group plans on having breakfast here, and I'm almost out of eggs. I hope they won't mind wheat mush."

Lucy, I noticed, looked pale and ragged this morning, as though she hadn't slept well. I wondered if she, too, had spent a sleepless night because of Verlan's late-night rendezvous with Lillie. No way, I concluded, I don't think she minds a bit. If she does, she sure doesn't show it. Verlan has Lucy well trained.

The kitchen sink was full of dirty dishes. I filled Lucy's blue kettle with water and put it on the stove to heat. Then I stopped at the window and stared out at the bleak, poverty stricken section of town. The cold, Baja wind was blowing again, stirring bits of dust, whirling it around the yard. The fog had lifted, leaving a gray sky that promised to bring a bone-chilling, drizzling rain.

How I wished Jay would pull into the yard! I ached to see his slender form, his blue eyes, reassuring me that I could make it through more of the dreary months that lay ahead. But the thought of Jay returning to Colonia LeBaron left hollowness inside me, a throbbing emptiness—and I didn't think I could bear to have him leave. My lonely existence loomed colorless and gloomy, like the gray winter sky that showed no promise of respite. How could I stand married life? Why couldn't I adjust and find happiness and satisfaction in doing the right thing? What was I going to do?

As I started to turn away from the window, Theron Leany's pickup turned the corner by the winery, then pulled to a stop by the front gate. Jay and Theron lumbered toward the house. I waved to them through the window, then ran to the door.

"There you are," I exclaimed, forcing cheerfulness. "I was hoping you wouldn't be much longer. Lucy has breakfast ready, if you're hungry."

"Sounds great; I'm starved." Jay yawned, stretched, then rubbed his stomach.

"Good," I whispered, "then you won't even notice the lumps in the mush."

He grinned and made a face. We followed Theron into the dining room, where Lucy had placed steaming bowls of cracked wheat cereal, swimming in milk. I sat beside Jay and watched as he daubed honey on his cereal. Then he glanced at me, his eyes roving my face. Keeping his voice low, he said, "You don't look so good, Sis—morning sickness again?"

I shook my head and mumbled, "I didn't sleep very well last night."

Jay thoughtfully stirred his cereal, mashing the lumps against the side of the bowl. Without looking at me he whispered, "How about coming home with me for a visit?"

Slowly, then faster, the warmth of newborn excitement seeped through me. My heart began pounding, causing my breath to catch. "Oh," I gasped. "Oh, Jay! Do you think . . . do you really mean it? Oh, do you think it would be all right?"

He spooned a bite of cereal into his mouth. "Of course it would, if Verlan will let you. There's nothing wrong with you going home once in a while." He grinned at my reaction, his blue eyes dancing. "Maybe we should check with Lucy and Charlotte, see if they can spare you."

"He has to say yes," I said suddenly, emphatically. "He just has to. Oh, Jay, I need to go home!" Desperate tears choked me, and I turned my face away, hoping no one was watching.

Jay's arm was firm and comforting around my shoulders. "He'll say yes or give me a good reason why not," he growled in my ear. "I already asked Theron if you could ride over with us. We're leaving this afternoon as soon as the meeting's over, so go pack your things. I'm going to talk to Verlan about it as soon as he gets here, and he'd better not tell me no."

"But, how will I get back here again?" I faltered.

"I'll buy you a bus ticket."

A sudden commotion in front of the house announced the arrival of more of the men. I wiped my eyes and kept my face averted as Verlan and Joel, followed by a dozen more men, tramped through the kitchen and on into the dining room. The room buzzed with male conversation as we placed bowls of cereal around the bar.

Suddenly someone leaned over and kissed my cheek. "Good morning." Verlan's voice sounded cheerful. Then he whispered in my ear, "I'll try to find some time to spend with you later on today, okay?"

I couldn't look at him. I knew he was trying to make up for last night. He was offering his version of an apology, and I was supposed to forgive and forget.

As soon as breakfast dishes were done, I headed toward my trailer, anger and hurt still smoldering. I wanted to go home. I jerked my suitcase from under the bed and threw open the lid. Suddenly Lorna's face crossed my mind, and my excitement subsided. How could I leave? How could I have forgotten Lorna, whose baby was due most any day? She was alone. I didn't know if she had reached Aunt Thelma or if my aunt would be able to come help her during and after the birth. I resolutely dropped the lid on my suitcase and pulled on my coat. I couldn't leave unless Lorna had things under control.

Skirting across the side of the yard, I ducked under the barbed wire fence, then ran through the shortcut past the back of the winery. The ground fairly skimmed under my feet as I raced toward Lorna's. Breathlessly, I pounded on her door, but no one answered. I pounded again. Impatient, I grabbed the doorknob, then frowned, backing away. Lorna's door locked? Where could she be? She had no car, and she wouldn't have walked far with Andrew and Tarsa. I hurried next door to the Sandoval's place.

The old woman who answered the door said, "Someone–a woman came in a car and took Lorna and the babies away this morning."

I thanked her and hurried back toward the winery. It must have been Aunt Thelma, I thought, relieved. She must have taken Lorna to Los Molinos. I wondered why they hadn't stopped at Lucy's, and then realized it was because of Ervil. Lorna was probably embarrassed because of Ervil's absence at the men's meeting.

I packed my suitcase, then sat on the small couch to wait for Jay. A full hour passed before he knocked on my trailer door. I swung it open, my heart pounding in anticipation. Well?" I demanded.

I knew the answer the moment I saw the grin on Jay's face. "Oh!" I squealed, flinging myself at him. "Verlan said yes, didn't he?"

"He wants you home in two weeks," Jay laughed, dropping onto the couch. "I told him I'd pay your way home. He seemed a bit worried, like he's afraid you won't want to come back, but I convinced him that you just need a visit with the folks."

"How soon do we leave?" I questioned eagerly.

"Well, the men have another meeting in fifteen minutes. It's going to be held here, in Lucy's living room." Jay hesitated and grinned a little. "Joel mentioned again that he wants to see me, and we haven't found the time yet. I'm going to go look him up right now before the meeting starts 'cause Theron wants to leave the minute it's over."

Jay stood up, ruffled my hair, and opened the door. "It's going to be great to have you home, Suze."

"Jay." I stopped him, my heart in my eyes as I said, "Thank you. I love you."

"I'll be back soon," he promised.

I straightened the trailer, humming as I worked. I was going home! Home, to see Mom, Dad and the little girls. Franny, Carmela, Debbie . . . Oh, it was enough to make me shout for joy.

Then I thought about Verlan. He had certainly agreed to my leaving easily, and the thought suddenly irritated me. I had expected him to initially argue and refuse. But according to Jay, he had readily agreed. Maybe he doesn't care if you're gone, I told myself. Maybe he thinks it will give him more time to chase Lillie. I shook the thought away, and hurried to Beverly's to tell her goodbye.

"I'm glad for you, Susana," Beverly said when I told her. "I wish I could go; I miss my family. Maybe next time."

"I'm feeling sort of guilty," I admitted. "I know it has been a long time since you've been home."

"When Lorraine is older, I, too, will go. Don't worry about it." She gripped my hand. "Tell my family that I sent my love."

Telling Lucy that I was leaving would be harder. I knew she had come to rely on my help, and caring for the household would again fall solely on her shoulders.

When I entered the big house, I could hear the men's voices in the living room. It sounded as if they were all talking at once, giving the impression that the meeting was coming to a conclusion.

I found Lucy lying down by little Norine in a back bedroom. She looked up as I entered and motioned for me to enter. "Lucy," I began. Then I stopped, noting her drawn, tired features. As I dropped down beside her on the bed, guilt flooded me. How could so many things dampen my joy?

"Jay told me you will be going home for a few weeks," Lucy's face brightened. "Don't you worry about me. I can manage. It will do you good to go home for a while." She patted me affectionately, and I hugged her, grateful for her understanding, then hurried back to the trailer. Two weeks wasn't a long time, and the girls would help her in the afternoons.

I checked again to make sure I had everything packed, then sat and looked around. It was going to be so good not to wake up to these honey-brown walls for a change. The only thing I wanted before I left was ten minutes with Verlan, enough time to tell him about the baby. No matter how upset I was at him, I realized that I desperately needed for him to know. I needed a bond with him—something to tie us together. Something to make him notice me, I thought sadly.

Jay's knock startled me. "Let's go, Sis," he breezed in. "Theron's champing at the bit." He grabbed my suitcase and started out the door.

"Jay, wait!" I called. He impatiently turned back to me. "Does Verlan know we're leaving now?" I asked hesitantly.

Jay stood holding my suitcase, his eyebrows wrinkling into a scowl. "Hasn't he been out to see you or talk to you about it?"

I shook my head and looked away from Jay's grim face. "He's been busy. He's had a lot of meetings."

"Yeah," Jay said shortly. "He's in another one with Brother Joel, right now, back in Lucy's bedroom."

My vision blurred as we walked to the front yard, and deposited my suitcase into the back of Theron's camper. I climbed into the truck and stared straight ahead as Jay got in beside me. My throat burned from the effort to hold the tears back. Verlan wouldn't even take the time to tell me goodbye!

The realization was staggering. I loved him so much and he couldn't even tell me goodbye. I clenched my hands and in stony silence stared down the road, away from the house, wishing Theron would stop fussing under the hood so we could leave. Suddenly Jay jerked the pickup door open. He said something to Theron before racing toward the house. No! I wanted to scream after him. If Verlan can't come on his own, I don't want him to come at all.

I waited, humiliated, unable to even look at Theron as he got behind the wheel. After a moment Jay emerged with Verlan in tow. Verlan hurried to the truck, a rueful smile on his face.

"So you're going gallivanting, huh?" he said. "Weren't you going to at least tell me goodbye?"

He leaned in the window and kissed me. Then straightening, he said, "Jay promised you'd be back in two weeks. Take care of yourself, dear. Give my mother a kiss for me." He squeezed my hand and swiftly stepped back, only stopping long enough to open the door for Jay. "You have a good visit. I've gotta get back in there; Joel's waiting for me." He turned and quickly walked toward the house.

"Verlan. Verlan," I called, suddenly overcome with love for him. I reached past Jay and out the window, desperate to tell him my news about the baby, desperate to know that he loved me.

He stopped on the porch long enough to call out, "Drive careful, Theron, you've got a precious bundle with you that belongs to me." He waved and hurried through the door.

As we started down the road, Jay slipped his arm around my shoulders. His gesture of sympathy threatened to snap the last threads of my control. I wanted to collapse, fold up against Jay's chest, and sob out my hurt and humiliation. Don't cry! I commanded myself. I stiffened on the seat as my pride warred with the emotions that knifed at my insides.

Chapter 21

J ust as we hoped, the Prophet Joel reinstated Jay into full fellowship. "He not only restored my priesthood; he told me that he plans to put me in the Bishopric," Jay told Theron and me. "He thinks I'll be an asset to the handling of church funds. Can you believe that?"

"I can," I said confidently. "Jay, you're a sincere, good man and you'll show that old Alma that he was wrong to doubt you and to judge you. He'll have to work beside you, and soon he'll have to acknowledge your talents. The whole church will benefit."

Jay glanced over at Theron and me. "We are so very blessed to be living during these last times!" he said fervently. "It's something, isn't it—to personally know a living prophet of God! To listen to him talk! Man, oh man. We are so lucky."

Theron nodded. "Joel's got his own way of handling things. He just lets them take their course, like with the problem between you and Alma. He just lets it happen, then he turns it right."

As the men talked, I settled sleepily in the seat. I refused to allow myself to think about Verlan as we rolled along the highway. Instead I concentrated on how great it was going to be to see my parents and sisters.

It was just past dawn as we covered the last lap of our journey, followed the gentle incline of the hill above the colony, and dropped into the valley. Colonia LeBaron sat before us, looking bleak and lifeless in the still winter air. Even the Blue Mountains in the distance seemed to have lost their majestic beauty. Their royal blue color had dulled to a drab gray. Trees on either side of the main road reached black witches claws heavenward into the cold February sky, accenting the barrenness of the little town. But still, it all looked wonderful. In my heart Colonia LeBaron would always be home. Inside the adobe buildings scattered across the valley were the people I loved—my friends and family. I wiggled with impatience as Theron guided the pickup through the morning mist toward my parents' house.

We had scarcely stopped when Jay opened the pickup door. Through the living room window I could see my mother's face peering out at us. As she and the girls dashed out of the house, Mom called exultantly, "Oh, Jay, you've brought her back!"

She threw her arms around me, seeming loath to let go so Fara and Ramona could have a turn. As I looked around at the old homestead, my heart wanted to burst. It had never looked so good.

Dad had been away for some time now, embarking on a new venture. He had moved Maria to a small Mexican village about a hundred miles from Colonia LeBaron. They were working a parcel of land, trying their hand at farming. Mom seemed skeptical about the whole thing as she told me about it. "Can you imagine your dad as a farmer?" she scoffed. "Oh, well, Maria wanted to try it. Maybe they'll surprise me."

For the first few days of my visit to Colonia LeBaron, I blocked Verlan and the others in Baja from my mind. I soaked up my family's love and attention. It came so natural to fall into the routine of home life. Helping Mom with the chores was so much easier than helping Lucy, and I enjoyed her company more than I ever had before.

"What a difference to see you pitch right into cooking and housework," she marveled. "You've changed, Susan. You're all grown up."

"I got plenty of practice at Lucy's," I assured her.

The days swiftly passed, and I dreaded the trip back to Ensenada and reality. One afternoon Mom casually said, "You know, I wish Verlan would just let you stay here with us. I doubt he'd notice your absence in Ensenada much."

Her words embarrassed me and made me wish I hadn't said anything to her about my life in Baja. But I knew that she had only voiced my own thoughts. Mother was right. Verlan would hardly miss me if I decided to not return to Ensenada. His life would go on as before, filled with his work in Las Vegas and his numerous wives and children to come home to. I began to wonder what he would do if I refused to go back.

I toyed with the idea of staying in the Colony as I renewed acquaintances with friends and relatives. Franny was still faithfully going to school and still dating Alma D. She told me Debbie and Ervil finally had a real wedding ceremony, the ceremony that married them for time. Debbie had returned to California and was staying with her parents until Ervil decided where she would live. I spent several hours with Carmela in the little house across the road. Carmela was extremely happy and contented in her marriage to Jay. He came home from his job in Deming, New Mexico, every weekend, and constantly brought new items for their home. He was even wiring their house for electricity, anticipating when the government would bring power from Casas Grandes.

I coveted the nonchalant way Jay gave money to Carmela. In almost five months of marriage, Verlan still hadn't given me a single peso. I had secretly hoped he would offer me spending money as we were leaving Ensenada. But he hadn't, and I hadn't dared ask. It was humiliating that I had to rely on my brother or mother to pay my way if we went somewhere.

A new resolution was forming. I was going to insist that Verlan start giving me an allowance. He was supposed to be the provider, wasn't he? Wasn't that his end of this deal between us? Well then, he could just start providing, and I certainly wasn't going to accept Charlotte's hard earned money.

I had been in the Colony a full week before I got the courage to visit Grandma LeBaron. I knew she would question me about Verlan and married life, and I didn't want to confess how neglected her son's families were, or how hurt I was at Verlan's new romance with Lillie. How could I admit to her that already I had serious doubts about my ability to endure and serve the Lord?

Grandma was so sure of her duty in life. In her own quiet way, Grandma was the strongest, most spiritual woman I knew and she thought the sun rose and set for Verlan. She believed he was a great man of God. I couldn't say anything about my unhappiness—it would break her heart. I would have to bluff my way through our visit.

I set out the following morning, determined to be cheerful and upbeat about my life, for Grandma's sake. I stopped for a while at Franny's, where her mother was teaching a German Cooking class to my old school mates. I stayed long enough to taste the Spaetzle and listen to the laughing and joking of the old gang. Gradually the realization dawned that while the girls were still the same teasing bunch of adolescents, hardly changed in five months, I was different. I no longer fit into the lighthearted crowd of teenagers. Their laughter seemed silly to me now, hollow and humorless.

What's the matter with you? I asked myself crossly, as I trudged through the bare peach orchard. *Don't you know how to have fun anymore? Have you completely lost your sense of humor and become a bitter old woman?* I knocked on Grandma's door, then boldly swung it open and entered. "Grandma, you home?" I called.

Ervil's wife, Kris, peered at me from behind the dining room wall. Her hazel eyes widened as she recognized me. "Susan!" she shrieked, dashing toward me. "I was wondering if I would get to see you. Heard you were in town—in fact, Mother LeBaron and I were just talking about you."

Grandma's blue eyes were swimming as she hastened toward me. I stepped back from Kris' embrace, once again in awe of Grandma's poise, of the dignified way she held herself in spite of her arthritis. Her eyes were glued to mine, and filled with love and pride in me, her darling son's new wife.

I reached out my arms and she silently walked into them. Her shoulders shook as she hugged me. Then she pulled back, smiling up at me through her tears. "I was afraid you weren't going to come see me," her voice quavered as she mopped at her eyes. "I was just telling Kris . . ." Grandma stopped, squeezing my hands. "I'm so glad you came."

Kris glanced at me over Grandma's head and she gave me an understanding smile. "I'm going to go, Mother, and let you and Susan visit. But first—Susan Ray, I want your promise that you will come and see Anna Mae and me before you leave. We miss you! We've talked about you several times. Will you come?"

"Kris," I began. "I'd love to see you both, but . . . Perhaps Sunday at church . . . "

"Oh," she said quickly, "You don't need to worry about Ervil. He's in Chihuahua City for a few days. He's not even around."

I grinned at her. "Okay. Then I'll come."

"Kris, dear, I'll walk you to the door," Grandma said. She twined her arm through Kris' as they strolled across the tile floor.

I didn't mean to eavesdrop. But as they stopped on the threshold, Grandma's soft words reached my ears. "You know I love my son, Kristina. I'd give my life for him in a minute. But I can't encourage you to stay with a man who is leading you astray. Sometimes, my dear, we women are forced to choose between love and loyalty to our husbands, and what our conscience tells us is right. Sometimes in a woman's rebellion there can be found wisdom and beauty. Perhaps Ervil will be jolted enough by your actions to think, really think about what he is jeopardizing."

I turned my back to the two women and quickly walked into the kitchen. So Kris was rebelling against Ervil! It thrilled me. Ervil didn't deserve a wonderful woman like Kris—or any woman, I thought contemptuously, remembering Lorna.

Soon Grandma closed the door and joined me in the kitchen. She bustled about, pouring me a cup of mint tea and slicing a loaf of banana bread. "Tell me," she began, "How's Verlan? How are the other girls doing?"

"Everyone's well, Grandma, all of them."

As we visited I tried to force enthusiasm about the circumstances in Baja. Grandma watched me closely, a pleased smile on her face. Suddenly she said, "Are you going to tell me when the baby is due?"

195

I almost dropped my cup. "How did you know?" I demanded.

She chuckled, her fine eyes twinkling. "You glow, dear, you positively glow."

Abruptly she changed the subject. "Susan, I wonder if you have any idea what a blessing you are in Verlan's life. If my son ever needed strong, supportive women behind him, it's now. I'm sure you're aware of the tension going on in the Church."

I nodded, avoiding her eyes as I spoke. "Ervil wasn't at the meeting in Ensenada. I've heard the rumors and I know that Verlan is worried. Do you think there will actually be a split, Grandma?"

She sighed and stirred her tea, gazing into the steaming liquid. "I pray not. It breaks my heart to see the way my boys are picking at each other, fighting over who's above the other one, who's right and who's wrong. I never thought such a sad day would come. Ervil knows that his father gave the mantle to Joel and he can't stand it; he's so jealous. I pray, Susan, every day, every hour, that they can resolve their differences, and united, go on with the Lord's work. If they don't, Satan will prevail. The Lord can't use men who want their own glory above all else. Sometimes I wish Ervil were small again, so I could give him a sound walloping and make him behave."

Grandma took a bite of banana bread, chewed it thoughtfully, then looked at me and said, "We need to go on, to be strong. We can't let Satan get a foothold." She set her cup carefully on the saucer. "Susan, dear, I realize being married to a man like Verlan is a challenge to a young girl like yourself. In the days ahead he is going to need you like never before. Trust his judgment! Stand firmly behind him and let him know that you're his and that he can count on your support. You must forget your own needs, put those of your husband high above your own. Be a prayer-warrior in his behalf. Prayer is a woman's mission if she's married to a leader in the Church of God."

I studied her face as she spoke, concentrating on the words. Somehow I felt like they were words of wisdom straight from the Lord. It was as if Grandma were His messenger. I tucked her message firmly into the recesses of my mind.

It was growing late when I finally said goodbye. As usual, Grandma had given me lots to think about. She never failed to amaze me—today more than ever. It was almost as if she could read my mind! I hadn't breathed a word, and yet she knew. She knew, and in her own way she had tried to bolster my faith and guide my steps.

I shook my head and breathed deeply of the crisp afternoon air. Grandma's advice to me was certainly different from the advice she had given Kris. She had encouraged Kris to leave Ervil, yet she had insisted that I completely trust Verlan. Grandma was a wise woman, who recognized the weaknesses in her sons but also knew their strengths. The only problem was, Grandma hadn't walked in my shoes. She didn't know the extent of my loneliness or realize that Verlan didn't even have enough time for me to tell him about the baby. She didn't realize that I felt like I was just another mouth to feed in Ensenada, just another burden on Charlotte. And she didn't know about Lillie.

Maybe the reason I had dreaded seeing Grandma was that I knew she would try to bolster my faith in Verlan again. Every time I thought of Verlan I saw Lillie's laughing face, with her eyes flashing up at him.

I was supposed to be packed and ready to go to New Mexico with Jay on Sunday night to catch the bus back to Baja. But as the time approached, I knew I wasn't ready to face Verlan and the rest of the family. In the back of my mind my mother's words re-played, how Verlan wouldn't miss me in Ensenada. He wouldn't care if I didn't return.

"Jay," I said, avoiding his eyes, "I just want a few more days. Verlan won't know the difference—he's not around there anyway. I can get someone to take me to the bus in Casas on Wednesday."

Jay shrugged, trying not to show his uneasiness. I knew he felt responsible because he had promised Verlan he would get me home. But I also knew that he understood my reluctance. He opened his wallet and handed me two twenty-dollar bills. "This will buy your ticket, Sis. Do what you think is right."

I stayed close to home Monday and Tuesday. In spite of Grandma's strong advice, thoughts of rebellion battled inside me. I wandered around in a stupor as I tried to decide what to do with my life. Nausea nagged at me, reminding me of the growing life in my body and adding to the burden of my depression. Was I being a spoiled, self-centered child, feeling sorry for myself and unwilling to do my part to serve the Lord? How could I think of my own unhappiness when Verlan's other wives were faithfully doing as he asked? They weren't complaining or looking for a means of escape. They were quietly supporting Verlan, just as Grandma insisted I do.

Grandma was right, of course. The last thing Verlan needed right now was problems in his own family. I had foolishly reasoned that I could stay in Colonia LeBaron, but the memory of Verlan's teasing, laughing eyes brought emptiness and longing to my heart. I loved Verlan. Oh, what should I do?

"Mother, I'm going to go see Anna Mae and Kris," I said abruptly. "I promised I would."

It was almost dark as I set off. A star or two twinkled above, already bright in the frosty desert sky. I pulled the collar of my jacket higher around my mouth, blowing against the wool collar to feel the warmth against my lips. Smoke from several chimneys along my path spiraled upward into the darkness, and I was glad that the people in the Colony had wood to burn, so they could keep their homes warm. I shuddered. How I hated the thought of going back to the big drafty house in Ensenada!

I had to make a decision, and I was hoping Kris could help me. She loved Ervil, yet because of his lack of support for Joel, she was thinking of leaving him. Perhaps she would have words of wisdom for me—different words—more earthy words than Grandma LeBaron's idealism.

I knocked on the door of Kris' house, then pounded again, louder. When she failed to answer I hurried toward the dim lights at Anna Mae's. I remembered how inseparable Kris and Anna Mae had always been, spending every spare moment together. The ideal sister-wives. Suddenly I wondered if Anna Mae, like Kris, had finally had enough of Ervil's nonsense. I couldn't even imagine it. She practically worshiped Ervil, was one of his "soldiers." Instinct told me that she backed Ervil's rebellion against Joel, which would mean that she and Kris weren't in harmony.

It was fully dark as I tapped on Anna Mae's door. She threw it open immediately, her broad, freckled face breaking into a smile as she saw me. "Well, I declare! She did come, Kris—Come in, Susan, come in!"

Soon the three of us were seated around the kitchen table. As I looked from Anna Mae to Kris I realized how much I had missed their friendship, and how badly I needed more friendships like this. Around us, children played, giggling and squealing, making it hard to hear. Anna Mae had to excuse herself several times, shouting at the kids to get ready for bed.

The children had just settled down, finally leaving us some peace and quiet, when a car turned into the driveway. The lights flashed across the kitchen window and Kris pulled the curtain back to peer out.

"It's Ervil," she announced. She glanced quickly at me. "I'm sorry, Susan. He was due back today, and I didn't get a chance to tell you."

I swiftly stood, alarm gripping me. "I don't want to see him," I hissed. "I'll go out the back door. I'm sorry. I hope you understand."

Anna Mae looked taken aback. She blinked her eyes as she curiously searched my face. "What, are you afraid he'll bite you?" she muttered.

Kris grabbed my arm, hurried me toward the back door, and quickly helped me into my jacket. Then she glared over her shoulder at Anna Mae and snapped, "Susan has her reasons."

She turned back to me and lightly touched my cheek. "Take care of yourself," she whispered.

The night was coal black, and I had to feel my way around the corner of the house. I stopped behind the butane tank, waiting for Ervil to enter the house so I could cross the front yard to the road. I could hear gravel crunching as he walked around the car. Suddenly the lights of another vehicle swung around the corner by Wakeham's chicken coop. I crouched behind the butane tank when the lights swept to the left, coming to an abrupt stop behind Ervil's car. The engine died.

"Hey, Brother," a man's voice called out in Spanish. Ervil grunted and stopped. The car door slammed.

"How did it go?" Ervil rasped in Spanish.

"It's done," the man answered. Then in a high-pitched voice he blurted, "But I hope you never have me do anything like that again."

I cautiously peeked around the steel tank, straining to make out the man's features. Ervil's broad back was to me; his light colored jacket visible under the starlight. Ervil put his arm around the smaller man's shoulders and led him to the corner of the house not ten feet from where I cowered between the wall and the tank. "Oh, come, now, you're letting your soft heart lead you around," Ervil said smoothly. "Those people won't even miss that car! That's why they pay insurance companies—to replace them in case of theft and the like. Insurance companies love car theft because it drives up the cost of premiums. See what I mean? You don't have to feel a bit bad about it."

"It's not just that!" the man hissed. "I almost got caught, man! As I turned the corner, the guy came out of the store and started chasing me. I think he saw my face!"

With pulse pounding, I listened to the exchange between the men. The stranger's voice seemed vaguely familiar, and I wished I could see who it was. I cautiously peered around the tank again.

"Then you'll have to lie low for awhile," Ervil's voice was gruff. "Go back home and go on with your life. I'll pick the car up tomorrow. Now tell me about the meeting in Ensenada."

I almost gasped aloud. The car thief had been at the men's meeting! Did Verlan and Joel have any idea this was going on?

The guy snorted. "It was run-of-the-mill. Things we've heard a hundred times. But I'd better tell you what Verlan said."

"What did he say?" Ervil's voice was impatient.

The man paused, then stammered, "He—he said he was aware there had been some stealing going on among some of us and that he didn't care if it was done in Babylon, he wouldn't tolerate it... Said we couldn't justify stealing, even from the Gentiles. And that if he heard of more of it, he would see that we were punished by the laws of the land and cut off from the church."

Ervil chuckled. "My, my. Since Joel gave baby brother the Presidency of the Twelve he thinks he can dictate. As usual, he can't see the forest for the trees. It's trivial squabbles like this that have delayed the Lord's work. Well, the Kingdom must be established. We'll do what we have to do."

Ervil straightened from his perch against the wall of the house. Grabbing the man's arm, he guided him away. "Don't worry about Verlan," he growled. "I've had about all of his mouth I can stand. I'm going back to Baja on the weekend. If he tries to cause us any trouble, I'll have him taken care of. Maybe you will do it, yes?" He chuckled again as they stopped next to the car.

I cautiously peered around the tank again, straining to see who the Mexican man was, silently cursing the stars for not giving more light. Yet at the same time I was intensely thankful for the darkness that hid me from Ervil's sight. I trembled to think what he would do if I were discovered.

The man's car was only a ripple of metal in the black night, and in reckless desperation I stood up as he opened the car door, hoping against hope that the interior light would illuminate his features so that I could identify him. Only a flash of light cut through the blackness, enough to show me the man's dark skin before he slammed the door. Ervil mumbled something, then the car backed away. It sped toward the corner and out of sight.

I ducked again, blending into the wall as Ervil strode to the front door. The minute I heard the door close I darted across the yard and into the street, running fast toward the corner. I was stunned with terror and disgust. Ervil LeBaron was having men steal for him! And, oh, God, he said he would have Verlan taken care of. What kind of sinister human being was he to even think that way—and about his own brother? Oh, he was sick... sick. And unless I had totally misunderstood him, he was ready to kill.

The wind was freezing against my face, and tears were flowing down my cheeks. Oh, Verlan, Verlan! I loved him so much, and his life was in danger. How could I have even considered staying away from him? He had to be warned.

Chapter 22

The Greyhound bus carefully maneuvered out of the Deming, New Mexico station, puffed its way to the on-ramp, then climbed onto the highway and picked up speed. After a good ten-hour bus ride to Calexico I would cross the border into Mexico again for the final three-hour ride to Ensenada, Baja California. When I settled back into the seat and closed my eyes, relief flooded over me at crossing the first U.S. border on my way home.

Directly in front of me a heavyset woman puffed on a cigarette. The smell wafted toward me and I gagged, my stomach churning with morning sickness. Opening the window, I stuck my nose out until the woman crushed her cigarette, then I leaned back in the bus seat, tense and miserable. As the hours dragged, filled with twisting, turning roads and the constant smell of the woman's smoke, I squirmed impatiently. The bus seat was putting strain on my lower back.

Repeatedly, Ervil's threat to Verlan pounded in my head. I was frantic about my husband's welfare; not only his life was in jeopardy, but also the well being of the whole church. Something had to be done and quickly. Surely Verlan and Joel would know how to handle Ervil. They couldn't delay it any longer.

I stared out at the countryside and thought about my mother's curiosity yesterday when I told her that I had to leave immediately for Ensenada. "What's the sudden rush, for heaven's sake?" she had demanded. I didn't dare say anything. Verlan was the only one I could talk to, and I prayed he could put a stop to Ervil's madness.

Mom had eyed me suspiciously and asked, "What's the matter with you? You were going to stay a few more days, remember?"

I had shrugged. "I just need to go, Mama. There's no reason to put it off."

She'd sniffed and looked away, letting me know she was unhappy, and that she didn't entirely believe my excuse. But she had helped me to pack and get a ride to the bus in Casas.

I carefully rearranged the guitar on the seat next to me, so that I could put my feet up. Mom and Dad had given it to me on my twelfth birthday, and were insisting I take it to Baja. I touched the strings, happy that I would have something meaningful to occupy my time once I got back to Ensenada. The guitar had meant much to me years ago. Perhaps now it would bring a touch of the warmth of home.

The bus crawled past each telephone pole, each mile an endless turning of the wheels that laughed in derision at my urgency. Finally the mountainous terrain became flat and the desert of the U.S. border town, Calexico, loomed before us.

The minute the bus stopped at the depot I grabbed the guitar and my huge suitcase. Placing my purse and other bags under my arms, I fought my way to the street and hailed a taxi. In moments we were rushing toward the Mexican border town of Mexicali.

The cramping in my back became intense—with pain shooting down my legs and knifing my abdomen. Something's not right, I shouldn't be hurting this way, I thought. Only a few more hours to Ensenada . . . Lucy will know what to do.

The cab driver screeched to a stop in front of the bus station. Again I filled my arms with my belongings, then struggled to the ticket window.

"One way to Ensenada, Senor," I said, digging into my purse for the money.

The Mexican gentleman behind the window eyed me suspiciously. "Your visa?" he barked.

I stared at him. "But, Senor . . . I don't plan to stay that long. I don't need a visa for a visit . . . just sell me a ticket, please."

I hoped the man couldn't tell that I was lying. Well, it was a necessary lie. Verlan had been very strict about my not telling officials or strangers that I was married. "Don't ever admit that," he had said. "If you do, they'll haul me in for statutory rape."

The man was looking me up and down. "Senorita," he said disdainfully, "Go back to the border and arrange for a visa, then I will sell you a bus ticket to Ensenada. You cannot go that far into Mexico without a visa."

I glared at him, picked up my bags, and struggled to the door, angry at myself for not having the good sense to ride the bus on to San Diego. There was no problem crossing the border between San Diego and Tijuana. I made my way to the street and hailed another taxi. "To the border," I snapped at the scraggly driver as I climbed in. I leaned back and closed my eyes. The pain became alarming. Lord, I silently prayed, don't let it be the baby. I can't have a miscarriage. Make the pain go away.

The cab driver deposited me at the proper building. Soon I stood in front of a fat official in a khaki-green uniform. "I need a visa, Senor, so I can go to Ensenada," I said, setting my suitcase and guitar down. I looked expectantly into the mournful brown eyes of the white-haired man behind the desk.

He stared at me until I began to wonder if he understood Spanish. Then his leathery face broke into a smile and he gently asked, "Am I to understand you are traveling alone, Senorita?"

"Si, I am going to Ensenada to see friends. The man at the bus station said I needed a visa, although I don't see why. I won't be there that long." I drummed my fingers on the man's desk impatiently, wishing he would hurry.

"May I see your birth certificate, please?" he said politely. I scowled at him as I dug through my purse. For some reason the man was laughing at me. It didn't show on his lips, but I could tell. I handed him my birth certificate and stood, fuming, as he looked it over. He grunted and nodded, then called out the open door, "Antonio! Antonio, come in here, please."

Antonio was younger than the man behind the desk, and from the look of the pins on his uniform, more important. He barely glanced in my direction.

"This young lady wants a visa," the first man chuckled, handing my birth certificate to Antonio. "She is traveling alone—to Ensenada." Antonio studied my paper, then looked up at me. "You're fifteen years old?" he questioned.

"Si, Senor."

"Where are your parents?"

"They live in Chihuahua. I'm going to Ensenada to see friends. I have the permission of my parents."

Antonio shook his head and handed me back my birth certificate. "It is not possible to let you pass. You're too young to be traveling alone in our country. Sorry." He turned on his heel and ambled back out the door, then turned back to me long enough to gesture in the direction of the American side of the border.

I stared after him in anger and desperation. My abdominal pain had become acute, but I forced myself to ignore it. Whirling, I faced the man behind the desk. "This is ridiculous!" I thundered. "I have been to Ensenada many times, and never has anyone insisted I get a passport. Ensenada is a tourist resort, for heaven's sake!"

The white-haired gentleman leaned back in his chair and lit a cigarette, then said mildly, "Go to the border at Tijuana. They can let you through there."

I wanted to scream in frustration and pain as I lugged my belongings back across the bridge to the American side of the border. The suitcase was heavy and the guitar was awkward and difficult to manage. To my right was the American Consulate. I glanced at it as I struggled past, noticing that two men in uniform stood by the door, curiously watching me. "Where are you going, Miss?" one of them called out.

I slowed my pace and set the suitcase down, panting and dizzy with the strain. "I'm going to the bus station in Calexico. I need a taxi. Could I call for one on your phone?"

The other man ambled toward me. "What were you doing in Mexicali?" he asked as he picked up the suitcase.

"Oh, thank you," I gasped. "I was planning to take the bus to Ensenada, but the men over there wouldn't let me get a visa. I will just go on to Tijuana and get a bus there."

I followed the man into the building. The ceiling seemed to be slowly spinning as I looked around. My eyes burned and my knees wanted to buckle. My peripheral vision was dark and shadowed, and I groped for the bench behind me, dropping unsteadily onto it. I had closed my eyes momentarily, and when I opened them, the uniformed man was standing before me.

"How old are you, and where are your parents?" he softly asked.

I squinted up at him, concerned with how blurry he appeared. I answered, "I'm fifteen. I'm traveling to Ensenada for my health, to spend some time with relatives there. My mother is in Chihuahua, where I live. She put me on the bus early this morning. Now, would you please call a taxi for me? Please."

The man reached down and grabbed my arm, yanking my to my feet. "Come with me," he demanded.

He hauled me into a tiny room in the back of the building and plopped me down on a chair. The room swam. In moments another officer joined the first. "What kind of Marijuana do you use, Miss Ray?" he sneered. "Cheap stuff, I'll bet. A girl like you wouldn't be too picky and Ensenada's full of friendly pushers. I'll bet those Mexicans enjoy trading favors with a hot little chickie like you, right? That why you're going there?"

The other man took over. "How'd you get here to Calexico? Did you hitchhike? Answer me, dammit!"

"What kind of dope are you on?" the first man snarled. I shook my head, stunned at the question. I had never been subjected to such humiliation, or felt so much physical pain, a pain that I had to hide. I couldn't let these men know about my pregnancy without implicating Verlan. I grimly ignored the pain.

"Do you have a pimp?"

"What's a—a pimp?" I stammered.

The men both snorted, and exchanged glances. "You're a runaway, aren't you?"

"No!" I screamed at them. "I'm not doing anything wrong! Let me go!"

"Is that a wedding ring that you're wearing?" one of them shot out.

I glanced in panic at my hand, at the circle of gold on my finger. "It—it belonged to my grandmother," I faltered. "She gave it to me before she died."

He grunted. "Give us a phone number, so we can reach your parents."

"They don't have a phone! We live in Mexico, in Colonia LeBaron. I've lived there all my life. I don't even know of anyone who has a phone. Why won't you believe me?"

I glanced toward the door. In the adjoining room, I could see another officer going through my bags. As I watched, he took a pocketknife to the inside of my suitcase and ripped the lining. I jumped to my feet, horrified. "What are you doing!" I screamed.

One of the men pushed me roughly back into the chair. "Sit down," he growled. "You know damn well what he's looking for."

Shocked, I looked up into the man's hard, cynical eyes. Behind me, the other man spoke. "You might as well tell us the truth or it's going to be a long night. Now, where do you live?"

I answered the same questions repeatedly. Tears of despair had replaced my initial confusion and anger, and I sobbed, terrified, as they discussed placing me in jail. How I wished I could just call Verlan and know he would come for me. I wished I could let these Babylonian monsters know that I was a married woman who was carrying a child. And that I was cramping, on the verge of miscarrying.

Suddenly the men stood up. One of them walked to the door and held it open. "Get out of here," he said quietly. "Go on about your business. We don't have enough evidence to hold you, but I do have a piece of advice. If your story's true, you're much too young to be traveling alone. You can tell your parents that for me. And if you're lying to me . . ." He paused, sizing me up, "Your ass is mine."

I gulped at the brutal warning. With averted eyes, I sidled past him, picked up my belongings from the next room, and crept out the door of the building. I dragged my things across the street, expecting at any moment to be called back, to be drilled again by those horrible men—or put in jail. I had to get away from there. I didn't understand why they released me, but I certainly wasn't going to question their actions.

As I struggled through the twilight, another sharp pain doubled me over. I gasped and stumbled, my head spinning. The streetlights seemed to be pulsing—

throbbing a pale glow on the deserted sidewalk. I searched the street for a cab as I forced my leaden body to carry me around the corner and out of sight of the consulate.

The air had cooled and I began to shiver. The muscles of my back contracted, then my whole body shook uncontrollably. The suitcase dropped from my fingers and I slumped down onto the curb, lowering my spinning head between my legs.

I had to get to Verlan. An occasional car cruised past, their occupants staring at me. I wrapped my arms around my body and dully looked up at them, past caring that I must appear a street bum. I waited, gathered my strength, knowing that I still had a long journey to make. San Diego was at least two hours away, and I would be lucky to have enough of Jay's money left to buy the ticket.

Behind me I heard the shuffle of footsteps on the sidewalk. I turned my head slightly, enough to see black, shiny boots come to a halt next to me. My gaze traveled up the white pant legs, past the white pullover top, and rested on the youthful, pimply face of a United States sailor. He stared down at me from beneath a jaunty sailor's cap.

"Hey, sister," he grinned. "What's goin' on?"

I dropped my head again, groaning to myself. "Go away," I growled.

He squatted down on his haunches. "Do you need some help?"

I exhaled, watching him out of the corner of my eye. His voice sounds friendly, I thought, and his face looks nice enough. He looks innocent. "You could find me a taxi," I whispered.

His eyes widened as he leaned closer to hear my words. Then he straightened upright, "You're sick, aren't you?"

I nodded, dropping my head. The sailor was gone when I looked up again. But in moments he returned and squatted down by me. "A cab's on the way. Where you going?"

"To the bus station. I need to get to San Diego."

When the cab arrived the sailor helped me inside, then climbed in next to me and directed the driver to the bus station. I slumped in the seat and closed my eyes, grateful to have someone take over.

The sailor talked amiably to me, telling me that his name was Jake Johnson and that he was stationed at the base in San Diego and was on leave. "I'd take you back myself, but I'm with a busload of friends. The other guys are visiting Mexicali; I was just out walking around when I saw you."

I felt as though I were drifting in and out of consciousness. When we arrived at the station, Jake practically carried me inside. "Isn't there someone in San Diego who can come for you?" he demanded. "You're in no condition to travel alone, at least not tonight. You should wait and go tomorrow."

That brought me to full consciousness. "No," I mumbled. I tightly closed my eyes as I tried to make a decision. Jake was right, I needed help. Suddenly I thought of Charlotte.

Charlotte was in San Diego, and if I could reach her, she would come for me. Finally I said, "Ask directory assistance for Charlotte LeBaron; ask her to come for Susan."

I watched Jake hurry away. Soon he was back, sitting close to me on the bench. "She'll be here in two hours," he announced.

Then Jake began to talk, telling me his life story. I only half-listened. His voice was soothing and I clung to it as I fought back tears. At some time during the narrative he reached out to rub my shoulder. Then he patted my hand. "You're going to be all right," he encouraged me. I gently pushed his hands away.

"You're married aren't you?" he asked abruptly. Picking up my hand, he looked at my wedding ring. "You're married alright. And you're pregnant. Aren't you?" I quickly pulled my hand away.

"Yes, I'm married," I snapped. "My husband's out of the country."

The wounded look that came over Jake's face suddenly made me feel guilty. "I'm—I'm sorry," I stammered. "I really do appreciate your kindness."

He stood up. "I'm going to get you a cup of coffee," he said.

Drinking coffee was strictly against Verlan's principles, but it smelled good and I hoped it would clear my head. The coffee was black, strong and bitter. I gulped it down. The nagging pain in my back was at last beginning to subside. The minutes slowly dragged by as I watched for Charlotte. I was glad she was coming. I knew that Verlan always picked Charlotte up before going on to Ensenada, and this way I would be seeing him sooner than if I'd gone straight there.

An hour went by. Digging in his pocket for more change, Jake made another trip to the coffee machine. "You're looking better," he said as he hurried back to me. "You had me worried for awhile."

Leaning over me, he held out the cup. "Thank you, Jake," I smiled up at him, reaching for the coffee. "You've been so nice to me."

He patted my arm reassuringly. "The U.S. Navy at your service, my dear."

Behind him, I glimpsed Charlotte striding across the station toward us. I quickly stood up.

"Charlotte! Thank you for coming for me. This is Jake. He's the one who called you. Jake, Charlotte."

"Hello," she nodded. Her face was set in hard lines, and she grabbed my arm with one hand, my suitcase with the other.

"I'll get that," Jake offered, reaching for the bag.

"No, thank you, you've done enough," she snapped, pulling it away from him and guiding me toward the door of the station.

I glanced at him, embarrassed. He ignored Charlotte's tone and hurried after us, carrying my guitar. Charlotte deposited my belongings in the trunk of the gold Chevelle, then opened the door and slammed it closed once I was inside.

She was furious because of Jake, but I didn't care. He had been kind to me, a gentleman in the midst of Babylon. I rolled down the window and called out to him, "Goodbye, Jake Johnson. You're a beautiful, wonderful guardian angel."

Charlotte's jaw was clamped closed as we drove to the outskirts of town. I knew I needed to explain, to tell her the details of the day so she would understand about Jake, but I wondered at the same time if it would do any good. She had already drawn her own conclusions.

"Charlotte," I suddenly said, "It's urgent that I see Verlan. When will he be home?"

Her voice was tight. "Well, he's due in tomorrow. I'm sure you're planning to tell him about your friend, right? It's better that you tell him, so that I don't have to. You should be ashamed of yourself! It makes me ill to think that one of Verlan's wives would be carrying on with a complete stranger—a sailor, no less! What a cozy little scene!"

I gaped at her. Sudden fury blurred my sight as I stared at her set face, at the tense way her fingers were gripping the steering wheel. "You don't understand," I muttered.

"Oh, I'm sure you have a good story. Go on, tell me about you and this Jake guy."

Rage caused my throat to constrict as I bristled under her accusation. "It's not like you think, at all," I choked. "Jake only helped me because I was sick. He was a gentleman, and I'll not have you thinking the worst!"

She snorted, then glanced over at me, looking me up and down, "What's the matter with you?

"It doesn't make any difference," I snapped. "I'm going to be all right. I just need to see Verlan. I have to talk to him."

She eyed me curiously. "What's this all about? Is something wrong in Colonia LeBaron?"

I dropped my forehead against the cold windowpane and closed my eyes. "Yes, something's wrong, but I'll save it to tell Verlan," I said coldly.

Charlotte could think what she wanted. The only thing that mattered was that I would see Verlan tomorrow, before he got to Ensenada. He would be warned about Ervil.

Chapter 23

T he threat of miscarriage subsided as I rested on Charlotte's couch the next day. I felt almost normal again, and I watched anxiously for Verlan's arrival. Late in the evening, his pickup finally pulled into the driveway. I sat quietly as he greeted Charlotte, then handed her his bag full of paint-splotched clothes soiled from his work in Las Vegas.

"I'll need those washed the minute we get back from Ensenada," he ordered. "I didn't have time to go to a . . . " His eyes widened and he grinned, suddenly noticing me. "Well, hello! What are you doing here? I thought you'd be in Ensenada by now."

"Susan has something urgent to tell you," Charlotte cut in.

Verlan looked from one of us to the other, but waited until Charlotte left the room before walking over and slipping his arms around me. Fierce love surged through me as I hugged him back.

Traces of fatigue had darkened his beautiful eyes, and as he smiled down at me, the furrows at the sides of his mouth were deeper than I remembered. He seemed much thinner.

"What's going on, my darling? What's Charlotte talking about?" he questioned.

Keeping my voice low, I said, "Something happened in Colonia LeBaron, Verlan, and it frightened me. I have to talk to you alone." I glanced at Charlotte in the kitchen. I knew she could hear us. Verlan grabbed my hand and pulled me toward her bedroom.

"We're going to go in here and visit for a few minutes, Charlotte," he informed her. I ignored Charlotte's stiff back and followed Verlan. "Go on," he said as he sat down on the edge of the bed and flipped on the lamp.

Quickly and unemotionally, I told him about Ervil and the Mexican man, about the car, and what Ervil said about "taking care of" Verlan in case of any more problems. "He meant it, too," I shuddered, "I could tell by his tone of voice. It was evil . . . scary. Did you know anything about this? What are you going to do?"

Verlan ignored my questions as he pondered my words. When he turned and faced me his eyes seemed even more haunted. "I want you to think. Who was the other man?"

I sighed and shook my head. "I couldn't tell. It was too dark, and besides, I was afraid they would see me if I looked around the tank. I've heard his voice before, but I don't know where. All I know for sure is that he's a Mexican who was at the meeting in Ensenada with you two weeks ago."

Verlan looked thoughtfully away. "That could be any one of two dozen men, now, couldn't it? Too bad you didn't pay more attention. It could be very important."

I stared at Verlan, shocked. Had he expected me to dash out from cover and walk up to Ervil and his fellow thief for a better look?

"Well," Verlan shrugged, watching me closely. "I'm not concerned about his threat to me. Ervil talks big— always has. What does worry me is the thing about the car. If he's really up to that kind of mischief, why, he's sicker than I thought. We'll have to get proof and somehow put a stop to it. If we don't, the authorities will tie the whole thing to the church and figure we're all in it together."

"Verlan! Ervil was not bluffing about having you killed!" I said angrily, wondering how could he be so stupid. "You weren't there—you didn't hear his tone of voice! He scared me, really scared me!"

Verlan cocked his head and regarded me. "How can you think my own brother would be capable of something like murdering me? Don't be ridiculous! Oh, he's power-hungry, and he resents my position in the church. That's his main problem. But he's not cracked enough to actually kill. Now, you stop fretting about it. You're overreacting. You misunderstood the conversation." Verlan chewed on his lip and shook his head. "About this other thing. I know how his mind works. He's convinced himself and some of the others that it's okay to steal something if it's used to build up the Lord's work. A ridiculous philosophy. He's bound and determined to force God's work ahead regardless. Anyway, you just put this all out of your mind." Completely dismayed, I protested, but Verlan waved my words away. "Now, I don't want you to tell a soul about any of this. Hear me? No one! Just forget all about it and trust me to handle Ervil." As if to himself, he murmured, "I hate the thought of telling Joel about this. Heaven knows he's got enough to worry about."

As I watched Verlan's face, the layer of ice that had formed around my heart since that night of seeing him with Lillie completely melted away. My husband was suffering, and I hugged him and patted him.

"There's something else I need to talk to you about," I whispered, trying to smile. Now would be a good time to tell him about the baby. Maybe my news would make him feel better.

He stood up. Kissing me quickly on the forehead, he said, "It'll wait until we get home, won't it? We'd better join Charlotte. Besides, we can talk on the way. I'm in a hurry to get down the peninsula." I pursed my lips, nodded, and followed him back into the living room.

I sat quietly next to Charlotte on the trip to Ensenada, deep in my own thoughts. The window felt cold against my nose as I stared out at the Baja coastline. The beauty of the sea by moonlight was lost on me, blurred behind a heavy blanket of fog that drifted into my own mind, clouding the events of the past few days. The traumatic incidents seemed unreal, almost like a figment of my imagination.

I longed to know what else Verlan was upset about. Why wouldn't he confide in me! I wondered if his anxiety had anything to do with Ervil. I told myself that I needed to trust him, put this all behind me, and go on with my life. But as we drew closer to the family home in Ensenada, the knot in my throat grew. I knew it was because I was once again faced with the situation of Verlan and the wives— the children, the loneliness, and new girlfriend. Yet all of that dimmed with the worry of Ervil and his horrible threat, and no amount of reassurance from Verlan would make it go away.

Where would it all lead? What would Ervil's rebellion do to the church? Was Jay right in thinking that Ervil would cause an actual split, that some of our people believed and trusted in Ervil as God's spokesman and would be willing to turn their backs to Joel? I couldn't even imagine it. Joel had inherited the mantle of God! How could this happen now, when we were so close to Jesus' Second Coming? We were supposed to be united and ready to receive Him. But Satan was at work among us, breaking up the Lord's people, just as it was foretold.

The ride seemed endless. My body still felt battered and bruised from the long bus trip, and the additional miles to Ensenada threatened to again bring on the horrible cramps. I longed to lie down in the quiet of my trailer.

The lights of the big house looked good as we pulled into the yard. I went directly to my trailer and fell into bed. I would see the family in the morning. I snuggled in and tried to push the turbulent thoughts away.

Sooner than I expected, Verlan's heavy step announced his arrival to tell me good night. I knew Beverly was waiting to spend the night with him. We would have only a few minutes alone together.

"So, did you miss me, and are you glad to be back home?" he began, lying beside me and pulling up the quilt.

"Verlan, I know you don't want to talk about Ervil, but I'm afraid for you. Afraid he will hurt you."

Verlan sighed, annoyed. Rising onto his elbow, he looked at me. "Susan, you have to understand. The Lord won't allow anyone to interfere with his plan for us. We are His chosen people. We have a tremendous mission, one that only we can carry out. Ervil is just trying to do what he believes is the Lord's work. He is a little misguided now—that's all. Joel believes he will repent. We're all praying for him."

He abruptly stood and stretched, and I could tell he was thinking that it was time to be moving on. A slow anger made my temples throb, and I spat, "Why are you covering up for Ervil! Why are you afraid to talk to me about it? I'm your wife, remember? If it were Charlotte you'd believe her! You'd trust her instincts, and you'd trust her enough to tell her what's upsetting you. But because it's me, and I'm young enough to be your daughter, you pooh-pooh it away—you tell me I'm imagining things. You're not being fair."

Verlan stared at me, momentarily taken aback. Then an amused look crossed his face, "That's not true, my little charm. No matter who told me those things about Ervil, I would take it with a grain of salt. I know my brother better than you do. He's a good man underneath all the blustering he does. He's a bit misguided, but he's done many good works for the church and God. As for something upsetting me, I'm just tired, that's all. It's been a long and hard two weeks."

He suddenly grinned. "What's this I detect in your attitude about Charlotte? Are there problems between the two of you?"

I slowly inhaled. I knew I might as well get it over with. "Has Charlotte told you anything about coming to Calexico to get me at the bus station?"

Verlan's grin vanished. "No, not a word. But then, we haven't had a chance to talk. Why didn't you just take the bus to San Diego?"

I sighed and began to explain, telling of my decision to cross the border at Mexicali and about my inability to obtain a visa because of my age. I decided to omit the part about the American Consulate interrogating me, afraid that Verlan would become angry and refuse to let me travel alone again to Colonia LeBaron.

"I was sick—too weak to take care of myself. Then this nice young man happened along and noticed that I was having some difficulty—so he offered to help me get to the bus station. It was a good thing, too. I almost passed out before we got there. It was awful. Everything went black. This man—Jake—kept saying that I was too ill to travel alone, and he insisted on calling Charlotte for me. He was kind enough to sit with me until she got there; wasn't that nice of him? Well, Charlotte walked in and saw me with him. She blew up, of course. She naturally thought the worst. She's never said a civil word to me, Verlan, not since the day I married you."

Verlan was silent, frowning. Finally he said, "You're not telling me something. What made you sick?"

I hesitated, my heart pounding. I had been waiting for this moment for six long weeks. Now it was here, but nothing was as I had planned. The renewed closeness between us had withered again, leaving only a stifling resentment in my heart. But I was beginning to show and I couldn't put it off forever.

"I'm pregnant," I said simply.

He sat beside me and took my hand. A growing silence, more eloquent than any amount of words, filled the trailer. I waited, sensing a battle within him. Finally he looked at me. His eyes were shadowed, but his voice was light as he said, "Well now, what do you know? Another baby. When's it due?"

I stared at him. "Another baby? Verlan, in case you'd forgotten, this is my first."

"Oh, I know that. What I meant was, Lucy told me two weeks ago that she's expecting, too. That'll be two more babies by next winter to add to the family. Let's see . . . that will make twenty seven, all together."

Suddenly he grinned and patted me, "So that's why you were sick, huh? I didn't expect you to get pregnant so fast. You're so young. It wouldn't have hurt to have waited for another year, but it's too late to think about that now, isn't it?" He smiled again, broader this time, resigned to the news. Then he leaned over and quickly kissed me. "Zion's certainly growing. Good for you."

He stood, grabbed his jacket, and stepped toward the door. Then he hesitated and turned, watching me with a strange look in his eyes. "Don't make a habit of turning to other men, Susan," he finally said. "I'm sure you know that I won't put up with it. You're my wife, and I expect you to behave as such. 'Night, sweetheart."

After he was gone I huddled in the bed, alone and desolate, crushed beyond belief. My hand went to the tiny lump in my tummy, feeling how hard it was. He's not one bit happy about the baby, I thought dully. It's just one more. Number twenty-seven. My baby is just surplus! Hot tears dropped onto my pillow.

I can't go on, I thought throughout the long night. I'm too weak and selfish to be a woman in the church, to live this way. Oh, is it wrong to need my husband's arms around me, to need the feeling that I'm loved and protected, to want to feel like my child is special?

"Lord," I suddenly cried out into the stillness of the trailer, "Oh, Lord, I wanted my husband to be excited about our baby!"

I tossed in the bed, suddenly remembering the thoughtfulness and concern the sailor, Jake, had shown me. I remembered the warm feeling of his arm around my shoulders, the caring way he had felt my forehead and rubbed my cold hands. He had truly seemed concerned about my welfare, had treated me as if I were special and important. I had liked the feel of his hands. I tightly closed my eyes, squirming with shame as an unbidden longing swept through me. But I couldn't deny it. I wished Jake were here, his arm around my shoulders, his eyes friendly and gentle.

"Oh, God in Heaven, no, no, I can't think such things," I groaned, sickened by my own weakness. "I don't want to think about another man—or wish for his presence. It's wrong! Sinful!" Yet, from the back of my mind surged the memory of Lillie with Verlan. How could it be right that Verlan could hold Lillie in his arms without a twinge of guilt? Even as the thoughts stormed inside me, I remembered that it was God's plan. A man was created to have several wives, as Father Abraham had. As King David of old had. All the Old Testament prophets had lived polygamy. It was the supreme test for God's chosen people, an opportunity for growth that the ordinary person didn't have. It was what separated the Christians who were merely saved, from those who actually attained godhood. Loneliness here on earth was a woman's lot, just as having to deal with, and support many women and children, was a man's. It would be different in heaven. I had to believe that.

It was late the next afternoon before I saw Verlan again. During the morning he had taken Beverly and Lucy to Ensenada to do the grocery shopping. While they were gone, I helped Charlotte's girls with the wash. Then I returned to my trailer and unpacked my clothes.

The guitar I had brought with me needed tuning, and I picked it up and fussed with it for awhile. The melancholy sound of the instrument fit my mood, and I soon lay back against my pillows, lightly strumming a Mexican folk tune. When Verlan stepped in the door, I was startled.

"I didn't know you played the guitar!" he boomed, dropping down next to me.

"I don't, at least not much. Mom and Dad gave it to me years ago for my birthday."

215

"It's a beauty," he said, fingering the blond wood. He took it from my arms and fretted the strings, his broad forehead creased in concentration as he struggled with a forgotten chord. For the very first time, he was actually doing something in my trailer other than sleeping with me. He relaxed like normal people.

Verlan eased the guitar onto his lap and said, "Honey, I've been thinking. How would you like to go to Los Molinos for a couple of weeks? Your Aunt Thelma and Uncle Bud are there now, and I'll bet they'd love to have you stay with them. Would you like that?"

I sat up straight and stared, excitement stirring inside me. "Oh," I exclaimed, "Oh, I would love to!" Then I thought of Lucy. How could I possibly leave her again? I hesitated, then added, "Verlan, I'd love to go, but what about Lucy? There is so much for her to do."

"Rhea and Laura will just have to help more," he said firmly. "And it wouldn't hurt for Beverly to help her, either."

He set the guitar aside and pulled me close. "Do you have any idea how much you mean to me?" he said gruffly against my hair. I pulled back and searched his face, again noting a trace of anxiousness in his blue-green eyes. "I want you to be happy, my little charm, and I know you're not happy living here. I know that you're lonely, and I feel bad about it. Sometimes I wonder what right I have . . . " Verlan hesitated. "Having a wonderful girl like you waiting around for me to come home. It doesn't seem fair, yet I don't know what to do about it. If it weren't for the promise of a blessed eternity, I would never put you through it."

I listened in shocked surprise. Verlan took a ragged breath, and as I looked up into his face again, I was astounded at the emotional struggle inside him that it mirrored. There was so much about my husband that I didn't know or understand. He had always kept his feelings hidden, at least, hidden from me. His outburst was an involuntary revelation of his inner self, letting me see just a glimpse of his heart. He closed his eyes for a moment, and I could sense the tears just beneath the surface. "I have got to spend more time with my family," he muttered. "I've got to work it out somehow. Beverly's just as unhappy as you are; she won't even speak to me half the time. I know it's because she's hurting, and I'm the one to blame." He looked down at me, his eyes dark as they met mine. "Do you love me, Susan?"

I blinked, astounded at his question. "You know I do." The words were almost a sob, coming from deep inside my soul. "I love you too much. So much that I ache inside, longing for you to be with me. How can you question it?"

He squeezed my hand and sighed, "You haven't told me for a long time, and I guess I wouldn't blame you if you didn't. I don't feel worthy of you. You've been so patient with me—so sweet and good. Susan, I will find a way to make a living in Mexico, where I can have my families around me. It's a priority, and I am making plans. My dream is to have my families all together in one place, where I can see each wife and each child every day. I've told you this before, but I want you to know that someday soon I'll make my dream into a reality. I've got to start putting my family first, and the church is just going to have to accept that."

"Verlan," I faltered, then continued, "Explain something to me. Why don't you let your wives take turns going with you to Las Vegas, so that we can spend some time with you? It seems so silly for you to spend so much of your life alone, when you could have someone with you. The Leany's wouldn't mind if you had a wife sharing your room. What would be wrong with it?"

Verlan shook his head. His jaw hardened in a determined line. "It would never work," he said flatly. "I've explained it to you before. If I should be pulled over by a cop and have one of you under-age girls with me, I could be slapped in jail on Mann-act charges. It's not worth the risk, especially now that you're pregnant."

"Couldn't you pass me off as your daughter?"

"It wouldn't work. It's not worth the risk, my love."

Verlan stood up. "I'm leaving for Los Molinos in an hour. Be ready to go, and have enough clothes packed for at least two weeks. We'll have a fun trip. It'll be just you and me," he nuzzled his face against mine, kissed my forehead, and stepped out of the trailer.

Chapter 24

"Los Molinos is growing fast; you'll like it there, Susan," Verlan sounded confident leaning back in his chair, his bright gaze languidly traveling the length of the tiny restaurant where we had stopped on the way to Los Molinos. He nodded to affirm his words. "You're going to feel right at home. I'll probably have to pry you away to get you back to Ensenada until we can move down for good."

I smiled and murmured a response, baffled by the change in his demeanor. He seemed so relaxed and different from the nervous, troubled man who had arrived at Charlotte's in San Diego two days ago. His eyes sparkled with renewed life, as though a heavy burden had been lifted from his shoulders. I didn't begin to understand him. He had waved Ervil's latest schemes away as though they were nothing, completely confident that the Lord wouldn't allow His plans for His chosen people to be thwarted. Verlan was behaving as though his decision to move the rest of his families to Los Molinos was the answer to all of his troubles.

"I can hardly wait to get all of you girls moved," he continued. "I've worried about this until my head ached, weighing the reasons for and against us moving on down. And, well, I've made up my mind to not put it off any longer."

I nodded and took a sip of water. "I could never understand why you moved the family to Ensenada in the first place, so far away from the rest of the church."

Verlan shrugged. "Joel thought it would be a good idea to have someone living there, and he was right. The place served its purpose for awhile, but it's time I got my family settled. Of course, Los Molinos is a long old drive from Las Vegas, so I won't be able to see you girls as often as before. At least until I scrape the money together to build you each a house. Then I'll find a way to stay home a good share of the time. But for now, I can't have you girls and the kids in Ensenada suffering any longer without the association of the church."

I nodded again, determined to enjoy Verlan's enthusiasm. But I wondered if the decision he had made to move us to Los Molinos was the only cause of his new excitement. I reached across the table and squeezed his hand. "I'm glad, Verlan, really glad. We'll finally all be together, as it should be. Especially Charlotte and her kids."

218

"Charlotte's agreed to quit her teaching as soon as school's out in San Diego. I plan to have her house built by then. She and Lucy'll have to live together until Lucy's house is built, but they'll manage. They've done it before."

I laughed, loving the way his eyes sparkled. "They're doing it now, remember?"

Verlan was quiet as the waitress served our food. Then he shook his head, "Can't please Irene, though. We finally got her house finished, and now she's complaining about having to live in it. She's just sick about having to give up her tent."

"Oh, go on!" I stared at him.

His eyes glistened with mirth. "She said she didn't have to mop the tent floor or do windows, claims it saved her hours." He chuckled and took a bite of his hamburger. "She's a true pioneer, that woman."

I giggled. Irene and her children had camped out for months without a real roof over their heads—and she joked about it! Verlan had every reason to be proud of her, and he was; it showed in his eyes.

I wanted him to be proud of me, too. I wanted to see that same glint of admiration in his eyes when he looked at, or talked about me. I wanted him to think of me as an asset to his family, just as he thought of Irene. Well, his pride in me would come. I would make it happen.

He suddenly squinted at me, his eyebrows drawing together in a scowl. "Why is all that black stuff on your eyelashes again?" he demanded. "You don't need it. I wish you'd quit wearing it. And I wish you hadn't cut your hair. I liked it better long."

I looked away. Well! I thought. So much for copying Lillie's haircut. He just loves her shoulder-length hair and made up lashes, but not mine. A frown of annoyance crept onto my lips, but suddenly I remembered my plan to earn Verlan's respect. Forcing a grin instead, I drawled, "Verlan, my dear, perhaps my new hair style and makeup doesn't make me look any better, but it makes me feel like I look glamorous. That's important, don't you think?"

He blinked his eyes, an amused smile beginning to play around his mouth. "I see. I guess it is, my little charm. Only remember: Destruction follows those who ride with vain spirits in saddles of pride. Keep that in mind. Now, hurry up and finish your sandwich."

At a small community called Guerrero we left the main highway. The winding dirt road that took us on over the hill to the new community of Los Molinos was rough. I held onto the door handle as I strained my eyes in the darkness for the first sight of the pioneer settlement I had heard so much about. The moon shone brightly, and as we came to the crest of the hill, its soft yellow light revealed the few scattered buildings below. I eagerly scanned the layout. To one side of the new colony, I could just make out a strange, round object suspended from the sky, like a giant spider on a strand of webbing. As we drew nearer I saw that there were three of the shadowy pendulums, at different locations across the valley.

"Verlan, what are they?" I asked in wonder.

He chuckled. "Hasn't anyone ever told you where Los Molinos got its name? They're windmills—molinos in Spanish. Joel and my brother Floren built them out of huge sheets of plywood. The wind blows constantly here, and those contraptions pump enough water to make this ocean-side desert blossom like the proverbial rose. Picturesque, aren't they?"

"That they are," I agreed. As we entered the settlement, I continued to examine the gigantic windmills, craning my neck to see the top of them. They looked like something you would expect to see in Holland, and lent an exotic touch to this tiny, moonlit, new colony.

Verlan pulled the car off the main road, parking it next to a pickup camper sitting on jacks. It was Uncle Bud's camper, the one he had brought to Colonia LeBaron. His pickup was parked close by, next to a partially finished adobe building. The camper was shrouded in darkness, and I hesitated, suddenly feeling uncomfortable.

"We shouldn't wake 'em, Verlan," I whispered. "Let's wait until morning."

"Nonsense," he whispered back, confidently tapping on the camper door. "They'll be glad to see you."

Stirring noises came from inside the tiny camper, then a light came on, the door swung open, and Aunt Thelma's youthful frame stood silhouetted against the light.

"Hi, Aunt Thelma!" Verlan practically shouted through the still night. "See who I brought to visit you!"

"Susan!" she squealed. "Oh, Bud, its Susan and Verlan! Come in, honey. My goodness, what a surprise."

As we crowded inside, Uncle Bud pulled on a robe and climbed from the bed. He planted a loud kiss on my cheek, then pumped Verlan's hand and playfully socked his shoulder. "It's about time you brought her down to see us," he groused.

I threw a quick glance around. The camper was warm and homey. It smelled of spaghetti sauce and homemade bread, exactly as I remembered Mom's kitchen back in Colonia LeBaron. In minutes Verlan and I were seated with them at the tiny table. Uncle Bud's arm was warm around my shoulders as we sipped cocoa and listened to Aunt Thelma talk.

"It's been an experience, with all of us living in this camper, I can tell you," she happily rattled. "Mark and Duane are sleeping under the stars, in what will be their bedroom once the house is finished. Rena's turned the storage shed into her room for the time being. Susan, you can sleep with her. It's crowded, but I'm sure the two of you'll manage. Oh, we're so glad to finally be here, Verlan. And we're having such a good time getting settled in. It's like playing house," her eyes twinkled as she glanced at Uncle Bud.

I chuckled, realizing from whom Lorna had inherited her ability to make the best of things. Aunt Thelma had spunk and spirit and had turned what normally would be a time of hardship and backbreaking labor into an adventure. I was going to enjoy staying here.

"Has Lorna had her baby?" I broke in.

"Yes, the poor dear had another boy. They named him Aaron. Aaron LeBaron. Isn't that awful?" Thelma shuddered. "I couldn't stay with her very long, since we were in the middle of moving. But she's doing okay. She's still in San Diego, waiting for Ervil to come from Colonia LeBaron to meet the new baby and take her back to that dump in Ensenada."

She sniffed, shook her head, stood, and poured more cocoa. "I'm certainly not happy about her going back there. I wish she'd move here, where I can keep an eye on her. But Ervil's convinced her that he needs a wife living in Ensenada, so she's going back. She's really enjoyed having you close, Susan. She talked about you a lot."

I felt Verlan tense at Thelma's words about Ervil. He drained the last of his cocoa in a quick gulp and stood. "I better go see how Irene and Ester are doing. I'll be back sometime tomorrow to see you, Susan. Thanks, Thelma, for letting her stay here." He squeezed my hand, grinned at me, and stepped out of the camper. "Night, everyone," he called.

As I watched Verlan go, I realized that for the first time since our wedding I felt no emptiness at seeing him leave. I knew it was because I felt at home with my aunt and uncle.

"That Verlan's quite a guy," Uncle Bud said. "Not as much sparkle as Ervil, but he's all LeBaron."

Aunt Thelma frowned and glanced pointedly at me. I stared into my cup, my face turning red. It was like comparing a snake to a bunny rabbit, and I began to say as much, then quickly decided against it. Ervil was Bud's son-in-law, and I didn't want to get our visit off on the wrong foot.

"I think I'll turn in," I said instead.

Rena's shed was drafty and cramped, the double bed barely leaving room to fit my body inside the door. I shivered as I undressed. The night air was cold and moist, and I crawled in next to my cousin's sleeping form, grateful for her body heat. I smiled in anticipation of the surprise on her face in the morning at finding me in bed with her.

I continued to smile as I settled into the soft pillow and began to relax. I was looking forward to spending time with my relatives. I would also get to see Irene. But mostly, my new happiness was because of the time I had spent with Verlan. The elusive closeness between us was back, and more wonderful than before. Again I felt in love with him. I had to cherish these feelings. Loving Verlan would carry me through the hard times.

Suddenly I jumped, my body tensing. What in the hell! There! There it was again, a tiny pair of pinchers on my thigh. Another nabbed onto my rump, and I howled as I scrambled from the bed and frantically shook out my nightgown.

"Rena! Rena, get out of the bed!" I screamed as my fingers reached for a match. Graphic pictures of spiders and centipedes flashed through my mind.

Rena turned over and blankly stared up at me, trying to focus her sleepy eyes. "Susan! What . . ."

"There's bugs in the bed!" I hissed. "Get out of there quick!"

Her eyes widened and she drew up her legs and began to roll. Then she stopped on the edge of the mattress and began to laugh. Sitting up, she pushed a mop of shiny brown hair from her eyes.

"They're sand fleas," she explained, grinning. "We have lots of 'em." She stood and tossed back the quilts. A tiny brown speck on the white sheet jumped. Another crawled under the pillow. Rena pointed to yet another one.

"See? I forgot to powder the bed this morning." She looked at my white face with a sympathetic grin. "You'll get used to 'em. When did you get here?"

As I explained, I reluctantly eyed the bed, wondering if I had the courage to crawl back in and let the fleas have a go at me. Rena settled down without hesitation, casually scratching her leg as I talked. "Come on, get in before you freeze to death," she chuckled. "They don't really hurt, you know."

In spite of her assurance, I spent a rather sleepless night. My every sense was tuned to the tiny fleas jumping around under the covers, and it seemed that each time I drifted, a sound pinch woke me again. The bites itched, and I was soon joining Rena and scratching throughout the long night.

As we changed the bed the next morning, the tiny drops of blood that were scattered over the sheets evidenced the feast that had occurred through the night. Rena handed me a can of flea-killer, and I powdered until I was satisfied that nothing short of a human could survive. As I dressed, I surveyed the red bumps on my body, the first drawback to Los Molinos.

After eggs and toast with Rena, my aunt and uncle, I followed Aunt Thelma to the outside of the camper for a look at the new colony. The smell of salt was in the air. The settlement sprawled on a rolling meadow about two miles from the sea. The land was barren, other than a few straggly eucalyptus saplings sprouting on the western edge of the lots for windbreaks. As we strolled around the acre parcel, Aunt Thelma pointed out the different homes that were situated around their place. She rattled off the names of the residents, some of whom were new to me. Most of the dwellings were ancient, single-wide mobile homes, with fields and gardens planted in between. But there were several adobe houses, and a few wood frame buildings under construction. Already I could hear the muffled sound of hammers and other tools. Just as Verlan had said, Los Molinos was springing up fast.

"Well, what do you think?" Aunt Thelma demanded, sweeping an arm around me. I chuckled, noting her smug gleam. The Chynoweths had only been living here a short while, but Aunt Thelma was as proud of Los Molinos as though she had planned and built it herself.

"I think I'm impressed," I grinned. "It's beginning to look like a real town. And Lucy and Beverly, and Charlotte and I will be living here soon. Verlan told me yesterday that he plans to move us down as soon as the children are out of school."

"Did he tell you that we have a school built?"

"A church-run school? No. Who will be the teachers?"

"Steve Silver will be the main one. See that adobe building over there, close to that windmill? That's the school. It's serving a double purpose right now. We're holding Sunday meetings there until we can afford to build a real church. We're super excited about having our own school, although it's going to take some more work and planning before we're ready to start classes."

Aunt Thelma glanced at me. "Steve's asked me to help him teach. I just couldn't say no to him." She sighed, but I could see a twinkle in her blue eyes.

I stared at her curiously. "Oh, I would think you'd enjoy teaching. Wouldn't you?"

She chuckled, "Truth is, I'm thrilled to death he asked me. I've always thought that I would make a good teacher. The problem is Steve and I won't be able to handle all the classes alone. We're going to have to find someone else for the younger grades."

Aunt Thelma's voice trailed off and stopped. She stared at me, her eyes widening as she grinned. "Susan! You could help us teach!"

I looked at her blankly. "Me! Oh, no. I couldn't teach school. I don't know the first thing about it, and I didn't even finish school myself."

"Well, honey, I don't know much about it, either. But that doesn't matter, Steve has experience, and he'll train us. Besides, you're smart. I know you could do it, and we need someone who's not tied down to a houseful of kids. There are so many children! Of course, the high school kids will still go to the school in Guerrero, the town just over the hill that you drove through on the way here. We'll have our hands full with the elementary ages. There'll be almost a hundred kids, once Verlan brings the rest of his family down."

"Wow!" I whistled in surprise. Zion was indeed growing, just as Verlan had said. Suddenly I laughed, becoming intrigued by the idea. "Teaching is something to think about, isn't it? It would certainly give me something to do, and I've been needing something. We'll see."

As we walked back toward the camper, I glanced again at the distant house that Aunt Thelma had identified as Irene's. Someone was on a ladder, painting the eaves a dull yellow. There's Verlan, I thought, shading my eyes against the rising sun. He's already hard at work. One of these days he'll build me a home, too, a home of my own. Tingles of excitement shivered through me. My life was beginning to come together.

Uncle Bud puttered around the unfinished building as we stopped in front of the camper. He had loaded tools onto the scaffold, and was hitching at his pants and glancing around.

"Thelma!" he roared, "Get those lazy boys up. Daylight's wasting—let's get some work done around here."

Mark and Duane were already up and hovering over the table, wolfing their breakfast. Mark grinned at me, his mouth full. "Hi, Suze! You sure showed up at the perfect time. Dad'll have you pouring cement before the morning's out, mark my words."

I laughed and flexed my muscles. "Right. The new house'll go up fast now that I'm here."

Thirteen-year-old Duane kissed my cheek, then glowered at Mark. "Just so you know, brother, dear. I'm not gonna be the go-fer all day again. I'm sick of it, and I'm going to talk Dad into lettin' me help him lay adobes. I can do it just as good as you."

"Okay, boys, your dad's ready to get started, so move out," Aunt Thelma broke in. She pulled on a pair of gloves and threw me a pair. "Let's go," she said. "Rena, you stay here and clean up the camper."

As we gathered around the work area, Uncle Bud pointed to a bucket and shovel. "Duane, start hauling water and get to mixing. I need mud," he ordered.

Duane groaned, looking at his mother with mournful, hazel eyes that were like Lorna's. "I'm sick of being the peon around here," he grumbled as he picked up the bucket. "It's no fun. Why can't I lay adobes for a change? I can do it."

Mark snorted and began loading adobes into a wheelbarrow. "It takes an expert brick mason, dummy. You just stick to something you can handle. Stick to the mud." He grinned. Grunting, he pushed the wheelbarrow of adobes to the work area.

Aunt Thelma opened a straw bale and scattered straw into the large mixing hole. "Come on Duane, pour some water in here," she said briskly. I pulled on my gloves, picked up a shovel, and helped Thelma mix straw into the soft earth in the hole. Duane sloshed water in, then waited as we mixed it together.

The morning hours flew; the wall grew higher. On the scaffold, Mark fit adobes onto a layer of mud, then smoothed the sides with a trowel. Uncle Bud placed another adobe, chipping at it with the edge of the trowel to make it fit. He dumped mud between the bricks, scraped the sides smooth, then used a level and checked accuracy.

"Hey, peon," Mark hollered over his shoulder to Duane. "Hoist that mud up here. And add a little more water in the next batch; this is too thick."

Duane glowered at his brother as he trudged closer and lifted the heavy bucket over his head. "It just ain't fair, Dad," he whined. "I have to do all the haulin' and mixin' and put up with him telling me what to do, when he's only a few years older'n me." Screwing up his mouth, Duane mimicked in a high falsetto: "Go add more water to the mud, peon."

Uncle Bud snickered. Then he roared with laughter. "Why don't you save yourself the work of hauling the water from the well, Duane, just go pee on the mud."

"Bud!" Aunt Thelma choked. "Don't you think these guys come up with enough of that sort of rubbish on their own, without you putting in your two cents worth? Why don't you let Duane have a turn up there with you? Mark can help down here."

"Aw, Mom . . ."

Duane shot a look of triumph at his brother. "You heard her. Climb on down, Smart Aleck." The switch was made. And in spite of Mark's lack of faith in his brother's ability, the adobe wall progressed beautifully.

The sun was beginning to set, and Aunt Thelma and I were preparing supper, when Verlan knocked on the camper door. "The boys and I just completed the finishing coat on Irene's house," he said as I joined him outside. "She's got a big supper cooked and asked me to bring you over. She was mad that I didn't take you to her place last night, but I explained that you wanted to see your relatives. So she's cooked up this big supper and asked me to come get you."

"Go on, Susan," Aunt Thelma called. "I'll save you a piece of cake."

As we tramped across the weed-covered meadow toward Irene's, a man working on a distant rooftop waved to us. Verlan returned the greeting, shading the sun from his eyes as he watched. "That's Joel, helping Fernando get his roof on," Verlan said.

I stared at Joel as we continued toward Irene's. His red hair glistened in the late afternoon sunshine, his head dropping with each stroke of the hammer. Building someone's roof seemed a menial task for a Prophet of God, who had the entire world to bring to salvation. I had always wanted to know Joel better. Perhaps now that I was here in Los Molinos I would have the opportunity.

I breathed deeply of the ocean air and looked again at the place that would soon be my home. There was something special about this colony. Something that drew me—excited me. These people were working to fulfill a God-given charge—to prepare a place of safety to which the people of the world could retreat when the time of the destruction came—the horrible end of times spoken of in the *Book of Revelations*. Joel's people here had a purpose—to help him build Zion. Of course, Colonia LeBaron had the same purpose since its founding, but I had been a child then. I had been too young to know the spirit of united effort toward a common goal that was manifested by the people there. But now I was a grown woman, prepared to join the rest of the saints and push the work of the Lord ahead, right here in Los Molinos.

Verlan and I skirted a fence at the back of Irene's lot. Goats bleated from a pen at one corner, and Verlan reached over the fence and patted the sleek black and white hide of a nanny. "How you doin', Heather," he murmured.

226

From what appeared to be a kitchen window, I saw Irene wave to us. Then she hurried out the back door. "Hi!" she called, her face creased in a huge smile. She hurried to me and hugged me tight, then soundly kissed my cheek. Her blue eyes danced as she held me away. "Let me look at you! Yep, Verlan was right. You're just as pretty as ever."

"Oh, Irene, I'm not . . ." I grinned and blushed, at a loss for words. She was as warm and friendly as ever. Surely this was what the Lord had in mind when He said that sister-wives should get along. How could anyone not want to be friends with a person like Irene?

She grinned at Verlan and took his arm, then twined her other arm through mine, and pulled us toward the house. "I really should feel jealous of you, you know," she teased me. "But somehow I'm not. I'm just tickled to death that you're here. I wanted Verlan to bring you down months ago, but he was afraid you wouldn't like our tent. It was rather nice, actually; not much housekeeping to do."

Verlan chuckled, glancing at me over the top of Irene's head.

"The house looks real nice," I said, admiring the paint job as Verlan opened the kitchen door. Suddenly clear was the reason Verlan hadn't finished the plumbing and the other devices in the house in Ensenada. He had known that the place there would only be temporary.

Verlan was certainly spending money on Irene's home, reminding me of my resolution in Colonia LeBaron to ask him for an allowance. I couldn't put it off much longer because I was becoming desperate for clothing.

We entered the neat, modest kitchen. The cement floors had been painted apple green, and had bright, braided rugs scattered about. A stainless steel cabinet with a built-in sink stood against one wall. In one corner sat an old refrigerator. A blond boy peered into its interior. He looked at me and gave me a shy smile.

"Kaylen, this is Aunt Susan," Verlan said.

The next few minutes were a carbon copy of my first day at the big house in Ensenada, with fewer new faces and new names to remember. Irene's ten, fair-haired children, along with one dark-haired little adopted girl, crowded around us. Irene introduced her brood to me, then shooed most of them outside for the evening chores. "You and Verlan sit down and visit while I set the table," she commanded, hurrying away.

Verlan had settled onto the couch, and patted the seat beside him. "Come sit by me, honey. Well, now, you've almost met the whole family, all but Ester and her kids, and you'll meet them at the church tomorrow." Leaning back, he shook his head. "I don't know what Ester's problem is, but she has never spoken to any of my other wives. She just refuses to have anything to do with them. She doesn't understand what a blessing she's missing."

The dining room table was covered with an eight-foot piece of plywood to make it long enough for such a crowd. We sat down to a meal of enchiladas, Spanish rice, and beans smothered in melted goat cheese. On the kitchen cupboard were three pies, topped with lightly toasted meringue.

"Susan, what do you think of our little town?" Irene asked as she dished up the food. Her voice rang with pride, just as Aunt Thelma's had.

"I like what I've seen of it," I said emphatically. "I'm looking forward to meeting everyone."

She waved her hand. "Oh, everyone'll be at church tomorrow, and tomorrow afternoon a bunch of us are planning to go to the beach for a picnic. It's still a little cold, but we'll bundle up. You'll come along, of course? I'm sure Thelma and Bud will be going."

As we ate, I watched Irene's children, and I had to smile. They were so much like their mother. They bickered as to whose turn it was to talk, telling me one exciting story after another. Verlan proudly observed them, laughing over their expressiveness and bragging about their small achievements.

The major dinner subject was the birth of a set of twin goats. Steven, the thirteen-year old, was insistent that he be the one to show them to me. "They're my goats!" Andre, the older boy, roared at Steven. "I'll be the one to show 'em to her! You just mind your own business!"

"Boys, boys!" Verlan broke in. "You can both show them to her. Steven feeds them too, Andre. He should get to show at least one of them to her." That settled the argument.

It was fully dark as we finished the meal, and Verlan excused himself to go say goodnight to Ester. The boys found a flashlight and led me outside.

"They are fine animals," I assured them, looking the goats over. "You must be real proud. Both of you."

"They're the nicest ones we've ever had," Andre bragged. "You wouldn't believe how much milk these two nannies give. We have cheese all the time now." We tramped back to the house, the boys keeping up a constant stream of conversation.

Irene looked at us, her arms filled with leftovers from dinner. "Let me just get these dishes done, then we can visit before Verlan gets back," she said.

"Can I help?" I offered.

"Sure," Irene pointed to a kettle, "heat the water in that. Andre, go get Aunt Susan a bucket of water."

The children crowded around as we cleaned the kitchen and tried to visit over the noise. "You kids, leave us alone for a few minutes, will you?" Irene finally hollered, exasperated. "Go on, now, every one of you. Get your clothes laid out for church tomorrow."

"We already did that," Steven said, grinning.

"Then go do your homework."

Andre looked at Steven. "I don't have any homework. Do you have any homework, Steve? Donna, do you?"

"Nope. Why can't we stay here with you and Aunt Susan, Mom?"

Irene glared at them. "Because we haven't had a minute alone! Go on, all of you, before I get mad."

They reluctantly left the kitchen, and I admired them, thinking that my own child would resemble Irene's, with their thick blond hair and blue eyes. I glanced at Irene, wondering if she would be happy about my pregnancy.

"Did Verlan tell you that I'm going to have a baby?" I blurted out before I lost the nerve.

She stared at me, her face breaking into a smile. "No! My goodness, Susan, you didn't waste any time. How far along are you?"

"It'll be the end of September."

I anxiously watched her, praying that her pleased reaction was genuine. Then I looked away, satisfied. "Susan LeBaron," she crowed, "You are going to give us a beautiful, beautiful baby. Verlan is going to be so proud of you!"

I smiled faintly. "I hope so," I muttered, remembering his rather cool reception of the news.

I could feel Irene's eyes on me. "What do you mean, you hope so?" she demanded. "Of course he will. There is nothing in this world that means more to Verlan than his children. He's told me that a hundred times. They are an eternal blessing to him, one that not even death can take away."

She paused, staring at me. "He said something dumb when you told him, didn't he? What did he say to you?"

"It was nothing," I said swiftly, regarding her flustered face. "I'm way too sensitive. I can't expect him to be as excited as I am; after all, he's been through having a new baby countless times." I slowly smiled. "But thank you for being happy for me. It means a lot."

As I walked with Verlan back to Aunt Thelma's later, I realized that I loved Irene. She was going to be a true blessing in my life. I now understood how a sister-wife could be considered real family.

Church the next day was a continual learning experience. Uncle Bud's group and I arrived early at the large adobe building, and as each Los Molinos resident arrived, Aunt Thelma introduced me. I knew several of the men, because they had come to Colonia LeBaron for the conferences. Most of them had also come to the priesthood meeting in Ensenada. But most of their wives and children were virtual strangers. I curiously observed the women of Los Molinos as they crowded around. They shook hands and hugged each other and me. Every one of them seemed in good spirits, excited, and truly happy. I sensed again the spirit of unity, the feeling that these people had a deep, abiding purpose in life, one that lifted them above their toilsome, meager existence onto a higher, richer plane. I determined to explore this attitude that they wore like a banner of success.

When Verlan and Irene arrived, Verlan grabbed my hand and marched me to the front, seating me on the piano bench. "You and Aunt Thelma pick out some hymns," he whispered, grinning happily. "You're going to be a real hit around here. You should hear Brother Castro try to play the piano." He rolled his eyes and motioned for Aunt Thelma. As the meeting started my aunt and I made an admirable pair, with her leading the hymns and me playing the piano. The congregation crowding the adobe building beamed at us.

Soon I returned to the audience, sitting next to Verlan and Irene. I unobtrusively glanced about, wondering which of the Mexican women was Verlan's wife, Ester. Well, I thought, I will meet her soon enough. I settled back, eagerly listening as Joel took the pulpit.

"Brothers and Sisters," he began, "only once, in the recorded history of mankind, did God speak from the heavens and give to His children a specific guide for their conduct. Only once did He come to earth in person to deliver those commandments. So important did He consider the law which He gave on Mount Sinai, that He wrote it with His own hand and spoke it with His own mouth. That law is known today as the Ten Commandments. It is the same law which Jeremiah said God would put in the inward parts of His people and would write upon their hearts. Then would it be said that He was their God and that they were His people. This law, my brothers and sisters, is the perfect law of liberty. This very law will have to be established upon earth, beginning with us here, in Los Molinos, before our Savior can come again.

Through our faithful dedication, we will one day become as a light on a hill, an ensign to the nations . . . "

As I listened to the familiar sermon, thoughts of Ervil crept into my mind. It was remarkable how both of these leaders had clung to the Ten Commandments as the basis of their doctrine. Yet they so differently interpreted how it should be practiced. Joel maintained that it would take long years of education before the law could be put into force; meantime we could live the positive side of the law—by doing unto others what we would have them do unto us. If we could do this, we would rise to heights of peace and prosperity never before achieved. Ervil, on the other hand, lacked the patience to educate the people. He was set on putting the punishments into effect immediately, thereby forcing people, on penalty of death, to keep the law. This very difference was what had caused the primary breach between Joel and Ervil. Still, both men preached their own interpretation of the law to whoever would listen.

Verlan followed Joel at the pulpit. He cleared his throat and looked the congregation over with a faint smile. "You all know that we have our work cut out for us. Sometimes it overwhelms me, how our Heavenly Father expects so few of us to carry His message of salvation to the entire world. But it must be done, and He has promised us that we will succeed. He stands behind us, my friends. His strength is ours. He has given us the authority to speak and act in His name. As the gospel is poured out to the nations, the people of the world will flock to these heaven-chosen places of safety. We will be ready for them. We will be prepared to teach them the higher principles of the Gospel to attain Godhood with us."

Verlan spoke convincingly. I watched the people of Los Molinos absorb his words, nodding their heads in agreement. Verlan's effect on the church members was similar to Joel's, I realized. They looked to him almost as they did to Joel, as a God-appointed leader.

Brother Castro closed the meeting at noon. When we left the church and the strong leadership, I knew a renewed sense of peace and fellowship, something I hadn't felt since leaving Colonia LeBaron. My soul had craved this very thing. Los Molinos was going to be good for me.

"Susan," Irene called, picking up her long skirt and hurrying toward me as I stood with Aunt Thelma and Rena in the midst of a group of people. I turned, smiling. She took me aside, slipping her broad arm around my shoulders. "Verlan said to tell you he'll be over to see you for a few minutes before he leaves," she forced a smile. "Run, run, run. That's all he ever does.

Sometimes I wonder if we'll ever have him home." She tossed her head as though pushing the thought away. "You're going to the picnic?"

"I guess so, I forgot to ask the Chynoweth's." I glanced around, whispering, "Which one of those ladies is Ester?"

Irene's eyes twinkled. "She's not here today. I wonder why."

"Is it because I'm here?" I asked, dismayed.

"I'm sure it is, but don't worry about it," Irene said darkly. "She acts so stupid. I don't know how Verlan can stand her. Well, she's his problem. I'll see you later." She picked up her skirt and dashed across the churchyard toward her old pickup loaded with fair-headed children in their Sunday best.

"Hmm," I thought. "So Irene and Ester don't get along. Ester must really be something."

Verlan had changed from his suit to a pair of jeans and a Western shirt when he pulled up next to the Chynoweth's camper to tell me goodbye. "Come get in here with me," he called.

I climbed into the car, suddenly feeling that old familiar knot of loneliness but also the nagging fear for my husband's life, a fear that I couldn't dismiss as easily as he did. "You'll be back in two weeks?" I asked, staring out the window to hide the strain on my face.

"Yep. Two weeks. I'm planning to break ground for Charlotte's house when I come down. Now, I want you to enjoy your stay here, my Sweet. Irene hopes you will go see her real often, and I'm sure you'll enjoy her company." He sighed. "I wish I could spend more time with you, but duty calls." I fidgeted, continuing to stare out the window. I could feel Verlan's eyes on me. "What's on your mind?" he finally asked.

I took a deep breath and turned to face him. "Promise me you'll be careful. I know what you said, but I can't forget Ervil's words. I'm far from convinced that he was only spouting off. I just don't trust him, Verlan."

"I'll be careful," he said soberly. He glanced at me again, then reached for my hand. "I'd better go. I've a long drive ahead of me."

I closed my eyes, little fingers of aversion tickling my stomach. I had to do it. He wasn't offering. "Verlan," I choked, "Do you think you could give me some money? There are things I need." There. It was out.

He was silent, his fingers drumming on the steering wheel. Then he said, "Well, I could let you have a few dollars, I guess. Honey, after paying for Irene's house, and trying to put a bit aside to start Charlotte's, that doesn't leave much. But here, take this. I'm sorry it's not more."

He reached into his pocket, extracted three one-dollar bills, and handed them to me. I stared at them, my face burning. My lips stiff with shame, I slowly took the dollars from his hand. "Thank you," I managed, wadding them in my fist.

He leaned over and kissed me, "See you in two weeks."

I numbly watched the old, battered Chevelle until it climbed out of sight over the hill. Then I opened my palm and meticulously smoothed out my money. Folding the bills, I shoved them into the pocket of my dress and entered the camper.

Chapter 25

Verlan didn't keep his promise to return in two weeks to Los Molinos. On the night that I impatiently expected him, the Chevelle pulled into Chynoweth's driveway with Charlotte behind the wheel. I looked at her curiously as I walked to the car.

"Verlan asked me to drive down and let you girls know that he's gone on a mission to Oregon," she said as she opened the car door, her voice strained, tired.

My heart sank at the news. I watched in dismal silence as Charlotte pulled a huge bag filled with my belongings from the back seat. Then reaching in again, she fiddled with an old sheet, extracted my guitar, and handed it to me. I stared at it in surprise. This was a thoughtful gesture—one that left me a bit baffled.

"Thank you," I mumbled. "I really appreciate this."

She briefly smiled. Rummaging through her purse, she pulled out an envelope and handed it over. Then she stood uncertainly, the silence awkward as we searched for something else to say.

"My girls said to tell you hello," she said as she slid back into the car.

I smiled nodding. "Are you staying for the weekend?"

"Just the night. I need to be in Ensenada in the morning. Well, see you later," she backed out of the driveway.

The night air was chilly as I stood watching the taillights of Charlotte's car wink out of sight toward Irene's. She was actually making a stab at being friendly! Her bringing me the guitar was above the usual call of duty. She was finally beginning to accept me, knowing that we were stuck with one another forever. She may as well. The Lord gave me little things like Charlotte's bit of thoughtfulness to cling to when I felt like screaming my protests about how unfair life was.

Taking my armload into the small room that I shared with Rena, I lit the lamp, tore open the envelope of Verlan's letter, and held it under the light on the dresser. His scrawled handwriting covered half a page. "There are some prospective families in Eugene, Oregon, who are considering joining the church, my love. They really need someone to spend time with them, and I should go. I will be back in about four weeks. I'm sure you will enjoy staying with your aunt awhile longer. Know that I love you and wish I could be with you. Please be patient. Be happy and wait for me, Verlan."

Dropping onto the bed, I sighed, subconsciously scanning for fleas on the bedspread as I thought of the days ahead without even a glimpse of Verlan's teasing, reassuring face. I had felt so content for the past two weeks, and now my chest ached with emptiness. In spite of my husband's new resolve to prioritize his family, he again considered the call of the church as the more pressing issue. Well, I couldn't expect less of a man like Verlan—he was a messenger for the Lord first and foremost. Just as Grandma had said, I must forget my own needs and support Verlan's work.

Leaning my head against the plywood wall and closing my eyes, I was determined not to cry. I must be brave and selfless, just as the other wives had to be. They missed Verlan as much as I did, and needed him just as much, and I was certain they didn't pout all the time. I would be fine! I had the Chynoweths, and Irene, and plenty of people around to help fill in the gap. At least I wasn't stuck in Ensenada.

Straightening upright, I re-read Verlan's letter, savoring the assurances of his love. Then I folded the note, and hid it in the bottom of a drawer, beneath a pair of pants that no longer fit around my growing waist. Placing the letter out of sight symbolized my marriage to Verlan. Our life together had been shoved to a back burner, saved for a time when the Church didn't require his presence so much, for when our marriage could actually be lived like most people's marriages. It wouldn't be like this forever. Lingering, I smoothed the rough material down over the top of the letter.

I was so glad I would be staying in Los Molinos while he was away. The past two weeks had been filled with interesting and dedicated people, and the realization that the new colony was beginning to feel like home. I would be just fine.

Thelma and Bud's household was a busy one, and I had fit into their lives with hardly a hitch. Of course, the camper was crowded, but no one seemed to mind. "Don't you worry, honey, we'll just add a bit more water to the soup," was the way Uncle Bud put my fears of being an intruder to rest. Rena assured me that she liked having someone share her cold bed, someone who didn't forget to powder the sheets each morning.

Much of my time had been spent with Irene and her brood. Being with Irene, I could count on lots of laughs and joking to fill my day. We also shared our personal joys and heartaches. On one occasion I had told Irene about my resentment of Verlan's courtship of Lillie. "I guess I don't have any right to feel this way," I had confessed. "After all, I didn't hesitate to marry him."

Irene had chuckled. "Don't worry too much about her. I don't think she's serious about Verlan. All she could talk about the last time she was here, was some guy she works with in San Diego. Lillie's seen too much of how her mother goes without, married to Joel and all, to want to jump into the same kind of boat." Irene sucked at her tooth, a twinkle in her eyes. "Besides, I think Verlan is beginning to realize he has enough wives, don't you?"

I stared at her, my spirits soaring higher and higher, and I grinned. Of course! How could I have not realized what had been going through Verlan's mind on the trip down from Ensenada? His courtship of Lillie had been nothing but an effort to fulfill some sort of misplaced obligation—one from which he now found himself free. He had finally realized that enough was enough, which was the reason for the new sense of peace I had witnessed. I'd have never recognized the reason for it on my own, but Irene knew Verlan well. Irene was perceptive. And of course she was right! I would be Verlan's last wife after all, and the thought made me almost dizzy with happiness and relief. Irene was such a blessing to have for a sister-wife.

The people who lived in Los Molinos were warm and friendly, and never missed an opportunity to invite me over for a visit and a meal. All, that is, except for Ester, Verlan's fifth wife. Ester coldly avoided me. She was a small, attractive Mexican woman, who lived in a trailer house at the far edge of town. I hardly ever saw her. She stayed far away from me at meetings, and although I glanced at her several times, she never looked in my direction. The minute the meetings were over she always hastened away, her back stiff and unyielding. Her sister, Isabel, was married to Joel. The two women had several other brothers and sisters who lived in town. According to Irene, Ester spent all her time with her family. "And that's fine with me," Irene informed me. "She's so stuck up. She's never even been decent to me."

One afternoon Irene stopped by the Chynoweth's in her old, dilapidated pickup to take me to the small general store in Guererro. She helped select enough material for a maternity blouse, which cost me two of my three hoarded dollars. When we returned home, she helped me cut it out, and guided my efforts as I sewed it together on her machine.

"One blouse won't be enough, of course," she frowned as I tried the completed blouse on. Digging through a sack of material in her closet, she said, "Here, this piece ought to be big enough to make you another one. Let's go cut it out.

And if you'll bring me some of your pants, I'll sew stretch panels in them. They'll get you by for awhile."

As the days passed, the Chynoweth's new house took shape. Uncle Bud and the boys worked on it from dawn to dusk. Once the roof was on and the doors and windows were in, Uncle Bud and Mark traveled to Utah in the Prophet Joel's big truck for a load of their furniture which was being stored by my older Chynoweth cousin, Victor, in his garage. The men were back within a week, the old truck loaded to the top. Joel and Brother Castro came to help unload. Aunt Thelma bustled about, supervising, as the men hauled precious articles into the new house. Great was my joy when I saw the upright piano at the front of the truck, carefully wrapped in old quilts.

The moment the piano was placed in the living room, Mark pulled up a chair. His fingers danced across the keys. In his rich tenor, the words of "Light My Fire," the new rock song by The Doors filled the room. I stood at his side, listening in amazed delight.

Joel stopped work and leaned on the other side of the piano. He appeared amused by the words of the song, and by the way Mark had drifted into his own world, oblivious of the clamor around him. Shaking his head, Joel finally walked back outside. "I don't know about the songs he sings, Bud, but that boy of yours has talent," his words drifted in to me. "If he'd guide his musical ability in the right direction, he could be a real blessing to the church."

Uncle Bud's voice growled in answer, "Well, why don't you try telling him there's more to music than that loud, modern crap! Believe me, it don't do no good, Joel. Thelma wanted him to take up classical music, but he won't do it."

After a few minutes Uncle Bud hollered, "Duane, go tell Mark to stop goofing off and come help."

"Oh, no, let him play," Joel insisted. "We can get by without him. Music's good for the soul."

Aunt Thelma set a box down, her eyes met mine, and we both grinned. Joel, our Prophet, was enjoying Mark's kind of music. I could just imagine what Alma would think of the trashy lyrics Mark was crooning—or Verlan, for that matter. They would label the words offensive and evil. But Joel allowed people to be themselves.

It was wonderful to finally have the use of the big house. After we were settled, Steve Silver, the man who had taken on the task of being the colony schoolteacher, stopped by. Steve was an energetic, vigorous man, whose blond hair swooped back from his broad forehead in a perfect wave. Behind glasses, his brown eyes were alert and intelligent. As I listened to Steve and Aunt Thelma talk, I remembered Verlan telling me the history of Steve's conversion.

Steve had joined the Church of the Firstborn of the Fullness of Times in 1958, along with a group of nine other people. These people had all been Mormon missionaries stationed in France. During their spare time on the mission, these fervent young people had involved themselves in an extensive study of their Church doctrine, a study above and beyond the usual requirements for Mormon missionaries. Rumor was, the group found things in the Church history books that disturbed them. After much study and prayer, dismayed, they concluded that the doctrine being taught by the modern day Mormon Church was incorrect. From what they'd read, it appeared to them that their beloved Latter-day Saints had changed the original teachings—teachings that Joseph Smith had professed to be "unchangeable and everlasting!"

One of the nine missionaries ran across a copy of *Priesthood Expounded*, a book Ervil had written under Joel's direction. This missionary shared the LeBaron brothers' book with his young friends, and together, they poured over its contents. They concluded that Ervil's book was based on correct, unchanged principles; the same principles that Joseph Smith had taught in the original Mormon Church. Excited, yet deeply troubled, they took the book to their superiors in the mission field. According to *Priesthood Expounded*, the Mormon Church was in trouble.

The nine missionaries were excommunicated for their efforts and sent home, causing a dreadful scandal throughout the L.D.S. Church. Subsequently, Steve and the others made their way from France to Mexico and Colonia LeBaron to find Joel. They desired to ask him more about the teachings in *Priesthood Expounded*. After talking with Joel at length, the missionaries accepted his claim to the Mantle, acknowledged him as the One Mighty and Strong (the name of the chosen Vessel of God), and joined Joel's struggling new Church.

Steve Silver was the only one of the original nine Mormon missionaries to move to Los Molinos. Joel had asked him to join the pioneer efforts at colonizing the new gathering place. Earning respect with his dynamic, positive personality, he attracted me as well as many others. I could see why Joel had selected him to be in charge of the school.

And now, Steve was explaining the tasks to be completed for the preparation of the new school, and he wanted to know if Thelma and I were ready to go to work.

"You bet," Aunt Thelma said promptly, answering for the both of us. "Just lead the way."

We started early the next morning, sorting and re-binding books. During the following days, we helped Steve paint blackboards, sand and re-varnish the old, donated desks, and follow up on other chores Steve put before us. I enjoyed keeping busy and knowing that I was accomplishing something worthwhile. More and more the thought of teaching at the new school excited me. Steve hadn't asked me personally yet, but I was hoping that he would. Of course, by the time school started in the fall, I would be far along in my pregnancy. But maybe I could teach for a few weeks, and then again after the baby was old enough to be left a few hours at a time.

Verlan showed up early one morning, worn out from his long and tiring, but successful, missionary trip. He was only able to spend a day with us in Los Molinos, during which time he organized a couple of the Mexican men to dig the foundation for Charlotte's house.

That night, Verlan spent the night with me in the room that I usually shared with Rena. I had looked forward all day to this time with him. The opportunity to spend the night in my husband's arms was rare.

He tossed and turned next to me once we were in bed, groaning restlessly. "Oh, Susan, I have got to get back to work! The funds are running out, and Theron is swamped with jobs to be done in Vegas. He's been carrying the ball on his own, but I've got to get back there and bail him out. I feel guilty even starting Charlotte's house, when I'm so broke. I don't know how I'm going to cover everything, and leave enough money for the family to get by..."

"Verlan, my love," I interrupted him softly. "Can't you just relax for tonight? Forget about all that. You can think about it tomorrow," I kissed his lips and snuggled against him, running my hand suggestively over his chest. His garment strings were in the way, and I pulled them loose so I could feel the crisp hair underneath. His skin was warm and soft as velvet. I planted a couple of kisses next to my fingers, and curled my bare leg over the top of his garment-clad ones.

He patted me affectionately, and mashed his mouth against mine in a quick, dry kiss. "Honey," he said, catching my roving fingers in his, "Let's don't start getting carried away. I love you so much, and I want you, I really do. But we have to remember you're pregnant now. We wouldn't want to do anything that might harm the baby."

I sat up in bed and stared down at him. The lamp was still lit, so I could see his face. "Do you mean..." my voice trailed. I gulped, embarrassed.

Verlan grabbed my hand, and gently kissed it. He pulled me back down beside him and wrapped his long arms around me. "That doesn't mean I can't hold you close, my Charm. We can still snuggle, and kiss, and enjoy each other's company. It'll be okay, and the next few months will pass in a flash. Okay?"

I lay stiff and still in his arms. In moments his loud snores roared in my ear, and I moved to the far side of the bed. Feelings of rejection and resentment flowed through me in huge, drowning waves. So this was the way things were! My limited sex life would be non-existent for the next six months. Wasn't that just dandy. Of course, Verlan would be set up just fine. He had other needy wives to turn to, wives who weren't pregnant and off limits. I wanted to scream with frustration. Here I was just beginning to really truly enjoy sex and lovemaking, to look forward to it, and now I had been cut off. Just exactly whose rule was this? I'd never heard of it before—not that I'd discussed sex much with anyone. Did every woman stop making love once she was pregnant? Man, was I ignorant.

Verlan left at the crack of dawn to tell Irene and Ester goodbye. "I hate to leave you so soon again," he said, kissing me at the door, "But I don't see a choice. I'm supposed to meet Joel and some of the other guys in San Diego for a meeting this afternoon. I don't know what it's all about, but I think there are going to be some changes made in the church organization."

I glued myself to the window throughout the early morning, watching as Verlan's pickup left Irene's and moved to the western side of the colony where Ester's trailer sat. I stared miserably at the tiny speck of gray, where it stayed parked outside of Ester's place for an interminably long time. As the minutes passed, my stomach clenched. Verlan might have some old fashioned and strange beliefs, but having sex during the daylight was not against his principles; I knew first hand. He had lain like a stone next to me all night, and now he was giving to Ester what should have been mine. My throat constricted and my head pounded with the certainty of it. With the soft, May sunshine pouring through her windows, that snobby little witch was writhing in pleasure right now, at my expense.

Suddenly, I hated Verlan. I hated him so bad, with all his excessive regulations and ridiculous fanaticism—his constant excuses and justifications for our having to live this rigid, unforgiving life. What was so godly and right about suffering and heartache and abstinence during pregnancy? My sexual desire was alive and well, and awakened like never before, and now I was cut off, while he took his pleasure all up and down the Baja coast. I hated that dark-eyed little witch.

Brother Castro brought news the following week from the meeting in San Diego, news that caused much speculation among the membership in Los Molinos. Joel had discussed officially stepping down from the position as president over the church. In his place, he desired to ordain Verlan as the new president—an office he would carry along with his duty as President over the Twelve Apostles.

When Irene heard about it, she wept. "As if Verlan has time to do more," she said bitterly. "We'll never see him now. I wonder what's going through Joel's head?"

I stared at her, shrugged and muttered. "Joel wouldn't give Verlan the office without direct guidance from the Lord. You know that."

She sniffed, biting her lip. "Yes, of course I know it." She finally sighed. "I shouldn't have said that, but dammit, Susan, I miss him! He's never been gone so much, and it just seems to go on and on. This new position is going to take so much more of his time, I wonder if he'll ever be able to come home. It's just not fair. Why does it have to be Verlan?"

The weeks passed, and my anger at Verlan slowly evaporated. I missed him desperately, and decided the sex thing was not that big a deal, and no reason to keep feeding the fire of resentment that had consumed me for the first week after he left. His face and voice haunted my dreams at night, and the precious intimacies we had shared in the past, though few, brought secret smiles to my face at the oddest of times.

One morning as Rena and I were outside hanging clothes, a long, gold Cadillac pulled into the driveway. We both stared open-mouthed at the fancy new car. Ervil swung the door open and got out, sauntered around the vehicle, and held the passenger door open for Lorna.

"Wow," Rena breathed, "Will you look at that." She tore off across the yard toward them, leaving me standing at the clothesline, staring at the man that I hated and feared most in the world.

I hardly recognized Ervil—no more demure long-sleeved white shirt and black pants. This garb had been replaced—an emerald-colored, flowered silk shirt, and hunter-green pleated britches, shouted for attention. The shirt was casually open at the neck, showing off his muscular, virile chest. His thin upper lip was graced with a new mustache.

The drastic change in his appearance took me by such surprise that I momentarily forgot my repulsion and fear of him. I gaped in open-mouthed shock. My, my, I thought. The snake has a shiny, new skin. His piercing, blue-gray eyes were the same, though, as they swept around the yard. They hesitated on me. Then Ervil threw me a stiff, crooked smile, and inclined his head in a taunting, half-bow.

My breath caught in my throat. I whirled around, showing him my back as I continued pinning clothes on the line. My hands shook. Oh, Lord, I thought frantically, I can't stay here! I can't walk over there, where he is! What'll I do? What will Lorna think, with me ignoring her like this?

My every instinct was to run. I wanted the ground to swallow me up so that I wouldn't have to face him and pretend that everything was normal. His presence flooded to the surface of my mind the horror of the night in Colonia LeBaron, the night I had cowered at the side of Anna Mae's gas tank and heard Ervil coolly say that he would have someone take care of Verlan.

"Well, hello!" Lorna's voice broke into the traumatic, seemingly endless moment. I closed my eyes tightly, forcing a smile into place. When I turned to her, she saw only friendliness and warmth.

"It's so good to see you," my voice was sincere as I embraced her. I stared at the baby in her arms, at the small, red face of Ervil's newest son. "This is Aaron," Lorna proudly held him out to me.

I took the baby reluctantly, and walked with Lorna toward the group of relatives gathered excitedly around Ervil's new car. Be cool, I told myself. Just don't look at him. You'll be fine.

Yet I couldn't help myself. Ervil was like a magnet, forcing my eyes to stray in his direction as he towered over the Chynoweths. His silk shirt glimmered and flashed in the bright sunlight, an outward symbol of the force and attraction of his personality.

"What do you think of Ervil's new love?" Lorna chuckled. "His wives call it his "Golden Calf." I glanced at the luxurious vehicle, suspecting where Ervil had gotten it. The paint was a soft, glistening gold, the interior creamy leather, the dash, wood veneer. A man's jacket was draped over the front seat. My fists involuntarily clenched and my lips tightened in repugnance. Ervil's brand new, Golden Calf. Oh, Ervil, Ervil. Grandma's precious boy. The Prophet's brother, stooping to such unbelievable depths.

Slowly I realized that a silence had fallen on the group of people standing at Ervil's side. My skin prickled. I sensed that every eye was on me. Pulling my gaze from the car, I glanced hastily around.

Aunt Thelma's eyes looked curious— guarded— as though she could read my mind. I blinked self-consciously, forcing a smile. "Some car," I mumbled.

Aunt Thelma turned abruptly away from me. "You must all be starved," she said briskly. "Come on in and I'll fix you some lunch."

From the corner of my eye, I saw Aunt Thelma twine her arm through Ervil's. Her action seemed deliberate, almost protective, and I stumbled hurriedly back to the clothesline.

Susan, you've got to stop this, I thought, as I hung the rest of the wet clothes. You've got to get control of yourself. Openly detesting Ervil will cause resentment from Lorna and Aunt Thelma and trouble from Ervil, himself. You can't let him know that you know anything. He's far too dangerous.

Ervil and Lorna stayed with the Chynoweths for the next two days. Ervil ignored me, for which I was deeply grateful. I watched from a distance as Aunt Thelma bustled around her son-in-law, going to great pains to treat him like royalty. Even his eggs had to be cooked to his perfect satisfaction. I cringed, sickened, one morning, when Aunt Thelma placed the plate in front of him, asking, "Will these do, dear?"

The finish-work on the new kitchen came to an abrupt halt, replaced by lengthy, private conversations between Ervil, Lorna, Thelma and Bud—that dropped in volume whenever I came near them.

My head and heart ached with fear. Right under my nose, Ervil seemed to be getting his clutches deeper and deeper into my darling relatives, and I didn't know how to stop it. Verlan had sworn me to secrecy about the incident at Anna Mae's, but if I thought it would do any good, I would have taken Aunt Thelma aside and told her about it anyway; however my sixth sense told me she wouldn't listen or believe me. Aunt Thelma was totally bewitched by her son-in-law—it showed in her constant smile and the proud, almost intimate look in her eyes as she regarded him. My heart felt like a heavy stone in my chest, my thoughts frantic as I searched for a way to warn her about the type of man Ervil was, that he was much more dangerous than people knew. Yet something warned me that I was too late. Ervil was carefully romancing my aunt and uncle, weaving an invisible web around them, a net with the strength to pull them to his side, away from Joel and the church body. In the Chynoweths trusting eyes Ervil was becoming God's champion, the real leader of the Church, the actual One Mighty and Strong. I could sense what they were thinking—I could read it in their eyes. Ervil was a born leader, where Joel was not; Ervil had charisma, where Joel had only humility and a strong and willing back. I knew without a doubt that Ervil's trip to Los Molinos had been for this very purpose. He intended to align the Chynoweths firmly behind him—soldiers for his army.

The morning of the third day of Ervil and Lorna's visit, I set off across the field to Irene's. I had wanted to go earlier, yet I was loath to leave my relatives alone with Ervil. Well, my stupid desire to protect them was doing no good whatever, and I had to get away from the stifling air in the Chynoweth home. Besides, I couldn't contain my anger any longer. I had to talk to someone about it.

As I tramped through the field, I glanced over at the distant walls of Charlotte's home that the men were working on. The house was going up much slower that Verlan had expected, I thought dully. But at least it was progressing some. When he returned, he would have a load of lumber for the roof.

I hurried to Irene's back door, changing my direction as I saw that she was in the garden pulling weeds with the boys. "Hi," I puffed, my breath shortened by the heavy load I was carrying in my belly.

She looked up at me, straightened up with a groan, and threw down her gloves. "Good," she grinned. "I needed an excuse to take a break. Let's go inside." She stopped at the gate and called back, "Andre, you boys finish two rows each now, you hear me?"

As we walked into the coolness of the house, Irene glanced at me. "So who owns the pretty Cadillac at the Chynoweth's?"

I looked meaningfully at the girls crowding around the kitchen and headed toward Irene's bedroom. She followed, waiting until the door was closed before demanding, "What's going on?"

"The car's Ervil's. He and Lorna showed up a couple of days ago, and I couldn't stand to be there any longer. Oh, Irene, I hate him so much!" I plopped down on her bed and buried my face in her pillow. "Ervil's!" Irene shrieked in surprise. "That fancy car is Ervil's? You've got to be kidding me."

I peered up at her. I knew she would be startled, but I didn't expect such anger. Her blue eyes flashed as her face paled. "Why that selfish... I can't believe him! How dare he buy himself something like that, when Joel doesn't own a decent car to his name!"

I sat up, puzzled and confused. "What do you mean! What does Joel have to do with it?"

Irene pursed her lips, her anger momentarily robbing her of words. She glanced at me, as though trying to decide if she should say what was on her mind. She decided and spat out, "The money that's making the payments on that car is obviously the money that Verlan and Joel give Ervil to support his families."

It was my turn to be shocked. "What! Verlan and Joel give Ervil money?" I gasped.

"They have for years. Ervil hasn't done an honest day's work since I can remember." Irene sat down on the end of the bed, her face ashen.

"It's Joel's fault in a way," she continued. "He felt Ervil was such an asset to the mission-field that he shouldn't waste time with physical labor. So Joel and Verlan agreed to support Ervil and his families, so he could be free to write church manuals and preach the gospel. They've had to occasionally use tithing to help with Ervil's bills."

I listened in consternation. "But surely they don't still do it? I mean, now that Ervil has been so against Joel, and all. They wouldn't still give him money, would they?"

Irene shrugged, "Ervil's wife, Delphina, was penniless and desperate in Ensenada a couple of weeks ago. She called Joel, and he made a special trip to give her what money he had. Jeannine was mad, of course, and she asked Joel about it. He said that no matter what Ervil was doing, he just couldn't sit back and see his poor wives going without."

I looked thoughtfully away. Respect for Joel's decency, for his willingness to return good for evil battled with my fear that Joel was indeed promoting Ervil's lack of responsibility for his families.

"I can't believe Ervil would stoop so low," Irene was saying. "How can he have the gall to flash around town in that fancy car, while Joel and Verlan work like dogs and drive old, beat-up pickups? I'd charge over there and slap Ervil's smug, ugly face, but shit splatters."

It was on the tip of my tongue to tell Irene my suspicions about Ervil's new car. But somehow I contained myself. It would doubtless get back to Verlan if I said anything. Irene was a wonderful, loving sister-wife, but she did have her weaknesses.

I breathed a heart-felt sigh of relief when Ervil and Lorna finally went back to Ensenada. The Chynoweths treated me well enough, although there was a subtle difference in our relationship. An invisible barrier, a sort of reserve, had crept between us, one that I knew Ervil had caused. Or, on the other hand, one I had caused by my cool treatment to their new champion.

It was six weeks before Verlan came again to Los Molinos. He was subdued and care-worn, and had disturbing news. One of the new members from California had loaned Ervil several thousand dollars. He was totally unaware that Ervil and Joel were at odds and that the money wasn't being used for the Church. The man had gone to Joel, expecting him to pay the money back.

"Ervil led John to believe that Joel asked for the money," Verlan groaned and buried his haggard face in his hands. "So, John handed it over without question. Now he wants it paid back, and Joel feels responsible. Oh—I don't know what we're going to do. We don't have that kind of money."

"Ervil's a grown man, Verlan," I snapped. "Make him responsible for his own debts. Let John take him to court for it."

Verlan jumped off the bed and paced nervously around Rena's and my new room. "That's not the worst of it, sweetheart. Ervil's been up to more of his so-called revelations. He's after brother Jensen's wife, Lawreve. He's convinced her to leave Earl and marry him. Joel's fit to be tied. Ervil told Joel he wasn't waiting for an official divorce, that it wasn't necessary for a man in his position to do so."

Verlan rambled on, freely wiping tears away as he relived the emotional meeting between Joel and himself. "First Anna Mae. And now Lawreve. And it would have been you, too, if we hadn't put a stop to it. Well, we're going to have to grind him to a halt, somehow. It'll be ugly, I reckon." Verlan shook his head, and stared at me in wonder. "Can you believe it, he honestly thinks he's above the law, both the law of the church, and the law of the land. He actually told me that blood would run to solve our problems! You should have seen his face when he said it."

I listened in paralyzed silence. Finally, Verlan believed me! Now he had heard it with his own ears, and it was all coming to a head. Ervil wouldn't allow himself to be shut down and humiliated without a fight, he was too fond of authority and power. "Promise me you'll be careful," I pleaded with him.

He gathered me into his arms and kissed my cheek and forehead. "I'm watching my step," he said quietly.

It seemed Verlan had barely told me hello, and now he was kissing me goodbye. As before, I watched from the window as his pickup disappeared over the crest of the hill above Los Molinos. Only this time I watched with much more anxiety.

Chapter 26

Convincing Verlan to let me go to back to Colonia LeBaron for the birth of my child was easier than I expected. I had a dozen good arguments ready should they be needed, but Verlan waved them all away.

"I think it would be the best thing to do," he readily agreed. "You should be with your mother. And you should leave soon, before you're farther along. I'll find you a ride to the colony right away."

He pinched my cheek and smiled. "Don't you worry. I'll be heading that way myself in time to be with you when the baby's born."

"Oh, Verlan," I said softly, "you're being so good to me. Thank you." I hugged him, noticing again how curious it seemed to have such a large lump between our bodies. After Verlan left, I sat down to write my mother a letter.

The following day Verlan did a bit of scouting around and found that his nephew, Joseph Butchereit, was in town. Joseph would be returning to Colonia LeBaron in a few days and would be happy to take me along.

As the appointed morning came, I waited expectantly, my bags by the door. Morning slowly dragged into afternoon, and still no Joseph. The sun was dropping toward the western horizon, and my nerves were raw with impatience when the young man finally tapped on the Chynoweths' door. "Wal, ready to go?" he drawled.

I controlled the urge to inform him that I had been ready for hours. I nodded instead and handed him my bags. Saying goodbye to the Chynoweths, I followed Joseph outside. He was a shy, dreamy man with a soft heart. I couldn't expect him to be perfect.

"Oh, hell-fire," I groaned, stopping abruptly as I got a good look at the pickup idling in the Chynoweths' driveway. Suddenly I wanted to back out of the offered ride. A gaping hole where the passenger door should have been plainly revealed the ragged interior. The engine appeared naked and ugly without the hood covering, and it spouted black smoke.

Joseph dumped my bags in the back and turned toward me expectantly, grinning as he noticed my dismayed face. "Oh, it don't look real good, Aunt Susan, but it runs," he assured me. "Just sit real close to me and you'll be fine."

"Are you sure that thing'll make it all the way to Colonia LeBaron?" I demanded, continuing to eye the old truck. I wondered if I dared risk the welfare of my unborn child in such a vehicle. And I also wondered if Verlan had seen it before asking Joseph to take me with him.

He patiently walked back to me. Taking my hand, he led me to the truck and helped me up onto the seat. "Don't you worry now. Scoot way over, away from the edge," he said cheerfully.

Well here we go, I thought. I set my jaw, averting my eyes from the enormous opening where the door used to be.

The long ride was a breezy one. But the old truck ran without missing a lick, reminding me that appearances aren't important. Showing sensitive concern for my welfare, Joseph fussed over me all along the way.

"You shore you aren't hungry?" he yelled several times above the noise of the engine. "You shore you don't need a bathroom? I know how you pregnant women are . . . "

I thought several times about Verlan's last words before he left me in Los Molinos. "I'll be with you in Colonia LeBaron in time for the baby," he'd promised.

Looking back, I was proud of how bravely I had smiled as he assured me of his plans. But even as he'd talked, I figured that something would doubtless arise to prevent him from keeping his promise. Not that he didn't plan to be with me. I knew he wanted to come, but his responsibilities were so very important, not to mention the burden of the new debt of Ervil's to which he and Joel had consented. If Verlan came, it would be a miracle. Still, I could hope.

Sixteen hours after we started our journey, Joseph deposited me, safe and sound, on my mother's doorstep. Mother and the girls danced around, excited at the prospect of a new baby in the house.

I sighed with relief as I settled back into the orderly routine of life in Colonia LeBaron. The Colony felt modern and slow-paced, after the hustle and bustle of the pioneers in Los Molinos. Fara and Ramona were busy with school, so Mom and I had the house to ourselves during the day. Dad popped in to see us occasionally. He was still occupied with his farming project and spent most of his time away. Maria had given birth to another girl, which increased the number of my father's children to fifteen.

The sultry, last days of my confinement dwindled slowly, and Verlan failed to arrive. I clung to the hope of his promise, believing that if it were possible, he would be with me for the birth. My awaited due date came—and went, with both baby and Verlan neglecting to make an appearance. I tried not to feel upset that Verlan hadn't made it, but the tears wouldn't hold. I paced my mother's living room in frustration.

"He'll come," Mom said soothingly. "Have faith, daughter, he'll be here soon."

The following night as I looked in the mirror at my hard, swollen stomach, I sighed. "Wait a few more days, Little One. Stay where you are until your daddy arrives."

I blew out the lamp and crawled into Mona's twin bed, turning awkwardly about as I tried to sleep. "Why, oh why, doesn't he come?" I moaned. "Lord, why can't he be here?"

Even as I spoke the words, a light tapping on the living room door startled me. "Anybody home?" Verlan's voice rang out through the still house.

A wild rush of joy flooded through me. I wanted to leap up and run to him, but as I sat on the edge of the bed, the muscles in my back suddenly knotted uncomfortably.

"Oh," I gasped, wide-eyed at the pain. I stood up, the contraction ripping around my back and clutching at my abdomen. Harder and harder it peaked, then faded.

Dazed, I heard my mother's voice blending with Verlan's in the living room. I paused for a moment next to the window as another contraction erupted through my body. I relaxed into the pain, allowing it to do its work as I looked out at the winking brilliance of the stars. Sudden tears choked me. "Lord," I thought, "This perfect timing isn't a coincidence, is it? You're much too great and loving. You care about every little thing."

"Melanie. Let's name her Melanie," I said, as I gently pushed the thick, black hair away from my tiny daughter's eyes. Her face was the most beautiful, delicate, pink. She wasn't the usual, wrinkled red color of most new babies. Not my little girl. She was a perfect little doll.

"Monica," Verlan insisted. "I thought you liked Monica."

"I did," I sighed. "But I don't anymore. I'm tired of that name—I thought about it too long. Don't you think Melanie sounds beautiful . . . sort of classical?"

Verlan leaned over and softly kissed his youngest daughter's tiny cheek. "I don't know what to think about it. I had my heart set on Monica. We'll have to see." Smiling into my eyes, he squeezed my hand, then stood up and grabbed his briefcase. "Got to go meet with Joel. Bye, sweetheart."

As I watched Verlan's long legs carry him across the front porch and out of sight, I thought, I've finally done it. I have finally seen pride in his eyes because of me.

I glanced down at the baby, my fingers straying to the soft, abundant hair that crowned her head. "Thank you, precious little bundle," I whispered. "You are the most beautiful baby in the world, the prettiest one your Daddy has ever seen, I just know it. Lucy's baby, your baby sister, couldn't be as perfectly lovely as you are."

I thought for a moment about Lucy and tried to imagine what her two-week old baby girl looked like. They named her Virginia, Verlan had told me. Well, Virginia was a nice enough name, but Melanie was a better one.

I moved gingerly in my mother's big bed, smiling as I remembered how wonderful Verlan had been these past twelve hours. Intense, burning love for me, and agony for what I endured, had shown in his blue-green eyes as he hovered throughout the labor and birth. He had never shown such gentleness, and the way he had held our baby, the pride in his eyes as he looked at her, removed every doubt that I had harbored about his wanting our child.

I was thankful that my mother insisted we have her bedroom once we returned from the hospital. Now there would be room for Verlan to sleep with me. Not that we would be staying long in Colonia LeBaron. Once his meetings with the men were over, he would be anxious to take me back to Los Molinos.

Joel had come to the colony with Verlan, with plans to take care of the official change in the church leadership. He would be returning to Los Molinos with his eldest son, Joel Jr., once the meetings were over.

Charlotte, Lucy, Beverly, and the children had moved to Los Molinos during my absence. They'd arrived a week before Lucy's baby was born, Verlan told me. Lucy and her children were living with Charlotte in her new house until Lucy's home could be built. Beverly was staying with Irene.

"I have a trailer lined up for you to live in, once I take you home," he'd said. "It's not a fancy one, but it'll do until I can build you a house. Just think, Susan, once I take you back, I'll have all my wives and kids together in Los Molinos for the first time." Remembering the sparkle in Verlan's eyes as he'd told me that, I smiled and drifted off to sleep with my baby's tiny back warm beneath my hand.

The next two days passed quickly as my strength returned. Several of the Colony women came over to see the baby and to visit. They brought covered dishes filled with tempting food, knitted booties, baby clothes, and blankets. On the second day, Franny dropped in just as Verlan was getting ready to leave for another meeting. "What's the baby's name?" she asked, picking her up.

I glanced at Verlan, noticing that he had hurriedly turned his back and busied himself at the mirror with his tie. "I'm not sure yet, Franny," I smiled. "We're thinking of Monica."

Verlan snorted. He picked up the card Franny had brought to me and scribbled on it, then leaned over the bed to kiss me goodbye, casually dropping the card on my chest as he straightened up. "Be back later," he said, winking at Franny.

I picked up the envelope. In scrawled letters next to my name, he'd written Melanie. I laughed softly. "That man spoils me so, Franny," I said happily. "Anything I want, he gives me."

The following afternoon I fidgeted at the window, looking out at the beautiful October day. "I'd like to see your mother, Verlan. I'm sick of being cooped up in this house. Why don't we take a walk?"

He eyed me suspiciously. "You sure you're up to walking that far already? The baby's only four days old; maybe you're rushing things a bit."

I laughed, delighted at his protective instincts. "I feel strong as a horse. Let's go, please!"

"Okay, but we can't stay long. Joel is expecting me at Jensen's by six." Verlan leaned over the bed and carefully picked Melanie up. "Come on, little chicken," he crooned. "Let's go see your Grandma."

I linked my hand through his free arm as we strolled down the tree-lined road. Melanie's blanket-wrapped body was tucked in the crook of his other arm, her tiny face squinting as she got her first glimpse of bright sunlight. Verlan chuckled, watching her expression. "Looks like a little wrinkled cabbage, don't she?"

"Verlan LeBaron, she does not!" I protested. "She's the most beautiful baby I've ever seen. She's also the most beautiful baby you've ever seen; you're just afraid to admit it. Isn't she!"

Verlan nodded, and was still chuckling as we crossed the wooden cattle guard by Esther Spencer's place. We stopped for a moment so that Verlan could visit with two Mexican neighbors who pulled up next to us in a mule-drawn wagon. After pleasantries were exchanged, the older man leaned toward Verlan, dropping his voice confidentially, "Is it true that you are to be the new presidente of your church now?"

Verlan nodded. "Si, it is true. Joel, my brother, desires to be the Prophet—nothing more. So I will fill the office of presidente."

"Ah . . . and what does your brother, Ervil say? Is he in agreement with this?"

I glanced quickly at Verlan's face, then looked away. Why did people have to be so nosy, especially when they were aware of the problems between the brothers?

"I understand that Ervil is in agreement," Verlan answered without hesitation. "I have not spoken to him personally."

"Ah . . . Well, perhaps today you will have the chance. He is just down the road, there," the man turned and pointed.

Verlan's head snapped up. Oh, no, I said to myself as I searched the road ahead of us, not Ervil again! At the far end of the road by Widmar's place I could see two men. A familiar knot of foreboding gripped me. Was Ervil's presence in Colonia LeBaron, at the same time as Verlan and Joel were here, a mere coincidence?

Verlan's face was expressionless as he said goodbye to the men in the wagon. He automatically began to move on down the road.

"No! No, Verlan," I pleaded, grabbing his arm. "Let's don't go this way, please. I don't want to see him; let's cut through the field."

"Don't be silly," he snapped. "I'm not about to avoid him, just keep quiet and leave the talking to me."

"Verlan, I whispered, "tell me how Ervil really feels about your appointment to the presidency. Is he upset about it?"

Verlan stalked along for a few steps before he answered. "It's just like I told Guillermo. I haven't seen Ervil since Joel asked me to take the office. Although Ervil agreed to it, I imagine he's not too happy about it. He knows I'm not the easy-going saint that Joel is. He won't have the free rein that he's enjoyed in the past."

Verlan glanced up at the two men ahead of us, then said, "I'll tell you one thing. Ervil had better watch himself from now on in regard to his so-called revelations. He's never written even one of them down in the past, at least, not to my knowledge, and I've become somewhat allergic to them. As long as I'm president of the church, I'll make him responsible for every revealed word he claims."

The man Ervil was talking to hurried away when he saw Verlan and me. Ervil turned toward us, watching our approach as he lounged lazily against the fence post.

"Well, hello, little brother, Susan," he grunted as we came within earshot. He nodded affably and switched the straw he was chewing to the other side of his mouth.

Verlan gripped his brother's hand, "Ervil, how you doing? I didn't know you was in town."

Ervil's mouth twisted into a smile. "I figured I should be around to congratulate the new church president." Eyeing the bundle in Verlan's arms, Ervil straightened upright. "Well, well," he said. "What do we have here, a baby girl?" He hurriedly glanced at Melanie's face, a dutiful smile on his lips. Then he leaned his huge frame back onto the fence post.

"Verlan, I want you to know you have been my choice all along for president. You're the perfect man for the job, and I told Sigfried so the day I released Joel from the office. I told Sigfried that I consider you one of the greatest princes ever born upon the earth. I meant it, too." Ervil nodded emphatically, his voice oil-smooth.

Verlan stared at him incredulously, ignoring the flattery. "You released Joel?"

Ervil shrugged. "He was interfering too much with the management of the church, by virtue of his higher office. He was stepping all over my patriarchal rights. Who else should release him?"

Verlan was silent. Ervil kicked his toe against a small bush, digging at it until it broke free of its roots. "Verlan, you know as patriarch I preside directly over the office of president and should have complete say over what decisions are made for the church. It was up to my discretion to release Joel, and I decided to do it weeks ago."

"Now, isn't that something," Verlan said evenly. "Joel told me that he released himself from the office, using his higher office of First Grand Head of Priesthood to do it."

Ervil shook his head. "I'm the one who released him, with you in mind as his successor. He wasn't cutting it as president, Verlan—you know that. I've no doubt that you're better qualified—you have the education and diplomacy that Joel lacks. A position such as president over the church needs a people-person."

A quizzical look flashed across Verlan's features. "Well, thank you for your vote of confidence. All we want, Ervil, both you and me, is to serve the Lord wherever and however best we can. Isn't that right?"

Ervil frowned, nodding.

I glanced at Verlan. The blue-green eyes locked with Ervil's were devoid of anger, and I instantly respected his self-control. In light of Ervil's lavish, insincere compliments and the derogatory way he spoke of Joel, I wouldn't have been surprised to hear Verlan lash out at him.

"Of course," Ervil drawled maliciously, "if you don't do a better job than Joel did, you won't last six months."

Verlan was silent. He kicked at a small stone in the grass, then he looked up again, and said, "I'll do my best and let God be the judge. Well, Susan and I had best be going. See you around."

My heart pounded as we rounded the corner toward Grandma's. In spite of the calm way the men had spoken to one another, the sparks had been flying. Verlan stalked along next to me, his hand squeezing mine until it hurt. I pulled it away and looked at his face.

"What did he mean, you wouldn't last six months?"

Verlan shook his head. "He means unless I run the church as he dictates, he will release me from the office. Just as he claims to have done Joel."

"Did he lie about that?"

"Whose word would you take, Ervil's or Joel's?"

Verlan shrugged off the black mood Ervil had left him with and seemed his usual self throughout the short visit with his mother. He walked me only part of the way home again, since he was late for his meeting.

That night when Verlan returned, his eyes were bloodshot. His face looked pale and set in hard lines as he sank onto the bed. Dismayed, I stared at him, waiting for Fara and Ramona to leave the room before I spoke.

"What's happened?"

Verlan raggedly exhaled. "I may as well tell you, I guess. It'll be all over town by tomorrow. Joel released Ervil from the patriarchal office a little while ago." He closed his eyes, his face gray with pain.

I watched Verlan's agony, tears of sympathy in my eyes. "Don't you think its high time?" my voice shook as I spoke. "You know it is, you knew it would happen, sooner or later. Ervil's like a possessed man—out to take whatever he wants, regardless of others. He wants to rule, Verlan, to take over the leadership and run things his way. Not God's way—his way, for his own sick glory!"

"Joel and I hoped—hoped he would change," Verlan dashed the tears from his cheeks, stood up, and pulled off his clothes.

"Maybe the humility of being stripped of his office will make him think," he whispered. "I pray, Oh, God in Heaven, I pray it does."

Chapter 27

We dropped off the hill into Los Molinos. The wind blew hard and cold, and Verlan scowled as he fought the steering wheel. Pulling the blanket tighter around Melanie's pint-sized body, I craned my neck to see around Babbitt's water tower, eager for a first glimpse at the new trailer that Brother Joel had moved onto the bare swell of ground across from the Babbitt's place. This was to be my new house, my first real, honest to goodness home since I married Verlan. No more living in with other people—not any more. I had a child now and had earned the right to have my own place. I hid a grin as I thought about it. My very own home.

Verlan swung the pickup around the corner and braked to a stop, and I stared in mounting horror at the long aluminum hunk of junk sitting on the windswept bare lot. The sun had already set, but there was enough daylight left to clearly reveal the mobile house before us. Orange rust wept down the dented sides. The windows were coated in dust and cobwebs, trash and tumbleweeds lodged against the un-skirted sides. A ragged screen door flapped back and forth on one hinge, banging dismally against the side of the trailer.

"Oh, Verlan! Is that it?" I wailed.

"It just needs a little work," he said cheerfully. "First thing, though, I've got to find you a gas tank. Take the baby in, and I'll see what I can do."

Swallowing the protests that arose, I covered Melanie with a heavy afghan, grabbed the diaper-bag, and stepped out, watching as Verlan backed onto the road. The wind whipped at my hair and at the baby's blanket as the gray pickup bounced down the dirt road.

I gingerly climbed up the rickety wooden steps and opened the trailer door. When I stepped inside, a musty, stale odor assaulted me. Slowly I looked around. Greasy filth clung to the kitchen cupboards, making much of the blond wood appear dark. The small stove was coated in burnt food. Thick dirt blanketed the peeling linoleum floor. The ledges of the bare windows were black with a lining of dead flies. Below the big window at the living room end of the trailer sat a solitary piece of furniture, a grimy orange couch, with cotton oozing out of the torn material.

Aghast, I held Melanie protectively against me. There didn't seem to be one decent spot where I could lay her down. I moved on through the kitchen and into the bedrooms, examining the broken, built-in bunks that clung to the wall in the middle bedroom. In the back, a bare double bed, its mattress heavily stained with urine spots seemed to be the best place.

Sinking cautiously onto the edge of the bed, I held Melanie close, rocking her and nuzzling my face against her sweet smelling softness. Oh, my darling baby. How could I make her live here? Where had Verlan and Joel discovered this filthy monster? Surely they hadn't paid good money for it. No doubt someone had donated it to the cause of the church, glad to have it taken off their hands. Lucky me!

Every cowardly instinct within me screamed to dash out of this nightmare to the warmth and safety of Aunt Thelma's home. I knew she would welcome us and would let us stay until I could get this horrid place mucked out. But I reluctantly shrugged off the thought. The Chynoweths had put me up for the past seven months, and I couldn't take advantage of their hospitality any longer.

"Okay then, Susie," I sighed aloud, my words echoing in the trailer, "Don't just sit here feeling sorry for yourself. You may as well get started." Spreading Melanie's new afghan over the mattress, I put her down and covered her with my coat. She slept peacefully on, her rosebud mouth sucking on a dream nipple.

I hurried outside, stopping momentarily to gaze around the windy little colony as I searched in vain through the twilight for Verlan's truck. Then I dashed across the road to Silvia Babbitt's place and pounded on her trailer door. Silvia was the first wife of Apostle Homer Babbitt. I didn't know her well, since she had only recently moved to Los Molinos now that there was a Church-run school for her children to attend.

Silvia's children were huddled around the table over bowls filled with delicious-smelling vegetable stew. The aroma made my eyes water with hunger. The children stared curiously at me as I asked their mother for the loan of a broom, soap, cleaning rags, and a water bucket. "Here," Silvia said, picking up a lamp, "Take this, too. You'll need some light." Smiling my thanks, I dashed back outside into the wind. Filling the water bucket at Silvia's pump, I hauled the water and the cleaning things back to my new home.

By the time Verlan returned and had the gas tank hooked up, I had the worst of the dirt and flies swept out and the cobwebs brushed down from the ceiling. As Verlan came in to light the pilots on the stove, I turned to him. "I don't want that couch," I said. "It stinks. And I'm going to need bedding and dishes, and some food . . . "

"Honey, I know," he interrupted, "I have some quilts for you in the pickup. Lucy and Irene'll go through their things tomorrow and find you enough of what you'll need to get by." He walked over to the couch and examined it. "Can't you beat the dust out of this and cover it with a nice blanket? It's not that bad. It's better than no couch at all, isn't it?"

I looked at it doubtfully, "Well, just barely."

Verlan grinned at me. "You won't be in this trailer very long. I'm sure you can clean it up and make it look real nice." He strolled over to the door and peered restlessly out the window, searching for a diplomatic way to leave me, to go to his other wives. I had been dreading this moment since we left Colonia LeBaron, and my vision began to blur—my chest raw with anger. Verlan watched me as I attacked a closet with short, sharp digs of the broom.

Suddenly he was next to me, unwinding my fingers from the broom handle. He set it aside and hugged me tight. "Susan, you know I've got to go," he whispered against my cheek. "I don't have much time to spend with the rest of the family before I leave for Vegas tomorrow. You're going to be okay here. You've got the baby, and you've got neighbors . . . and I'll be back in the morning with some stuff for the house." He forced my chin up with his finger, making me meet his gaze. "I love you," he whispered. "See you in the morning, my charm."

I turned my back as Verlan stepped out the door. How? My rebellious thoughts screamed through my mind, how can he bring us to a run-down, drafty place like this and just dump us off? How can he do it? I slumped against the wall of the trailer, my shoulders shaking with fresh loneliness and despair. Oh, I wanted my mother—I needed to feel her comforting, warm presence. I had never appreciated her enough, growing up, or realized just how much I loved her. Why had I left her? I was so stupid to think I was ready for life on my own. What a little fool I was. I didn't know how to take care of a new baby by myself! What would I do if Melanie got sick, and Mom wasn't there to help me? What a cocky, obnoxious girl I was, to think I could handle married life on my own. I was nuts.

"Stop it, Susan. Stop it," I finally sighed, wiping the wet, telling proof of my childishness away. I lit the lamp. The trailer looked huge in the shadowy light, and felt uncomfortably cold. Pulling a sweater from my suitcase, I put it on, then turned on a burner and set the bucket of water on the stove to heat. For hours I stubbornly blocked Verlan and my mother out of my mind as I scrubbed the trailer, carrying the lamp back and forth. Melanie awoke around midnight. I nursed her, then moved her to the blanket-covered couch and attacked the bed, beating the dirt and dust out of the mattress. Tomorrow I would take it outside and scrub it. For now, it would have to do. No smooth sheets tonight, I thought, as I spread out the remaining quilts and placed Melanie between them. Shivering, I undressed and got in next to her. I pulled her tiny body into the crook of my arm and blew out the lamp.

As I lay in the ghastly shadows of the trailer, the wind rattled and beat against the metal sides, causing my exhausted body to flinch with nervousness. I finally allowed myself to think about Verlan, to remember how wonderful he'd been during our time together in Colonia LeBaron. I had become accustomed to being with him, to the warmth of his body lying next to mine at night. Between us had sprung companionship and closeness. For a week or so, I had actually felt like he was my husband. Well, now we were back to the reality of polygamy. My possessive dependency on Verlan had been ripped away the moment we entered Los Molinos, with its various houses filled with his other wives and children. He'd spent so many days and nights with just me, that I would be the last on his list of priorities for many weeks to come. I couldn't expect anything else. I would have to get used to being on my own again. Slowly I relaxed and drifted into unconsciousness.

I slept late the following morning, loath to pull my exhausted body from the warm blankets. The wind had died down a bit, but still rattled the windows. Shivering, I dressed and put my sweater back on. My stomach growled, and I longed to go to Aunt Thelma's and beg something to eat. Just as I made my mind up to do it, Verlan arrived, bringing Irene and Lucy to see me.

The women had their arms full of sheets and towels, dishes and cooking utensils. They presented them to me, waving away my thanks. "They're not much," Irene shrugged. "They're not new, but they'll get you by. And here, I brought you a plate of potatoes and eggs."

"Well, where is she?" Lucy demanded as I shoveled food in my mouth. "We want to see that new baby. Verlan says she's just beautiful."

"She is," I smiled, putting my plate down and leading the way to the back bedroom.

"Oh, Susan! Look at all that black hair!" Irene crooned, unwrapping Melanie and admiring her from head to foot. "Verlan's never had a more lovely baby, has he, Lucy."

"Never," Lucy agreed. She smiled at Verlan, who had followed us and was lounging against the closet. He was fresh-shaven, and dolled up in his pale-blue Western shirt and creamy Levi's. He looked relaxed and wonderful, and had no doubt spent a comfortable, intimate night with some lucky woman, somewhere.

Irene straightened upright. "Well, Dearie, I'd like to visit, but we can't stay. I've got the washing machine running. But I'll be by to have a long visit with you when I'm done."

As Verlan followed the ladies out the door, he slipped me a ten-dollar bill. "Charlotte'll come by to take you to town for groceries later on this afternoon," he said. "I'll stop in to see you before I leave town."

Yes, I thought, watching his silver pickup pull away. Then you'll be gone again, for a month or six weeks perhaps . . . I shrugged the thought. I couldn't think about that now.

In the early afternoon, I walked down the gentle incline of the hill the mile to Aunt Thelma's. I needed to let them know I was back and to introduce Melanie.

Once the baby had been passed around, admired, and the family news caught up on, Aunt Thelma looked me speculatively up and down. "How soon do you think you'll feel like getting involved with the school, Susie? We really need you, now that Lucy and Charlotte's kids are living here."

"As soon as I'm settled and can find someone who'll take care of the baby," I said promptly.

"Good. Talk to Steve as soon as you can, will you? He needs to know what to plan on."

I nodded, watching Aunt Thelma's deft movements as she put dough into bread pans. How strange it was that life seemed to be going on just as usual for the Chynoweths. They made no secret of backing Ervil's rebellion against Joel, yet Aunt Thelma continued to teach at the school and still led the music at church. Where, I wondered, would it all lead? What would be the outcome? I stayed and visited for an hour, then Mark loaded my few belongings into their pickup and carted me back up the hill to my trailer.

"It's gonna' seem strange not having you live with us," he commented as he carried my guitar and bags up the steps. Once inside the door, he stopped short and looked around, his hazel eyes wide. "Wow! I figured this place for a dump, but . . . When's ol' Verlan going to make you a decent house?" He dropped my things on the couch, then wrinkled his nose in disgust.

"Soon. It won't be much longer, and this will do just fine until then." My voice had sharpened at his critical tone.

Mark shook his head but refrained from further comment. He stayed and

259

visited with me for a couple of hours, and I knew he hated to leave. He sensed the emptiness I felt, and in his own fumbling way wanted to make up for it.

I dove busily into fixing up the old trailer. In the bottom of one of the boxes Irene had brought, I found some long, ruffled yellow curtains, enough for the living room windows. Silvia loaned me her iron and ironing board, and soon the curtains were hanging in front of sparkling clean windows. I stood back and admired them, delighted at the way they brightened up the atmosphere in my new abode. A tablecloth covered the rust on the tabletop, and turning one of Lucy's old Levi quilts over to the plain blue underside, it made a fine enough bedspread. By the time Verlan returned to tell me goodbye, the trailer actually looked presentable.

"See," he said approvingly. "I knew you would manage. You're going to get by just fine, sweetie. And I'll be back before you know it." His fierce hug enveloped me. Then with a smile and a wave, he was gone.

It was late in the day when Irene and Charlotte came to take me to town for groceries. Charlotte sat behind the wheel of the old family pickup, lightly tapping the horn as she drew to a stop. Her oldest daughter, Rhea, hurried up the steps and pounded on my door.

"I'm so glad you're finally here," Rhea declared, a happy grin spreading across her face as she saw Melanie. "Oh! Susan, she's precious!" she exclaimed. She took the baby from my arms, her eyes soft with instant devotion. "Hi, Melanie," she crooned, moving to the couch and cradling the baby in her lap. "I'm your big sister, Rhea. Aren't you just the sweetest thing . . . "

The blare of the pickup horn pulled Rhea's eyes from Melanie's face. "Oh! Mama said for me to tend her while you're in town, so you don't have to take her out into the wind."

"Are you sure?"

"Hurry up, they're waiting," she grinned. "We'll be just fine. I'm sure I can find everything I'll need."

Charlotte's brown eyes held a friendly smile as I climbed in next to Irene. "Welcome home," she said cheerfully. "I want to see the baby of course, but I'll wait until we get back from town. How's she doing?"

"She's . . . "

"Charlotte, I told you, she's just beautiful," Irene interrupted. "She's the picture of health, and she looks like Donna did when she was a baby. She has the LeBaron eyes."

It was strange to hear Charlotte visit so freely. And it was even stranger to be buying my own groceries. I followed the two women down the aisles of the small store as we filled our baskets. Irene kept a critical eye on my selections.

"Don't forget baking powder," she ordered. "You'll need yeast, salt, flour and oil. No, don't get beans, we have a big sack in the shed, and don't buy potatoes. Joel has a truck-full that somebody donated, and he said to take all we wanted. Don't forget soap."

The money Verlan gave me went fast. Once we were back home, the women helped me carry my groceries into the trailer. Irene pitched right in and helped me put them away. It was almost dark by the time they left.

An odd type of contentment seeped through me as I finished straightening the kitchen, then paused to admire my neat, clean home. True, it wasn't fancy or snug. The furniture left much to be desired. The wind sung its way in through various ill-fitting windows and the cracks beneath the doors. The only heat I had was to light the oven and leave the door open. But I had my own food—in my own cupboards! If I were careful with my money, I would eventually accumulate the other things I needed.

I picked up my guitar and settled down on the couch, idly plucking at the strings as I looked around me. Well, I thought, I have my own place now, and I have a child of my own, which makes me a respected and valuable part of Verlan's family. I'll be teaching school soon. It'll give me something useful to do, something with which to occupy my time. Yes, Lord, I thought, I have a lot to be thankful for.

Melanie hated the goats' milk Irene and Donna fed her during the hours I spent at school. She fussed and cried, taking days to become used to the taste. Then she settled down and gulped it like a greedy little pig. She was growing fast. Her black hair was becoming lighter every day, her eyes changing shades of blue.

"Irene, I've got to get Melanie some clothes," I said one Saturday. "She's outgrown almost everything she's got."

Irene frowned at her hand of pinochle cards, and then glanced at me. "Well, I'd give you some of Verlana's hand-me-downs but there wasn't many of 'em, and Lucy asked if she could have them for Virginia. Have you got any material? We could make her some clothes."

I shook my head. "Not a single piece." I glanced at Melanie as she kicked and squirmed on the blanket, then I said quietly, "D'you suppose Verlan would let me have some extra money?"

Irene hooted. "Are you kidding? I had to sell my gas heater to Betty Tippetts when Margaret got the flu last month, so I would have the money for the doctor. When Verlan came home do you think he would give me an extra dollar or two for cough medicine? No sir." Irene shook her head and hatefully threw a queen of hearts on the table, trumping Donna's black ace. "He told me to make onion syrup."

I nodded, thinking about how tight the money had been since we came back to Los Molinos. There was rarely a spare peso for luxuries such as margarine or Colas. I had stopped turning the oven on for heat, as it used up the butane too fast. Eight dollars a week was the amount allotted to Melanie and me, and sometimes it was dropped to five dollars, on weeks when Verlan Jr.'s paycheck wouldn't allow more.

Charlotte's oldest son had been working in San Diego for the past four months, sending every possible dollar home to support the family. The thought of the seventeen-year-old boy carrying such a responsibility angered me, yet his father seemed to feel that it was right and just. "It teaches him responsibility, Susan," Verlan said flatly. "Until he either marries or turns twenty-one, I plan to have him help out. He's agreed to it, so stop feeling sorry for him."

Well, I did feel sorry for Verlan Jr., living alone in San Diego, working hard on a construction crew to support his father's wives and children. And I knew Lucy's son, Chad, would be expected to do the same as soon as he graduated. Meantime, Verlan was still giving his own hard-earned money to the church.

"Play, Donna," Irene demanded, breaking into my thoughts. I looked up from my hand, waiting for Donna to lay a card down. But she was staring out the trailer window, following the progress of a blue Ford sedan that was climbing the incline toward us. "Mom, isn't that Lillie's car?" she asked.

"It looks ... yep. It's Lillie, all right. I wonder how long she's been in town?" Irene's eyes met mine.

Rising discomfort nagged at my chest as the car edged up the hill and stopped in front of my trailer. I hadn't seen Lillie since that night in Ensenada, so many months ago, when she had been snuggled up to Verlan. Irene had said she'd been in Los Molinos a couple of times, but somehow I had missed her. And now she was getting out of her car and was walking toward my trailer on small, feminine feet, each step somewhat hesitant, as though she wondered if she would be welcomed.

Fourteen-year-old Donna jumped up and threw the door open. "Hi!" she beamed, pulling Lillie inside. "My, don't you look gorgeous. When did you get here?"

"Last night," Lillie grinned. She looked at me over Donna's shoulder, her eyes questioning as she searched mine.

"Hello, Susan," she said softly.

"Lillie." I nodded.

She hesitated when I didn't say more, the room suddenly quiet. Shrugging her shoulders, she looked at the floor. "I wanted to come see you," she mumbled.

I forced myself to stand, laying my cards down on the table. "I'm glad you did," I lied. "We're playing Pinochle . . . would you like to join us?"

I sounded stiff and cold and Irene kicked my leg to let me know it. It was over between Lillie and Verlan, so I should behave and act nice to her. I managed to smile reassuringly into Lillie's dark blue eyes.

"Did you come down alone?" Irene asked smoothly, scooting over on the couch to make room.

"No, Daddy and Uncle Floren rode down with me from San Diego."

"Floren?" Irene's face broke into a delighted grin. "Floren's back from Nicaragua? Well, for heaven's sake! Where is he?"

Floren, another of Verlan's brothers, also one of the Twelve Apostles of the Church, had been in Nicaragua for the past year or so. He had been searching for Book of Mormon relics and archeological facts. Verlan had told me of Floren's belief that Central America was the land inhabited by the Book of Mormon people. Being extremely interested in such things, Floren had gone to explore, moving his two wives down to Nicaragua, so that he could spend some time there.

"He's somewhere with Daddy, getting ready to witch a well for Brother Zarate. That I gotta see," Lillie giggled. "Then tonight Dad plans on taking Floren grunion fishing. Mom and Aunt Gaye are making a picnic lunch to take along. The whole family's going, I guess."

Irene scooped up the cards that were spread across the table. "Well I think I'll go over and see Floren! How about a ride, Lillie?"

"Sure," Lillie agreed. Her thin face looked anxious as she turned to me. "Come with us, Susan?"

"I can't," I said swiftly. "Melanie needs a nap."

"Oh, come on, Susan." Donna said, exasperated.

"Come with us!" Irene wheedled. "She'll go to sleep anywhere."

Out-numbered, I shrugged and nodded. Wrapping a blanket around the baby, I followed Irene to Lillie's car. In uncomfortable silence, I listened to the three of them talk and joke as we skimmed across the small colony in the direction of Jeannine's trailer. The car radio was on—some kind of debate about President Nixon's election to Office, and I tuned into the news and ignored the chatter around me. I wished that I could be as friendly as Irene. It wasn't fun to feel resentment and anger, especially toward someone as nice as Lillie.

As we turned the corner by the Zarate's lot, Irene pointed out the window. "Look, there's Floren now! Witching away."

Word seemed to have gotten across town that something exciting was going on. A dozen or more people stood at the side of Zarate's lot, watching intently as Floren paced across the weed-covered soil with his arms straight in front of his body. As we drew closer, I could see that Floren held what appeared to be two long willows in his hands, stretching them out across the ground.

"What's he doing?" Donna gasped. "Witchcraft?"

"Not exactly," Irene chuckled. "He's water-witching. Some people can find under-ground water. Floren can do it, or so Verlan says. He holds green willows out like that, and they cross each other when he walks over an under-ground stream. Don't ask me how. It's sounds kinda fishy to me."

Lillie stopped the car next to the fence, and we joined the crowd that had formed. I could see Brother Zarate, shaking his gray head doubtfully as he watched Floren's progress across the lot. "I don't know, Joel," he muttered. "Is this actually going to work?"

My brother-in-law's sunburned cheeks creased into a smile, and he patted Brother Zarate on the back. "Have a little faith, Benjamin," he whispered confidently. "Have a little faith."

I glanced at the huge mound of dirt at the far corner of the Zarate place. It marked many days of effort on the part of the Zarate family to find water on this piece of land. All that digging had resulted in nothing but a dry hole. But watching Floren's antics, I completely understood Brother Zarate's skepticism.

Behind us, observing quietly as Floren paced, stood Steve Silver, and his new wife, Carolyn. Three of Joel's wives, Jeannine, Gaye, and Kathy huddled by the fence, firmly holding onto the collars of several small children. Two of the Castro boys and brother Zarate's family stood back at the corner of the front yard. Everybody seemed to be holding his or her breath as the minutes passed. Every eye was on the willows held loosely in Floren's hands. Suddenly the willows swung toward each other, crossing in the middle. Floren stopped. With the toe of his boot, he scratched an X on the ground. Then he walked swiftly to the opposite corner of the lot and again began his careful pacing. As he crossed in direct line with the spot he had marked before, the willows slowly swung in his hands. "Here!" he shouted. "Right here."

Joel, Steve Silver, and Brother Zarate rushed to the spot, examining the ground. Floren's homely, yet arresting face broadened in a happy grin. "There's water down there. Right there, or my name ain't Floren LeBaron," he crowed jubilantly.

Joel laughed out loud and clapped Floren on the back, then pulled his thin body close for a brotherly hug. "Praise the Lord!" he shouted, "I knew you could find it. Benjamin, get your boys to digging. Now, now," Joel grinned as he saw the look on Brother Zarate's leathery face. "Remember what I said, Benjamin, have a little faith."

"Floren, put those sticks down and say hello," Irene demanded, hastening toward him. Lillie, Donna, and I followed her. I felt a bit self-conscious as I reached my hand out to Floren. I hadn't seen him for a couple of years. I wondered if he knew of Verlan's and my marriage, and if he recognized me.

"Well, hello, Susan Ray," he said cheerfully, putting my fears to rest. Below Floren's honest, hazel eyes, his grin made deep furrows in his cheeks. "What is this? Is a handshake all I get from my new sister-in-law?" Grabbing my hand, he pulled me into his arms and planted a noisy kiss on my cheek. Then he held me away from him, looking me up and down. "Verlan's certainly got an eye for a good lookin' woman," he teased.

I could feel myself blush and I hastily drew back, embarrassed that Irene and Lillie had heard his comment. But Irene was her usual, jocular self. "Verlan's got good taste," she nodded proudly. "Hell, Floren, you knew that when he picked me out of the crowd."

Everybody laughed, and I quickly looked at Joel's face to see if Irene's swearing bothered him. But he looked jolly and his eyes sparkled, so I figured he didn't mind.

"Hey!" Joel said. "Let's put all this hard work aside and go fishing. Irene, Susan, why don't you girls go with us!"

Without waiting for an answer he turned and strolled after Benjamin Zarate. "Why don't you guys put the well digging off till tomorrow and find some buckets and come with us to the beach?" he called. "The grunion are running tonight, and I'm taking Floren fishing. What d'ya say?" As Joel neared Benjamin, he motioned with his hand toward the Zarate family. I knew he was telling Brother Zarate to bring the whole group.

From the corner of my eye, I noticed Joel's wives, Jeannine and Gaye, quietly conversing together. Gaye whirled on her heel, stomped over to Joel's old pickup and got in, slamming the door closed behind her.

"Oops, Gaye's mad," Lillie grinned.

I nodded and glanced at Lillie. "Do you know why?"

"Oh, because she and Mom planned for this to be a family outing. They've made a picnic lunch and everything, and now Daddy's inviting half the town to come. Gaye says he always does that and the family doesn't get any time alone with him."

"Well then, I'm certainly not going to go." I started toward Lillie's car, needing to check on my sleeping baby.

Lillie hurried after me. "Oh, Susan, don't worry about Gaye. Everyone else is going, so you may as well. It'll be fun. Irene, you'll come, won't you?"

Irene looked at me, her eyes twinkling. "Have you ever been grunion fishing?"

"No, I don't even know what they are," I confessed.

"Then you should go. Let's stop by my place and pack a lunch. Donna, will you tend Melanie?"

Donna glared at her mother and snapped, "Since I wasn't invited to go along, I might as well."

An hour later, a small caravan of vehicles moved across the barren land to the beach. In spite of my sympathy for Joel's exasperated wives, I couldn't help but admire him for inviting everyone to the outing. His kind of love was all encompassing. Joel considered all of his people as family and wanted to share everything with them—even something as simple as a fishing trip. Steve Silver's Volkswagen had fallen in behind Lillie's car. I turned and peered through the dust, making out three other vehicles behind his, each one loaded with people and fishing buckets. Ahead of Lillie, Irene and I, Joel's pickup raced toward the beach. Floren was huddled down in the back of the truck with Joel's kids, his balding head sticking up above the rest.

The sloping ground became sandy. We parked the vehicles, and gathering up blankets, buckets, and picnic sacks, the crowd hurried over the steep dunes to the ocean.

"Let's gather some driftwood and make a fire," Joel called to the men. Within minutes a roaring fire invited cold palms toward its warmth. Blankets were spread over the damp sand and everyone gathered around, our backs to the incessant wind. A blessing was asked, and baskets and bags were opened. Everyone snooped into each other's grocery supply, looking for tempting morsels. Talk and laughter defied the snapping of the fire and the deep, rolling rhythm of the ocean waves.

"Let's sing a hymn," Gaye called once the food was gone. The strum of her guitar wafted through the salty air, blending with her clear voice. The song she had chosen was an old and familiar one, of the joy and beauty life offered when people's homes were places where love was shared. One by one the crowd joined in, eyes meeting in meaningful looks across the flames as friends and family sought one another. This was the wonderful unity that Joel inspired, this belief that we were a chosen people—a special people, called of God to lead the inhabitants of the world heavenward. And before us, like Moses of old, was our beloved prophet.

We sang around the fire until the moon appeared, then Raul Perez, a young, fun-loving man, hurried away to the pounding water's edge. He ran back, his eyes flashing. "Grab your buckets," he shouted above the wind. "The grunion're here!"

A dozen men jumped to their feet and headed to the water. Some of the women gathered up sleeping children and took them to the warmth of the vehicles. Lillie, Irene, and I hurried after the men toward the froth a giant wave left on the sand. Just below the high tide mark, small, flopping fish glistened in the moonlight.

"Grab 'em, grab 'em!" Lillie giggled. We dropped to our knees and grappled for the plentiful, squirming fish, throwing them into a bucket. Then as the tide rolled toward us again, we raced, laughing, out of its reach.

I breathlessly pulled the wet sleeves of my sweater up, getting ready for another race against the tide. All along the beach on either side of us, a full moon revealed dark figures heading toward the spawning life left on the sand. Oh, this was fun! The pounding waves rolled in and out as the fish were gathered. To our right, I could see Joel and Floren, working together.

I grabbed for a fish, flinging its slimy, blue and silver body into our five-gallon pail. "What do we do when the bucket's full?" I shouted to Lillie.

"We empty it into that barrel in Daddy's truck."

"Then we'd better go. They're beginning to jump out again."

Lillie grabbed hold of her side of the bucket handle. We dashed over the sand dunes to the pickup, emptied the bucket, and laughing, raced each other back again.

As we topped the dune, a scream floated toward us. It was a man's scream, high, thin, and weak. Prickles of fear raced down my spine. Then another

267

scream—a woman's this time. Lillie and I stared at each other, our eyes wide with growing dread as we ran to the beach.

"It's Joel . . . " The wind carried Irene's voice to us. "He's out past the tide . . . It's dragging him out, pulling him under! Oh God! Please . . . "

Lillie dropped the bucket, racing toward the water. "No, no!" Irene shouted at her, grabbing her arm. "Floren's gone out after him. The undercurrent's too strong for you."

From every direction people raced toward us. Shouted questions and answers, calling and screaming filled the air as we frantically searched the pounding sea for Floren and Joel. The crests of the waves looked fluorescent under the moonlight, as though mirroring innocence and beauty instead of a skulking, hungry evil with the power to snatch our spiritual leader from us.

Raul Perez and Fernando Castro raced into the water, striking out for the open sea beyond the breaking surf. Raul carried a rope over his shoulder.

Gaye stood calf-deep in the boiling water. She was silent, searching the waters for sign of her husband. Jeannine shouted above the roar around us, "Pray! Everyone pray."

"Oh, Father in Heaven," Steve called loudly, looking up into the starlit sky. "Still the waters, Lord! Just as you did during the storm of long ago on Simon Peter's fishing boat. Still the waters and bring Joel back to us. Bring him back, Lord . . . " Steve's voice broke and his shoulders shook. His cheeks glistened with tears as he dropped his hands into the sea that suddenly swirled around his thighs.

Every second crawled as we waited—huddled together in desperation, each of us tortured with our own thoughts. Joel had to come back—we couldn't go on without our prophet. God wouldn't take him from us. But what if He did? What would we do? Oh, Lord in Heaven, what would we do! How could Joel survive so long out in that wild ocean? What if Floren and the others were dead, too? What if . . .

Suddenly a shout broke through the ominous silence. Raul's muscular shoulders appeared through the water's surface, fighting his way toward the shore. "Help, help!" His voice sounded weak. Steve and Brother Zarate plunged toward him. Raul turned around, pulling on the rope. Out of the midst of a ten-foot wave, Floren and Joel were washed toward us. Behind them, Fernando Castro's head stuck out above the water. Steve and Brother Zarate grabbed hold of Joel's limp body, pulling him to shore. Behind them, Floren struggled to his feet, dragging his exhausted body to the shoreline. He crumpled to his knees.

"Lay him on his stomach! Lay him on his stomach," Irene shouted, pushing the men away. "Someone get a blanket! Bring flashlights. Stand back, now! Stand back and give him some air."

Seventeen people crowded around Joel as he lay death-like on the sand. Jeannine and Gaye dropped to their knees beside their husband, willing him to live. Irene pounded his back with several quick thrusts, forcing water from his lungs. Then turning him over, she started C.P.R. Jeannine breathed into his mouth, working rhythmically with Irene. Suddenly the prophet's eyes opened, and he gagged, choking up salt-water.

"Joel! Joel, can you hear me?" Gaye sobbed. "Joel, darling, say something! Tell me that you're okay."

Every eye was glued on Joel's face. He looked deathly gray in the yellow gleam of the flashlights, his eyes two cavernous circles staring up at the faces above him.

Suddenly his mouth moved, his hand motioning weakly toward the ocean. "A—a river—undercurrent—going out fast. Be careful, all of you," he croaked. "I'm okay. I'm fine, now. You—all fish."

"Now, Joel, you just relax. We're through fishing for tonight," Floren's voice shook. "You're not out of danger yet so take it easy. Man, I've never been so scared in my life."

Struggling, Joel sat up, ignoring his wives' protests. Floren dropped down beside him and gently pushed on his shoulders, trying to make him lie back again.

Benjamin Zarate had stood quietly at the side of the crowd, his brown eyes filled with misery as he watched his friend. Suddenly he pushed his way through the kneeling people to Joel's side. Joel looked up at him and lifted his hand. Benjamin gripped it, pulling the Prophet to his feet. He slid an arm around Joel's waist and looked up into his eyes.

"Joel, my friend," the old man's voice quavered. "I thought we had lost you. I thought Satan had won and snatched you from us."

Joel's voice was still feeble, but his eyes were steady, as he answered, "Benjamin, the Lord's plan for His people won't fail. Our mission has hardly begun, so you know it's not my time to go. Remember what I told you earlier today, when we were looking for water? Have a little faith, Brother. Have a little faith."

Chapter 28

I sprinkled the last of my cornstarch on Melanie's raw bottom and pinned her diaper on, careful not to make it too tight around her legs. She sniffled, stood up, and looked at me with bright, pain-filled eyes. Gathering her close, I hugged her, my chest aching as I felt how thin she had become.

"I'm so sorry, baby," I whispered. "I've got to get you some decent food, something besides beans and carrots. Oh, and beets, we can't forget the beets."

I dropped back on the couch, sighing as I watched Melanie toddle across the floor toward a toy. She'd had diarrhea for a solid month, caused from improper food for her sixteen-month-old stomach. The medicine Lucy had given me for her wasn't working. Neither was the salve for her bleeding bottom. I needed to take her to a doctor.

I need to see a doctor myself, I thought ruefully. I hadn't had the money for a check-up since realizing that I was pregnant again. My second child was due in three months.

This past year had been a long and hard one—months of watching from a painful distance as Aunt Thelma's family became even more engrossed in Ervil's affairs. Since Ervil's removal from the patriarchal office, he had kept a low profile around the colonies. I knew he came and went occasionally—his car could be seen parked in the Chynoweths' driveway. He had made their home his base in Los Molinos. Although I still dropped in to see the Chynoweths on a regular basis, I gave their place a wide berth whenever Ervil was around.

There were several people in Los Molinos who now openly sided with Ervil, attending the private meetings he organized in the Chynoweths' home. One of these people was a man named Conway LeBaron, a cousin to the LeBaron men and a rather recent member of the church. Another of Ervil's new followers was one of Brother Zarate's sons. It angered me to see Benjamin Zarate's lovely, close-knit family being torn apart.

It seemed to me that Verlan and Joel ignored what was happening, and it angered and frustrated not only me, but Irene as well. She and I had discussed it just the other day. Joel had even agreed to let Ervil's group use our Church building for their Sunday meetings, with their meeting starting as soon as ours adjourned. The tension between the two groups of people, as Ervil's group took possession of the church, and Joel's group left, was revolting. Irene had ranted to me about it, saying, "I can't believe what ostriches Joel and Verlan are! Why don't they do something? How can they just sit back and watch that snake weasel his way into people's heads? Oh, Susan, it worries me to death. I wish they'd ban him from the colony."

Well, I had other things to worry about at present. I closed my eyes and leaned my head back, reluctantly considering Lillie's offer, yesterday at church, to buy my guitar. The thought of it caused bitterness to rise in my throat—the dreadful thought of selling my prized possession to Lillie, of all people. Especially now that I knew for certain of her plans to marry Verlan.

It wasn't just speculation now. No sir, Verlan had secretly told Irene about their plans, and the moment he was gone from town, she had come to my trailer and told me.

According to Irene, Verlan had persistently asked Lillie to marry him over the past months, and she'd finally accepted. It was as simple as that. The wedding would take place in a couple of weeks.

And to think that I had actually started liking Lillie again! Ever since that night on the beach, the night of Joel's accident, I had tried to put the past aside and forgive Lillie for her secret involvement with Verlan. On her weekend trips home from San Diego we had even spent a bit of time together. And now she had changed her mind again and was planning to marry Verlan after all.

Verlan, of course, hadn't confided in me about their plans. He knew my feelings on the matter very well. So to avoid a problem, he'd said nothing at all. The thought caused rage inside me, hot, hateful rage.

I fidgeted restlessly on the couch. In spite of my anger toward Lillie, I had to consider selling her my guitar in order to have doctor money. Verlan, I knew, wouldn't be coming down to see us until after he and Lillie were married. There was no way to get in touch with him, so I couldn't count on him for advice or help. Verlan Jr. had sent us all the money he could, with instructions to make it last for two weeks. It was substantially less than we were used to, my share barely covering the cost of filling my empty butane tank. It left me no choice but to rely solely on the family garden and the big bag of beans in Lucy's shed for food—which explained Melanie's condition. Beverly's new little girl had diarrhea, too.

Suddenly Melanie let out a cry. She turned and looked at me, her pale face contorted with pain, her legs spreading stiffly apart.

"Oh, doggonit! Not again," I breathed, hurrying to her. It hadn't been ten minutes. I laid her down and changed the diaper, washing the acid liquid from her blistered bottom and spreading on a thick layer of Lucy's cow-teat salve. Blood oozed through the yellow covering, staining my fingers.

Picking up my sobbing little girl, I rocked her as I struggled with the decision before me. She needed to see a doctor. I would have to bury my pride and resentment and sell Lillie my guitar.

"Knock, knock, Aunt Susan." Kaylen, Irene's blond, twelve-year-old son, stuck his head inside my doorway, interrupting my gloomy thoughts. Kicking the mud from his shoes, he lumbered in.

"Here's your milk. Mama said to tell you she sent you part of our share for Melanie. How's she doin'?"

He set a half-gallon jug down on the table and picked Melanie up, talking gently to her as he nuzzled her cheek.

"Thanks, Kaylen," I smiled tiredly, "She's still the same." I patted the seat beside me, impressed at how gentle the boy was with his little sister. He dropped down next to me, snuggling Melanie onto his lap.

"How're things at school?"

He shrugged, making a face. "Same ol' crap. I don't learn nothin'. I can't wait until I'm old enough to go to San Diego with Verlan Jr. and Chad and earn some money." He looked out the window at the rain, his eyes shadowed, "When I do, I'll promise you one thing. My money's going to the family! You and Mom and Aunt Lucy'll have what you need. I'm sick and tired of seeing y'all go without. It ain't right."

I looked at his serious, youthful face, my heart bursting with love for him. "Kaylen, that's the nicest thing anyone's told me since I can remember when," I declared, squeezing his arm. "But I hope by then we won't need to use you boys' money. You'll have families of your own to support. By then, your dad'll figure something else out."

Kaylen glanced at me. "I'm willing to do my part," he said shortly. As he shifted Melanie on his knee, she whimpered and looked up at him, her blue eyes bright with sudden tears.

Kaylen's gaze narrowed as he scanned her pale face. Suddenly he looked at me and roared, "Aunt Susan, you need to take Melly to the doctor. She's been sick for too long. Just look at her! She's flabby, like her flesh's turning to water. Look at the purple around her eyes. You've got to do something."

I looked away from Kaylen's earnest face and nervously chewed my nails. He was absolutely right. I had been acting stupid and childish not to put my baby's well being above my own pride and anger at Lillie. I should have jumped at the chance to sell her my guitar yesterday, when she first offered to buy it. I could have had Melanie to a doctor by now.

I abruptly stood. "Kaylen, I want you to go and find Lillie. She's most likely at Jeannine's. Tell her I need to see her and ask her to come. Will you do that for me?"

Kaylen's eyes met mine as he got to his feet, but he didn't say anything, just nodded, content to trust me. Glancing from Melanie to me, he headed for the door. "I'll hurry," he promised, dashing out.

I rocked Melanie in my arms and watched Kaylen from the big window until he disappeared behind Silver's place. Then I slowly walked to the middle bedroom, put the baby in her bed, and picking up my guitar, carried it to the couch. I had a bit of furniture oil left, and I cleaned the light-colored wood, buffing it until it glowed.

Why, I wondered, did I feel so sad? Was it because the guitar meant so much to me, or was it because she would be taking possession of it? I wondered again what had motivated Lillie to finally choose Verlan for a husband. I knew there were several other men interested in marrying her; as was my cousin Mark. Mark liked her a bit too much—it was obvious by the way he mooned around her whenever she was in town. I shook my head, thinking about it. The way Mark was involving himself with Ervil's group made me glad for Lillie's sake that she paid no attention to him.

But why Verlan? Lillie saw how his families lived—how we did without. She was aware of how much Verlan was gone from home. Our family was one of the largest in the church, yet Lillie had chosen to be a part of it.

Placing the guitar strap over my shoulder, I stood, lightly strumming the chords to a favorite tune as I watched out the window.

Lillie had a good job in San Diego. She owned her own car. Irene told me she had even purchased her own furniture and placed it in storage, so that when she had a house, she could furnish it. I could just imagine how fancy and comfortable Lillie's home would be. Verlan was going to love staying at her place.

And then there was me. I had little of value, little of my own. Looking around at my trailer, I realized that everything in it had been loaned or given to me—the dishes, bedding, table and chairs. Every item had been used, and certainly looked it—except for my guitar. It was the nicest thing I owned, other than my wedding ring. And now my guitar would belong to Lillie, the girl who was marrying my husband—the girl who had everything.

I shook the thought away as Lillie's car turned the corner. She pulled up next to the trailer, waving as she saw me through the window. Opening the door, I stood on the threshold, watching as she walked toward me. Her steps were small and modest, feminine as a cat's.

"Hi," her voice was soft. "Kaylen said you wanted to talk to me."

"Come on in," I held the door open and stepped back.

As she moved to the couch and sat, I could sense her nervousness. Her lips were in a tight line, her bright blue eyes determined-looking. Suddenly I realized she was expecting me to chew her out about marrying Verlan, and she was steeling herself in preparation for it. Her gaze swept around my trailer, taking in the scattered toys and littered table, then resting on me in surprise as I held out my guitar.

"You said you wanted to buy it," I said shortly. "Well, I'm ready to sell."

Startled, she took the guitar from me. "Are you sure . . . ? I thought you didn't want to do this." Her eyes probed mine as I tried to hide my unease.

"I need the money." I stood up and turned my back to her. Lillie sat uncertainly, holding the guitar on her lap. I could feel her watching me, and I knew she realized how upset I was.

"Susan, if it's money you need, I could loan you some. I would be glad to."

"That won't be necessary, thank you just the same. If you're interested in buying my guitar, it's for sale. If you're not, I'll find someone else who wants it." I took a deep breath and stared out the window.

The contents of her purse rustled as she dug into it. Then she hesitantly said, "Here, I checked on prices for used guitars in San Diego, and ones similar to yours are going for fifty dollars. Will that be okay with you?"

Fifty dollars! My hand shook as I held it out and took the money. I had never had fifty dollars all at once in my life. It would pay a doctor, and buy so many other things that I needed . . . "This will be just fine," I said, keeping my tone expressionless.

"Susan, please . . . " Lillie's voice dropped and failed. I glanced up at her face, noting the pleading in her eyes. "Please don't hate me."

As I realized what she was referring to, the blood immediately rose to my face. "I can't promise you that," I snapped. "My feelings aren't to be considered in your plans, so what do you care how I feel? It wouldn't change your mind, now would it?"

Lillie hesitated, the color rising in her cheeks. Visibly swallowing, she said, "I'm doing what I believe is right. You have to understand that. I don't mean to hurt you. Verlan doesn't, either. You have no idea what he's going through!

Verlan is more upset over how you will take this than over any of his other wives. He feels so deeply about you . . . "

"Oh, I just love hearing from you how my husband feels!" I sneered. "I suppose he tells you everything, right? All of our little secrets, all of his fondest desires—I suppose the two of you are just so close . . . "

I turned away, hiding from Lillie's red-rimmed eyes the torment of my own. The seconds ticked by as I fought back tears. Why didn't she just leave! Our business was over with. Couldn't she see I hated being around her now—that just looking at her made my heart want to break?

Her voice was muffled when she spoke again. "It amazes me that you think you have reasons for jealousy about me! It just amazes me. How do you think I feel, listening to Verlan talk about you? Susan, his eyes sparkle when he talks about you. His voice fills with laughter and he looks so young . . . Oh, he talks of the others, too, but it's not the same. The more I'm around him, the more I'm convinced that you're the very heart of him. I'm marrying him knowing that." Suddenly she was beside me, forcing me to look at her. "Do you understand what I'm saying?" she whispered.

Staring into her eyes, I slowly shook my head.

Lillie shrugged lightly and let go of my shoulders. "Verlan has a favorite wife. It's you. You're it. I can't take your place in his life, no one can. There is no reason for you to be jealous of me."

I stared incredulously at Lillie as her words rang in my ears. His favorite wife? Me?

"That's . . . that's not true!" I stammered. "You're just saying it. You're trying to make me feel better, hoping I'll ease your guilt and welcome you into the family. Well, I'm not going to do it."

Lillie's hand dropped from my arm. She backed away and, picking up her new guitar, walked to the door. Stopping with her hand on the knob, she turned back to me. Her voice was flat as she said, "One of these days you're going to realize that I'm right about this. I just hope you don't hold it over my head."

As the screen door closed, I stared blindly at the wad of money in my hand. Lillie was being ridiculous. She didn't know what she was talking about. How could she—she hadn't been around enough to know anything about Verlan's and my relationship.

I shoved the money Lillie had given me into my purse. Bundling Melanie and lifting her into my arms, we set out across Los Molinos toward Irene's. I would borrow the pickup and take my baby to a doctor.

The suggestion haunted me as I struggled over the damp trail. Me, Verlan's favorite wife. He didn't have a favorite—he was much too fair a man for that. And even if he did, it was Charlotte—Charlotte, his first love, his educated, right-arm of a wife. Or Irene, perhaps! Irene was such a happy, jolly person. I remembered the way Verlan's eyes danced when he joked with Irene . . .

The trail joined the main road. Shifting my tiny daughter's weight against my growing tummy, I rounded the corner and continued toward the distant yellow house that was Irene's.

Ahead and to the left of me sat a white and green trailer house. I looked up as its screen door closed with a loud bang. Involuntarily, I slowed my steps as Joel's third wife, Isabel, and Verlan's fifth wife, Ester, walked swiftly toward the road. Turning, they came directly toward me.

"Oh, boy," I groaned. "I wonder if they'll speak to me."

As the sisters approached, I glanced quickly at Isabel. Her plump, dark face was set, angry at me for her sister's sake. Looking at Isabel, I remembered the story of how she and Joel's first wife, Magdalena, detested each other. Word was that their mutual jealousy and hatred was the reason Magdalena had refused to leave Colonia LeBaron along with the rest of Joel's wives, when he had moved his families to Los Molinos. Magdalena had coldly informed Joel that no one town was big enough to hold both her and Isabel. Isabel had fervently agreed.

I turned my attention to Ester's marble-like features. Slender and petite, Ester walked with her head held high. In spite of her stiff back, each step she took was graceful and fluid. Jet-black hair hung in a single, heavy braid down her back and gently swayed with each step. Regal. That was Verlan's word for Ester. Verlan had said that when Ester was dressed in her Sunday best, she looked like a regal queen. Ester, my sister-wife whom I scarcely knew.

The women and I were almost opposite one another now, and still both of them were snubbing me. Well, I wasn't going to be as low. "Good afternoon, Ester, Isabel," I nodded cheerfully.

Ester's almond-shaped eyes met mine for a split second. Then pursing her full lips, she carefully, deliberately, spat on the ground between us. I whirled to stare at her. Just as haughty and superior as royalty itself, she moved on down the road, her steps light and lithesome.

Of all the cheap, disgusting . . . My face flamed. She even had the callousness to spit. Boy, wasn't she something! Cold as ice . . .

Hot tears forced their way to the surface. I brushed them hastily aside as I neared Irene's gate. Everything was going so wrong. My baby was sick...my beloved guitar was gone, Lillie was marrying Verlan, and Ester . . . snobby Ester treated me like dirt. The saddest part was, I didn't blame Ester. I understood her heartache. How could I blame Ester for hating me, when I resented Lillie so much! It seemed that I was Ester's cross to bear—just as Lillie was mine. The Lord had planned it that way.

Not even the huge amount of money in my purse, or Irene's company on the way to town could cheer me. Once again everything was so confusing. How, Lord, I silently pleaded, how am I supposed to handle all of this? Why can't I, like Lucy and Irene, just accept things and be happy? What's wrong with me?

Irene swiftly shuffled, then dealt the cards clockwise around the table in a smooth and experienced motion. Her face was sober, her blue eyes carefully following every movement of her hands. The silence in my trailer hung dismal and heavy as Beverly, Donna and I picked our cards up and examined them. I mentally decided not to bid, placed my cards face down in a perfect fan, and hurried to the stove to shake the pan of exploding popcorn on the burner.

Then I walked to the open north window of the trailer and, grabbing the four bottles of soda pop from the sill, unwrapped them from the wet towel. They felt pretty cold. Now would be a good time to serve them. The Cokes should make my guests happy—at least, as happy as possible under the grim circumstances. Verlan and Lillie's wedding was occurring in San Diego.

At this very instant, Lillie was becoming Verlan's seventh wife. And, Charlotte—Verlan's right arm—was standing next to our husband and his new bride at the wedding. The thought was nauseating.

I sniffed as I vigorously shook the pan of popping corn. Verlan had decided Charlotte should be the one to present Lillie to him during the ceremony. He'd discussed it with her last time he was home, asking her to do the honors.

It wasn't suggested that the rest of us be there. In fact, Verlan had stubbornly refused Irene's plea to go, saying he didn't want Lillie to feel uncomfortable. No, we certainly couldn't have that.

Of course Lillie's wedding reception would be a fancy one. She wouldn't settle for anything less. If anyone could present a gala occasion properly, Lillie could. Half of Los Molinos had left this morning to attend the wedding, leaving us wives of Verlan's conspicuously behind. Joel naturally was performing the ceremony.

I shook the popcorn pan once more, and poured the savory-smelling kernels into a bowl, adding melted margarine and salt. Then I hurried to the back bedroom to check on Melanie. She was still fast asleep, healthy, and gaining weight now, thanks to Lillie's money, the medicine the doctor had prescribed, and the jars of actual baby-food I had purchased. I tucked the covers tightly around her, touched her cheek, and hurried back to my company.

Donna, my pinochle partner, was getting impatient. She looked pointedly at me and demanded, "What'er you going to do, Suze?"

"Let you do the bidding." Carrying the popcorn bowl to the table, I set it in front of her.

Donna glanced at me and frowned. "Again? Aren't you even going to open?"

I set the bottles of Coke on the table, and glumly said, "Okay, I'll open and bid once."

"Thanks for the Coke, Susan. I'll bid two-sixty," Beverly intoned without looking up.

"Two-seventy," Donna said promptly, taking a swig of her pop.

Irene shoved a huge bite of fudge into her mouth before glaring at her cards again. Her brow wrinkled in concentration as she mumbled, "I'll bid three-fifty."

As if defying us to outbid her, Irene's eyes roamed around the table in an effort to read each face. Her gaze hesitated on each one, taking note of our long expressions.

With a sudden, exasperated snort, she threw her cards down and snapped, "Okay, dammit, I've had enough of you girls' mournful expressions to last me a lifetime. I say we cheer up."

She looked from Beverly to me, her blue eyes angry. "Look at all these expensive goodies you've bought, Susan! If it weren't for Donna and me, they'd be going to waste. Beverly, eat some fudge; what's the matter with you? We're at a party, girls—a party! Let's forget all about that damn wedding." I peered over the top of my cards at Beverly's swollen eyes. She'd cried plenty over this, too.

I took a slow breath and forced a smile. "You're right. We're being stupid. What do we care about Lillie, anyway? We can't do anything about it; we might as well have a good time." I picked my cards up again and threw an ace of clubs on the table.

"Play, Beverly," I nudged her and smiled.

Donna casually sloughed a card as the play moved to her. "Look at it this way," she said, "if Daddy had to marry again, you girls ought to be glad that he chose someone nice like Lillie."

Beverly glared at Donna. "Oh, fine! Wonderful. That's just what we need here tonight—someone on Lillie's side."

"I'm not on anyone's side, I'm just telling you how I feel. I'm glad Lillie's nice."

"Well, I happen to be glad she's skinny," Irene grinned wickedly, "skinny as Lucy's poor dog. Verlan's in for a big disappointment. I can just imagine him trying to cuddle up to Lillie's sharp bones."

Beverly looked at me, and we both giggled. Lillie wasn't as wretchedly thin as Irene suggested, but Irene's way of trying to cheer us up was so typical.

"Did I ever tell you girls what happened one night when Charlotte, Lucy and I lived together in the old, three story blue house in Ensenada? It's the one we lived in before Verlan built the big house."

Irene's eyes were dancing in a manner that I recognized. A long story was imminent, and setting my cards down, I relaxed to enjoy it.

"Well," Irene sniffed, "life was hell with the three of us living together like that—absolute hell. All those kids under one roof. Charlotte, of course, figured because she was the oldest and the first wife, she could boss Lucy and me around. I wasn't about to let her! She was always on such a high horse, telling Lucy and me what to do and acting like she was insulted if we didn't obey. Boy, she made me mad! I finally got tired of arguing with her, so I started ignoring her. She'd stick her nose in the air, stalk to her bedroom, and spend hours sulking over my 'negative attitude.'"

Irene made a face and shook her head, warming up to her story. "Verlan always sent Charlotte the household money," she continued, "and it griped me to death. Charlotte and I would go grocery shopping together, and she'd try to tell me what I could or couldn't buy. If I put a container of Cokes in the basket, Charlotte would put them back on the shelf and tell me I couldn't have 'em. I'd put them back in the basket and tell her to mind her own business, and she'd stalk out of the store, mad as a wet hen. Well, this one time Verlan was home with us, and it was my night with him. Charlotte, of course, had the big bedroom on the main floor. My tiny bedroom was directly above hers on the second floor, and Lucy's was down the hall from mine.

"That night I knew that Lucy was really depressed. She'd had a miscarriage and was having a hard time getting over it. You girls know Lucy—nothing phases her—so I knew she was bad off. When Verlan came on up to bed that night, I spent a few minutes with him, then I asked him to go spend the night with Lucy. She needed someone to cheer her up and I didn't care, I was tired anyway. So Verlan told me good night, went on into Lucy's bedroom, and went to bed."

I glanced at Beverly and Donna. Our card game had completely stopped, and the two of them were raptly listening to Irene, the hint of a grin on their faces. I took a slow, contented breath, cut myself a piece of fudge, and turned my attention back to Irene.

"I lay in bed awhile and couldn't seem to sleep, and suddenly I got this idea." Irene's eyes twinkled, and I grinned, watching her. "I knelt up on the bed and began to bounce, real rhythmic-like. Slow at first, then faster and faster. The harder I bounced, the harder I had to smother my laughter so Charlotte, in her bedroom below me, wouldn't hear it. I knew Charlotte thought that Verlan was with me, and I could just imagine the look on her face as her imagination ran away with her."

Beverly and I choked with laughter. "Oh, Irene," Beverly gasped, "I can't believe you did that! What happened then?"

"Well, every hour or so, all night long, I knelt up and bounced again. Now, you girls know Verlan. He's never gotten sexually carried away like that in his life, at least not to my knowledge, but I sure tried to make Charlotte think he was. You have no idea how much I enjoyed that! You should have seen Charlotte's face the next morning when I went down to breakfast," Irene giggled. "Her eyes were swollen, and she was pale and quiet. I acted real happy, and asked her what was the matter. I told her she didn't look so good. She just turned away, real quiet, and went to her bedroom. It was great," Irene chuckled again in remembrance.

I shook my head, wondering how Irene had the nerve to do it. "Did Charlotte ever find out the truth?"

"Oh, I'm sure she did. I imagine she accused Verlan of over-indulging me, and he let her know he'd spent the night with Lucy. I told Lucy about it the next morning, and she got a big kick out of it."

"Speaking of Lucy," I changed the subject, "I wish she would have come to my party. I imagine she could use some cheering up, too."

Donna hooted. "Aunt Lucy thinks playing cards is wicked. She'd never come to a card party. Besides, she doesn't care if Daddy gets married again. Aunt Lucy likes Lillie."

Irene glared at Donna, then abruptly changed the subject. "Well, guess what girls. Guess who visited me yesterday?"

"Who?" Beverly and I said in unison.

Irene rolled her eyes. "None other than Ervil the Great, in his fancy gold car. We had a long visit."

I pursed my lips. "What did he want?"

"You won't believe what he talked about. He was so affable and friendly, and acted like he and I were best of buddies. He wants to start a target practice for the women of Los Molinos."

"A what?"

"Target practice. You know, guns. He wants to teach all of us women how to shoot guns in case we should ever have the need to know how. He plans to talk to every woman in Los Molinos about it, so you two can expect a visit," Irene sniffed. "He's crazy as a loon."

"What did you tell him?"

Irene snorted, "That I wasn't interested, thank you. I told him to cross me off his list and not to bother coming back to see me."

I shuddered. "Well, I hope he knows better than to come to my house. He's well aware of how I feel about him. Beverly, if he comes to talk to you, don't let him in. Just tell him to go away."

She nodded in agreement.

"I'll be seeing Ervil before too long, though," I grimaced. "You girls know that Uncle Bud is taking a plural wife—Naomi Zarate, Benjamin's daughter, the young widow from Mexico City with the two children. Aunt Thelma and Uncle Bud are insisting that I come to the wedding. Ervil, of course, is performing the ceremony."

"How nice," Irene said sarcastically.

I nodded and paused, reflecting. "You wouldn't believe how happy Aunt Thelma is about Bud's marrying Naomi. She's absolutely thrilled. It almost doesn't seem genuine."

We settled into our pinochle game for the rest of the evening, and in spite of the anguish in our hearts, we enjoyed each other's company. It was midnight by the time we put the cards down.

"Do you know, I still can't believe how happy Thelma is about Naomi," I muttered as I sorted cards.

Beverly shrugged. "Things are different in their case, Susan. Thelma is Bud's only wife; why should she mind sharing him with Naomi? It's different with us. You can only cut the pie in so many pieces before no one gets enough."

Irene glanced at her and stood up. "I've heard enough talk about pies and weddings for one night," she yawned. "Come on Donna, let's go home." Cutting herself one last piece of fudge, Irene shoved it into her mouth. She waved goodnight to me and headed out the door toward the old pickup. Beverly and Donna trailed through the darkness behind her.

Chapter 29

The coal oil lamps resting on either end of the Chynoweth's piano and coffee table cast uncertain, ghostly shadows along the walls of their living room, shadows that at first held suspiciously still; then they wavered and dissolved as the warm bodies in the room merged closer together.

"Congratulations, Bud, Naomi!" A chorus of voices rang out as Ervil LeBaron's ceremonial words of Sealing for Time and Eternity came to a halt. The circle of guests moved in for the traditional hand shaking and backslapping.

I watched from my seat in the back of the room. I knew I should congratulate my uncle, but Ervil's people possessively surrounded him, leaving me little desire to barter for standing room. Other than the Chynoweths, not one of the group had spoken to me. I linked my fingers together around my swollen middle.

I had purposely arrived late. Knowing full well I would be the only one of Joel's followers invited to attend, I was hesitant to come, especially as I had sensed that Uncle Bud was the only one of the family who really wanted me here. All I desired to do, now that the ceremony was over, was give my uncle a quick hug and slip out the back door.

For the past few months, Aunt Thelma's natural warmth had slowly disappeared. Although the outward sham of being close, loving relatives still existed, complete with invitations for occasional Sunday dinners, there was a barrier in our relationship, an underlying strain between my aunt and me. Yet Uncle Bud treated me with more love and consideration than before. I knew, of course, that Aunt Thelma's coolness was because of my open contempt of Ervil.

And now as I watched the middle-aged groom, I swallowed an affectionate grin. Miserable in his Sunday suit, easy-going Uncle Bud kept craning his neck around and tugging at his tie. Sweat glistened on his sunburned forehead. He mopped at it, then grinned at his new wife. Naomi Zarate Chynoweth's dark eyes shyly met Uncle Bud's hazel ones. Covering her embarrassed smile with her palm, she quickly dropped her gaze.

Aunt Thelma stood straight and proud at Bud's right side as the guests lingered in the line to visit. Strikingly elegant in her pink and white outfit with the matching necklace and large, pearly earrings, her brown and silver hair had been gathered high on her head in soft curls. With her hair up, Aunt Thelma dwarfed Uncle Bud. A constant smile played across her glossy pink lips as she watched the events in her living room, yet the smile didn't reach her eyes. Obviously Aunt Thelma didn't consider Naomi a threat to her and Bud's relationship; Naomi wasn't in the least pretty—she was quiet, unassuming, and half Uncle Bud's age. But she was a stepping stone into the Celestial Kingdom—a necessary tool so that the Chynoweths could attain Godhood.

The bride's face brightened and was transformed into near-beauty when Mark, Rena, and Duane pushed through the small crowd to embrace her. Naomi's own son, twelve-year-old Alejandro stood shyly apart from the others, his brown eyes studying his new relatives.

As the group of young people moved on toward the kitchen, Mark casually draped his arm around Alejandro's shoulders, and pulled him along to the refreshment table. My cousin's action was gentle and protective. Mark will make a good stepbrother for the boy, I thought.

Rena was the last to excuse herself from her father and Naomi. As I watched her hurry across the room, I noted again that she'd certainly grown out of the gangly stage this past year. She'd become tall and graceful, and was budding into a beautiful young woman. Glistening, brown-gold hair hung to her waist in a mass of curls, sensuous against her cream-colored satin dress. The men would begin noticing her soon.

I looked back at the tight ring of well-wishers around Uncle Bud. Andres Zarate, the bride's younger brother and the only member of the large Zarate family to attend the wedding, crowded in close. Andres smiled broadly as he leaned an ear toward Ervil in order not to miss a word his idol said. Old Benjamin Zarate's absence from his daughter's wedding was, of course, conspicuous; religious arguments among the close-knit Zarate family were reaching the boiling point. Watching Andres, I realized that his father's passionate efforts at defending Joel's doctrine were useless. Andres beamed with pleasure as Ervil absentmindedly patted him on the shoulder.

Ervil ignored Andres, and extended his hand to his cousin, Conway LeBaron. Conway and one of his wives made up the outer edge of the circle. I looked quickly away, a hard lump in my throat. A month ago, Verlan had confided in me that Conway, our church treasurer for the past several years, had frozen all of our church funds and records, refusing to release them to Joel and Verlan. He had turned them over to Ervil, of course. Our church was penniless.

My heart was heavy as I watched the group. These people had believed in Joel, but now because of Ervil's demand for complete power and authority, they had not only rejected Joel, they blatantly ridiculed and threatened the very man they had previously revered as a prophet of God.

Ervil's quest for followers had expanded to people outside of Joel's disciples. Next to the piano, wearing an expensive suit and an arrogant smile stood a gray haired gentleman who was a stranger to me. Seated in front of him, his mousy little wife kept her eyes fastened on the floor as though ashamed and confused by the happenings in the room. Her husband was Ervil's honored guest. A diamond pinkie ring on the man's finger flashed and glimmered in the lamplight, and I suspected he was Ervil's latest answer to financial freedom.

From the other side of the room, Lorna caught my eye. Grinning, she pushed through the crowd. "How are you, Suze?" she whispered. "Everything okay?"

I nodded and gave her a stiff smile. "I'm just hot and tired. I think I'll go give Uncle Bud a kiss and then leave."

Lorna looked me over, her understanding gaze resting on my tummy. "When's the baby due?" she asked sympathetically.

"In a month," I sighed, then grinned at her. "Will you be staying down for a few days?"

She shook her head. "Ervil needs to get right back to San Diego. He's bringing Debbie down here, did you know? She's going to move back in with her parents for awhile."

"You're serious!" I squealed in delight. "Debbie's moving here? Well, that ought'ta liven this dead town up a bit!"

I grinned, my thoughts flashing back to three years ago, to the pretty girl from California who had pleaded with me to join her in marriage to Ervil. Debbie Bateman, the hilarious, foul-mouthed, gum-chewing girl, rumored to be terribly unhappy in her marriage. Debbie's parents had moved into the place across from Lucy's only last week. I'd been so busy with my own affairs I hadn't had a chance to go see them, and so hadn't heard about Debbie.

I glanced again to the front of the room. Most of the wedding guests had meandered into the kitchen where Aunt Thelma was busy at the refreshment table. I frowned, noting that Ervil still hovered over Bud and Naomi. The crowded room was like an oven, and I longed to get the amenities over and go out into the fresh air.

Awkwardly passing time, I turned to Lorna. "What do you think of your father's new wife?"

She glanced at the couple, shrugged and whispered, "Dad's going to have his hands full with that woman. If he can keep her in line, I guess she'll be okay."

Shocked, I stared at Lorna. "Why do you say that? Naomi's so quiet and sweet, you hardly know she's around!"

"Ervil thinks she's trouble..." Lorna's words trailed off, and she glanced guiltily at me as she remembered I was a "Joelite" and couldn't be trusted. Sickened, I quickly looked to the cozy picture Ervil, Bud, and Naomi made, standing by the piano.

"How proud I am of you," Ervil was saying to Bud, his voice floating above the noise in the room, "I'm sure you'll honor the Lord with a house full of new sons." Ervil patted Uncle Bud's back and smiled patronizingly down at the bride. "Strong sons, who will be soldiers in our army; what do you say, Naomi?"

Naomi's bowed head lifted. She looked directly into Ervil's eyes and whispered something; then with a scornful expression, she pointedly turned her back. Ervil frowned, muttered something to Bud, turned on his heel, and stalked from the room.

My heart skipped a beat and my eyes widened in surprise. "Well, well," I mumbled under my breath. "Naomi Zarate, no wonder Ervil thinks you're trouble! Your father would be proud of you—fancy a tiny, shy woman like you turning a cold shoulder to Ervil LeBaron! There is finally a woman in the Chynoweth family who doesn't trip over herself to lick his boots!"

"Come on, Lorna," I said triumphantly. I grabbed her arm and pulled her along with me toward Uncle Bud and his bride. Naomi was someone I wanted to know better.

Bud's leathery cheek felt smooth against mine as we hugged. "I was afraid you weren't going to show up," he growled into my ear. "I was about to have Mark go get you."

"Now, Bud, I wouldn't miss your wedding, you know that." As I looked up at the teasing, laughing face that I loved like my own father's, tears filled my eyes. A foreboding came over me, the sense that my adopted family would soon be whisked away, removed forever from my sight because of Ervil's schemes.

"Susie, honey, this is a happy occasion!" Uncle Bud reproached. "I hope those are happy tears."

I whispered, "Nothing—nothing will ever change the fact that we're family, will it, Uncle?"

"No, Darlin', nothing ever will change that."

I squeezed him again, then turned to his bride. "Welcome, Naomi," I whispered to her. I searched her eyes. Oh, God, I silently thought, let me see some stability in her. Please...

Naomi's usual shyness had disappeared. As I took her soft hands, a small flame of hope for the Chynoweths began to burn within me. Perhaps she could talk some sense into Uncle Bud, make him see how fanatical and dangerous Ervil was. Maybe in her own quiet way, Naomi would be able to do what my open anger and disgust hadn't accomplished.

The guests stood around the kitchen, loudly visiting in little groups, as Lorna and I joined Aunt Thelma. She handed each of us a saucer of wedding cake. Glancing briefly at me, her eyes narrowed. "Susan, you look miserable. Should I have Mark drive you home?"

I shook my head. "No, thanks, I can walk. I did want to talk to you about some things going on at school, but it'll wait until Monday."

She nodded, then briskly said, "Did you notice where Rena went? She's supposed to be serving the punch."

I glanced around. "Maybe she's gone outside. I'll go have a look."

"I'll check the bedrooms, Mother," Lorna offered, hurrying away.

The night air felt cool on my hot cheeks. I took a tired breath, glad the evening was over. A fragment of the dread I had felt while talking to Uncle Bud still gripped me, and I exhaled, trying to ignore the vague emptiness.

Somewhere in the moist darkness, a faint sound—soft, girlish laughter mixed with the lower tones of a man's voice, wafted toward me. The tones sounded intimate, and I sensed I was intruding on something private. I hesitated, then continued around the corner of the house and stopped in the shadows of Uncle Bud's fig tree.

Silhouetted against the gray plaster of the house, Ervil held a woman in his arms. Pale moonlight glistened off of Rena's light-colored satin dress. Ervil's voice was gentle and soothing, his words muffled against her hair.

No! I thought wildly. My heart leaped into my throat, my hands suddenly clammy. No! Not Rena—not my baby cousin. Ervil can't have her—I won't let him.

I moved out of the shadow of the tree just as the kitchen door opened and Lorna stepped onto the porch. Rena pulled herself from Ervil's grasp.

"Oh, there you are," Lorna said, peering at Rena. She laughed and walked closer, her laughter abruptly dying as she noticed Ervil's arm around her sister's waist.

Ervil casually dropped his hand. His eyes darted from Lorna to me, then he brushed past his wife and stalked into the house.

Lorna stood as though frozen; her startled gaze fastened on her sister, the light-hearted voices from inside the house mocking the rigid moment. Rena's chin came up and she boldly met Lorna's eyes. "What did you want?" she snapped.

Seconds ticked by as the sisters stared at one another. "Mother was looking for you," Lorna finally whispered. She abruptly turned and stumbled after Ervil.

Annoyed, Rena tossed her head and called after her, "Well, I wasn't exactly lost!" She sighed with exasperation and bounded up the steps. Hesitating a second, she threw a glance at me and mumbled, "Night, Suze." She turned the doorknob.

"Rena, wait!" I commanded, suddenly finding my voice. I hurried to her side, yanked the door shut, grabbed her arm and pulled her away from the house. My hands shook.

"Rena, honey, listen to me!" I whispered urgently. "You don't know what you're doing, Rena. Please stay away from Ervil!"

Light from the kitchen window softly illuminated her face as she regarded me. "I don't know what you're talking about," she said mockingly.

"Yes you do!" I snapped. "I saw the two of you, I know what was going on. Rena, Ervil is not the great man of God that he would have you think he is. He's trouble, Rena, more than you could ever understand right now. Please, oh, please, believe me and stay away from him!"

Rena's laughter was insolent. "You're the one who doesn't understand! He and I were just talking. Now let go of me."

I grabbed her arm tighter, and hissed, "I'll bet he told you he had a revelation that you were to marry him. I'm right, am I not?"

Even in the poor light I could see the startled flash of impact in Rena's eyes. She swallowed, slowly dropped her gaze from mine, and began to twist her hands together. "How did you know?" she finally whispered.

It was my turn to laugh, but the sound was tight and humorless. "Oh, Rena—I know because he pulled the same thing on me. I almost married Ervil myself; did you know that? I was stupid! He used the revelation trick on Debbie too, and I don't have to tell you how miserable she is. Teresa Rios is another of Ervil's victims. Pretty convenient, isn't it, Rena? He preys on young, innocent, unsuspecting girls and has them married to him before they know what's happening."

She listened to my heated whispers, her eyes on the shaft of pale lamplight that fell between the house and the shadows of the tree. As my words ceased, she inhaled and looked me in the eyes.

"There's no sense in wasting your breath," she said curtly. "You don't know what you're talking about anyway. If I were you I'd mind my own business. Good night." Rena's feet made no sound as she walked to the door and slipped from my sight.

"Teacher! Can I go to the out-house?" Someone yanked on my sleeve, and I looked up at Sam Babbitt, Jr.

"Yes, Sam, go on," I said guiltily, his insistent demand bringing me back to the hot schoolroom filled with eight, nine, and ten year olds.

I had to stop this. I couldn't let Saturday night's incident with Rena and Ervil distress me so much. Chances were, my fourteen year-old cousin was already sealed to him. She would become like Lorna and Anna Mae, another one of Ervil's soldiers, ready to do his bidding in his attempt to take over Joel's church, and eventually, the world. Rena was young, loyal, energetic and fearless. She was exactly the material Ervil wanted.

I jerked the thought from my mind, stood, and forced myself to concentrate on my students. For the rest of the afternoon I listened to the children read aloud, then had them study for their spelling test. School would be out for the summer on Friday, and I had impatiently marked off the days for the past month. My advanced pregnancy made me restless, the hot classroom leaving me drained each afternoon.

When the final bell clanged I shooed the children outside. As I rummaged through my desk, gathering papers and belongings, the dividing door between my classroom and Aunt Thelma's opened. Aunt Thelma strode toward me.

I glanced up at her, "Ready to go?"

"No. Not quite. You and I should have a little talk before we call it a day," her voice was soft and even, but the look on her face belied her tone. Grabbing a chair from behind one of the children's desks, she placed it next to my desk and sat down.

"What? Aunt Thelma, what is it?"

"I want you to stay away from Rena."

"Stay away from—What do you mean?" I gasped, paling.

Her blue eyes, cold with anger, filled me with alarm. "I'll not have you criticizing Ervil to her," she softly continued, "she's young and impressionable and easily swayed. Her guidance is not your responsibility, so please keep your negative thoughts to yourself."

"Do you mean you want Rena to marry Ervil? You want her to be as unhappy and–and neglected as Lorna is? Oh, Aunt Thelma, I can't believe you would–"

"Just like I said, stay away from Rena," she interrupted. "I know what's best for her." She stood, shoved the chair out of the way, and stared at me for a long moment. "Do you know, I feel sorry for you, Susan," her voice was still quiet. "You've been given every chance to accept Ervil. You can never use the excuse that you didn't know any better. The Lord gives each of us the opportunity to repent, then it's up to us."

I gulped, my hands shaking.

The tiny muscles in Aunt Thelma's jaw and temple quivered. Suddenly she blurted, "I love you. You know that. But you have a closed mind, and I refuse to allow it to affect my family. I'm afraid I'll have to ask you to not come over again." She strode determinedly to the door and jerked it open. Hesitating with her hand on the knob, she looked back at me. "By the way," she sweetly added, "you're mistaken about Rena and Ervil."

My heart pounding, I slumped in my chair and stared at the rough-hewn, homemade door. The dark rectangle of wood blurred in and out of my vision, and I closed my eyes, the pain in my chest suffocating me.

"Cry!" I finally screamed to myself, "just cry it out so you can breathe." But the tears wouldn't come. The minutes silently ticked by, the late afternoon sunshine steadily streamed through the western window. Its rays danced across the width of the desk before me, and disappeared, as the ball of fire crept into the ocean. Soft purple shadows bathed the adobe schoolroom.

I shuddered with the effort to breathe, to make myself think. I had to think . . .

Rena must have been more shaken by my words than I'd realized. I had sown doubt in her mind about Ervil and she had discussed it with her mother. Why had Aunt Thelma reacted so violently? How could my warm, motherly, fun-loving aunt have changed so much in the past year? Her icy request that I stay away from her family astounded me. That she would allow Ervil to become a dividing factor between her own family was something I wouldn't have dreamed possible. Why had she bothered to deny Rena's and Ervil's involvement? Why the deceit?

I leaned back in my chair and stared up at the open-beamed ceiling, my thoughts racing. I knew now. I suddenly understood the depth of the harm Ervil's rebellion could do. It had been the question in my mind for the past three years, and now I had the answer.

Father against son and son against father, mother against daughter and daughter against mother, mother-in-law against daughter-in-law—." The words of the scripture played like a broken record in my mind; This passage in the book of Luke had never made sense to me, and I had skimmed over it as so much garbled poetry. It spoke of the division that would come in the last days, caused by evil, sinful teachings.

Believers against unbelievers. I now recognized its prophetic meaning. The inclusive evil of Ervil's doctrine—the power it had to physically and emotionally tear families apart, limb by limb. The LeBarons—the Zarates—and now the scripture had become a reality in my own family. How would I ever stand Los Molinos and this lonely way of life without the comforting association of the Chynoweths?

Chapter 30

D ebbie Bateman LeBaron lifted my baby son high above her head and wiggled his little body back and forth. Grinning up at him, she said, "This little James Val is sure a lot bigger than my baby was at two months. He's all LeBaron. I thought you were going to name him James Bruce?"

"Oh, I was, but I like the name Bruce so much, and hate to waste it on a middle name that James'll rarely use. I told Verlan I want to save it for my next boy—Debbie, give him to me!" I gasped.

She dodged my attempts at rescue, giggled, and continued her chatter. "I thought my Jeremy was going to be the runt of the LeBaron kids for the longest time. He's outgrown the runt-stage, but he still doesn't look at all like his daddy." Debbie muttered under her breath, "Yep. Jeddie's ol' daddy, bless Ervil's peaked heart."

At that, she handed me my baby. Leaning down, she picked up her own toddler and hugged him tight. "Weren't you, Jeddie?" she murmured, "You were a little blond runt-baby."

As Debbie dropped down beside me on her mother's sofa and placed her little boy on her fast-dwindling lap, her playful attitude slipped away, replaced by the morose, withdrawn young woman who had met me at the door an hour ago.

I laid James down, turned, and contemplated Debbie. The emptiness in her hazel eyes, the tightness around her mouth, looked nothing like the pretty, vivacious girl with whom I had gone to school three years ago—the girl who had pleaded with me to join her, in the same ceremony, in marriage to Ervil.

Glancing toward the kitchen, I wondered if Debbie's mother could hear us. Although I knew the Batemans were staunch followers of Joel, I wasn't certain how Ruth would react to what I planned to say to her daughter. Debbie had weighed heavily on my mind for days, ever since Aunt Thelma, Mark, Duane, and Rena had moved to San Diego.

One by one in the past two months, Ervil's followers had abandoned Los Molinos, all but Uncle Bud and his wife, Naomi—and Debbie. The tension between the "Ervilites" and the "Joelites" had gotten completely out of hand of late, to the point of ugly and heated arguments between the two groups.

Ervil was claiming ownership to the church land in Baja, which had Joel's people furious. They bickered over who got to use the church building and to whom it belonged. Some of Ervil's men had been seen around town with weapons in their belts. Unpleasant and uninvited visits were paid to many of Joel's people, visits laced with underlying threats; along with advice to pay tithe to Ervil, to be re-baptized, to align ourselves at Ervil's side, or be under the wrath of God. The whole town was immensely relieved, therefore, when the "Ervilites" packed their belongings and moved away. Aunt Thelma and her children were among the first to go.

I had run into Uncle Bud a couple of times at Castro's little grocery store, and I asked him why he and Naomi were staying in Los Molinos instead of moving away with the others. Uncle Bud was evasive, withdrawn, and appeared to be confused and unhappy. I guessed things weren't going well between him and Aunt Thelma, although Uncle Bud was driving back and forth each week between Los Molinos and San Diego to see his two families. Bud did say that he had moved Naomi into Aunt Thelma's house, and he had offered the news that his new wife was pregnant.

And now I wondered about Debbie's position. Since her arrival in Los Molinos, I knew she had scarcely left the privacy of her mother's home. In our two prior visits she avoided talking about Ervil at all, yet I sensed the cloud of depression that surrounded her.

Keeping my voice low, I suddenly pleaded, "Debbie, why won't you talk to me? I'm your friend, remember? Please let me try to help."

She stiffened, glanced at me, shrugged, and nervously began to twist her wedding ring. "What's the use of talking about my hang-ups? Just so you can say I told you so?"

"I wouldn't do that, you know."

She looked away, fidgeting, then spread her hands in surrender. "Okay—Ervil lied to me—I haven't learned to adore him like he promised I would, and I'm unhappy as hell. That's the least of it. It's killing me that he's splintered off from the church! I don't know what to do! I'm torn between my mom and dad, and my husband. I don't know what's right anymore . . . There. Just like you thought." She closed her eyes and leaned against the couch, absently patting Jeremy's back with soft, even strokes.

I nodded and forced back the lump in my throat. That I wasn't in this same situation was nothing short of a miracle. She restlessly moved Jeremy off her lap, walked to the window, and stared out at the weed-covered meadow across the road. "It's been easy, most of the time," she muttered, "because Ervil's gone so much. It's when he's around that life's so unbearable. I hate his preaching at me, Susan—I hate it! All the pressure to be his "loyal and dedicated wife" like Anna Mae is, and to back him up in his rebellion against Joel. To "leave father and mother, and cling to my husband," she mimicked. "I can hardly stand to be around him. But . . . Now I'm having another kid—"

She glanced at me and shrugged. "I have no choice but to stay with him. There's no use whining about it."

"That's ridiculous," I snapped, jumping to my feet. "You always have a choice, do you hear me? You have a choice."

I began to pace around the Bateman's living room with furious memories of Ervil's arms around Rena. I wondered if Debbie knew about his latest conquest. My innocent young cousin would end up in the same situation as Debbie, in time. I whirled to her, and through clenched teeth, said, "There is a solution. Just tell that—that bastard to forget about you, to leave you alone and not come back. Debbie, he's headed down a path of destruction, and he's dragging his families and followers along with him. You don't need me to tell you that. The guy has big problems. Get out of the mess while you still can."

Silence after my outburst. I watched Debbie, hoping to see a change in her expression, but despair clouded her eyes. She felt trapped—bound and sealed to Ervil for eternity.

James began to fuss, supplying my excuse for departure. Calling for Melanie, who was playing outside with the Bateman children, I told Debbie good-bye.

The trip back across the colony was a slow one, with Melanie's short legs wandering across the road. My thoughts were filled with Debbie. What would I do if I were in her place? Would I have the courage to leave my husband, take my children and start a new life of my own? The church regarded divorce as shameful, but Debbie's case was different. Joel's people would support her decision.

As I rounded the corner by the largest windmill, I shifted the diaper-bag strap on my shoulder, rearranged James in my arms, and kept my eyes firmly on the road ahead of me. At the far end I could see my trailer. I was careful not to waste a glance at the new home being built on the corner lot opposite from the windmill.

Debbie wasn't the only one with problems. Who would have ever thought that Verlan would wait until just this past month to move my trailer-house down from the hill, so that I could be conveniently closer to the well and washing machine at Irene's. Now every time I stepped outside, absolute proof that Lillie was extra-special, and of great importance to Verlan, slapped me in the face. All I had to do to was look to the corner lot where three hired men were feverishly building her house.

The injustice was, that I had been married to Verlan for three years, had given him two children, and I still lived in my old, ugly, drafty trailer. Lillie, on the other hand, had been married only six months, and already Verlan was ensuring that she be the recipient of a brand new house of her own.

The Saturday morning, two weeks ago, when I had seen her parading around her new lot, giving directions to the hired men had angered me to no end. I didn't care if she was pregnant; Verlan's building her a home before me still was the height of injustice and it was beyond me how he could do it. He was due home tonight, and I could hardly wait to give him a big, fat, piece of my mind.

"Come on Melanie, stop goofing around!" I snapped, yanking on her hand as she leaned down to pick up an interesting rock.

Behind us, the roar of a small engine turning the corner all but drowned out the boyish voice that hollered, "Hi, Aunt Susan!" Ivan LeBaron, Lillie's thirteen-year-old brother, careened to a stop next to us.

"Hello, Ivan. What have you got there?" I forced my voice to be calm, and I looked curiously at the contraption Ivan sat upon. Three bicycle tires, odds and ends of lumber, and a small gasoline engine, hooked by pulleys to the rear tires, made up the tricycle.

Bright blue eyes and a freckled face grinned up at me from the low seat. "Figured I'd show off my new 'sheen. Pretty neat, huh?"

"Oh, yeah, it's quite the—the—interesting looking cart. Did you build it by yourself?

"Yep. Had to take my motorbike apart, though. The motor used to be the one on Aunt Gaye's well, but it burnt out, so Daddy gave it to me. I had to re-wind it. It works real good now. Want me to give Melly a ride home?"

I looked doubtfully at Ivan's "sheen". "Are you sure it's safe?"

"Course it is. I'll go real slow. Here, give me your diaper bag. Come on Melly, come to Ivan." Gently lifting Melanie up on the seat in front of him, he put an arm protectively around her waist. With a wave of his hand, they putted on down the road.

I grinned and shook my head, glad for the interruption to my ugly thoughts. Ivan LeBaron was quite the boy. I had come to know and like him during my months of teaching at the school. Although slow to grasp the basics of reading and history, Ivan was a whiz at math, and according to Steve Silver, a genius at mechanics and electronics. Thus, his new motor-cart didn't surprise me.

As I neared the trailer, they were seated on the front step. "Safe as a passenger car," Ivan grinned smugly.

Laughing, I tousled his dark-brown hair. "Come on in, you two. I'll bet I can find a cookie."

"Sounds good to me," Ivan agreed.

Soon the three of us were seated around the kitchen table visiting over milk and cookies, and when Verlan's silver pickup pulled up next to the trailer, it surprised me. I hadn't expected him to arrive until late in the night.

He bounded up the steps, threw the door open, and joyfully shouted, "You home?" In two giant strides he was at the table, his blue-green eyes dancing with happiness. "Hello Ivan. Hi, Melanie, sweetheart!"

He squeezed Ivan's shoulder and planted a sound kiss on the top of Melanie's head. Then grinning at me, he crowed, "You beautiful doll, it's so good to see you! Come give me a kiss."

It had been six long weeks since I had last seen Verlan. I desperately wanted to jump up and fling myself at him. I wanted to, but just as I pushed my chair back, I remembered Lillie's house. I relaxed back into the chair.

"Hello, Verlan," I said coolly. "It's nice to see you. I didn't expect you so soon."

Verlan ignored my coldness. Grabbing me bodily from the chair, he pulled me tightly against him and forced me to meet his kiss. Over his shoulder, I caught sight of Ivan's bright eyes watching our every move.

"Well for heaven's sake," Verlan grumbled as I pulled myself from his arms. "Aren't you glad to see me?"

"Oh, yes, just thrilled," I whispered scornfully. "I've been wanting to have a long visit with you for weeks."

Verlan's eyes darkened. "Oh, boy," he groaned. "You're mad about Lillie's house, aren't you?"

"An excellent guess," I whispered, darting a furious look at Ivan to see if he'd heard. "Tell you what. Let's don't discuss it right now."

Ivan casually stood and stretched. "Well, I better be goin'; it's about supper-time. Thanks for the cookies, Aunt Sue. Uncle Verlan, do you want to come outside and have a look at my new putt-putt?

"You bet," Verlan agreed a bit too heartily. Winking at me, he followed Ivan out the door, and his voice droned on as he exclaimed over his nephew's new toy. I knew he was biding his time and hoping I was cooling off. As I changed the baby and began to nurse him, I rehearsed what I would say to Verlan. Before I was through, he would be one sorry man who would think twice before stepping on my rights again.

Finally the noise of the motor started, and Verlan leaped up the trailer steps. Dropping down beside me on the couch, he lightly touched James' velvet skin. "He's growing like a weed, the little angel," he commented. Settling back, he sighed and looked at me expectantly. "Well, I'm ready. What's on your mind?"

I swallowed hard, fastening my gaze on James' plump cheeks as he drank my milk in huge, hungry gulps. I suddenly didn't know where to start.

"Go on," Verlan prompted.

Taking a shaky breath, I began. "It's not fair, Verlan. How could you build Lillie a house before Beverly and me?" My voice started out low and quiet, but as I continued, it ended in a wail. "All this time I thought you were a fair man. I thought you loved me—thought I was special to you. But, no! All that changed the day Lillie married you! What Lillie wants, Lillie gets! All she has to do is bat her lashes at you, and her wish is your command. Here I've lived in this old, drafty trailer for years now, with the dirt and the bugs ... You don't care! Just as long as precious Lillie gets a fancy new house before her baby's born, all's well in the Verlan LeBaron family." Grabbing a clean diaper out of the diaper bag, I shook it out and blew my nose.

After a moment I peered up at Verlan. His face looked grave, but as I met his eyes, the tiniest hint of a twinkle in the very center of his iris began to glisten, then to snap and dance. The twinkle sparkled and grew, and suddenly Verlan's mouth twitched.

My own mouth dropped open in shock. He was laughing at me—laughing at my tears! He was a heartless—I jumped off the couch, my swift movement yanking my nipple out of James' mouth. His sleepy eyes flew open in surprise as I dumped him onto the sofa. Immediately he started to holler.

"Verlan LeBaron, how dare you laugh at me!" I hissed as I buttoned my blouse. "You can just leave! Get out of my sight! You and Lillie deserve each other!" I whirled around, dashed into the bedroom, and dropped onto my bed in a heap of misery.

How, I wondered, could he be so uncaring? How in the world could I love a man like him, who didn't care a drop about me? Hadn't I been a good wife? Hadn't I—

A warm hand on my back made me look up. Verlan stood over me, the baby in the crook of his arm. His face was sober.

"Susan, sweetheart, I didn't mean to laugh. I'll leave if you want me to, but before I do, I have something to tell you." Taking my hand, he pulled me up and led me back to the couch. He sat me down, handed the baby back to me, then perched on the edge of the kitchen counter and soberly regarded me.

"To begin with, I'm not paying for Lillie's house. She wanted to continue working during her pregnancy so that she can pay for her own, which leaves me free to plan and pay for yours and Beverly's. Lillie insisted on it; the whole thing was her idea."

I blinked, trying to follow his train of thought.

Verlan looked at me calmly, "I arranged for your lot last time I was here. The lumber for your roof is already ordered. The boys and I will break ground first thing in the morning."

"Break ground? Tomorrow? Tomorrow?"

Verlan grinned. "I wanted it to be a surprise. I had it all planned out, see. I was going to take you out there to the lot and make a ceremony of it. But it seems that didn't work out," he chuckled. "Oh well. This was more fun anyway, don't you think?"

I stared at Verlan, his words beginning to make sense. A house. My house. Verlan was building me a house. Standing up, I dumped James back onto the couch. I ran to Verlan and flung myself into his arms.

"Oh, Verlan," I whispered against his chest, "How could I have thought... You do care, don't you? You don't love Lillie more than me. You're the fairest man in the whole world, and I was such a little idiot to doubt you. My own house? Oh, Verlan, can you ever forgive me for being so mean?"

He threw back his head and laughed. "Mean? You? My little charm, you don't have a mean bone in that cute body of yours. To tell you the truth, I rather enjoyed your version of meanness. I like it when your eyes snap like blue fire and you toss that golden hair. It's enough to make me—"

I didn't hear the rest of his sentence. His words were consumed by my lips.

For the next five days Verlan and the boys worked steadily on the foundations to Beverly's and my houses. They dug dirt, hauled rock, and poured cement before Verlan had to leave again. Then our new foundations sat untouched for weeks, while the walls to Lillie's house steadily took shape. Beverly and I tried to understand.

"It's because Verlan's broke again, and Lillie has her own money," Beverly concluded. "That must be the answer."

"Oh, I'm sure it is." I took another sip of Beverly's brand of 'coffee'. "Do you know, Beverly, Lillie's gone out of her way to be so nice to me every time she comes. She stopped by my trailer a few weeks ago and said that when she moves down she plans to share her car with me. She said that I could consider half the car as mine. I didn't know what to say."

Beverly grunted, "Well, say yes! That way you can loan your half to me, and we'll all have a car."

I chuckled, then immediately sobered. "Oh, Lillie puts on a selfless act, all right. But before long she'll be down here with the rest of us, demanding a lion's share of Verlan's time. She'll be moved into her fancy house and have everything just so-so before a single adobe is laid on our foundations. Watch it happen, Beverly."

I was halfway right. The rainy season began, the heavy fall rains pouring down on our bare foundations, while the men steadily worked on Lillie's house. They wore rain slickers and stepped gingerly about on the roof as they pounded in the nails. Lillie's baby was due soon. They would have to hurry if she was to be moved in by then.

As the weeks passed, a constant loneliness for Verlan consumed me; loneliness that Irene and Beverly's company didn't begin to diminish. When would the enormous hole in my heart be filled? Would the time ever come when we could be a real family? Was this day by day existence what I could expect for the rest of my life? Where was the excitement and romance I had anticipated as the wife of a leader in God's church? We were supposed to be an army for the Lord, and yet babies, dirty diapers, back-breaking work, and never enough money to go around, was the lot of a polygamist's wife. All around me were poverty-stricken homes filled with lonely women and children, living for the scattered moments when our husbands could find time for a hurried visit home. And yet the time Verlan spent at home was the most frustrating time of all. Knowing that Verlan was close, yet sleeping in another wife's bed only blocks away, was the purest form of torture. The irony of it all was the fact that when he was with me, I felt sorry for the others.

Early one October afternoon Verlan's pickup pulled into Los Molinos closely followed by Lillie's car. The truck was loaded high with furniture. They stopped at Charlotte's long enough to collect her two boys. Then they drove on to Lillie's and unloaded the truck.

An hour later Verlan dashed into my trailer. Quickly pressing his lips against mine, he said, "I don't have time to stay and visit right now, sweetie. I want you at Lucy's in half an hour. We're having a family meeting."

At the scheduled time I knocked on Lucy's door and followed her into her cramped, cluttered living room. Glancing around, I looked for a place to sit. Charlotte and Lucy had pulled up kitchen chairs and were quietly visiting together. Beverly and Irene shared the sofa, and they scooted over to make room for me.

As I sat down, Irene nudged me in the ribs, then casually inclined her head toward a corner of the room. Ester stood with her back to the group, loftily refusing to waste a glance on any of us. I nodded, amazed, as Irene was, that Verlan had managed to convince Ester to come at all.

Lillie slowly rocked back and forth in Lucy's rocking chair, and when I glanced at her, her blue eyes met mine. She smiled and said hello. I nodded and smiled, forcing myself to return her greeting. From the look on her face, she was nervous around so many of Verlan's wives. Living in Los Molinos was going to be a change for her.

Verlan paced until everyone was quiet, then he cleared his throat. "Girls, I want us to have a special family dinner this evening. I've brought an ice chest full of chicken and other goodies, and once the meeting's over, I want you all to get to work and cook up a feast."

He waited for our nods, then continued, "Now, the reason I've called you all together is to let you know I've arranged to stay right here at home for six weeks. That's why we're having the dinner, so we can celebrate."

"Oh, Verlan!" Irene and Lucy exclaimed in unison. "Six weeks? Six whole weeks?"

Verlan grinned, nodded, and continued. "Now, during this time, I plan to get Beverly's and Susan's houses built. I don't have the money to hire the work done, so we'll have to do it ourselves. We'll need to get organized and work together. Make a family project of it. Anyone have any suggestions?"

We women looked at one another. Then Lucy spoke up. "The older kids won't be much good now that school's started. And Susan and I have nursing babies. So I suggest that the two of us stay home and take care of the other wives' kids, which will leave them free to help you with the building. Susan and I can do laundry and cook for the other girls, too."

"Well, Lillie can't be doing much, of course," Charlotte snapped. "And Beverly's not up to hard labor. She's pregnant, too, and it won't do." Charlotte threw a meaningful glance at Ester's coolly averted face, then she looked back to Verlan in an unspoken message. "So I guess that leaves Irene and me to be your helpers. The boys can work in the afternoons and on weekends."

"I can help, too, Verlan," I broke in. "There's no reason why I can't leave my kids with Beverly and go home for a half hour at nursing times."

Irene chuckled. "Personally, I'll be glad to get out of the housework. Slinging mud sounds nice for a change. Lucy's welcome to do my wash and house cleaning. Oh, and my cooking."

Verlan grinned at her and ruefully shook his head. "Then it's settled. First thing tomorrow morning I want Charlotte, Irene, and Susan ready to go to work. We'll start making adobes out on that vacant lot past Charlotte's. I figured there would be more left over from the ones made for Lillie's house, but there aren't near enough. Once the bigger boys are out of school, they can come and help. Now, about the dinner tonight. Irene, will you make the pies?"

"I'll make a dozen if Susan'll help me."

I nodded.

The rest of the menu was discussed and the work was divided, with everyone offering to help but Ester. Then the women stood and headed for the door.

I glanced back at Lucy's house as Irene, Beverly and I hurried away. The back door opened and Ester slipped out. She looked small and alone as she scuttled across the field. Suddenly I felt sorry for her.

That evening Verlan sat at the head of the table and looked proudly down at the long lines of his offspring seated on either side of him. Their ages ranged from seventeen years to three months. The freshly scrubbed faces showed anticipation as their mothers served the special meal and tried to keep a serenity and order.

For the first time in several years Verlan's whole family other than Verlan Jr. and Chad, who were in San Diego, were together for a family dinner. Of course, the family was larger than the last time its members were together. We had grown a lot in the past four years. There were twenty-seven children with just Charlotte's, Irene's, and Lucy's. With Ester's four, Beverly's three, and my two, that made thirty-six. Lillie's baby was due in a few weeks. Every one of Verlan's children was mentally bright, and reasonably handsome; his wives were loving and loyal. He had a lot to be proud of; God had richly blessed him.

Now, if Verlan could get Beverly and me into sturdy homes of our own, he would finally have things under control. Each of his seven families would be living in the same town, with each of us in our own home. Verlan's long-time dream was at last becoming a reality. One day soon he would find a way to support us, right here on the Baja peninsula, where he could stay at home. He would let the younger men of the church do the biggest part of the field missionary work. He would actually be able to breathe, to slow down and live like a normal man.

The evening went by in a flash of noisy activity. Once the meal was over and the mountain of dishes was done, Verlan gave each of his wives, along with their smallest children, a ride home. Passing out goodnight kisses at each stop, he headed back to Lucy's for the night. Once my children were settled, I fell into bed, completely worn out by the excitement of the day.

As Verlan had requested, Charlotte, Irene, and I were at the vacant lot west of Charlotte's place by sun-up the next morning.

"We'll dig a mixing hole right here," Verlan announced, pointing with his toe as he passed the shovels around. Lifting a pick high over his head, he plunged it into the soil.

The ladies and I glanced at one another and awkwardly fingered the tools in our hands. "Well, just like he said, we may as well get started," I said grimly. Sinking my shovel into the loosened earth behind Verlan, I lifted the dirt, turned it, and slapped it back down again. On either side of me, Charlotte and Irene began to do the same.

By the time we had a circle of earth twelve feet in diameter and a foot deep loosened, my back ached and my hands were raw. In this "mixing hole" we would mix dirt, straw, and water into mud for the adobes. As we needed more dirt for mud, the size of the hole would increase.

Once the loosening of the soil was done, Verlan straightened and wiped the sweat from his brow. "Susan and Irene, you girls finish scooping this dirt out while Charlotte and I go haul water and straw. We won't be gone long. Come on, Charlotte."

As they hurried toward the pickup, Irene leaned on her shovel and glared after them. "Just as I thought," she snapped contemptuously. "Charlotte's right at his elbow. She'll do the running around with him and keep her hands clean, while we stay here like good little wives and slave away. No, sir! I'm not going to put up with it; I just won't. He's going to be fair or I won't help."

For the next couple of days, in spite of Irene's complaints, Charlotte rode with Verlan each time there was a load of something to be hauled. Irene scowled and griped about it, and periodically threatened to quit, but each morning she came to the work site and out-worked the rest of us. She never hesitated to roll up her pant-legs, climb barefoot into the mixing hole, and stomp and stir the huge amount of dirt, straw, and water into mud for the adobes. Then using a shovel, she slapped the muddy mixture into the wooden adobe frames, scraping and patting the mud flat with her bare hands. Lifting the mold clear, she left perfectly formed adobes on the field to dry.

One morning after Charlotte and Verlan returned from hauling a load of straw, Verlan stood over our work, carefully scanning the rows of adobes. "Beautiful! Just beautiful. Charlotte, look at all these adobes. Irene does a good job, doesn't she? And so fast!" He winked at me and drawled, "Maybe I should pass the word around and hire her out."

Irene straightened up, wiped her muddy hands on her pants, threw a scathing glance at Charlotte, and retorted, "One thing's for certain, Verlan. I'm the only wife here who would be worthy of her hire." Charlotte glared back at Irene, then shrugged, turned on her heel and walked to the pickup.

Each day, Lucy, Beverly, and Lillie took turns preparing our lunch and bringing it to the work site. Our break time was always brief. Verlan, never one to waste a precious minute, would hustle us back to work hardly before we swallowed our last bite. "Okay, okay, let's stop fooling around and get this show on the road," he would holler.

At nursing times, Charlotte drove me to Beverly's to attend the baby. Verlan ignored my insistence that I was fully capable of driving myself. Although it angered and insulted me that he didn't trust me to drive his pickup, my anger was colorless in comparison to Irene's.

"Dearest Charlotte's the only one with brains enough to drive Verlan's truck, don't you know," she growled sarcastically. "Don't waste your breath arguing with him about it. I've tried. Believe me, I've tried."

I nodded, knowing she'd tried. I had heard her try numerous times, to no avail. Verlan remained adamant. Charlotte was his right arm, and Irene and I both might as well accept it. Charlotte was careful not to flaunt her position. She coolly carried out her privileged duties, with only an occasional, superior sniff.

Each afternoon when the older boys arrived to help, it surprised and annoyed me how much their father snapped and yelled at them. I'd never seen this side of Verlan, the side that wasn't loving and affectionate. As the days wore on, it became evident that Verlan had little patience for his children and that being around so many of them on a continual basis made him nervous and ill tempered. Even in his various homes, I noticed for the first time how quickly he greeted the kids, then practically shoved them aside, or out the door, in order to spend time with one of his wives behind a closed bedroom door. I wondered if having him home full time would be different, or if he felt extra pressure because of our tight schedule.

Within ten days, Irene, Charlotte, and I working steadily at Verlan's side made enough adobes for both houses. Verlan hounded us like a slave driver, pushing us to hurry as he anxiously watched the sky, hoping the autumn rains had indeed quit for the season so that the adobes, at last drying in the field, would have a chance to mature. We were in luck. Each day dawned bright and cold, with few clouds. "There's no doubt in my mind that the Lord's behind this project, girls," Verlan declared as we surveyed the huge lot of adobes. "I'm feeling better and better about the time I took off from work to do this. It was the right thing to do."

Once the earthen bricks were completely dry, we loaded them into the pickup and hauled load after backbreaking load to the building sites. Then followed the actual building of the houses.

The walls of Beverly's house were slowly constructed, with Verlan and Irene laying the bricks, while Charlotte, the boys, and myself kept them in supplies. Once the adobes were up, the roof trusses, and the windows and doors in place, Verlan had two of Brother Castro's sons pour the cement floor. Meanwhile, we moved our equipment down the road to my new lot. The building process began all over again.

Early one morning, Irene came by my trailer. "Lillie's finally in labor," she informed me. "She's had contractions since midnight. Verlan said we'll take a break for the day."

"Who's with her?"

Irene turned to the stove and dipped a fork into my fry pan of sizzling diced potatoes, speared one, blew on it, and popped it into her mouth. "Charlotte and Verlan," she mumbled. "So is Jeannine. I offered to stay and help, but Verlan told me to go home. Said they didn't need me."

I glanced sympathetically at Irene. Even in the dim, pre-dawn light in my trailer I could see that her eyes were swollen. "Oh, well," she sniffed, "just as long as Verlan has Mrs. LeBaron at his side, everything's under control."

She popped another piece of potato in her mouth and chewed thoughtfully. "I can't help it, Sue, it gripes me to death. Charlotte's always the one he counts on! The only time he turns to me is if he's short a strong back to haul a wheelbarrow of sand for one of his wives' new homes. Good ol' Irene, always available for the dirty work."

"That's not true, and you know it," I retorted swiftly. "He counts on you all the time. He'd be lost without you. You've worked harder than any of us, and you lay adobes better than he does."

She snorted and headed for the door. "Well, he can forget about me helping him anymore on the houses. I won't do it. He can just have Charlotte finish up the damn work. I'm gonna stay home with my kids and keep my wash done up," The trailer door slammed shut behind her.

I sighed, turned off the stove, and crawled back into bed. Irene didn't mean it; she was only spouting off, but I didn't blame her for feeling left out and taken for granted. And now, with Charlotte being the one Verlan had asked to deliver Lillie's baby, I could understand her pain. Verlan's constant dependence on his first wife would naturally get on his second wife's nerves. It angered me, as well, but I felt differently about it than Irene did. Charlotte was Irene's competition, while mine would be giving birth shortly.

Lillie's baby boy was born late in the afternoon. They named him Christian Bruce. Bruce—the name Verlan had agreed to save for my second son.

Chapter 31

"Susan, you do know that Joel is planning to begin a mission in the San Diego area?"

Setting my bucket of paint down on the window frame of what was soon to be my bedroom, I held the brush suspended and curiously regarded my visitor, Lillie's mother, Jeannine LeBaron. What, I wondered, did this have to do with me? "Yes, I remember Verlan mentioning something about it."

Jeannine fidgeted and pulled her jacket tighter around her thin body. Damp November wind blew hard against the west wall of my new house, rattled the windowpane in front of me, and seeped in cold gusts through invisible cracks. Tiny grains of sand began to stick to the fresh paint on the sill. Disgusted, I tapped the lid back on the paint can and gave Jeannine my full attention.

"Joel asked me to go to San Diego for a few months and keep house for him and the other men. I'd love to do it; I could use a break. Would you consider keeping Ivan for me?"

As I cleaned the paintbrush and other tools, I considered and nodded. "I'll be moving in a week or so. Meantime Ivan could sleep on the trailer couch. Sure, Jeannine, sure he can. I'd love to have him."

She grinned her relief. "He'll be more help than trouble," she promised. "Lillie will be taking care of the little girls. She offered to keep Ivan too, but I don't want to burden her with all three kids, with her new baby and all. The girls will be right next door in case Ivan gets lonesome, and I'll be coming down on the weekends. I'll have him get his things together." Smiling brightly at me, Jeannine dashed out the door and cut across the field toward Lillie's.

I'd always liked Jeannine, even though she was Lillie's mother, and never hesitated to sing her perfect daughter's praises. Having Ivan around would be good for me. He would be someone at home to visit with who didn't talk baby talk.

The tarring of my roof was a big day for Verlan's family. It completed our frantic six-week building project, and life for Verlan's families returned to normal. He immediately left for Las Vegas, and I began the move into my new house.

True to Jeannine's word, Ivan was a great help. With the old family pickup and Ivan's and Kaylen's assistance, the trailer was soon cleared of everything that wasn't glued in or tacked down. The thirteen-year-old boys worked hard and steadily, and once my belongings had been hauled to the new house and unpacked, I gathered James into my arms and slowly, almost reluctantly, wandered through the half-finished rooms.

For the past three years I had looked forward to this day with excited anticipation, fantasizing how wonderful it was going to be to have my very own house. I'd looked forward to making it a comfortable, warm, and cozy home for Verlan, and he would love to stay with me. My home would be filled with good smells and laughter and beautiful things.

Wryly, I glanced around. The walls were of rough gray plaster, the floors cold gray cement; dismal winter sky showed through the bare windows. The bedroom doors needed to be hung, and kitchen cupboards needed to be built. Trash and leftover building materials, in piles around the yard, were too trivial for Verlan to worry about.

The furniture in my bedroom consisted of a double bed—its box springs resting on cinder blocks—James' crib, and a kitchen chair. No time or material to build closets, so my clothing hung on a broom handle suspended from the ceiling by baling wire. In the kids' room, a cot for Melanie and a mat on the floor for Ivan were the sole furnishings. Cardboard boxes along the wall held their clothing.

The old orange couch, brought from the trailer, was the solitary piece of furniture in the living room. The kitchen boasted an old stove, a table, and three rickety chairs. My dishes, pots and pans were in boxes on the floor.

I sighed and looked out the kitchen window, past my new outhouse, to the desolate, treeless field between my lot and Charlotte's. "You knew in your secret mind it would be like this," I reminded myself. "At least you have a real house of your own now. One of these days Verlan will get you the other things you need. Until then you will just have to make do."

Yet as I remembered the scanty furnishings in Lucy's, Beverly's and Charlotte's houses, I knew that it would most likely be years before I had much. Verlan was a fair man. He wouldn't fix my place up until the others had what they needed.

Of course, I couldn't compare Lillie's house to mine because she had bought her own furniture. I'd seen the inside of her house the day Beverly and I had stopped in to see her baby. White metal cupboards and sideboards, a lovely oak table and matching chairs, bedroom groups, plush couches, and over-stuffed rockers. Carpets, drapes—everything a woman could want.

I shook the thought away. "I won't do it!" I said through clenched teeth. "I

307

will not allow myself to envy Lillie!"

"What, Aunt Susan? What did ya' say?" Kaylen called, peering at me.

"Oh, nothing. I was just rattling to myself." I kicked a scrap of sheetrock out of the way, then grabbed it up and slung it into a box of trash.

Ivan glanced up at me, his lips tightly pursed over the nails held in his mouth. His eyes briefly met mine, then he dropped his gaze, and began hammering nails into my new water bench. I watched him in silence. Ivan was a quiet boy, but there was an active brain behind those bright blue eyes. At times I felt as though he could read my mind—kind of depressing because my thoughts today were anything but cheerful. I was all moved in, finally into my own place, and it was absolutely dreadful.

"There!" Ivan announced as he pounded the final nail. "It's sturdy as can be. Go ahead, Aunt Susan, just try to wiggle it."

I sniffed and turned my back to the boys, pretending not to hear, as I fought back tears of dejection.

"Come on, it's solid as a rock and big enough for two buckets. Just try to wiggle it!" Kaylen insisted.

"I don't want to wiggle it!" I snapped. Striding to the door, I yanked it open. "You boys leave me alone for awhile. Go on over to Aunt Charlotte's and fill those buckets with water. Go! Now!"

Kaylen's and Ivan's mouths dropped as they stared at me. They glanced at each other, picked up my empty pails, and strolled out the door.

From her seat at the table, Melanie watched me with tears in her eyes. "I'm goin', too," she sniffled. Grabbing her coat, she hurried outside, her tiny body braced against the wind, as she struggled to catch up with the boys.

I stared after her until she took Ivan's hand, and then I closed the door and leaned against it. "You ugly old witch!" I said out loud. Startled, James turned in my arms and regarded me with solemn eyes as I scornfully whispered, "Now look what you've done! Your own little girl can't even stand you. Those boys have been so good and tried so hard, and you've been mean as hell just because your house isn't as fancy as Lillie's. Stop feeling sorry for yourself; you've got a lot more than you've ever had, and crying about it won't solve a thing."

Carrying James to his crib, I laid him down and looked around me again. I needed to think positively, that was my problem. If I took one project at a time and practiced a little ingenuity, I could make this place livable. I would do it! I had to do it.

I wandered through the empty rooms, my thoughts racing. A sheet, dyed and cut in half, would make presentable curtains for the kids' windows. I could hang another sheet up to my bedroom door for privacy.

I stopped in the kitchen and thoughtfully eyed the boxes of odds and ends littering the floor. I needed something to store my dishes in, and obviously I was going to have to solve the problem myself. Frowning, I searched my mind. If I remembered right, there was a piece or two of plywood out behind Lucy's in the goat sheds. If I scrubbed the manure off them and rounded up some two-by-fours, I could build a cupboard and sideboards for the kitchen. Ivan was good with tools. He would help me.

By the time Melanie and the boys returned with the water, I was in a better mood and ready with an apology. Holding the door open for them, I offered my best smile. "Hey, you guys, I'm sorry that I yelled at you. You've all been such good helpers, and I'm ashamed of myself. The water bench is a master-piece, Ivan. I didn't mean to be so cross."

Kaylen set his bucket down on the new bench, lazily scratched his thigh, and grinned at me. "Cross? You call that bein' cross? That was nothin'. You should hear my mother. She hollers so darn loud at us, the Tippetts can hear her swear—" Kaylen bit off the last of his sentence and looked guiltily at me.

"Don't worry," I chuckled, "I won't tell her what you said."

He nodded, relieved. "I wasn't worried. Well, I've got to go, Ivan. I gotta milk."

Thanking Kaylen again for his help, I escorted him to the door and watched him saunter to the road. Suddenly I giggled. Kaylen walked with the same loping gait as his father and the rest of the LeBaron men, definitely in the blood.

Ivan puttered around the kitchen, putting away his tools and sweeping up the sawdust, and he seemed absorbed in thought. I caught him glancing at me several times as I sat on the couch and nursed the baby.

"What's on your mind, buddy?" I finally asked.

He took a breath and mumbled, "I, uh, I...would it be okay if I go to see Lillie for awhile?"

"Of course you can! Anytime you want to, you can go. Whenever you start to feel lonesome, or whatever, you just go have a visit with her. It'll make you feel better." I inclined my head toward the door. "Don't be gone too long, though, 'cause I'll be making supper soon, our first meal in the new house." I grinned at him.

An hour later I stepped outside into the cold, early evening air. The wind had died down, and the sky had cleared somewhat. Half the sun was visible through pink and red clouds dipping into the ocean.

I glanced around, located Melanie's blond head on the other side of the sand pile left over from the building project. She'd become bored watching me make supper, donned her coat, and headed outside to "dig."

"Mel," I called, "come on in now, it's time to eat." While I waited for her, I glanced toward Lillie's, wondering about Ivan. I'd had guilty thoughts ever since he left—aware that he had gone to his sister's place because of my wretched attitude. I'd upset him, and he'd gone for comfort. It rankled me.

Bright orange rays from the sunset glistened off of Lillie's dining room window and off of the old family pickup that was backed up to her front door. Shielding my eyes, I stared. What was that woman doing now?

The pickup was piled high with furniture. Even as I watched, Lillie and Ivan loaded something heavy onto the end of the truck and slammed the tailgate closed. The two of them climbed into the cab, then Lillie started the truck and pulled it onto the dirt road. It swerved in my direction and slowly bumped through the potholes, drawing closer and closer. "What is she doing?" I muttered. "What on earth is she up to now?"

Melanie's cold little hand slipped into mine. Together we stood on the cement step and watched Lillie maneuver the pickup through the break in the barbed wire fence that was someday to be my driveway. She stopped in front of us, opened the door, and stepped out.

"Hi." Her voice was low, her dark blue eyes holding a hint of embarrassment, "I brought you a few things."

A knot began to form in the pit of my stomach, spreading heat upward to my face and cheeks. My heart pumped shallow surges of guilt and shame. "What—what things?" I croaked.

"Uh, just some furniture for your house. I couldn't stand to have so much when you don't have anything. I wanted to share with you."

In a daze I stumbled to the pickup. Lillie's gold bedroom set, complete with dresser and huge mirror, were carefully arranged along one side. Another smaller dresser, Lillie's nice, plush sofa with the oak trim, and her old-fashioned green rocker with the cream ruffles, the one I had secretly admired the day I'd gone to see her baby, filled the remainder of the truck bed.

"Oh!" I gasped in horror. "Oh, Lillie, no! I don't want it. These are your things that you worked for! No, don't do this. Just take them home again where they belong!"

She determinedly reached out and opened the tailgate. "I want to give them to you! See? I can't stand to live next door to you and know that you don't have anything, and I do. Now, don't argue, Susan. I'm giving you this furniture, and that's that."

I stepped past her and slammed the tailgate closed again.

"Nope. Uh, uh!"

"Yes," she shouted, wrestling with me over the tailgate. "Yes! I want you to have nice things. Susan, can't you understand? I—I love you! We're family!"

Suddenly Lillie's arms were around me and she was croaking into my ear, "I don't want you to hate me anymore! Please don't hate me anymore."

Tears blinded my eyes. Wrapping my arms around her thin waist, I buried my face against her shoulder.

"I don't hate you," I choked. "I never did. Honestly I didn't. It's just that..."

"I know. I know." She sniffed. "I love him, too, remember?"

"How can you be so good to me?" I wailed. "I don't deserve this; I've been so rotten to you—so mean! Oh, Lillie, I can't take your things."

She dabbed at her eyes and grinned at me. "You might as well. I asked Mom a week ago to stop at garage sales in San Diego and find me some more, so you'll have to take these or there won't be room in my house when she brings the new ones. Come on, now," she ordered, opening the tailgate again. "Stop your blubbering and help me haul this stuff inside. We're going to fix your house up, and I can't wait to see what it will look like! Can you?"

Lillie grabbed a firm hold on one end of the long dresser. "Hurry, it's getting dark!" she giggled.

My brain began slowly to function when I backed into the house with my end of the heavy dresser. It was something how she brought the furniture on this very day, when I had been feeling so low.

Behind Lillie, I caught sight of Ivan as he followed us inside, his arms full with the rocker. Suddenly I froze in my backward movements and searched his freckled face. A dawning realization clutched at my mid-section.

No, he wouldn't have! Ivan wouldn't have said anything. Yet, he avoided my eyes. Why?

I stood at my kitchen window watching the first golden rays of a beautiful April dawn creep over the distant highway. I caught a flash of metal. I immediately recognized Uncle Bud's blue pickup slowing down for the bend in the road by the eucalyptus trees. The pickup gained momentum for the short stretch to my place, and with a quick spin of the wheel, Naomi Zarate Chynoweth pulled through the opening in the barbed wire fence that marked the boundary of my lot. Wrapping my robe tighter around me, I opened the back door as she stepped out of the truck.

She smiled a shy greeting and in Spanish said, "Susana, my sister-in-law Victoria is in labor, and my mother isn't feeling well enough to help deliver the baby. Can you come?"

My eyes widened in surprise. "Why, yes, Naomi. I'd be glad to help, if you're sure I'll do. I've never attended a birth before."

"That doesn't matter. I'll tell you what needs to be done."

"Then I'll go get dressed," I motioned for her to come inside.

"My brother Benjamin came by a few minutes ago," Naomi called after me as I headed down the hall. "Victoria has had contractions most of the night, so we need to hurry. Is there someone who can stay with your children?"

"I'm here," Ivan answered for me. He had passed me in the hallway, yanking a shirt over his head. "Don't worry about the kids. I can handle them."

I pulled my clothes on and ran a brush through my hair. Giving Ivan quick instructions, I followed Naomi outside. As we drove toward the Zarate's, I stole a sidelong glance at her. She still appeared a bit pale, and I remembered that her own baby boy was only a few weeks old. She didn't look as though she were back to normal health yet.

I understood why Naomi had chosen me to assist her with Victoria's confinement. Because of Uncle Bud, Naomi felt a kinship with me. And also, because of Bud's association with Ervil, she felt uncomfortable asking the other, Joelite women of Los Molinos for help. She knew that I was aware of her dislike and mistrust of Ervil. Her life had to be one of constant stress, with Uncle Bud's home being Ervil's headquarters in Los Molinos.

Benjamin Zarate Jr's two-acre parcel of land was located to the right of his father Benjamin Sr's place. Between the younger man's trailer and his father's small adobe home was the well Floren LeBaron had witched. New saplings had been planted along the borders of the lots, their green leaves attesting to the success of Floren LeBaron's trip to Los Molinos. Benjamin's youthful, dark face broke into a relieved smile as he opened the door of the small trailer for his sister and me.

"Victoria's lying down," he said nervously, motioning toward the back end of the trailer. "The pains are too severe for her to walk around anymore. I have hot water on the stove."

"Good," Naomi squeezed her brother's arm, then set her medical bag down, poured hot water into a wash bowl, and began to scrub. As she lathered her arms, she glanced at Benjamin. His angular face showed signs of weariness as he paced back and forth. Stopping a moment, he chewed at his thumbnail and gazed longingly out the window.

"Now, Ben," Naomi said, "you don't have to stay unless you want to. We can take care of things. Why don't you go on outside for awhile? If Victoria needs you, Susana'll come and get you."

He nodded, "Okay. I'm going. But I won't be far."

I followed Naomi to the sink and scrubbed while she entered the bedroom to examine Victoria. Emerging after a few minutes, she shook her head. "She's got a way to go yet, Susana; she's small, even for a first birth."

Filling a basin with cool water, I entered the dark, cramped bedroom. Victoria lay on a lumpy mattress, her child-like face beaded with sweat. She smiled up at me as I bathed her forehead and arms and quietly visited with her. Once I was through, Naomi took her sister-in-law's hands and pulled her up off the pillow.

"You need to walk a bit, Querida. Come on, you can do it."

With Naomi's help, Victoria stumbled through the small trailer as one contraction followed another. I watched Naomi, sensing her inner strength. Uncle Bud had indeed found himself a fine woman. Thinking about Bud reminded me of Aunt Thelma, and sudden loneliness for her left an ache in my chest. I missed her so much—all of them, Mark, Duane, Rena...

An hour dragged by, then another, as Victoria endured the excruciating labor. Watching her, I recalled James' birth, nine months ago. I hadn't been nearly as strong as this girl.

The sun was high in the sky, radiating a still, breathless heat into the little trailer. Outside the window, I could hear the rise and fall of the Zarate men's voices as they lounged in the shade at the far end of the trailer to await news of the birth. Well, they wouldn't have to wait much longer. Victoria was once again lying down, this time on the sterile sheets Naomi had pulled from her bag.

Victoria gripped my hand, staring wide-eyed and unseeing as she struggled against the pain. Tossing her head, she moaned, "Benjamin—Benjamin..."

"Susana, why don't you—"

Suddenly from outside the window, a man's high-pitched Spanish voice rose in an angry tone, drowning out Naomi's words. "...This land is our land, Benjamin! If you want to go on living here, you will pay us for it, or by damn..." Something vaguely, hauntingly familiar about the man's voice prickled along my spine. What was it about that voice?

A cacophony of protests and threats interrupted the first man. Several began to talk at once. Startled, Naomi and I stared at each other, then our eyes dropped to Victoria's face.

The girl's agonized gaze lit on the window as she breathed deep with the labor, her eyes dilating as she looked away again. "No, no!" she gasped, rocking her head wildly back and forth. "Jesus, no."

"Get out there and tell those men to move away from the window!" Naomi snapped to me. "Don't they realize what's going on in here? Tell those *estupidos* to go argue somewhere else!"

I hurried to the door; Naomi talked soothingly to Victoria.

". . . Isn't that right, Ervil?" the first voice I had heard, the high-pitched one, started in again when I reached for the doorknob.

My heart skipped a beat as I swung the door open. Ervil LeBaron's back was to me—that enormous back, covered in a bright silk shirt. His balding head was nodding an agreement. "We can arrange this amicably," he reasoned smoothly. "I have no desire to evict you people. I'll accept a transfer fee of a hundred and fifty dollars per hectarea, if you like. It's a fair price."

"Ervil's a fair man." This was the high-pitched voice again, and as I recognized its owner, I gasped and stumbled backward.

My breathing almost stopped; my head reeled. The short, wiry man standing beside Ervil was the same man I had seen with him that night as I crouched behind the butane tank outside of Anna Mae's home in Colonia LeBaron! Gamaliel Rios. The driver of that stolen car had been Gamaliel Rios, a boy I had gone to grade school with. "Maybe you will take care of Verlan, yes?" Ervil had laughingly said to him.

"Oh," I groaned, suddenly sick to my stomach. It couldn't have been Gamaliel! He wouldn't be stealing for Ervil and discussing such a horrible thing as murder. He had always been a good boy.

"Joel gave these acres to us, you know that. He gave mine to me, and he gave Benjamin's to him." The man who quietly protested was Fernando Castro. He stood solidly in front of Ervil and Gamaliel, his thin body dressed in patched and faded clothing that perfectly suited his simple, unpretentious bearing.

As I stepped out onto the porch, the huddle of men seemed oblivious to my presence. Behind me I could hear Victoria moaning, and I knew that Naomi needed me. I had to send the men away and get back—but I stood frozen, unable to tear myself free from the drama unfolding before me.

As Ervil shifted his weight, I caught sight of Dan Jordan's smirking face behind him. He seemed content to stay in the background and let Ervil and Gamaliel do the talking. I hadn't seen Dan since my honeymoon three years ago, when Verlan and I had spent our wedding night in his and Sharon's spare bedroom in Chihuahua City.

Why were all these Ervilites here on Zarate's land? What could they possibly hope to prove by their ridiculous claims against these poor people?

I scanned the faces of the six men at the end of the trailer, quickly noting that Benjamin Jr. hovered protectively at his father's side. The older Benjamin's agitated face was beaded with sweat, his chest beneath his ragged cotton shirt heaving with anger as he faced Ervil. Benjamin Sr.'s attention shifted to the young man on Ervil's left, his old leathery face wrinkled with pain. Andres Zarate returned his father's appraisal, his features cold and mocking.

My blood chilled. How could Andres be a party to Ervil's efforts at taking his own family's meager little acre of land? Oh, the wickedness of it! How could he side against his own flesh and blood?

Ervil ignored the looks that passed between the Zarates. He stared unblinking down at Fernando Castro. "Now come, Fernando, Joel had no business giving this land to you. It wasn't his to give! The land on which Los Molinos sits was mine in the first place. It always has been. But as I said before, we can come to an understanding, one that will prove beneficial for all of us."

Ervil cleared his throat, squared his huge shoulders, and puffed out his chest. "I want you men to know that I intend to bring about a great economic project here that can help the situation of you poor Lamanites. Look around you, man! This great valley will give us thousands of dollars if we only do a few things here to attract the gentiles.

"Look over there by that salt flat, old Benjamin. We can build a grand, fancy hotel there with all its conveniences. We will put signs along the highway so the gentiles will come here and leave their money with us," a conspiratorial look flashed across Ervil's face. His voice lowered in a confiding tone. Cupping his huge hands, he slowly moved them up and down. "Have you men ever held millions in your hands? Millions of pesos?"

Fernando Castro's eyes briefly shifted to Old Benjamin's disdainful face. Then he shuffled his feet, scratched his head, and grunted.

"Well, if you choose to side with me, you will have millions—but dollars, not pesos!"

Dan Jordan lazily drawled, "We want ten men. Both of you, Fernando and Benjamin, along with young Benjamin, here. Ten men who will not betray us. Find us the others, join our ranks, and we will make you rich."

Fernando studied Dan's swarthy, insolent face for a moment, then he turned back to Ervil. Somehow his voice remained calm. "We don't need your promises of wealth. What's the matter with you guys, anyway? Have you forgotten that our mission here is not to become rich, but to spread the gospel of Jesus? As for joining your ranks, Joel is our prophet. You used to believe that too, Ervil. You are the one who converted me to the church, remember? You came on a mission to my home in Mexico City, where you baptized me and swore to me that Joel was a prophet of God, sent to deliver the world from the hands of Satan. I believe that today with all my heart! We don't need your money. We are already wealthy! We have the priesthood of God, and Joel in our midst."

"Besides," Benjamin Jr. spoke for the first time, cutting off any retort by Ervil, "your big plans won't work, because the land is rightfully ours. We are building our own city, which one day we will call the City of Zarahemla, a refuge for the righteous. God is blessing us here. As you can see, this desert is blossoming, just as the promise reads, becoming green and fruitful with the water pumped by the big windmills Joel built."

Ervil threw back his head and laughed soundlessly, then wiped his eyes. "Those unsightly, farm-boy specials? Come on! They're practically from the dark ages. Joel never has learned to change with the times." He laughed again, shaking his head.

Andres snorted and motioned toward a distant windmill. "Take a good look at them, Benny boy. Those rickety old things are the best Joel will ever have to offer you."

Gamaliel Rios impatiently waved the small talk away, intent on getting back to business. "Enough. You men have made your position clear. If that's the way of it, then there is no deal, so we demand an immediate payment."

Gamaliel's words trailed off. A breathless, uncomfortable hush fell over the small crowd as Joel LeBaron strolled around the corner of the trailer.

Upon catching sight of the men in their rigid huddle, the tune Joel was whistling abruptly ceased. He looked from one tense face to the next.

"Well, here's the farm boy now," Ervil jerked his hand in Joel's direction, not bothering to hide the sneer on his face as he looked him up and down. From his work boots and faded jeans to his sweaty, checked flannel shirt with

316

its rolled-up sleeves, Joel indeed looked the part. The slight sunburn on his nose and broad forehead enhanced the image. He smiled good-naturedly and shook hands with Ervil and Dan. "Hello, didn't know you men were in town." He nodded to the other men. "What's going on?"

"Unfinished business. I was letting these men know the land they're on belongs to me." Ervil coughed into his hand and casually leaned his shoulder against the trailer. "I'll take a hundred and fifty an hectarea for it. They've expropriated my land long enough, Joel. If they want to stay, they'll pay."

Benjamin and Fernando glanced at Joel, their expressions taut.

The prophet's eyebrows slightly raised. "You know that the church gave these men this land years ago. It's theirs, free and clear. I'll not have you hounding them."

Ervil's eyes narrowed. "I don't want there to be any trouble, Joel, I really don't. But I'm the one who arranged for this land in the first place, and since we no longer see eye to eye and have come to a parting of the ways, I plan to take my belongings, or at least the value of them, with me."

Joel's voice was so low I had to strain to catch his words. "You may have 'arranged' for the land, but you used church money to do it."

The men surrounding Joel and Ervil stood silent, almost receding into a backdrop for this strained meeting between the LeBarons. Joel spoke again, his voice even. "Take anything of mine you want, but if you begin to take that which belongs to the needy Lamanites, I'll stand in your way. If it becomes necessary to protect their interests, I'll take you before the courts of the land."

Ervil's head snapped up, his face becoming a dull red as he stared at Joel. "You'll what!" he rasped. "How dare you—" Growling deep in his throat, Ervil took a threatening step toward his brother.

Joel didn't flinch. He stood in front of his followers, his legs slightly apart, his body relaxed. His eyes were devoid of anger; I sensed only sadness as he looked at Ervil.

Just as suddenly as Ervil's violent anger flared up, it cooled off. "Do you know something?" he suddenly chuckled. "You make me laugh. A goat farmer whose convinced himself he's a spiritual leader! Ha, ha! You're a dry well, Joel. You're all washed up, and it's a sad thing that these men can't accept it!"

Ervil's voice rose again, his eyes glowing with that unearthly light I had come to recognize. "You've let the Lord down, Brother. You've failed your mission, and you're leading precious souls astray. You're standing in direct opposition to Jesus Christ's personal representative, and you'll have to answer for it. Take warning, Brother Joel. The Lord requires payment for your sins. He requires a day of atonement. Blood atonement."

Fernando and Benjamin Sr. gasped.

I frantically searched my mind, knowing I had heard the term "Blood Atonement" before. What was it?

Joel bowed his head. A heavy, unnatural silence hung over the group of religious rivals. Then Joel slowly looked up into his brother's eyes. "The only thing the Lord requires, Ervil, is a broken heart and a contrite spirit," he answered.

Ervil's sensuous lips twisted. He began to say something, then bit the words back. Turning abruptly on his heel, he stalked around the corner of the trailer and headed for the road.

Dan Jordan, Andres Zarate, and Gamaliel Rios stood uncertainly. When Joel searched the faces of his former disciples, his eyes mirrored the deep, heart-wrenching sorrow in his soul. The three men looked away. Without another word, they scurried after Ervil.

Joel sighed as he watched them go. His shoulders suddenly sagged with weariness. Then turning back to the three men who remained, he draped an arm around old Benjamin's stooped shoulders. In a comforting voice, he began to reassure the men of their ownership of the land.

My legs trembled as I stepped off the porch. Suddenly Joel straightened, turned, and regarded me. Concern creased his brow as he saw the terror in my face.

I searched his hazel eyes. Lifting my hand, I placed a shaking finger to my lips.

He threw me a quick, understanding smile. Grabbing Fernando's arm, he led the men away from the trailer.

I fled back up the steps. As I pushed the door open, from the bedroom at the back of the trailer came the gasping wail of a newborn baby.

"There!" I took a step back from the table, set my hot-pad down, and sniffed at the glass pan filled with steaming, gooey, cheesy enchiladas. Verlan loved enchiladas. This supper was going to be the beginning of a special and intimate evening. Verlan, praise the Lord, was finally home from his mission to Utah, and for the first time in almost two months, tonight was my night.

"No!" I screeched as Melanie, a spoon in her pudgy hand, headed toward the pie sitting on the end of the table. "No, Melanie. That's Daddy's pie, his surprise. He's coming to spend the night with us."

Melanie frowned. Standing on tiptoe, she eyed the golden brown swirls of toasted meringue. Then she demanded, "Well, where's my lemon pie?"

"If you're a good girl, I'll save you a piece of Daddy's for tomorrow. Okay? But you have to go to bed early."

Her rosebud lips pouted for a moment as she considered the deal. "Does Ivan get some, too? Does he have to go to bed early, too?"

"Ivan's spending the night at Lillie's. And, yes, he will have a piece of pie tomorrow."

I smiled as I thought about Lillie. She had come over earlier today, through the field on the little path that had formed between our houses. Glancing toward my bedroom where only a sheet hung in front of the doorway, she had made a cheerful suggestion. "Why don't you send Ivan to my house for the night? That way you won't be so crowded."

My face reddened a bit, but I immediately agreed. Lillie wanted my night with Verlan to be a memorable one.

Over the past eight months, Lillie and I had become the closest of friends. Time after time she had proved what a gracious and lovely person she really was, with constant thoughtfulness. Lillie had not only become a wonderful example for me, but a source of strength and moral support, as I knew I had become for her. I guiltily tried to ignore the memory of the long months I had allowed myself to openly resent her. I was amazed that true esteem and respect for my sister-wife allowed me to suppress the natural jealousy of knowing my husband loved her and spent time with her. I actually found myself wanting her happiness above my own. And now Lillie had out-done herself by wanting

319

my night with Verlan to be a special one.

It will be special, too, I thought grimly, as I scurried around the house making certain everything was ship-shape. But as I worked, a tiny finger of guilt persistently plagued me.

I had a secret—one that I knew I should share with Verlan. Yet telling him my secret would put a quick end to my plans for an intimate night in his arms. Past history reminded me of Verlan's firm belief that it was morally wrong to have sex during pregnancy.

"You need this time with him, Susan," I sternly told myself. "You're lonely, and you're only human! If you don't take advantage of your night with him now, it'll be too late for months to come. Stop feeling ashamed! One night of secrecy won't hurt a thing. It's not your fault he's a fanatic." Yet all the reasoning in the world didn't change the nagging feeling that I was somehow culpable.

"You've been so down in the dumps, lately," I grimly carried on my silent monologue as I fed the children and put them to bed. "You need your husband's lovemaking. A woman needs that once in awhile. So just keep your mouth shut, and Verlan won't know the difference."

Shadows filled the house; I lit my lamps, then walked to my bedroom window and peered out through the darkness toward Lucy's. Then I looked down the road toward Irene's. Verlan's lanky figure wasn't in sight. Where was he? It was getting awfully late, even for him. He knew, of course, that I was expecting him. Maybe he'd run into Joel.

Turning on the oven, I re-warmed the enchiladas, and then wished I hadn't as the minutes dragged by and Verlan didn't show. With the children asleep, the house seemed terribly quiet, and I fidgeted. Rearranging the table settings took my mind off my absent husband for a few minutes, as did sewing the buttons back on James' shirt. In desperation, I cleaned out my silverware box. And when I finally allowed myself to look at the clock on the wall, it was after eleven o'clock.

Listlessly strolling outside, I searched through the damp, ocean-side darkness toward Charlotte's house, straining my ears in hopes of hearing a familiar step in the underbrush. The faint noise of a cricket off in the distance was the only sound. Why didn't he come? How could he do this to me, when he knew how much I needed him and how patient I had been? Oh, life wasn't fair. My night was almost over, and Verlan was leaving for conference in Colonia LeBaron tomorrow, to be gone for weeks. Where was he?

And yet I knew, of course. Verlan wasn't in a meeting with Joel. Not this time of night. Somewhere within the boundaries of Los Molinos, my darling lay in another wife's arms. He held another lonely woman close to his warm body, caressing and loving her instead of me. On my night!

Anger surged through me, blinding me with the force of it. Every one of Verlan's wives knew whose turn it was; we all kept track. Yet one of them had contrived a reason for him to stay with her. I knew it as surely as I stood here alone in the darkness. Oh, how I wished I knew who it was! I would never forgive her. Who would do this to me?

Was it Charlotte? I quickly discarded the thought. Charlotte was a stickler for the rules. Lucy? No way, Lucy would never presume to take advantage of Verlan. Ester? Of course not. I knew it wasn't Lillie. Beverly, perhaps! Or Irene.

Yes, Irene! She had always been one to send Verlan to another wife if she thought he was needed. She was like that, Irene was; selfless. So if she happened to be having a rough time, she would expect me to do the same. Well, maybe someday I would be willing, but tonight I wasn't. If Irene had conned Verlan into spending my night with her, I would never forgive her. Never!

I stomped back into the house and stared for a moment at the cold dish of food on the stovetop. I had saved my goat cheese for a week for those enchiladas, knowing Verlan was coming. What a fool I was. Picking up the lamp, I stormed into the bedroom.

Misery and loneliness consumed me as, fully clothed, I tossed back and forth on the bed. Oh, how empty and damned pointless life was! Never a moment of true and lasting happiness. If not for my beautiful children, and Lillie, my friend, I would be wishing for a black hole to swallow me up and take me away from this dreary existence. How did a woman keep her faith while living like this? What in the hell had ever possessed me to think life married to a leader would be an adventure? We women, soldiers in the glorious army of the Lord—bullshit. We were nothing but mindless cows in a pasture, waiting for our time of the month so our bull could pay us a visit and start another jewel for his heavenly crown.

We lived in such isolation. We were veterans of loneliness. Whose fault was the greater, the man's for his neglect, or the woman's for accepting it? "Be a good little wife, Susan, and when I come home... Be patient, my darling. The day will come when our life as a family will be normal..."

A normal family life would never happen. As long as I was willing to put up with Verlan's excuses and warped priorities, my life would remain in the same, intolerable rut. Lucy's pale face flashed before my eyes. Uncomplaining Lucy, always the quiet and long-suffering saint. A stoic, complacent martyr, and I was becoming just like her. But what could I really do about my situation?

I sat up on the edge of the bed, then restlessly paced around my dimly lit bedroom. I could always rebel; I could refuse to stay home and wait for Verlan any longer; I could threaten divorce. I could! I could demand that he treat me like a real wife, and if he couldn't stay at home, then he could just haul me along with him.

But would his fear of losing me prompt him to act? Did I mean as much to Verlan as he constantly assured me I did? As much as Lillie thought I did?

Striking a match, I re-lit the lamp. I placed it on the dresser and took a long, earnest look at myself in the mirror. At nineteen, a soft, ethereal beauty had replaced the child-like prettiness that was mine on the day of our wedding almost four years ago. Ash-blond, shoulder length hair glistened in the lamplight. An oval face and creamy complexion accentuated the striking, sea-blue eyes that stared back at me from beneath dark, delicately arched brows. Full lips, naturally curved upward at the corners, smiled experimentally back at me, revealing the tips of even, white teeth.

I slowly unbuttoned my blouse and pulled it off. Then I slipped out of my jeans. With only my bra and panties hiding my nakedness, I stared at my reflection. My figure was a bit more slender than it had been before, but still showed supple, womanly curves in the right spots. I had to be honest. I looked better than I ever had. Something about the way Verlan's eyes followed me of late told me he thought so too. But would my sensuality be enough? What about the conspicuous age gap that caused lulls in the conversation if we happened to spend much time around one another?

I unfastened my bra and slipped a nightgown over my head. Blowing out the lamp, I pulled back the covers and settled into the pillow. The difference in our ages and interests had nothing to do with the fact that I deeply loved Verlan, and that I needed him more than I ever had. I needed him and I deserved him, and God willing, I was going to fight for my rights. Maybe Lucy and the others were content with their lot in life, but I wasn't. I had shown Verlan a complacent, obedient little robot for far too long. Time for a change!

Verlan leaned over me, waking me with a quick kiss on the lips, "Hi, my love, I hope you're not mad. Say you're not, and I'll promise to spend some extra time with you today before I leave for San Diego. Okay?" His fingers gouged into my ribs, tickling me, his eyes pleading for understanding.

Pushing his hands away, I sat up in bed and looked coldly back at him. His casual manner and cheerful attitude made my blood boil. Instantly awake, I ran fingers through my hair, then grabbed the covers and held them tightly to my chest.

"Oh, I see," I said slowly. "Pacify the little woman with a bit of 'extra time.' A little hug and a little kiss. Well, it won't be necessary, thank you." My voice was suddenly crisp and in control. "I've decided to go with you to Colonia LeBaron, so you can just spend your 'extra time' with your other wives."

Verlan stared at me, his eyes widening. Then he shook his head. "Nope, that won't work. I'm sorry. You can't go this time. I've already promised to take—"

"Oh, no. Don't you dare!" I leaped out of bed, my control snapping. "Verlan LeBaron, you have neglected me for—for too damn long! I absolutely refuse to be left behind, so you might as well change whatever plans you've made."

"Well, I can't do that. I'm telling you, I already—"

"No!" I shouted. I shook my head and stamped my bare foot, my eyes blazing as I stood half-naked in front of him. "You're not leaving me again, Verlan! I've thought and thought all night long about you and me, and something's got to change. I'm tired of waiting around for you, hoping you'll find some time for me in your busy life. That's all I've done since the day we were married, is wait, wait, wait. Well I'm not going to hang around and be patient and understanding any longer. Do you understand what I'm saying? I'm going to conference with you. I'm your wife, and you owe it to me to treat me like one."

Dropping his chin onto his chest, Verlan slowly shook his head and sighed. Then he was silent, his eyes flitting around the room as he searched for a way out of the box I'd put him in. I pretended to ignore him as I dressed and put on my shoes, but I watched him stew in the reflection of Lillie's big mirror when I brushed my hair. Finally Verlan patted the bed. "Sit down for a minute and listen to me. I want to explain to you about last night. Last night as I—"

"No!" I snapped, slamming the dresser drawer closed and whirling to face him. "I don't want to hear where you spent my night. I'm too damn mad. Besides, it doesn't matter now because I'm going with you."

Sighing again, Verlan stood up. "I wish you'd quit that language, and I wish you'd listen to me. Ester was really unhappy last night—"

"Ester?" I shrieked, my blood running cold. "You spent my night with Ester? Oh, that's just lovely. Of all the raw, low down nerve . . . How could you even bear to touch that—that bitchy little snob!"

"Sweetheart, she's not like that, really. She can be such a gentle, queenly woman . . ."

323

"Well, I don't want to hear it. I'll never forgive you for this, Verlan. Never! I made such a nice dinner, and I waited for you for hours."

Verlan regarded me for a long moment, then walked to the window. His shoulders were bowed as he pulled the curtain back and stared across the vacant field toward Lucy's house. As I yanked the covers over the bed, I couldn't help but notice that he looked really haggard. For a fleeting moment I felt sorry for him, and I regretted my ugly show of temper. My loneliness and jealousy had caused me to forget that he had his own side to this story.

I didn't doubt that it was real hell for a man to be emotionally torn between so many wives. Verlan wanted to be there for each of us. He loved and needed us, and wanted to make all of us happy. Well, this whole mess was his own fault. He should have thought of that before he married us. He always wanted to. Wasn't it something how his intention and his follow through somehow weren't connected?

"Okay." His voice almost startled me. He turned and gave me a brief smile. "You can go. Go ahead and pack for you and James. Plan on two weeks. I'll have Reenie take care of Melanie."

I gulped, an abrupt, unexpected guilt causing my hands to shake. He had given in so easily! I'd expected such a battle... "Thank you, Verlan." I plumped the pillows, somehow keeping my voice even and sophisticated.

He walked to the doorway, hesitated, and looked back at me. I met his gaze, hoping that he would see only confidence and self-esteem in my eyes. I didn't want him to know that I was suddenly feeling darting little arrows of shame. Ducking through the doorway, he dropped the curtain back into place and quietly left the house.

I sank down on the bed, my knees weak. I shakily exhaled. All right, you should be happy, I thought. You've pulled it off. You've bullied him into taking you to Colonia LeBaron. You are special to him; Lillie was right. He wouldn't have given in to anyone else. So he's leaving someone else behind. That's his problem. That's her problem.

I bit my lip and rubbed my forehead, my temples beginning to throb. I hadn't even had the guts to ask Verlan who? One of his other wives was going to be terribly disappointed and angry with me. I gulped in growing misery. I was so selfish.

From the corner of my bedroom, a faint smell of urine wafted toward me. James had awakened and was standing in his crib. He stared at me from between the bars, his sleeper sagging between his legs. After a moment I stood up, went to the kitchen, and put a bucket of water on to heat for his bath. I told myself that Verlan's other wife didn't matter, I was going with him! That was the important thing. Verlan and I were again going to become as one flesh, just as the Bible said we should. We had to do this! We had to build a relationship once again—I couldn't bear this way of life any longer if we didn't.

I resolutely planned for the trip, and packed Melanie's clothes to take to Irene's. Surely Irene would agree to take care of her, she loved Melly, and besides, she had Donna and Kaylen and the others to help. Lillie, of course, would keep Ivan.

I ran down the little path that was forming between Lillie's house and mine and explained to her about my intended trip. "Will you mind keeping Ivan?"

"Of course not. Go, and have a good time. Verlan should take someone, and it's your turn."

Her words salved my guilt as I waited for Verlan to arrive. He came for Melanie shortly after lunch. "Come on, baby," he called for her as he picked up her bag. Turning to me, he said, "I'll be right back for you."

I frowned. "Why don't I just come with you now? I'd like to tell Irene good-bye, and thank her."

"We don't have time for that; we're getting away late as it is. I'll tell her good-bye for you. Now Melly, give your mom a kiss."

She hugged me, looking at me with a trace of tears in her eyes. "You won't be very long, will you, Mama?"

"A few days, but you'll be fine with Aunt Reenie and Kaylen. Be a good girl, and I'll bring you back a prize." I kissed her cheek, a growing lump in my throat.

Twenty minutes later, Verlan, James and I bumped along the road and climbed up the incline above Los Molinos. I looked back at Irene's yellow house in the distance, wondering if Melanie was crying. This was the first time I had left her for so long, and I felt like a traitor. She was so little and so trusting, and I was dumping her on Irene to satisfy my own selfish needs. I blinked rapidly to block the tears and erase the growing fear that I was a horrible mother and a self-centered, demanding wife. As we sped along the highway, the knowledge that one of Verlan's wives was being left behind because of me kept crowding to the forefront. My feelings of justification in what I had done were dissolving like drops of water on a hot stove.

Verlan seemed distant and silent for the first half-hour, hardly noticing that I was with him. Suddenly he brightened, smiled at me, and said, "What is this?

Are you going to stay clear over there the whole trip? Move that big hunk of a boy over, and come sit next to me."

I lifted James from between us and scooted him next to the door. "He really is getting big, isn't he," I forced a grin, "I'll bet he's as tall as you when he grows up."

Verlan glanced at him. "Oh, at least. Just look at those feet. He'll be as tall as Ervil."

"Verlan," I took a deep breath, "There is something I've been needing to tell you about Ervil. Something happened the other day. Did Joel tell you about the fight between Ervil and the Zarates and Brother Castro?"

Verlan's eyes darkened. "He told me some of it, yes. Go ahead, tell me what you heard."

As I related to him the incident at Victoria's trailer, I watched his face. His expression hardly changed throughout my account, only a grinding of his jaw showing his emotion. "Gamaliel Rios was the man who was with Ervil that night in Colonia LeBaron," I said soberly, "the night I heard Ervil say he'd have you killed. Oh, Verlan, Ervil's not rational! He knows he can't bully those men out of their land, and they won't be threatened into joining his group. And yet, something is building. I can feel it. Ervil talked of blood atonement. What does that mean?"

"It's an old Brigham Young doctrine, one, I'm glad to say, that quickly bit the dust. It means that if a person sins against the Holy Ghost, or in other words, against personal knowledge of what's right, then that person is executed for the salvation of his own soul. Ervil's professing to be in charge of seeing that the doctrine is put into practice once again. Claims God told him to clean house." He snorted. "It's pure hogwash. He'll never do it."

I frowned. "So what's going to happen? I can't picture his threatening these things and not carrying through with some action! He would look stupid. I don't know," I shook my head worriedly, "I think you're kidding yourself if you think he is just going to let it all go away."

Verlan yawned. "You know what? I don't want to talk about Ervil anymore. I'm sick of the subject. Let's just enjoy our trip together, hum? Because once we get to San Diego, we're going to be picking up a couple of brethren to ride on to Colonia LeBaron with us. I was originally planning to stay in San Diego for a couple of days, but since you're going with me we may just as well leave immediately for the colony. That way you'll have a chance to spend some time with your folks."

He patted my knee as I snuggled against him. This was the Verlan I had been missing so much ... This was why I'd thrown the fit this morning, so that I could once again have my husband to myself. He was so different when we were around the rest of the family—so harried and stressed out. But now that we were alone, he was affectionate and considerate. I pressed a kiss against his shoulder and said a silent prayer of thanksgiving. For the next few days, Verlan would be mine. The choking, dried out garden of our love would be watered once more, given a long, deep drink that would have to last for weeks, or possibly months, until my turn came again. I had to make the most of it.

Chapter 33

I awoke as we rattled over a cattle guard. "Where are we?" I yawned loudly, rubbed my eyes, and peered out the bug-spattered windshield.

"We're here, honey. We're at the colony," Verlan yawned in response and patted my knee.

Colonia LeBaron's main walnut tree-lined road, dark and silent under the pale ghost of a late moon, was a welcome sight and I immediately felt the familiar excitement of being home again. Mom and Dad, Fara and Mona, oh and Jay— I couldn't wait to see them! My hands drifted up to my tangled hair in an effort to make myself presentable, then I fished in my purse for a brush.

"Hey, what's going on here?" Verlan muttered, suddenly braking the car when the shadowy figure of a man waving a flashlight stepped out of the trees to the driver's side window. After Verlan rolled the window down we both recognized Beverly's father, Delfino Paisano, although his head and shoulders were covered by a serape. More figures emerged from the shrubbery hurrying toward us. A man on horseback galloped close, abruptly reigning the horse to a halt.

"Delfino! Nephi! How you guys doin'? What's going on here?" Verlan's hearty voice woke James, who was lying on the seat next to me. Immediately he started to wail, drowning out Nephi's shouted response. I shushed James, but Verlan had already opened the door and joined the men. They'd gathered in a huddle, the car-lights outlining the group.

"What in the heck?" I muttered, peering at my watch. Almost midnight and five men, one of whom appeared to be Verlan's brother Floren, were out in the chilly night air, conversing with Verlan. Something was wrong.

"Abel, wake up." I reached into the back seat and nudged Verlan's snoring nephew who had shared his sedan with us for the trip from San Diego. "Go see what's going on out there, will you?"

Abel sat up with a start, groggy from having driven most of the long trip. "What? What's happening?" he mumbled, leaning over my shoulder as he squinted out the windshield. A quick glance was all he needed. "What the heck . . . ?" He hurriedly opened his door and joined the others.

Although Verlan's window was open, I couldn't hear the men's voices over the engine. I turned it off and doused the headlights. Suddenly I realized that beyond the group of men were other figures further down the road, some of them carrying lanterns. This was too strange! I wrapped a blanket around the baby and hurried to the group of people surrounding Verlan.

Several of the guys were talking at once as I approached, with Floren's voice being the most dominant. "Absolutely not," he was insisting to Verlan. "You aren't going anywhere without a body guard. Nowhere, you hear me? Abel can take her to her Mom's. Sigfried and Ossmen are waiting for you at Magdalena's; let's get over there!"

"Verlan, what's going on?"

As I grabbed Verlan's arm, Floren shoved me away. "Don't! Stay away from him, Susan," he commanded. "Get back in the car and Abel will take you to your Mom's. Hurry up, now, get out of here. Verlan's busy, so you're on your own."

My eyes practically popped out in angry surprise. "What's happened?" I demanded. "Somebody tell me what's going on!"

"Joel's been killed!" Verlan said hoarsely. His face was hidden in the shadows, but his voice held the same shock and disbelief that the words hit me with.

"What?" I gasped. My eyes roved frantically over the men huddled around us. They settled on Delfino, whose face was somewhat visible because of the flashlight in his hand. "Joel?" my stiff lips whispered, scanning Delfino's black eyes for verification. As he nodded, my arms holding James weakened, and my blanket-clad little boy slipped to the ground.

Abel grabbed and steadied me, and one of the Mexican men scooped up a wailing James. Dizziness and nausea swept over me, the men surrounding me fading in and out of my vision.

"Put your head down," Abel's voice came to me from far away. Then Verlan's arms were around me, his rough whiskers against my cheek. "It was Dan," he croaked. "Oh, my God! It was Dan Jordan. Dan shot him—in Ensenada—Oh, my God. Oh, my God, no! Joel, Joel!" He rocked me back and forth, his body shaking.

"It can't be true," I babbled, my mouth dry as cotton. "Oh, Verlan, it's a lie! It's just a lie! Joel couldn't be dead; his mission isn't over yet! Don't you remember, he's supposed to be here until Jesus comes! Don't cry, honey, he's not dead!"

Floren yanked me out of Verlan's arms. "Let's go," he barked at him. "You're a target, damn it! You want her in danger? Now, let's go take care of business. Abel, take this girl to her family."

I got back into the car and watched through the rear window as Verlan and Floren disappeared from my view. When Abel maneuvered the car around the potholes, I hazily noted the huddled groups of people gathered on the street corners of Colonia LeBaron. Their faces mirrored confusion, their eyes incredulous. They carried on a lantern-lit vigil in honor of our fallen leader. I knew they were harboring the same questions, the same denial, and the same horror as me. Oh, how could this be? Joel, dead? It couldn't be true! God wouldn't allow it—it was all a mistake, a sick, Satanic hoax. Either that, or—or the end of the world was actually here—it was happening right now! These were the only possible explanations.

Abel opened the car door for us in front of my parents' dark, silent home. His round, bespectacled face was a mask of shock, and he wordlessly pulled my suitcase from the trunk and set it on the porch. Then he climbed back in the car and drove away.

Shifting James' weight onto my hip, I pushed open the door to my mother's bedroom. "Mom, it's Susan," I croaked. "Mom?"

Only silence and the smell of stale air greeted us. I hurried across the porch and into the living room, but even as I felt my way into the kitchen, I knew there was no one home, that the house had been deserted for some time. The musty odor attested it. One-handed, I felt for a box of matches, found one in a kitchen drawer, and lit a lamp.

Dust covered the counters and table. Dirty dishes piled in the sink, the old food hard and moldy, was causing the smell. Adding to it was a half-filled, rotting garbage can. My stomach rolled, my second month of pregnancy once again making itself blatantly apparent.

Where was my mother and sisters? Carrying the lamp in one hand and James with the other arm, I wandered through the deserted house. How could they be gone, when the whole world was spinning out of control? Maybe with Joel dead they'd been translated up to heaven like Elijah in the Bible. Stranger things had happened—were happening even now.

I sat at the kitchen table, rocked James back to sleep, and stared at the smoking lamp. My mind reeled. The world had gone crazy—it must be coming to an end. The Church had constantly preached about the end of the world coming soon, ever since I was a little child, and if the prophet was actually dead then there was no other answer. Joel was supposed to be here until Jesus' return; at least, that's what I'd always been taught. So if he were really dead would he come back to life as Jesus had?

I blew out the lamp, grabbed my purse and suitcase with one hand, arranged James' sleeping little body against my other shoulder, and left my mother's empty house. The suitcase was unbearably heavy and cut into my fingers as I hurried across the dark colony toward Grandma LeBaron's. Oh, Grandma, I thought, her sweet old face haunting my thoughts with every step, how can you possibly live through this unspeakable tragedy? This will kill you if it's true. Oh Sweet God in Heaven, don't let it be true! Please, please . . .

A small group of people, huddled in front of Esther Spencer's rock fence, was singing "We Thank Thee, Oh God, for a Prophet" as I stumbled toward them. They turned towards me as I approached, the hymn dwindling away as Maria, my father's second wife shouted out, left the group, and hurried to me.

"Susana, honey, what are you doing here?" she asked amazed, taking my bag and wrapping her free arm around my shoulders. "Is Verlan with you? Did he get here safe?" I nodded as the others crowded around us.

"Uncle Verlan's here? You were with him?" Sammy LeBaron, Abel's brother, eagerly questioned me.

"Yes, we arrived a half hour ago," I answered. "Verlan's with Floren and Sigfried. He's fine, safe." I hesitated, loathe voicing my horrible question. "Is it really true? Oh, Sammy, is Joel actually dea–gone?" The words choked in my throat.

His colorless lips trembled. "That's what they say–I don't know. Velma Jones, Ossmen's wife, called from San Diego and said Dan Jordan murdered Uncle Joel in cold blood. She said my little cousin, Jeannine's boy Ivan, saw it happen. Ivan saw Dan shoot his dad! That poor little boy." Sammy turned away, his shoulders hunched.

My heart nearly stopped, my mind exploding with renewed grief and horror. Ivan! Oh, dear Lord, my sweet Ivan, my little buddy–my little helper. I'd left him–just two days ago I'd left him with Lillie in Los Molinos. And yet, somehow he was in Ensenada yesterday and witnessed his own father murdered? Oh, Lord no, no! Not my Ivan. Oh, and Lillie! Joel was her stepfather! She had to be beside herself with grief. And Jeannine . . . her husband dead. It was all too much, too much. I stumbled to a large rock at the edge of Esther's lot and sat down. Burying my face in James' soft shoulder, I sobbed.

Maria's arms crept around me, her tears mingling with my own as she tried to comfort me. "Is okay, Susana, is okay. God is in control. He knows what he's doing, is okay," she crooned.

"Where are my mother and sisters?" I asked her when I could talk.

"Oh, honey, your Mama's in Utah. I'm so sorry, Querida! Your Grandma got really sick, and your Mama had to go. Two weeks ago, she left—your Papa took her. Fara and Mona are staying at Jay's ranch out at Spencerville. Pobrecita Susanita." She patted my shoulder and kissed my hair.

I sobbed again, harder. I needed my mother right now! How could she be gone when I'd come all this way! But I couldn't think about that—there were too many horrible things happening; I couldn't be thinking about myself right now. I blew my nose on the edge of James' blanket. "Does Jay know? About Joel?"

"I don't know," she shrugged. "I haven't seen him and we all just found out late tonight. But he probably knows. Someone probably drove there to tell him, I think."

"Maria, this is going to kill Grandma LeBaron," I whispered, my chin trembling.

"I know, honey. I know."

"I need to go there. Will you help me?" I asked.

"Yes, but Sammy has his truck here; he'll take you, I'm sure. Momento, I'll ask him."

I climbed into Sammy's pickup, grateful for the ride. James was so heavy, and with the suitcase, more than I could handle.

"Sam, what's going to happen to us?" I asked as we moved toward Grandma's. "How will we possibly cope if Joel's really gone?"

"I don't know. I don't know!" He wildly shook his head. "I can't imagine it, it's so against everything we've been taught would happen. Who would have ever thought Uncle Ervil would actually do such a hellish thing? Yes, he's been threatening to, but, to actually carry it out! It's just—just unbelievable!"

"Ervil?" I echoed in a whisper. My lips felt stiff. Until this moment I hadn't truly connected the dots. The possibility, then the knowledge, of Joel's death had shut my brain down, and it had refused to accept the appalling fact. Ervil!

"Of course, Ervil!" Sammy snapped bitterly. "Maybe Dan shot him, but Uncle Ervil's the one behind it; you know that! Dan was just the hit man. And, from what I gathered from Ossmen Jones, Uncle Verlan was supposed to have been killed, too. But you guys left San Diego a day early, right? Before they could get to him, thank God! Did you know that? We're mighty lucky that Uncle Verlan's not dead too."

I bit my lip, trembling. Because of Abel's offering us a ride to Colonia LeBaron, we had left sooner than originally planned! No wonder Floren had acted as he had and was talking about body-guards for Verlan! Maybe you will take care of Verlan, yes? Ervil's haunting words reverberated in my ears.

As we pulled into the driveway I peered at my watch, then hurried onto Grandma's front porch. Almost two o'clock. As I waited for someone to answer the door, I remembered another late-night visit I'd made to Grandma LeBaron's house. Ervil's evil had been at the center of my visit then, too, but that had been nothing in comparison to this. How could I stand to look into Grandma's eyes tonight?

Lawreve Jensen, the woman whose home I'd stayed in the night of my wedding, answered my timid knock. Behind her, Esther Spencer sat on the couch with Grandma LeBaron. They were clasping hands, their faces masked in sorrow and disbelief.

"Susan! Oh, sweetheart," Grandma's knobby hands reached for me. I handed James to Lawreve and hurried to her, kneeling and wrapping my arms around her thin shoulders. She shook as she sobbed and moaned, clutching me tightly while rocking back and forth.

"Grandma, oh, Grandma," I whispered, kissing her cheek over and over. "I'm so sorry. So sorry! I don't even know what to say... Oh, I love you so much, and I'm so sorry you have to live through this—this nightmare... How I wish I could take it all away from you." I buried my face in her neck.

"I know, dearie, I know," she sobbed. "I wish I'd died before this happened, because I can't bear it. My precious boys..." she turned her wet face away, her anguish more than she could stand for anyone to see.

Esther patted my hair and touched my cheek, her face stiff with sorrow. I squeezed her hand and pulled away from Grandma's arms.

"Mother needs to get some rest," Esther whispered. "Help me get her to bed."

Amid Grandma's protests, we walked her to her bedroom. Esther turned down her bed and I helped her into her nightgown. "I'll stay with her awhile, dear," Esther said. "You must be exhausted. Verlan sent word he would be here soon. Mother has the corner room ready for you. Make yourself at home."

It was an hour before Verlan crawled into bed next to me. He was beyond exhaustion, and regardless of his deep sorrow, began snoring immediately.

The scorching, August sun was well into the sky before Verlan's stifled sobs woke me. I wrapped my arms around him, reliving the horror of the past few hours. His body was rigid with grief and hot as fire. As I kissed his wet cheek, my exhausted brain searched for words of comfort. But they wouldn't come. I couldn't find the words. So I patted him and kissed him and said, "Shush,

333

shush, its okay, honey. It's okay."

"He was my brother," Verlan moaned, shuddering. "He was my brother, my precious brother. Oh, Susan, how can we go on without Joel?"

The brethren decided that conference should proceed as scheduled. The timing of Joel's murder left little doubt that the Ervilites anticipated enough turmoil that conference would be canceled. We couldn't allow them to defeat us. First, we would have Joel's funeral, followed immediately by the scheduled, three-day event.

Joel really, truly was dead. No hoax, no misunderstanding. Family members had hastened to the mortuary where Joel's body lay and verified that the prophet had been shot in the head.

Phone calls from members in San Diego flooded the message phone in our neighboring village of Galeana. The calls related that Joel and his wives, Jeannine and Kathy, along with several of his children, Ivan included, had stopped in Ensenada to pick up an old car of Joel's that was parked in front of the home of Benjamin Zarate. Somehow the keys to the car had been left at another residence across town, so Joel sent his wives, along with Benjamin's son, Andres, to locate the keys. All the children rode with them except Ivan, who had remained behind to help Joel work on the car.

Meanwhile, Ervil's follower, Gamaliel Rios, had showed up, approached Joel, and said that he and Dan Jordan had questions of a religious nature for him. So Joel and Gamaliel walked inside the Zarate house and visited while waiting for Dan to arrive. Outside, Ivan, patiently awaiting his father, climbed into the front seat of the old car they had been working on. Its dusty windshield hid his small, slumped figure from Dan Jordan's view as he approached the house. Ivan witnessed Dan shake hands with Joel through the open living room window, then enter the front door. Within minutes Ivan heard raised voices, sounds of a scuffle, a window breaking, and gunshots. Immediately Gamaliel Rios jumped out an open side window and Dan walked out the front door of the house. Both men fled down the street.

Meantime, Jeannine and Kathy had been sent on a wild-goose chase. Andres Zarate led them across town to where the elusive key supposedly was—only to be told that Andres' brother had it and had gone to a swap meet. They drove to the swap meet, where Andres left them to locate his brother. The women waited for more than an hour, becoming annoyed and mystified. Andres had disappeared! Finally they decided to leave, return to the Zarate house, and tell Joel what had happened.

As they approached the house they became alarmed. Crowds hovered on the sidewalk and people peered in the windows. Neither Joel nor Ivan could be seen. Kathy and the children waited in the pickup and Jeannine entered the house and called for Joel. No one answered. Blood was all over the floor! Jeannine frantically questioned a bystander and was told that a tall, blond man had been shot. "Who did it?" she choked.

"Daniel," a Mexican man answered. "Daniel Jordan."

Jeannine and Kathy raced to the police station. When they entered the building, Ivan ran to Jeannine, sobbing, "They killed Daddy!" When she asked him who had done it he answered, "It was Dan."

That same afternoon Ervil's son Arthur, along with one of Anna Mae's boys, Eddie Marston, went to Los Molinos looking for Verlan. But he, James and I were en route to Colonia LeBaron.

The following evening, a large group gathered at the airport in the colony's neighboring city of Casas Grandes. It seemed the whole town was here; everyone desired to be present for the arrival of our leader's body. Fear for my husband clutched me as I waited with the silent crowd. I could see Verlan, his bodyguards hovering close.

I'd ridden to the airport with Jay and Carmela. The men surrounding Verlan refused to let me near. Though I understood their actions, I was angry. He was my husband; he needed me, and I needed him even more now. I felt ill with worry as the details of Joel's murder came to light. Verlan was in grave danger and I couldn't bear to be parted from him. But my pleading was of no avail. Floren and Sigfried surrounded him, and they treated me like an annoying fly and shooed me away if I got too close.

The men's meetings had been interminable since we'd arrived at the colony, and were only now interrupted as we watched the black sky for the plane lights. Jay had been included in the meetings and I'd only gotten to see him tonight, when he and Carmela, Fara and Mona, had picked me up at Grandma's for the forty-mile ride to the airport. Our usual, joyful greetings had been subdued, our whispered visiting during the long ride minimal. Keen shock and vague unease hovered over us. The question on everyone's mind seemed to be, what now? Is this the end of the world as we know it?

Standing behind me, quietly scanning the sky, I suddenly recognized Joel's seventh wife—his last—Priscilla, a half-sister to Lane Stubbs, my old flame. She stood a bit apart from the rest of us. I stared, my heart breaking for her. By the dim light of the overhead flood-lamps, I studied her lovely face, surprised at how calm and collected she seemed. She was awaiting the body of her slain husband, yet her eyes held no tears and her features appeared normal. And here I was, my own husband nearby, alive and well, and I was trembling with fear for him and shock for us all. How did Priscilla control her emotions so well?

I hastened to her side and kissed her cheek, and she gave me a small, tremulous smile. "Oh, Priscilla, how can you stand this?" I blurted. "How can you be so strong?" I dabbed at my eyes and squeezed her cold hand.

"I don't know, I guess his death hasn't hit me yet," her graceful shoulders raised in a slight shrug. "I'm just numb right now. I don't want to feel yet."

I nodded and squeezed her hand again. How did you express your sympathy when there were no adequate words?

Magdalena, Joel's first wife, and her family waited next to the gate. The plane was landing now, then taxiing toward us. When it stopped, Joel Jr., Magdalena's and Joel's eldest son, was the first to step out. Even at this distance I could see his thin, solemn face scanning the crowd. Some of the men rushed forward, and soon they were carrying the gold casket toward us. They placed it into the back of Ossmen's pickup, and we all crowded silently around as Joel Jr. hugged and wept with his mother, brothers and sisters. Jeannine had come on the plane, too. I wanted to get to her, hug her, and to ask her about Ivan and Lillie, but the crowd was too dense.

We formed a long, mournful caravan behind Ossmen's pickup, the slow, sedate trip back to the colony taking two hours. Little was said. Fara and Mona sat on either side of me in Jay's back seat, our arms around each other. They missed our mother so much, and I was the next best thing. Dad would be here in the morning. Somehow we all had to survive one more night.

Charlotte, Irene, Lillie and Beverly had all come from Los Molinos for Joel's funeral. To my horror, I learned from Irene that my little Melanie had been in Ensenada with Joel, Jeannine and Kathy, along with Ivan and several of their children, the day Joel had been shot. Irene, much to my dismay, was the wife Verlan had left behind in order to take me with him to conference. Irene was furious at Verlan, first for leaving her, then for pawning Melanie on her as well. She had finally rebelled.

Learning that Jeannine planned to go with Joel to conference, Irene had coaxed them into taking Melanie along. In her slow-boiling anger, she knew sending Melanie to me would get her scathing message across loud and clear.

Consequently, my precious little daughter had been taken to San Diego and was being cared for by church members there. Irene coolly told me all this. In spite of the distressing reason for her ensuing trip to Colonia LeBaron, her hostility toward me increased. For the first time in our relationship as sister-wives, Irene viewed me as a conniving, self-serving scoundrel.

Members from the United States and Mexico had put their affairs on hold and hastened to Colonia LeBaron. The colony swarmed with grieving humanity, with every residence bursting at the seams to accommodate so many.

Time was at a standstill. Every person inside the colony's boundaries, from the priesthood-holding men to the smallest child, openly watched the skies and counted the seconds expecting to see the clouds roll back and Jesus appear. Many hovered over Joel's body as it lay in state in Magdalena's parlor, and prayed that he would rise from his coffin and gather his flock into his arms. Speculation as to the church's future was on every tongue, and everyone expectantly looked in Verlan's direction. He was the next in line of our leadership. Surely he knew what to do; surely he had the answers. God wouldn't leave us without a leader and the proper priesthood! He had promised us that the priesthood office, which included the Keys of Sealing for Time and Eternity that Joel alone held, would never again leave the earth. The church couldn't go on without this, so if Joel were truly gone, then Verlan, or perhaps one of Joel's sons, must have it.

The old adobe church was packed to overflowing for Joel's funeral. His widows were seated on the bench directly in front of the casket, and placed in the order of their marriage—Magdalena, Jeannine, Gaye, Isabel, Kathy, Claudine and Priscilla. Nestled in her arms, Gaye held her week-old infant son, whom Joel had never seen. Grandma LeBaron sat in a padded chair at the family's side.

I was sitting with my father and Maria, Fara and Mona, and I anxiously looked back to where Verlan sat, surrounded by his new bodyguards, against the back wall of the church house. My heart ached for him, and I feared for his life. I tried to imagine his burden, the unexpected weight on his shoulders. He looked so solemn, his face as pale as his crisp, white shirt. How I wished I could hold his hands and kiss his mouth and tell him how much I loved him.

The church house windows and doors were left open, with those mourners who couldn't fit inside crowding at the openings. Hoards of Mexican neighbors had flocked to Colonia LeBaron to pay their last respects. Although most were of the Catholic faith, they all knew Joel and revered him as a great man of God. Many of them stood outside in the stifling heat throughout the long service, then waited in reverence as Joel's casket was carried past them and placed into Ossmen's pickup bed for the twelve mile trip to the cemetery on the outskirts of the neighboring village of Galeana.

The scorching afternoon sun beat relentlessly on the caravan as we followed Ossmen's pickup with its precious load. The small, fenced cemetery, bare of greenery, was filled with dusty mounds marked by Catholic crosses. The huge crowd silently traipsed behind the casket as we threaded our way between the graves and circled around the freshly dug hole. As Verlan raised his arm in the dedication of Joel's resting-place, his voice quavered. He prayed that the ground might be hallowed and safe until Joel was resurrected. After prayers and songs, the coffin was lowered into the rocky ground. Sobs and groans filled the stifling, hot air. I stood on the edge of the grave and said a silent, private farewell to my prophet. Shovels, manned by several of the men, began to fill the hole with the powdery earth.

I dizzily stumbled back through the crowd, weaving my way through the graves toward Dad's pickup. The fierce heat suffocated me, pounding down on my head like a hammer. The hot air shimmered, and I was desperate for something to drink. My throat felt parched and my mouth was dry. Every pore in my body screamed, begged, pleaded for water. I had never felt so completely thirsty, so totally desperate for liquid. The bright blue sky blackened at the edges of my vision and my knees buckled. Someone grabbed me, sat me down on a cement grave covering, and shoved my head between my legs.

"Susan, you can't do this now," Helen Leany, Theron's wife, whispered, shaking me. "You must be strong, you hear me? Verlan needs you to be strong for him right now. You can't let him see you like this—he's got other things than you to worry about. So snap out of it—you'll be fine!"

"Okay." I forced the word past my swollen tongue and through dehydrated lips. I blinked my eyes, tried to focus. "Water. Get—me—water."

Helen patted me and hurried off. As I battled against the encroaching dizziness, Joel Jr. struggled past me, carrying the limp form of his half-sister, Fawn, in his arms. Her face was beet-red and her eyes closed. Her head lolled on his shoulder. Sorrow, stress, and the horrible heat had gotten to her, too, the poor thing. So many widows and so many orphans! What would happen to them all? How would they go on without their husband and father?

Fresh grief for them, and for us all, consumed me. Weak, dry sobs wracked my desiccated body. I leaned my head back against the hot cement tombstone, my anguish a high-pitched keen.

Chapter 34

Fara, Mona, baby James and I moved back into my mother's house for the remainder of my stay in the colony. With Charlotte and Irene both at Grandma LeBaron's, there was no room for me—not that I wanted to stay on with both sister-wives hovering. Irene continued her coolness, and I was unhappy with her for shipping Melanie off, and thus putting my tiny daughter in harm's way, so close to such unspeakable horror. I was desperate to get back to San Diego and hold her in my arms again. But I had no way of leaving Colonia LeBaron until conference was over on Sunday night. Meantime, I spent the endless days after Joel's funeral with my sisters, Jay and Carmela, and my father.

Under the direction of Verlan, Alma, Sigfried Widmar, and Ossmen Jones, our three-day General Conference took place on schedule. As usual the church-house was packed, but the meetings, understandably, were not the joyous reunions of the past. Faces were grim and somber; distress and bewilderment was in the minds and hearts of all.

Where did we go from here? Who was in charge now, who had the Keys? Had Joel secretly passed his priesthood authority on to someone, or would God appoint us a new prophet? Could we continue on as a church without the Keys Joel held?

For three days, our leaders took their turn at the pulpit. Varying degrees of confusion were apparent in each man—a few feeling that the platform they had built their lives and their family's lives on had been jerked from under them. But though shaken, most of the men seemed steady in their faith and they tried to bolster us, each in his own way.

On the last day—Sunday—Verlan finally spoke, making it clear to everyone that Joel had definitely not passed the Keys to him. Verlan knew that God had a plan for us, but presently he was as much in the dark as we were. He assured us that the church had everything needed in the way of priesthood authority to carry on until such a time as God's new leader stepped forward. Meantime we should walk in faith as the followers of Jesus had after his crucifixion, and continue on with the building of the church.

Then Alma took the stand. Openly wiping tears, he began, "Joel was one of the great prophets of the earth. He said he had the promise from God that he would not fail and would live till his mission was fulfilled. Brothers and Sisters, God knows what He's doing! Joel's martyrdom will prove, as in all ages past, a greater benefit to the people for his having gone to the other side. The righteous in heart will look more deeply into church history and the works of righteousness. The enemy will step back. When Joseph Smith was martyred, the enemy thought Mormonism would end. And now, our enemy thought if Brother Joel was killed, his people would be stopped, and those who are jealous would gain a following. The sincere and honest will see that those who have been instrumental in taking the life of our prophet have been traitors and hypocrites. Now, let us prepare our hearts to uphold the new prophet whom God will raise up. Who it will be I do not know for sure. I expected Joel to lead us right into the millennium." Alma shook his head, blew his nose, mumbled a closing phrase, and sat down.

From out of the congregation, a stranger to me stood up, a thin, bald man in his fifties. "I'd like to say a few words before the meeting closes," he said. Making his way to the podium he stood nervously blinking his eyes, then cleared his throat and in stilted sentences began, "Uh, most of you don't know me. Some of you do. My name's Timothy Neil and I'm from Sandy, Utah. Joel converted my wife and me to the church about a year ago. He's been a guest in our home on several occasions. He seemed to me to be the godliest man I'd ever met and knew more about the scriptures than anyone I've ever talked to. I was finally convinced he was a prophet of God, and believed with all my heart he was the One Mighty and Strong talked about in the 28th Chapter of Isaiah, and in the 85th Section of the *Doctrine and Covenants.* My wife and I were baptized last January, and we've been making plans to join the colony down in Baja ever since."

He cleared his throat and looked nervously around. "Friends," he continued, "I have to tell you that I'm shaken to the very core by Joel's death. I don't consider his mission hardly started, let alone finished! Why would God barely begin His mighty work in these final days, only to allow His prophet, his Mouthpiece, His One Mighty and Strong, to be snatched away at the hands of some madman? Joel himself personally told me that he would be here to usher in the Millennial Reign of Peace. We talked for hours about all the missionary work that has to be done, about all the souls that need to be reached. And now, poof! He's gone. Joel's gone, people, and left us all holding the bag."

He shook his head and glanced behind him at the leaders seated on the bench. "You guys can fool yourselves on and on, and say the Keys Joel had, the ones that were never to leave the earth, are here, somewhere among you. Where, I ask? Verlan says he doesn't have them. No one else has stepped forward. Some of you are speculating that maybe Joel's young son, Joel, Jr., has them, or one of his other boys. Well, as far as I'm concerned, all that's irrelevant. As I said, Joel told me personally that he would be here until Jesus comes. That didn't happen, and that speaks volumes in my opinion."

He pursed his lips and let his gaze rove slowly over the silent congregation; then grabbing the pulpit with each hand he took a deep breath and continued. "I want to state here and now that I'm backing away from the church. I'm doing this for two reasons. One, I refuse to put my family in harm's way, and with Ervil and his people threatening more murders and the like, I feel it would be irresponsible of me to maintain an association. Two, we joined this church believing in Joel and his mission. With him gone I feel confident that God is trying to tell us all something. The question is, are we smart enough to understand, or will we just hold on and watch this organization crumble around our heads?"

He paused. His eyes flit around the congregation, lighting on various faces as though seeking support for his reasoning. Then shaking his head, he chewed on his bottom lip a moment, and continued. "I highly recommend that the rest of you get on your knees and ask God for personal guidance. That means you women, too! Stop looking to your husbands to carry you into heaven—stop leaning on the arm of flesh. You'll stand naked and alone before the judgment seat of God! Don't cling to something that is disintegrating before your eyes. Don't be blind. Think for yourselves. Read! Pray! Don't stop searching until you find the truth. That's what I intend to do. May God bless you all." With that, he shook hands with all the men seated behind the pulpit and walked down the long aisle and out the door.

Silence for a full minute, then Franny's dad, Sigfried Widmar, stood and took the stand. "Brothers and Sisters," he said in his crisp German accent, "That's the good thing about free agency. We are all entitled to our own opinions and free to voice them. I pray that Brother Neil's faith will be restored and he will get over the shock of Joel's murder, just as we all have to do, and that he finds his way back to us again. Let's keep him and his family in our prayers.

"I ask each of you to keep the faith and be patient. Remember that the Lord is in control and has not forgotten us, His Church. Be alert. Watch for His hand, but also, watch for the enemy. The evil ones are out to do us harm and are waiting to pounce on us, just as they did our dear brother Joel. Be on the lookout! Satan is standing by and will do anything in his power to lure us, the Hope of Israel, away, or to harm us. So go now, on about the Lord's business, with God's truth as your armor and shield."

Hymns were sung and prayers said, and amid tears and pleas to one another to be on the lookout for the Ervilites, the final meeting of conference was adjourned.

As I made my way home, the words of the varied men played in my mind. Verlan, adamant that he didn't have the Keys, but reassuring us that in spite of this minor set-back, everything would be fine. Alma, emotional but faith-filled, awaiting the appearance of a new prophet. These attitudes I had expected. But this brother Neil, this new guy—he had given me tons to think about . . .

His words raised so many questions! What about Joel's claim that he would be here until the Savior came? How did Verlan and the others wave this away? I personally didn't remember those exact words coming from the prophet's mouth, but it was generally understood. No wonder Tim Neil was leaving us— in truth I was shocked that more of our church body hadn't left. Verlan's intervention and reassurances were all that was holding us together.

Brother Neil was certainly right about another thing—none of us should be leaning on the arm of flesh. I, for one, needed to continue my studies.

The long journey back to Los Molinos was a nightmare, filled with hot, wailing children and the constant smell of soiled diapers. Joel's widow, Kathy, and her three small children rode with Abel, Lillie, our two babies, and myself. As sorry as I was for Kathy, I found myself biting my tongue to keep from repeating my plea to her to contain the soiled diapers instead of leaving them on the floor under our feet. Lillie and I helped her as best we could, but we had our own babies to care for. Abel drove doggedly through the night and into the morning, ignoring the chaos around him.

Early afternoon we stopped at the Jones' home in San Diego to pick up Melanie. She stared at me, her blue eyes wary with distrust. I knelt and hugged her tightly, fighting back tears as I reassured her that I wouldn't leave her again. She sniffled and turned her head away, refusing to trust me so easily. She had been dumped on strangers and forced to stay with them for days. Her three-year old brain was aware of her mother's neglect, and forgiveness came slowly. She clung to me all the way down the Baja Peninsula as I held her on my lap whenever James would let me put him down. Between the two, I was too occupied to think of what life held in store for us once we reached home.

Before leaving Colonia LeBaron, Verlan had sent for Lillie and me. He'd spent a hurried moment with each of us, telling us goodbye and letting us know he would be going on an extended missionary trip with Sigfried. For safety reasons he couldn't tell us where he would be or when he would be back. During his absence he wanted us to live together, to keep each other company and to be there for one another. He felt we'd be safer and happier that way, so I was to move into Lillie's home for the next few months.

Well, why not my home? I'd asked. Well, because Lillie's was more comfortable and nicer, and she had a washing machine and a closer well for water. Didn't I think that was a better idea? She'd already agreed and was glad to share her house. Couldn't I be just as gracious and show a bit of gratitude for her sweet hospitality?

You mean her sweet charity, I'd thought. But I'd swallowed the words and reluctantly nodded. Verlan didn't need my nasty mouth to add to his troubles. Besides, I was feeling too desolate and frightened not knowing when, or even if, I would see him again.

Upon our arrival at Los Molinos, I dutifully packed the children's clothing and necessities. I would no longer have Ivan, since Jeannine was staying on in San Diego for awhile, and had kept him with her. I boxed up his few remaining things. Then we left our little house with its bare, cheerless kitchen and frugal belongings, and trudged over to Lillie's. She'd made a pallet for the kids on the living room floor. She and I would share her bedroom with the frilly lavender curtains, matching bedspread, and soft purple rugs.

With reluctant acknowledgment, living with Lillie was comforting. She was a meticulous, organized housekeeper and I learned how to keep ahead of housework and laundry. Her special rule was—don't make a mess and you won't have to clean one up. She was also a great cook and could make a variety of dishes from our meager supplies. We did everything together—the laundry with her gasoline-powered Maytag, the cooking and cleaning. We even prayed together at night for Verlan's safety and quick return to us. Together we did the grocery shopping, attended church on Sundays, and occasionally invited Donna, Rhea and Laura over for cards and fudge. Irene seldom joined us. She was in a world of her own, and refused to let us share her private anguish.

The people of Los Molinos continued with life in a daze. Church meetings still took place every Sunday with some of the Mexican brethren presiding, but the heart and drive and joy of serving the Lord was missing and seemed out of reach. The once booming little town was hushed. Children played quietly, and the streets were desolate.

As for me, I locked my sorrow and confusion far away into the back of my mind. I couldn't bear to dwell on the Chynoweths, Lorna, Ervil, Joel, the church and what was happening. I was afraid that if I started thinking, I would lose my mind. I tried to not think of Verlan often.

As the weeks passed, Lillie missed her period. She'd become pregnant in Colonia LeBaron, on the night she'd spent there with Verlan. I didn't let her know, but I was angry. In spite of Verlan's grief over Joel's death, he'd obviously been able to make love to Lillie. He'd hardly even spared me a kiss the whole week, but Lillie had managed to pull him away from his cares long enough to get her pregnant. I enjoyed the feelings of anger. I could deal with anger better than loneliness.

The days slowly passed, with little change in our routine. One day while the children were napping I walked to my house and wandered through the dusty rooms. I'd stayed with Lillie long enough. The steady, close association was beginning to get on our nerves. I was tired of her constantly cleaning after me. If I pulled something from the cupboard and left it sitting more than a moment, she would be at my elbow, putting it away. And if I left my dirty plate on the table while I attended to my children, she was right there, scooping it up and hauling it to the sink. She had the bed made before I was hardly up, and was continually scolding Melanie for picking her roses. If this continued, I feared that our relationship would suffer. I didn't know when Verlan would return, and I decided I couldn't wait for his permission. He'd been gone for two months and we hadn't heard a word from him. People said they'd heard he was in Illinois, visiting Nauvoo and other famous historical places where Joseph Smith had lived, but that was just a rumor. I had begun to miss him terribly, and felt awkward letting Lillie see how forlorn I was. She seemed to stay cheerful and upbeat and had accepted his lengthy absence in stride. She never complained, as I did occasionally.

I stopped in my kitchen and observed the bare room. My house needed kitchen cupboards and work areas desperately. The makeshift boards I'd used for a temporary work-counter had to go. This was a start.

I hurried across the field to Lucy's and searched through the goat sheds and storage room. Leaning against the back of the goat sheds I discovered several two-by-fours and a couple of old, manure-stained sheets of plywood. A filthy porcelain sink, lying in a mud puddle, caught my eye. I gleefully examined it. In the shed I found another treasure, an almost-full gallon of white enamel.

Elated, I hurried to Irene's to borrow the pickup. I had to load the items myself, since the big boys were all in school. Struggling with the sheets of plywood and the old sink, I eventually got them loaded. Then I raided the storage shed for tools, nails and a paintbrush. Grinning, and truly excited for the first time in weeks, I hauled the supplies to my little house.

As I wrestled with the big sheets of wood, Lillie hurried across the field and gave me a hand. "What are you doing with all this stuff?" she asked curiously. She turned her nose up at the dirty sink and wiped her hands on her pants.

"I'm making myself some kitchen cabinets," I announced, laughing. "Wanna help me?"

"You're kidding," she scoffed. "You need some decent wood, for one thing. That stuff's gross. Do you know how to build?"

"No," I said cheerfully. "But I'll figure it out."

She shrugged. "I honestly think you'll be wasting your time. I'll watch the kids for you, but I don't think I'd be any use to you here."

"That's fine. Thanks," I smiled, refusing to let her dampen my spirits.

I worked for days on my new project. I drew my plan up on paper, then bravely measured, marked, and began cutting with my handsaw. I had no wood to waste, so I had to be careful. Most of the time, I took the children with me and let them play as I worked. One day when we went to Lillie's for lunch, she didn't join us as usual, but stayed busy washing windows as we ate. I put the kids down for a nap and returned to my project. That evening, she hardly spoke to me, and when I asked what was wrong, she answered that nothing was wrong. The next day she was the same—silent and preoccupied. I was putting the final coat of paint on my cupboards and anxious to see the finished results, but I finally threw my brush down, frustrated. I stomped across the field and onto Lillie's utility porch where she was doing the laundry. "Okay," I snapped. "What are you mad about? Tell me, dammit!"

She scrubbed at a sock, her face red. Then shrugging, she said, "Okay. I'm mad because you hardly help me around here anymore. You don't do a thing except take care of your kids and work on your cupboards! Susan, you've lived with me for almost three months now, and you haven't washed windows even once! I've washed them every time they've been done! I don't think it's fair!"

I stared at her in consternation, my eyes wide. "You mean you wash your windows that often? Gosh Lillie, if they were my windows, they'd be lucky to get washed once a year. It just never occurred to me that you should wash 'em more than that. I never even thought about it. Why didn't you ask me?"

She shrugged again. "I just thought you'd offer on your own, I guess." Her mouth formed a thin smile. "Okay. Now I understand. And it's okay, really. It's my mistake. I'm sorry I got so mad. It was dumb."

Her smile slowly dissolved, and tears flooded her cheeks. Dropping the wet towel she was wringing into the tub, she sat on the edge of the porch and began to sob. I sat beside her and put my arm around her shoulder. I hugged her and kissed her cheek, and she cried harder. "What is it?" I whispered. "What's the matter?"

She shook her head, unable to speak. I waited, and finally she hiccuped and moaned, "I miss Daddy so much! Oh Susan, I can't believe he's dead! He was so good to me! And I miss Verlan so, so much! Do you think he's okay? Why doesn't he write to us? How can he be gone so long, and not even send word that he's all right! I'm just, so—so sad! I never thought I'd hate anybody, but I'm so mad at that damn Ervil I could shoot him myself!" Her body shook with misery.

I jumped up and stomped my foot. "Yes!" I hollered. "Let's do it! Let's find us some guns and go track him down, you and me! We'll blast him into Kingdom Come, the old bastard! Come on, Lillie, go change your clothes!"

I hitched at my pants, fiercely yanked my hair back and started braiding it, and Lillie burst out laughing. She leaped up and hugged me, and together, we went inside to check on the children.

Chapter 35

Verlan's long legs, muscular and sexy in his baby blue Levi's, swung freely from where he sat perched on my new countertop. I stood in front of him bristling with fury and scorn, while his blue-green eyes pleaded, begged, and insisted that I accept the current, sharp knife he was plunging into my very soul.

He'd arrived from his eleven week absence today, a few minutes ago, and the first thing out of his mouth was that he had to leave again, tonight. Why? Because he had to go back to San Diego to see a young woman named Kim.

"Honey, she likes me, I know she does, and if I don't get back there now she'll take off with Steve Silver to Israel. I've got to stop her—don't you see? Before she's gone and out of my reach. Please understand!"

"Oh, this is just wonderful!" My voice was cold and insulting. "Here, the whole foundation of the church is at stake, and you're wanting to go off chasing another woman! Aren't there more serious issues to deal with right now, such as putting the church back in order? How can you even consider pursuing another girl?"

My anger, my reasoning, and my tears had been to no avail. Numbly I stood at my front door and watched his retreating back as he dashed on over to Charlotte's. I could only imagine how she would take this latest news. When had Verlan found the time, or the inclination, to court Kim? I just couldn't believe it! Where were his priorities? I shook my head and went back inside.

Steven Silver, our schoolmaster at the Los Molinos School—the man who had been one of the L.D.S. French missionaries, had left us right before Joel's death. To the shock of the whole church body and especially to us at Los Molinos, he'd given up on our religion, abandoned his first two families, and had only taken Carolyn, his third wife, with him. Lanky, redheaded Kim was Carolyn's teen-age sister. According to Verlan who had received this bit of information from Irene only minutes ago, Steve had convinced Kim to go with him and Carolyn on their journey to Israel to join a Kibbutz. Hence we had Verlan, earnest knight in shining armor, to the rescue. I wanted to slap his handsome face.

Joel had been dead for almost four months, during which time Verlan had been traveling around the United States and staying out of Ervil's way, while at the same time working with the authorities to have Ervil arrested for master-minding Joel's murder. He and Sigfried had also notified the FBI and the California State Police, and had contacted rival polygamist groups throughout Utah, along with the Mormon Church leaders in Salt Lake, warning them of Ervil's madness and his written intentions to mete out further punishment.

In his ongoing pamphlets that were sent to our people, Ervil had threatened: "The first thrones that will be cast down in this great work are the thrones of the false kings in the priesthood of the different groups of Mormondom." In another pamphlet Ervil wrote: "The most flagrant and criminal violations must be stopped first. The one single violation of the law, which God hates more than any other, is the crime of ecclesiastical treason. This monstrous crime is presently being openly and flagrantly committed by almost all the different sects and churches of Mormondom. All those who should not hear the word of the Lord that this servant would bring forth would be destroyed."

Ervil, Dan, and others of his group signed these types of warnings, couched in religious jargon. They were either sent by mail to our church members or handed out on our meetinghouse doorsteps by the handful of Ervil's followers who still lived among us. Most of his people had gone into hiding, as had Aunt Thelma and her children. Uncle Bud occasionally came to Los Molinos to see Naomi, who was still refusing to leave her Zarate relatives and join Ervil's followers. The few times I'd bumped into Bud, I'd gotten the impression that he was straddling the fence between Joel's people and Ervil's group. He refused to discuss his position, and would only tell me that Aunt Thelma and the others were somewhere in the San Diego area. The whole situation made me nauseous.

I wondered what the Chynoweths' lives, as Ervil's puppets, were like. How could they stand living in hiding like wanted criminals? But that's what they were. Police investigators had circumstantial evidence that Mark was involved in the plot to kill Joel. I could see Dan Jordan being a murderer, but my sweet cousin, with all that musical talent, conspiring with these horrible men to kill our prophet? It was more than I could comprehend. Uncle Bud had told Naomi on his last visit that Mark had married Ervil's daughter, Lillian, a girl I'd gone to school with in Colonia LeBaron. So now Mark was Ervil's son-in-law. And, Rena was most likely married to Ervil by now. Lorna, Rena, and Mark, all now in Ervil's immediate family. His carefully spun web around the Chynoweths was complete.

And here was Verlan, running off to chase yet another girl—Verlan, who had left his seven families practically destitute and ignorant of his whereabouts. The audacity and stupidity of his latest urge continued to stupefy me. How, Lord, how could I uphold my husband in this? How could he justify it? I was truly confused.

I'd begun to study the scriptures in an effort to find for myself what I believed in. Ervil's writings were what triggered my interest—as had the provoking words of Brother Tim Neil during the last conference meeting in Colonia LeBaron, when he'd challenged the church's women to read and study, and stop leaning on the arm of flesh. Tim Neil's accusation had made me realize how well I fit into that category. I was no longer a child; I needed to know for myself that our church doctrine was true, especially now that Joel was gone.

Until Joel's death I'd never had a single doubt that the Church of the Firstborn was all it professed. But what, now that Joel was gone? Still no one had come forward claiming his Office of Moses, the Office that was never to leave the earth again, according to the *Doctrine and Covenants*. Verlan and the other leaders were standing in as best they could, but they didn't hold the Mantle of the True Priesthood, or the Scepter of Power, the Authority needed to set in order the house of God. Nor did they hold the sealing Keys to perform Celestial, or plural marriages. Something was amiss, and I felt a growing anxiety. Evenings of late I sat at my kitchen table and pored over the books our church considered as scripture, the Bible, the *Book of Mormon*, the *Pearl of Great Price* and the *Doctrine and Covenants*, in an effort to understand what God required of us. There were so many of them that I felt overwhelmed at the task.

Although my study plan was our doctrine as a whole, I found myself becoming focused on what the scriptures said about plural marriage. This unorthodox practice of ours was a major part of our lives and beliefs; it had to be God-ordained, and must stand up to scrutiny, or the very foundation we based our church on was wrong. I searched every reference I could find. I started with the Bible.

In Genesis of the Old Testament, the subject was first mentioned. In the sixth chapter, men, whose normal life span exceeded 800 years, began to notice the beauty of the daughters of men, and began to marry as many of them as they chose. The Lord said to this: "My Spirit will not contend with man forever, for he is mortal, his days will be a hundred and twenty years."

I gaped at the verse, grabbed my dictionary and looked up the word contend. Its meaning was, "to fight, to argue, to strive with." I sat back, excited. God obviously was angry at these men's choice to take more than one wife, and to punish them, he shortened their life span by hundreds of years! I read furiously on in Genesis.

Chapter six, verse five, went on to say that the Lord had seen how great man's wickedness on the earth had become, and that men's hearts were filled with evil all the time. The Lord was grieved that he had made man, and His heart was filled with pain. He would wipe humanity from the face of the earth and start over.

The only righteous man was Noah, who had one wife. Noah was commanded to build the ark and take his one wife and his monogamous sons and their wives, into the ark. Even the animals that were taken into the ark were in pairs, one male and one female. Then came the rain for forty days. The flood wiped out everyone on the earth but Noah's righteous family. And what started all this? According to my understanding, it was God's anger at man for his corrupted ways, which included his plurality of wives.

God promised Noah that never again would He destroy the world by flood, and that men should live out their lives as long as the earth endured. After many fruitful years in the New World, man began the practice of polygamy once again. Along with the other laws and ordinances God gave to Moses was the one which said that if man should marry a virgin, and desire to marry another, that he must not diminish the first wife's raiment, apparel and duty of marriage. This was not a commandment to live polygamy, but a rule to abide by if man chose to do so. In other words, God was saying okay, do what you will, but you must at least be able to afford the luxury of more than one wife before indulging in this practice; this, I do command.

I turned to The New Testament. It hardly mentioned plural marriage, except for both Paul and Timothy's warnings that leaders in the church shouldn't practice it.

The *Book of Mormon* mentioned the practice in several places, and each one condemned it as being evil and disgusting, and not to be lived by God's chosen people. In Jacob 3:5 it said: "Behold, the Lamanites your brethren, whom ye hate because of their filthiness and the cursing which hath come upon their skins, are more righteous than you; for they have not forgotten the commandment of the Lord, which was given unto our fathers—that they should have save it were one wife, and concubines they should have none, and there should not be whoredoms commited among them."

Whoredoms! How could this clear message of warning be ignored? All Mormons revered the *Book of Mormon*. It was written from the ancient records

Joseph Smith found with the help of the angel Moroni, records that were written on golden plates and translated, with God's help, into English. If God were truly the same yesterday, today, and forever as the Bible said, why had His strict commandment changed, according to Joseph Smith, for our time?

I searched feverishly on and finally found what I was looking for. It was in the *Doctrine and Covenants*, the book of revelations the Prophet Joseph Smith claimed were given to him from God. The 132nd section talked about the Old Testament, saying that God commanded Abraham to live polygamy. Abraham was commanded by God to take Hagar, his wife Sarah's maidservant, as a plural wife. This was called the Law of Sarah, according to the *Doctrine and Covenants*.

I opened the Bible again, read the story in Genesis, and discovered that the whole Hagar thing had been Sarah's idea in the first place and not a commandment from God at all. Sarah was barren. Desiring that her husband Abraham have offspring, she gave Hagar to him in order to produce a child. Why was the *Doctrine and Covenants* calling this a law, and a direct command from God to Abraham?

Totally confused, I looked from one of our scriptures to the other. Why were the stories so different? Why were the scriptures so hard for me to understand? Maybe it's because I was a woman, and didn't have the benefit of a man's sharp brain. Maybe that's why the men insisted that women leave the heavy scripture studying to them.

I went back to the *Doctrine and Covenants*, starting at the beginning of the 132nd section, and found where polygamy was called the New and Everlasting Covenant. Here God commanded that all those who should have this law revealed to them must obey the same or be damned. Men should go and do the "Works of Abraham." The section went on to say that the prophet's first wife, Emma, was strictly commanded to accept all the wives that had been given to the prophet or she would be destroyed. She must cleave unto her husband and to none else. God would destroy her if she didn't abide by His law.

I had heard this section read before, but I'd never paid attention until now. According to this, God had created women for one purpose alone—for the enjoyment of the men. Women were possessions, just like cattle. We had no rights in and of ourselves. God had created the world and the heavens above so that men could reign, and the women were given to the men as wombs to bear their children. The man could espouse as many virgins as his heart desired, and be blessed by God, and become a god himself. But a woman was allowed only the man to whom she was given. If she should be with another, she would be an adulteress and be destroyed.

I sat back, totally bewildered. What was I to believe? If the *Doctrine and Covenants*, the book of revelations given to Joseph Smith from God, were true, our Father in Heaven obviously loved and valued his sons so much more than his daughters! How could this be possible? We were created in His image, weren't we? Did He love and value my little James more than my sweet Melanie? Oh, this just didn't make sense.

Shaking with emotion, I read it through again, and as I got to the end I was totally distraught. "God, Oh, Heavenly Father," I wept, slumping over my table. "Can this be true? If it is, then you obviously love your sons much more than your daughters! Aren't we just as lovely and valuable a creation? Why should a man deserve so many women to love and care for him, to desire and adore him so that he's never lonely, and yet his wives are heartbroken, abandoned and forlorn? We raise our children by ourselves and they hardly know their father—I don't understand! Why? The men get to be gods, and we're just their handmaidens! Is that fair? Is it? Can this be right? God! Why did you bother to give women a heart and a mind—and a brain? Please help me. I'm confused and my faith is weak."

I closed my books and put them away. I would leave them alone for now. I was in too deep, and I no longer understood anything. Verlan seemed to have no problem with the conflict in scripture. Maybe it was just I; as a woman I was too ignorant to understand the intricacies of God's Word.

As the days passed, I found myself carrying on a silent conversation with the Lord at every opportunity. I begged Him to open my eyes to His Word and His will, and to help me stop questioning the church because of what I'd read. I needed to accept the fact that He was in control. But if the *Doctrine and Covenants* were true, why was He so partial?

Lillie had left Los Molinos on an extended visit to her mother in San Diego. I sorely missed her companionship, and found myself withdrawing from the other family members and the residents of Los Molinos. Day after day I spent alone with my children, finding little in life to look forward to except for my time at the piano. Our diet was more meager than ever, as the family garden was through bearing for the year. We lived on ground wheat bread, beans and rice. Lillie had left her chickens for me to care for, and the luxury of having a few eggs partially made up for her absence.

As the weeks passed and my abdomen grew huge with my third pregnancy, my loneliness and confusion consumed me. How I needed someone to talk to!

Mentally I journeyed throughout the colony, my thoughts resting on each woman as I searched for someone who would spare me her wisdom and friendship. Irene, who was pregnant with her twelfth child, had her own problems and spent her spare time with her best friend, Betty Tippetts. Beverly and Lucy each had tiny new babies and were too depressing to be around. Charlotte was aloof. The rest of the colony women were so bogged down with their many children and chores, and so filled with worry and cares, that none of them could meet my need. The only bright spot on my horizon was the fact that Kim had turned Verlan's marriage proposal down flat.

As I went about my lonely days, I continued my habit of talking to the Lord. I constantly asked Him to strengthen and guide me, to help me accept my lot in life, and not be bitter.

One day, word came to Los Molinos that Ervil, weary of dodging the law, had gone to the authorities in Ensenada and turned himself in, expecting to clear his name of masterminding Joel's murder in a rapid manner, and go free. But to his consternation, several of our people promptly arrived to bear witness against him, and he was arrested and thrown into the Ensenada jail.

We were all ecstatic. Certain that justice would be served, everyone in Los Molinos said fervent prayers of thanks. Verlan and the other men determined to double their efforts in catching Joel's actual shooters, Dan Jordan and Gamaliel Rios, in hopes that they could make a clean sweep of the Lamb of God's leadership, and douse Ervil's evil purpose forever. I celebrated along with everyone, yet I knew that nothing could ever bring Joel back, or my beloved Chynoweths, for that matter. As the weeks passed and we settled back into semi-normal life, melancholy once again engulfed me.

One cold, December afternoon I had the best surprise—my brother Ross, along with his wife, Bobett and their baby son, Jared, drove into my yard. They had come to San Diego on vacation from their home in Utah, and decided to drive on down the peninsula to see me. Thrilled, and determined that they wouldn't see how cheerless my life in Los Molinos had become, I enthusiastically showed them the town and drove with them to the beach. But as the afternoon turned to evening, I became plagued with embarrassment. I had no eggs left, no beans or bread cooked, and nothing else to feed my guests but one small sack of pasta. Verlan Jr. had sent no money for the family this week.

Verlan was in town after another long absence. He'd arrived just the day before, and though I knew he was in an important meeting with some of the brethren, I quickly, unobtrusively, sent Irene's son Brent with a note. I had company, I told him, and I was in desperate need of grocery money. His scribbled reply was for me to make do with what I had.

I resolutely pulled out the Mexican pasta and sent Brent to Beverly's to beg a can of tomato sauce for seasoning. Using the last of my ground wheat, I mixed bread dough and fried some scones. As I dished up the small portions to my guests, I tried to hide my embarrassment.

Ross and Bobett were effusive in their praise for the wonderful meal. It was so delicious, they reassured me—such light, wonderful scones and such flavorful Mexican pasta!

We visited until the wee hours. Ross updated me on all the news of my older brothers and sister who lived in Utah. My mother had returned to Colonia LeBaron because Grandma Susie was finally well again. Ross also informed me that Jay had taken a second wife, Karen, the daughter of one of the church brethren. And Fara, at seventeen, had become the plural wife to a relatively new member of the church.

I had mixed feelings about this news from our sister-colony. How could I be so out of touch with my own family—as though Los Molinos was on a different continent! I should have known these things without my brother from Utah having to bring the news from Colonia LeBaron to me. Our mail system here was pathetic; taking at least a month, and more often, the letters didn't arrive at all. As Ross talked, the feeling of dejection and of being ostracized from the planet overwhelmed me.

So Jay had finally done it, he'd joined the ranks of polygamy, and Carmela was getting a taste of having to share her husband. And Fara, my saucy little sister, was now a plural wife. I should be happy for them, but instead I felt they had nailed themselves to a cross.

Ross wanted to know the details of Joel's death and Ervil's part in it, and about Aunt Thelma and Uncle Bud. In spite of Ervil's incarceration, Ross appeared worried about our safety and suggested more than once that the children and I should return to Utah with them for a lengthy visit.

I reluctantly declined. Oh, how I wished I felt free to discuss my new and growing questions where the church was concerned! But I knew he would leap into the opening with heated arguments against the Church of the Firstborn. He would demand that I leave it behind—and I wasn't prepared to turn my back on my life's beliefs.

An answer for the turmoil in the church would come; I just had to have faith and be patient. As hard as it was to see the purpose of my being here, I was still Verlan's wife and my job was to be supportive.

As much as I enjoyed the time with my brother's family, I was relieved to see them go. I had no food left except beans and whole wheat. Besides, having the happy, carefree couple here caused me to wonder more than ever about the existence I'd chosen. The children and I stood at the edge of our yard, smiling and waving until they were out of sight, but as we trudged back inside, the hard lump in my throat melted into a stream of despair and poured down my cheeks.

"Verlan, would you please explain this to me?" I demanded one January afternoon. I thrust my open Bible into his hands and pointed at First Timothy, third chapter. "Bishops and deacons shall be the husband of but one wife," I read aloud. "And here, further down, verse five. If anyone does not know how to manage his own family, how can he take care of God's church?" I glanced at him and raised my eyebrows.

He read it slowly, grinned and shrugged. "In the first place, this was written way before God gave the New and Everlasting Covenant of marriage to Joseph Smith. We're in the latter days now, and we've been commanded to live plural marriage." He readjusted his pillow, snapped the book closed, and set it on the nightstand. "And as to the other verse, what are you trying to say? Don't you think I manage my family well?"

"No, I don't," I said dryly. "You're never here to do it. When you're not out running around for the church, you're marrying other women and traipsing off to Nicaragua. I don't call that good management." I pulled my nipple from my newest daughter's mouth and laid her down on the bed.

"Well, I'm here now," he said with a chuckle. "So stop trying to make me feel bad." He tickled baby Jeannette's plump toes and blew on her bare tummy. She rewarded him by grabbing a firm hold on his large nose and yanking as hard as her seven month-old fingers could.

"Ouch!" he whined, pulling loose. "I'm being attacked by two girls at once. That's not fair."

I grimaced. "I suppose you thought it was fair for you to marry Helen Leany. What did you have to offer an elderly widow like her? Companionship, maybe?" I yanked my arm from his roving fingers.

"She needs someone to look after her. Darn it, Susan, why do you have to question everything I do? I owe it to Theron to take care of his family, don't you think? He gave his life to the church; that's the least I can do."

"Oh, yes, Sir Verlan to the rescue. Again." I bounced off the bed and stomped out of the room to check on Melanie and James. I needed to get their things together to take to Irene's. She was leaving for Nicaragua with Verlan tonight, and I'd agreed to help Donna take care of her kids.

Nicaragua was Verlan and Floren's latest project. Before Joel had died, he had talked of going south, and Joseph Smith and other early Mormon leaders had foretold the time when the Saints would move into Central and South America. The men had made two scouting trips down there so far, with the last trip doubling as Verlan and Helen's honeymoon. They were impressed with the land and intrigued with the thought of how well goats and cattle would do on such abundant vegetation, and also they were excited by what foods could be produced in such a moderate climate. Land was cheap, and government officials had made it clear that the LeBaron people would be welcomed.

I was appalled at the whole thing. Here we were, finally settled in Los Molinos, with Verlan's dream of having a home for each of his wives a reality. And now he was chasing another whim. Life for Verlan was always better and greener over the distant hill.

Verlan was taking Irene with him on this trip, to get her support for a move south with some of his families. Well, they could go and explore the jungle to their heart's content. I would never go. In fact, I'd made up my mind that as soon as they returned I would leave Los Molinos for good. Verlan was practically never around, and with the Chynoweths gone, there was nothing left here for me. If Verlan wanted to see me, he could just come to Colonia LeBaron. With or without Verlan's permission, I was going home.

Chapter 36

s soon as Irene and Verlan returned from their six-week trip to Nicaragua, I began to pack my bags. Verlan didn't battle my decision to move to Colonia LeBaron—he was much too occupied with the preparations to move Irene and Lucy South. Also, after almost a year's incarceration, Ervil's case had finally gone to trial in Ensenada, and of course Verlan was in the thick of it. Reports from the courtroom were phoned in to Colonia LeBaron on a daily basis, the details passed throughout the colony. Several of our people were absent, and now in Ensenada to witness against Ervil. Other than a wild rumor that his followers were raising money in the hope of purchasing his release, things were looking good for a long sentence. God was smiling on us again.

Once Ervil was imprisoned, Verlan would head south with Irene and Lucy's families. I could hardly believe they were actually planning to move—and to a jungle, so far away! The trip would take six days of driving around the clock, plus numerous borders to cross to get to Matagalpa—the small Nicaraguan village close to the piece of land Verlan had bought.

I wondered if he'd lost his mind altogether. What could possibly be the purpose of starting a new colony thousands of miles from civilization? Who would ever want to move there, and what was wrong with finishing and improving the two colonies we'd already started? We had plenty of land already—we should be concentrating our efforts in the mission field and fill the land we already had. We were supposed to be saving souls—wasn't that more important than starting a new venture and raising goats? I was aghast that Irene had gone along with it. Lucy, yes, she would do anything Verlan asked without question, but Irene? According to Verlan, this new dreamland of his was in the middle of nowhere. Who would Irene visit with besides Lucy? Well, it wouldn't be me. Maybe Verlan could sweet-talk the two of them into moving into a bamboo hut and starting over from scratch, but the Lord Himself would have to order me to take my tiny children into the wilds. My soul longed for the tree-shaded, peaceful streets and green fields of my childhood, and that was where I would live.

Within two weeks, Charlotte loaded the children and me into Verlan's pickup, hauled us to Colonia LeBaron, and dropped us on my parents' doorstep. Once again, my mother wasn't there to welcome us. Grandma Susie's health had gotten worse, and Mom would be staying with her indefinitely.

Maria and Dad had given up on their farming project and moved back to the colony. They were living at Mom's. With six children now, they no longer fit into Maria's two-room adobe out back. Dad promptly offered me the use of the vacant house. He was glad to have us home, but scowled at the mention of Verlan's name.

"He couldn't even manage to bring you here himself, could he now?" he snapped. "He just ships you back here and expects us to find you a place to live. He sure didn't have any problem marrying you, but that's where he thinks his responsibility ended. Guess he's too busy running around the countryside. Well, don't worry, honey, I'll see that you're taken care of."

Dad bustled around for two days, taking me to Casas Grandes to buy groceries and fill my butane tank, and finding me odds and ends of furniture and household items to get me by. I had nothing, as Verlan had insisted I leave everything in my house for some other needy family to use. Dad even talked Harv Stubbs, my sister Rose Ann's husband, into loaning me a fridge. He was attentive and considerate, and determined to tuck the kids and me under his wing. It felt wonderful to have someone looking out for us, and I didn't know how to thank him enough.

I learned immediately upon arriving at the colony, that Debbie Bateman had indeed divorced Ervil! She had just re-married. She was now the third wife to Ritchie Stubbs, Harv and Lane's half-brother. What wonderful news; I couldn't wait to see her and find out how her new life was going.

Grandma LeBaron was looking a bit better than the last time I'd seen her. She was still teaching piano, she told me, but only to a handful of students now. They helped her temporarily forget her dear son Joel, and her precious son Ervil. She kissed my children and fed them bread and honey, and she wanted to know all about Verlan and the other girls. I didn't want to talk about them, and I left as soon as I could. Being around Grandma made me feel guilty.

My sister Fara was living in El Paso with her husband John and his first wife, Robin. Fara was doing well—Dad told me—and seemed to fit right in with her new family. They were planning to move to Colonia LeBaron soon.

My youngest sister, Mona, had been staying with Dad and Maria, but to my delight, she immediately hauled her few belongings across the back yard and announced that she was my new roommate. At sixteen she was a shy girl with immense, dark-lashed cerulean blue eyes and long, honey-blond hair, and a soft little chin that quavered at the slightest harsh word or look. She was in her junior year of high school, and caught the bus at the highway every day to Buena Ventura. She was so homesick for Mom and deliriously happy about having me home again.

Jay had moved Carmela and his new wife Karen to the acres of land he'd purchased twelve miles from the colony, parcela land. As the other American men had done, he'd secured it in Carmela's name, because she was a Mexican citizen. He'd built two homes and was planting pecan orchards. He already had several acres of baby trees that his wives took care of during the week while he worked in New Mexico. Carmela had three children now, and Karen, a slim, attractive blond, had a baby daughter. Carmela confided in me that Jay was in the process of courting another Mexican girl, Luz Vila, the daughter of one of the colony residents. Carmela was incensed about it. "He doesn't even have time for us, Susan!" she declared in exasperation. "He's only home on the weekends, and he has so much work to do, with the orchards and all. We hardly see him . . . I just don't know what to do."

How well I understood! I nodded in sympathy and bit back a nasty comment regarding my brother's increasing lack of devotion to her, his childhood sweetheart, as he became more and more important in the bishopric of the church. Carmela didn't need to hear that from me, and I certainly didn't want to begin my new life with a negative attitude toward my darling sibling. I felt wonderful being away from Los Molinos and all my sister-wives and heartache, and even to be away from Verlan and the constant reminder of how topsy-turvy my own emotional life was.

I knew my spiritual life was suffering. I still prayed every day, but my prayers were perfunctory words that I no longer felt in my heart. I couldn't feel close to a God who was so solidly aligned with his sons, and who valued his daughters only as vessels for bearing more sons. I tried not to be angry, but I couldn't seem to control my feelings. Maybe someday I could accept it, but for now, I didn't want to think about it. All I wanted was to relish the associations of my family and friends, enjoy raising my children, and keep all thoughts of plural marriage and what it entailed far away. Verlan's new wife, Helen, his cousin Theron's widow, lived across town, but I hardly saw her except at church, and I'd managed to steer clear of her even then. I had three lovely, healthy children, and that was plenty for me. I didn't need Verlan anymore. The others could have him. Just as long as his three boys working in San Diego kept my twenty dollars a week coming, I would be just fine.

On November 9th, 1973, Ervil was sentenced to twelve years imprisonment by the Ensenada court. Although the sentence seemed ridiculously short for such a crime, we at the colony rejoiced that justice was finally being served, and we breathed a sigh of relief. Our joy was short-lived, however. The following month on December 14, a higher court in Mexicali, Baja California, ordered Ervil's release. Lack of evidence was the reason given for the change of verdict, but bribery was of course suspected. Dismay and apprehension once again reigned throughout the church. So much effort on the part of Verlan, Sigfried Widmar, Ossmen Jones and the others, and all for nothing! Ervil again roamed free.

The sound of someone knocking woke me from a sound sleep. I pulled my robe around me, hurrying to see who needed me at this hour. I glanced out the kitchen window as I unbolted my door. The first whispers of a rosy, late December dawn were creeping across the sky. The year 1974 was fast coming to a close.

Joel LeBaron, Jr. pushed the crack of door I was peering through further open, and unbidden, stepped inside. Even in the poor light I could sense the fear and horror in the brown eyes of the late prophet Joel's twenty-two year old son. Joel Jr. had been only twenty when his father was killed. The past two years had matured him into a true leader among us.

"The Ervilites just attacked the Los Molinos colony!" he rasped. They shot people...some are dead...burned the whole town... Grab your kids and find a hiding place; they're headed here next..."

"What?" My heart leaped into my throat. My body began to tremble as his words sank in. The past year since Ervil's release had been one of constant foreboding. We lived each day expecting another disaster, and now it had happened. I grabbed Joel's icy hands, needing the human feel of his closeness. "Oh, my God!" I moaned. "Who's dead? Who, do you know? Charlotte and her kids are still there... and Ester...Oh, Joel... Who...who all, how bad is it, and how do you know the Ervilites are headed here?"

"I don't know the details...just that thirteen or more are wounded and at least two are dead... Alma's wife Luz called from San Diego. They're all certain Colonia LeBaron's next...We need to be ready!" He squeezed my hands, then pulled away from my frantic fingers.

"Find a spot out in the peach orchard, or somewhere. Take water and blankets, and a gun if you have one... The cowardly bastards threw cocktail bombs on the houses, so we need to expect the same here. I've got to go—and warn the others."

Within minutes, Mona and I had the children bundled up and our necessities thrown together, and we headed out into the frosty pre-dawn. We scurried around the barn and chicken coop, then ducked through the barbed wire at the back of Dad's lot.

"Run! Run!" I gasped, pushing at Melanie's back. I clutched James' hand and half-dragged his small body across the uneven ground. We had to make it to the trees. They wouldn't find us in the trees. Mona raced next to us, baby Jeannette bouncing up and down in her arms.

Our rushing steps through the frozen underbrush crashed in my ears, and I cringed. The early morning silence seemed ominous, and I darted a quick look behind us. Halfway through the orchard, I found a tree with a particularly large ditch bank around it. We dropped a blanket and hunkered down under the low, frost-covered branches, then covered up with a heavy quilt.

"What's happening, Mama?"

The terror in my oldest daughter's eyes mirrored my own fear. She was so little, so helpless. How could she ever comprehend that her own uncle wanted to kill us?

Mona's gaze met mine for an instant. Then she buried her chalk-white face against Jeannette's blanket-wrapped body and slumped against the tree trunk.

My voice quivering, I whispered, "All of you be very, very quiet. Be real good and don't worry! We have to stay here for awhile, so let's just get comfortable and take a little rest."

I peered over the ditch bank. I could just make out the back of Dad's barn through the bare trees. Dad and Maria had gone to El Paso on business, and their kids were staying at Maria's parents' place across town. Oh, why weren't they here with us?!

Thoughts of Los Molinos, Verlan's families, and the others there—bloody and dying—God, please, let them be okay, just let them be okay, my mind chanted. Just let Charlotte and the kids, and Ester and her little ones, the Tippetts, the Babbitts, the Castros, the Zarates... Please Lord, please! Don't let them be dead or hurt!

Thank God I had decided to leave... And, oh! Thank God that Verlan and the others were in Nicaragua! He would have been their prime target.

Los Molinos was burned. My house there, with its rose-colored windowsills that I'd painted so carefully, was it still standing? Well, it didn't matter. If only our people were all right. But some of them weren't; they were wounded and dead, Joel Jr. had said ...

Who of Ervil's people had done this dastardly act? Gamaliel Rios, probably, and Andres Zarate, the young man who had led Jeannine and Kathy on the wild-goose-chase in Ensenada when Joel was killed. Ervil himself wouldn't dirty his hands—and Dan was still in hiding.

Roosters were crowing. A dog yapped, and another one answered. Jeannette began to squirm and fuss, and James raised his blond head and whined that he had to pee. His nose was running and he was shivering. We were all freezing— how long were we supposed to stay here? I took the baby from Mona's arms and shushed her. Mona helped James unzip and had him kneel in the bushes. Next to me, Melanie began to sniffle.

"Suze, how long should we wait?" Mona whispered. "We can't stay here all day, it's too cold! What should we do?"

"I don't know! I don't know," I whispered back. Not even an hour had passed. The sun was up now, but was heading into a mass of heavy gray clouds, and at best would give little warmth. But if we went back, we could be in danger. What were the rest of the colony people doing? Everything was so silent!

"We'll hear them if they come! We should go back home; I'll keep watch!" Mona pleaded. "Besides, we can't stay here all day! We need to find out what everyone else is doing and if everyone's okay."

She was right. I nodded and straightened my cramped body upright. Jeannette's round face was ruddy with cold, and I pulled her blanket over her head. "Okay, let's go," I whispered. "But quietly. No talking."

The children trotted obediently after me, with Mona and her armload of blankets acting as rear guard. We scuttled across the yard and into the house like a strange assortment of burglars. The house was chilly with no fire. I hesitated to start one for fear the smoke would broadcast our presence.

"Feed the kids, and stay inside," I ordered Mona. "I'm going to Nadine's to find out what's going on."

I dashed across the street and tapped on the door of Jay and Carmela's old dream-house—a bigger and nicer place now—where Joel Jr. and his second wife, Nadine lived. There was no answer. I tapped again and called out. The house remained silent. I ran up the street to Elizabeth Jensen's place. She opened the door immediately and pulled me inside.

Elizabeth, an attractive, middle-aged widow, was alone but didn't seem frightened. We would be okay, she assured me. Some of the men had gone to Casas Grandes and were bringing back the National Guard to keep watch over the colony until the threat was over. I should go home and take care of my children.

The only new details she'd heard about the raid on Los Molinos was that it had been a pickup-load of men with guns and Molotov cocktails; Babbitt's tower had burned to the ground, and the roofs of several homes had burned, and two young Mexican men had died. She didn't know their names.

Young Mexican men. The relief I felt was overwhelming—quickly followed by guilt for being so happy it wasn't women or children. None of Verlan's family was dead, if Elizabeth's information was correct. How long before we would know? And how long would Ervil and his followers keep us captive in our own homes? His lunatic doctrine was plain and simple: If we refused to be his disciples, he would kill us. And if we joined him, we would be the killers of others. How could this happen to us, the Church of God? Was this part of the test we had to endure, to earn our way into the Celestial Kingdom? I hurried back to my family, my mind a whirlwind.

Jay arrived at noon to take us to his "ranch" at Spencerville. As we left the colony, guards with khaki-colored uniforms stopped Jay's pickup, recognized him, and waved us through. Seeing rifles in their arms was scary; yet, it was comforting to have the soldiers hovering at the colony's entrances. How long they would stay, no one knew. But I guessed not long—perhaps a few days.

The two young men who had died were new to Los Molinos, Jay told me. They had just come from Puebla, down past Mexcio City, and weren't even members of the Church. Ossmen Jones and brother Perez had brought them and several others to Los Molinos, promising them a better life with our people, and land of their own. They had never even known Ervil.

Thirteen others had been wounded. Among them was an old Mexican grandmother, two pregnant Mexican women, one being Victoria Zarate, the brave young wife of Benjamin Zarate—whose baby I'd tried to help Naomi Chynoweth deliver. Benjamin himself had been shot in the head and was in a coma. Two of Fernando Castro's sons were also wounded—Fernando Jr.'s hand had been severed.

The next bit of news was the worst of all. Mark, Duane, and Rena Chynoweth had been recognized among the group of Ervil's people who raided Los Molinos. They were in the back of the pickup, and threw the bombs and shot the rifles at the innocent residents of the tiny town where the

Chynoweths once lived.

For two days Mona, my children and I stayed at Carmela's. Their place was a mile from the highway and hidden by trees, and Jay was certain we would all be safe. He didn't return to the states to work, but spent every day in the colony, holding meetings with Alma and the other men. It seemed wryly weird to me that Jay was a counselor in Alma's bishopric, and his right-hand man—since Alma was the one who had objected so strongly to Jay marrying his step-daughter, Carmela. Mean old Alma had eaten crow where Jay was concerned. Maybe my brother got along with him now, but I still couldn't tolerate him.

Dad and Maria were finally back from El Paso, and Jay took us home. The soldiers still hovered at the entrances to the colony. They were supposed to stay on guard for a month, Jay told me; then the colony men would take turns. Each family was to have a place of hiding prepared, and in the event of a warning by the guards, we were to go to our hideout and stay until further notice. Our plan wasn't foolproof, but the best the men could offer for now. Surely the authorities would catch the people who had executed the raid soon, he said.

I shuddered when I thought of my cousins going to jail. Even Rena, with her laughing eyes and smiling lips, had taken part in the raid! I wondered what Aunt Thelma thought of her precious children now? Was she proud of them, thinking they had done a service to God? Or was she sickened and desperate to get them away from Ervil's clutches? In spite of what they'd done, I loved them still. They were under Ervil's malevolent spell, and my heart ached for them. But for God's intervention through Verlan and Irene, I too, could have been doing those wicked, horrible things.

Slowly, we all in Colonia LeBaron became accustomed to our new way of life. I showed Maria and Dad our peach tree with the high bank around it, and we cached water and plastic-wrapped blankets there. Dad oiled his old 30-30 and rarely left the house. Our church meetings went on as usual, but men with rifles stood outside the doors, bundled and braving the cold winter air.

Verlan had immediately flown back from Nicaragua, arriving at Los Molinos in time for the funeral of the young men who died. I got this information from Ossmen. Verlan had called him on church business, and given him a message for me. He loved and missed me and hoped we were all well. He had lots to tell me, and he would come as soon as he could. I was to please go see his mother and give her his love.

I had news for Verlan, too, for when he found time to come see us again.

As careful as I'd tried to be, the one time I'd been with him on his last, quick visit to the colony had left me with a tiny keepsake. The thoughts I'd been toying with—to become independent and live a carefree life as a single woman— were dashed away. I couldn't deny it to myself any longer. I was pregnant with my fourth child.

Chapter 37

After several days of rain and wind, the sun had finally returned, and the chilly March morning was just warm enough that I allowed Melanie and James to bundle up and play in the yard. They'd been cooped inside long enough—we couldn't hide forever.

While washing my breakfast dishes, I watched them through the window. Melanie was squealing excitedly about something she'd found and babbling to James nonstop as they wandered around. He followed her like an adoring puppy, and looked so cute in his red coat with the hood covering his wavy, platinum blond hair. He was getting so big! He'd be three soon. Born on his late Uncle Joel's birthday, on July 9th.

In the back bedroom, Jeannette had awakened. I dried my hands and threw another quick peek out the window, then hurried to her. Her sleeper was soaked— I would have to put some water on to heat. I put her in the highchair, and as I reached for the water bucket, Melanie's piercing scream electrified me.

She was always squealing about something, but this was different, and I glanced, startled, out the window. The children weren't in sight. Rushing out the door, I scanned the yard—nothing. She screamed again from the well house, and I dashed inside.

Melanie's terrified eyes met mine from where she knelt on the boards covering the well, over a hole left by an eight-inch steel pipe that Dad had removed. Her arm to the shoulder was in the hole, clutching something I couldn't see. I dropped down beside her, reached in, and grabbed James' wrist from her tiny hand. His little body swung back and forth beneath the boards under our feet, and Melanie's grasp was all that had kept him from falling into the deep well beneath us.

I tightened my hold on his wrist. I could barely see his little face looking up at me. As I tried to lift him back through the hole, his head, together with his raised arm and shoulder, wouldn't fit. How he'd fallen through such a tiny hole was a mystery, but I couldn't get him out. I was kneeling on the eight-foot boards, so I couldn't move them.

"Go get Maria!" I screamed at Melanie. She dashed out into the sunlight, sped across the back yard, tearing around the side of Mom's house. James was whining in terror, his voice echoing against the cement sides of the well. I tried to reach my other hand in to get a better hold on him, but the size of the hole wouldn't allow it. I grimly held on to his wrist, my fingers becoming slippery. How had four-year-old Melanie, who weighed almost the same as James, managed to hold on until I got here?

Oh, where was Maria? At least a minute had passed, the seconds ticking away maddeningly, as my hand became numb and my fingers so very slippery. My heart thudded with fear. If I dropped him, I'd never get him out of the water in time. The well was so deep—how would I get down by myself? "Maria!" I screamed, knowing she couldn't hear me. "Maria, help! Help!"

Suddenly she was running toward me, her thongs flapping against her bare soles. Melanie was hard at her heels. "What's a matta?" Maria shouted.

"My boy's in the well!" I screamed in Spanish. "I'm losing him—Help me!"

Maria dropped down flat beside me and slipped her arm in next to mine. She grabbed James' wrist above my hand and allowed me to flex my fingers.

"I got him," she said. "I got him tight. Now move the boards on your side."

"Stand back, Melly," I ordered, pushing her to the doorway. Carefully, I pried the heavy, tarred boards from their concrete border and set them to the side. Once the opening was large enough, Maria pulled James up and thrust him into my waiting arms.

"Thank you, Lord! Oh, thank you, dear Father!" I quavered fervently. My festering anger at God dissolved in an instant. Shaking and crying, I hugged James and rocked him, and covered his soft face with kisses. Then I reached for Melanie who still waited in the doorway.

"Come here, my brave girl," I croaked. She hesitantly walked to my outstretched arm. "You saved your brother's life, Mel," I whispered. "You are the strongest, and the very bravest girl in the whole world, and I love you more than—than I know how to say, and I'm the luckiest mother I know to have you for my daughter. You saved your little brother."

Tears began to stream down her pale cheeks as I talked, and she buried her face in my shoulder and sobbed and shook.

"Hey, is okay!" Maria laughed and patted Melanie's back. "Pobrecita, she so scare. When she come to get me, she not say anything! She so scare she can't talk, but I know something is wrong, so I run..." She laughed again and dabbed at her eyes. "Everything is okay now. You boy is fine, so don't cry no more, be happy!"

I kissed her brown cheek and hugged her. "Thank you, my sweet little Mother," I smiled at her through my tears.

Naomi Zarate Chynoweth, my Uncle Bud's Mexican wife, had disappeared. The Ensenada police were still looking for her, Verlan told me. But she'd been gone for over three months now from her house in Ensenada, where Uncle Bud had moved her and her five children. According to Naomi's children, Aunt Thelma and one of Ervil's wives, a woman I barely knew named Vonda White, had taken Naomi from her home. She hadn't been seen since, and Verlan was certain she was dead. "She wouldn't go along with Ervil's orders; she kept inviting her family and other members of our church to her house. I'm guessing Ervil's had her eliminated."

I felt sick to my stomach at the news, especially hearing that Aunt Thelma had taken part in it. Oh, how could she do it? She had become a party to murder! Ervil had corrupted her and all her children, had brainwashed them, and was using them as pawns and puppets in his evil game of blood atonement. I remembered Naomi's strength and fire while delivering Victoria Zarate's baby, and her flashing black eyes at her wedding to Uncle Bud, and how she had stood up to Ervil. I had admired her spirit and thought she was so brave. But she had probably paid for her defiance with her life. She was a heroine in my eyes.

Ervil had continued his ominous written warnings, giving them colorful names such as Hour of Crisis and Contest at Law, and now he was not only sending them to us, but to other fundamentalist, polygamous groups in Utah. In a nutshell, we were all told to repent, and accept him as God's chosen one, or suffer the wrath of God. The groups in Utah were also taking his maniacal warnings seriously, Verlan told me, and had tightened security. Anxiety mounted on all sides.

After the Los Molinos Raid, Verlan and his Counselors decided to send a written petition to Ervil for peace. It was titled The Church of the Firstborn of the Fullness of Times Raises a Standard of Peace to Its Attackers. The single-page document pled for Ervil and his followers to "Restrain themselves from any further acts of violence against our people." It asked them "To respect our God given rights to life, property and the free exercise of conscience and no more proceed criminally against us in treading down our inalienable civil rights," signed, Verlan M. LeBaron, patriarch over the church.

Ervil responded with another written attack, labeled "Response to an act of war." The pamphlet, from the Church of the Lamb of God—the name Ervil had given his group—was addressed to its "attackers," meaning us, the Church of the Firstborn. Ervil classified Verlan's appeal for peace as "an overt and premeditated act of war." The pamphlet accused Verlan and his "coconspirators" of capital crimes. Ervil obviously had convinced his followers that we were dangerous criminals and out to get them; but, did the demented lunatic actually think anyone else would believe this?

I had read each of Ervil's pamphlets, but they were so disturbing and hard to follow, filled as they were with hundred-dollar words—the same way Ervil talked. The man was an educated loony, as evil as Satan himself. After muddling through "Response to an Act of War," I determined I would read no more of his high-sounding garbage. I would pray, and be careful of my children, and refuse to let him or his threats dwell in my mind.

The problem I had was that everyone in the colony talked of little else. Verlan had come to visit us twice since we moved to Colonia LeBaron, and he was consumed with worries about his mad brother. He was determined to see that Ervil, Dan and the others were put behind bars for the atrocities they'd committed, and he was working with the authorities in Ensenada, and with the Secret Service in the states, to apprehend them all before anyone else was killed. At the same time, Verlan knew that he himself topped Ervil's hit list, so he had to be constantly vigilant. He actually was packing a pistol at the insistence of the police. He knew nothing whatever about guns, and one night as I lay in bed, waiting for him to undress and blow the lamp out, he shot a hole into the plastered adobe wall when he checked to see if the safety was on. His carelessness scared us all to death. He swore me to secrecy.

With all the Ervilite business, Verlan's Nicaragua project was on hold. He had Irene and Lucy and their kids living there, but he was too occupied to spend any time there, himself. I wasn't surprised.

My baby was due in a month, and Verlan let me know that he wouldn't be able to get back to the colony in time for the birth. He was needed in so many places, and I would have to understand. I would be fine, he assured me, and he would come as soon as he could.

My mother had settled into living with Grandma in Pleasant Grove, Utah. Dad went to see her occasionally, and she'd been here for a short visit a few months ago. Mona and I missed her terribly, but when Dad announced that he had decided to move Maria and their family to Southern Mexico—and without further ado proceeded to pack up and drive off, our sense of abandonment was complete. I knew my parents had become disillusioned with the church. Especially Dad—he rarely attended the services anymore, and had started smoking again, and was openly showing disgust with most of our leaders,

Verlan included. Joel's death had hit him hard, and Ervil's "shenanigans," as Dad called them, left him incensed. That his own dear sister Thelma and her family had become Ervil's champions was more than he could take. Dad felt responsible because he had been the one initially to coax the Chynoweths into listening to our missionaries. He, personally, had taken Ervil to their home in Utah and made the introductions. Ervil's first visit to the Chynoweth home had resulted in his courtship of their seventeen-year-old daughter, Lorna.

And now, Dad needed space. His Social Security checks would nicely cover their needs in Southern Mexico, and it was a beautiful place to live. They would give it a try.

At Dad's insistence, we moved into my mother's larger home. There wasn't much to move, as Dad and Maria hadn't had room to take household goods. But the place needed a good cleaning, and Mona wasn't much help these days. She was in her final year at school, and she was head over heels in love with Joel LeBaron, Jr. Her life was full, and she could spare little time.

I rushed madly around in an effort to be settled and have everything organized before the baby came. My sister Rose Ann offered to help the colony midwife with the birth. Mona also wanted to attend since she hadn't seen a baby's birth. I searched the countryside for a work-girl to help me for a few days after the baby came, and finally located one who was available. Breathing a sigh of relief, I relaxed, content to patiently await my due date. Everything was set.

My labor started in the early evening, and I sent Mona for the mid-wife Linda, and for Rose Ann. Then I had Mona go inform the work-girl that I would need her the following morning. Not until after my new son was born did Mona tell me the work-girl's mother was sick. She wouldn't be coming after all.

"You'll be okay," Rose Ann cheerfully assured me. "You have Mona here, and I'll try to stop by sometime tomorrow. Just get some rest."

The baby was healthy and beautiful. He possessed a powerful set of lungs and the deep chest and broad shoulders of a future linebacker. His appetite was enormous—he nursed hungrily the moment Rose Ann put him to my breast.

I was happy to see the women leave for the night. My after-pains had started, and I felt exhausted and wanted to collapse and cry without an audience. But rest was not to be. Mona had gone straight to bed in Mom's old room off the front porch, and didn't hear Jeannette crying in the middle bedroom. I called and called for her, but she was sound asleep. Groaning, I put the baby aside and stood up, my body sore and shaky as I shuffled down the hall. I lifted

Jeannette from the crib and half-dragged her to my bed.

My night remained a sleepless one. The baby wailed, and Jeannette refused to sleep, and my uterus contracted harshly, making me want to scream. Melanie and James awoke and joined us in my bed. They were excited about the new baby and needed the comfort of Mama's presence in a house gone suddenly nutty. Mona slept on.

Total exhaustion overcame me as the late November sun was rising. The children had all finally settled down, and slept like little angels all around me. With the baby in the crook of my arm, I relaxed and fell asleep.

"Breakfast, everybody!"

Startled, my eyes flew open. Grinning happily, Mona stood at my bedside, a plate of pancakes and eggs in her hands.

"Oh, Mona, shush, not now!" I moaned. "These kids barely fell asleep..." But it was too late. James popped his head up, then Jeannette rolled on top of the baby and he started to bawl. "Dammit, you guys!" Melanie cussed, sounding just like me as she rolled off the bed.

I dutifully ate my breakfast while Mona took the children to the kitchen. Their noise was deafening, and I sighed. I felt like crying myself. You just need a few hours of uninterrupted sleep, I told myself, and you'll be all right. Mona will take care of the kids and you can take a nap.

But this also was not to be. She came to my room for my plate, and said, "Suze, Joel invited me to go to Casas with him this morning. I'll be back late this afternoon. Will you be okay?"

I glared at her through swollen eyes. "You are kidding me!" I hissed. "I just had a baby, remember? You're not going anywhere! I need your help, dammit. What, do I have to beg?"

She glared sullenly back at me. "Do you realize this is the first time Joel's asked me to go with him? The first time! I'm sorry, but I have to go. Besides, Rose Ann said she'll be here later on today... and the kids'll be just fine. They can play in the other room while you sleep. He's going to be here any minute, and I have to get ready," she flounced out of the room.

I closed my eyes. I didn't have the strength to argue with her. She was so in love—she couldn't think of anything else. She was only seventeen and didn't realize what she was doing.

I'd turned twenty-two last month, yet I felt so much older. I would manage.

Melanie brought me clothes and a diaper for Jeannette and I got her dressed while the older ones dressed themselves. Then I tried to rest through the morning as five-year-old Melanie did her best to entertain her brother and sister. Linda, the midwife, stopped by at noon to check on me, but she could only stay a minute. She had another birth across town to attend.

James and Jeannette had both fallen asleep on the foot of my bed. My eyes burned from lack of sleep, but the potty under the bed was beginning to smell. I would have to empty it. I carefully stood and pulled on my robe and slippers, wondering how I would make it across the back yard to the outhouse. It had to be done, and no one else was here to do it. Rose Ann had still not shown up. I retrieved the potty and started down the hall.

"Mom," Melanie dawdled in the hallway, looking doubtfully at the curtained doorway of the unfinished bathroom, "What is that thing?"

"What thing?"

She pointed, "That ugly thing in there."

Sighing, I set the potty down on the hall floor and pulled the curtain back. Bile rose in my throat. Amid a pile of blood-soaked sheets, the white bedpan Linda had used last night sat on the cement floor. My huge, purple lump of placenta, swimming in blood, was drying in it.

I let the curtain fall into place as I backed away and slowly dropped my head against the opposite wall. My body tingled with shame—then anger choked me.

What was wrong with everybody?! How could Mona, Rose Ann, and even Linda, leave me here alone with all this! I couldn't stand it! My poor little kids were fending for themselves, and I was shaking with pain and exhaustion, and nobody cared!

My legs were cramping, and I slid my back down the wall and sat on the floor. After a moment, Melanie sat down beside me and put her head against my shoulder. We sat together in total silence, but then her small, comforting hand patted my arm, and I could stand it no more. I burst into tears.

I sobbed hard, for Verlan and for my mother, and for my sweet little children who had to take care of themselves. And I cried for Aunt Thelma and Lorna, and dead Naomi, and for my new little baby, who I hadn't even wanted at first, but who I wanted now, so much. The tears streamed down my cheeks.

Suddenly I realized Melanie was crying too. Her shoulders were shaking, and I glanced at her and saw the tears raining down her smooth cheeks. I gave her a fierce hug and cried a minute more; then I mumbled, "I'm sorry, honey. I'm so sorry! I didn't mean to cry. Everything's going to be fine, so let's cheer up and be happy. Okay?"

She nodded and sniffled, her chin quivering. Then she whispered, "I'll

372

empty the potty for you, Mama."

As hard as I resisted, I erupted into new wails of despair. After a few minutes I was all cried out, and I dried my puffy eyes and blew my stuffed nose. Together, Melanie and I carried the chamber pot outside, through the disaster of Mona's kitchen mess, and into the crisp, late autumn sunshine. We emptied the potty, then together, we sat on the two-holer and emptied our bladders.

I waited until it was nearly dark before taking the bedpan and a shovel to the garden. I couldn't stand to dump this part of my own baby's existence into the privy, and had determined it needed a proper burial. I dug a shallow hole, plopped it in, and covered it up. Then I went inside and lit the lamps.

Chapter 38

"Forrest Lane LeBaron!" Verlan insisted—his voice filled with wonder at the beauty and creativity of the name he'd chosen for my new son. I argued and pleaded, but his mind was made up and no other name would do. Verlan gave the baby his blessing in church the following Sunday, then he kissed us all goodbye and was off again to San Diego.

Forrest was six months old when Mom moved back to Colonia LeBaron. She'd come home just in time for Mona's wedding, riding down from Utah with my three oldest brothers and their families. They, also, had come for the sending off of their baby sister. Even Dad showed up from Southern Mexico for the big event. Mona had handled most of the wedding arrangements herself; the reception was held in Grandma LeBaron's front yard.

The wedding seemed more like a funeral than like a joyful occasion. Surely a more somber union never occurred. Joel Jr.'s second wife Nadine was the love of his life, and it was practically killing both Nadine and Joel himself to have another wife join the family. But he was determined to earn his eternal blessings, so he proceeded with the marriage vows. Joel's two wives sat on the sidelines during the ceremony, with Tina appearing pale and stoic, and Nadine's chalky cheeks wet with misery. Joel's expression was tortured and sorrowful and my sweet little sister looked as though she might collapse at any moment. I was disturbed at the whole thing and wondered how this could possibly be God's will.

I was ecstatic, though, to see my older brothers, Perry, Dale and Ross, and to get to know their families a bit. We all drove into Casas the next day and went shopping and out to eat, and we played cards and had a party that Mona didn't get to join since she was on her honeymoon. The Utah relatives stayed for three days. Dad stayed a week to spend some time with Mom.

Mother herself looked rested and happy. She'd bought new clothes, and a pair of the stylish new, Nike brand, running shoes. She'd cut her hair into a short, wavy style and had gained a bit of weight. She said it was from all the ice cream she'd eaten at Grandma Susie's, but I personally thought it was from living a stress-free life for the past two years. She told me that the kids and I could continue to live with her, but I knew my rambunctious children would quickly get on her nerves.

Fara was also living at the colony now, with her two-month-old son, Sam. Her marriage had crumbled right before Sam was born, and she had quietly settled back into single life. She'd moved into an adobe house near the highway. Another house close to hers sat vacant, and she suggested that it should be my new residence. We could live by each other, and keep each other company, which sounded good to me.

Jay made the arrangements for me to use the vacant house and offered his pickup and services for the move. His new Mexican wife, Luz Vila, came with him to help, and soon I was all settled into the "hill house'".

Verlan came back to town a week later. He arrived in the middle of the night, and brought Charlotte and all but her three oldest children with him. They'd spent the night at Grandma LeBaron's. Verlan was in the process of moving them to Nicaragua.

"Honey, I'm planning to get them settled, then I'm coming for you," he announced. "I don't like having you live here; I never get to see you. I'll be spending lots of time in Nicaragua now, and I want you there with me."

"Absolutely not. I won't go," I said stubbornly. I stirred the eggs I was scrambling and added salt, then I opened the oven and pulled out the toasted bread. I spread butter on, my shoulders stiff with determination. He couldn't make me go. I'd barely gotten settled, and I had my family all here. My life was orderly and pleasant. I wouldn't do it.

I'd reluctantly let him in last night. He'd knocked and woke me, and though my heart had skipped with excitement at the sound of his voice, I'd reluctantly unlocked the door.

I'd discovered something in the past several months—a feeling I hadn't felt in years. I was actually happy! I'd learned to manage my four children just fine by myself. I had the association of my mother and sisters and brother, and I didn't have the heartache and loneliness that had been mine on a continual basis. Though I felt a twinge of guilt and pain when I thought of Verlan and the rest of the family, mostly I was content. True, I missed Verlan's kisses and lovemaking—but the lack of turmoil in my life more than compensated.

I placed the plate I'd prepared in front of Verlan and sat down at the opposite end of the table. My coffee cup, filled with hot water, was grasped firmly in my hand, and I spooned instant coffee grounds in and added sugar and cream. I stirred and took a sip, then boldly met his eyes.

"What do you think you're doing?" he roared. He picked up the small bottle of Folger's Instant and examined it at arm's length. Then he screwed the lid on tight and rolled the bottle across the cement floor. "Susan LeBaron, I'll not have you breaking the Word of Wisdom!" he flared. "Put that in the garbage where it belongs, and stop acting like a rebellious child. What's gotten in to you?"

I calmly took another sip. "This is my house, not yours. I arranged for it, I moved myself here, and I'll drink coffee under my own roof if I feel like it."

He jumped up and wrestled the cup out of my hand. He dumped the creamy brew into the sink and slapped the cup on the counter, then picked the jar up from the floor and threw it in the garbage can.

"I'm the patriarch of this church," he icily reminded me. "If I can't control my own wives, how do you expect me to control anything else? How do you think it would look to have my own wife acting like this?"

I sniffed. "I don't care how it looks. It's just coffee, for heaven's sake. I'm not running around with another man or anything, although I've thought about that, too. What do you care, you're not around anyway."

His face was grim as he stood over me. He stared at me and slowly shook his head. "So, this is what I get, for being good to you and letting you live here so you can be around your folks." He shook his head again and sat down to his cold food.

He took a bite, then shoved the plate away. "I'll be back from Nicaragua in two months. I have to spend a bit of time in San Diego, then I want you packed up and ready to move. Can I count on your support?"

"Why me?" I snapped. "Why not Lillie, or Beverly, or Ester? I don't have the slightest desire to move to the jungle, Verlan! You won't stay there, anyway—its just another one of your crazy ideas, just like Los Molinos was. I'm happy here! This is my home, and I'm not going to Nicaragua, not even if you beg me."

He stared at me, his eyes cold and stormy. "You want to know why you?" he asked. "I'll tell you why. The other girls aren't rebellious like you are. I'm not worried about leaving them! I hardly dare to leave you, just look at the way you're behaving!"

The children, awakened by all the noise, trailed into the kitchen, and Verlan cheered up and passed out hugs and kisses. Jeannette refused to go to her father at first. He had to coax her to sit on his lap, and she stared at this huge stranger with big, troubled eyes. "I'm your daddy, precious," he assured her, kissing her round cheek. She looked to me for verification, and I bit my lip and turned my back.

He stayed and played with the kids for an hour, then promising to be back later to finish our conversation, he climbed into his truck. "There's another matter I need to visit with you about also," he casually said when he backed away.

What he wanted to discuss I had no idea, but in any event, I wasn't interested. I went inside and shut the door, then dug my bottle of coffee out of the trash and hid it in the cupboard. I made my bed, memories of the wild night I'd spent with Verlan haunting me. Thank God I'm still nursing Forrest, I thought grimly. I don't have to worry about becoming pregnant.

The "other matter" Verlan had mentioned was Elizabeth Jensen, the widow lady who lived close to my mother. She became Verlan's ninth wife the following evening, in a simple, private ceremony in her home. Verlan stayed with her for two days, then he and Charlotte's family left for Nicaragua.

In spite of my anger at the suddenness of it, and at the whole idea of Verlan marrying widows, I liked Elizabeth. She was bubbly and friendly, and I decided I didn't mind too much that she had joined Verlan's family. She occasionally came to the hill house to visit with me during the next few weeks, and I could tell she was independent and wouldn't be demanding on our husband's time. She had simply chosen Verlan to be her "spiritual head" as single women were supposed to do.

According to a rule of the Church, single women had to choose a holder of the priesthood to make all the hard decisions for them, whether they chose to marry the man or not. Women weren't considered fit to make their own decisions. I sniffed when Verlan explained this rule to me. I'd made my own decisions for some time now, or hadn't he noticed? Besides, as soon as Verlan and Charlotte left, I became more determined than ever that I would separate from Verlan. The time I'd spent with him only served to make me realize how little I needed him or wanted him in my life. I cared about him and his family, but I was no longer in love with him. The relief I felt at this realization was enormous. Where this all would lead me, I had no idea, and at this point I told no one.

Something else I couldn't tell anyone was that I was attracted to another man. David Stubbs, Lane and Harv's brother, belonged to another fundamentalist organization in Arizona. David came to Mexico occasionally to visit his relatives. He was young still—only in his thirties. He had two wives, but that didn't bother me; I was used to polygamy, and I knew David would never have a harem as Verlan did. He wasn't a member of our church, of course, but at this point, it didn't matter much. The thought of going to the Celestial Kingdom didn't appeal to me as much as it used to, now that I fully understood that even there, women were subservient to the men.

David had flirted with me outrageously at the Saturday night dance last weekend. He was blond and gorgeous, with the sexiest blue eyes and smile, and he could sing as well as any country star I'd ever heard. Naughty thoughts of David filled my head. I fantasized about him for several days, until the horrible realization that my period was way over due. My wicked thoughts came to a crashing halt.

Oh, how could this be?! I'd spent only the one night with Verlan, and I'd been so sure I was safe! Never before had I gotten pregnant while nursing—everyone said it was the perfect form of birth control. I'd barely got my figure back! I couldn't possibly handle another child! What was I going to do?

My unrealistic fantasies of David and freedom vanished like an illusion, and gloom, thick as heavy fog, encompassed my soul. I had no choice. There was no way I would go through my pregnancy as a single woman and have to deal with the wagging tongues and the suspicious glances I knew would be cast in my direction. With one hasty roll in the sack, for the time being, Verlan had won.

Nicaragua was like being in another world. Endless coffee-bean fields grew on rolling hillsides, surrounded by thick, dark jungles. Villages were few and a good distance from one another, though an occasional bamboo hut was seen along our route. The village people were fairly well dressed but the dark-skinned country-natives wore scanty clothing. The terrain was unbelievably beautiful with lush vegetation and the strangest trees I'd ever seen, many covered with vines and flowers. I looked for monkeys, but didn't spot any although Verlan assured me they were out there. A panther did run across the narrow road ahead of us, and I was satisfied that indeed, we were in a jungle as savage as Africa's.

Once we left the pavement, we traveled for thirty or more miles on a narrow dirt road. Then Verlan drove through a two-foot-deep creek surrounded by willowy bushes, spun the wheel to the left, and navigated up a little hill. A huge, faded red barn sat before us. Verlan stopped the truck and turned off the engine. "We're home!" he said cheerfully.

As wives and children ran out to greet him, it reminded me of that day, seven years ago this month, when Verlan had taken me as his new bride to the house in Ensenada. I had been so full of excitement and anticipation then. Now all I felt was a dull dread. I smiled though, and hugged everyone, and pretended to be happy. Charlotte, too, hugged me tight and treated me with such warmth that I was amazed.

Verlan had tried to prepare me for the dwelling, but he didn't do it justice. It was a nightmare. The barn was drafty and had dirt floors. Lucy and Irene and their combined eighteen children lived in it, with all the kids sleeping in the ladder-accessible loft. Verlan had built Charlotte's family a small, four-room house higher up on the hill. Behind the barn was a storage room where we would sleep.

The creek ran around the hill, which was the cleared side of the property. Verlan and the older children took me on a tour of the much larger, jungle side, where we walked single file through the trees, then over a log spanning a rivulet, until we came to a large clearing where Verlan and the boys had planted a garden. The corn was already two feet high, and Verlan was ecstatic when he examined all the growing vegetables.

"This is wonderful!" he shouted. "We don't even have to water it, what with all the rain. Honey, this is the main reason why I wanted to come to Nicaragua. We can grow anything here!"

I tried to be happy for him. But I felt hollow inside, and without a word I started back down the path to the barn. The sky had been blue and sunny on our way to the garden, but now the sky was gray, and the rain came swiftly. I was soaked through as I walked into the kitchen.

Irene's older girls were feeding my children beans and bread at the split-log table. I dropped down beside them and lifted Forrest onto my lap. The open kitchen door allowed the rain to blow in onto the dirt floor, where water puddles had turned into mud. Flies carpeted everything. The girls and I shoed them from the food, but they returned in swarms, and I wanted to scream.

Instead, I handed Forrest to one of the girls and hurried outside, where the rain had become only thin drizzle. The storage room had been cleaned out before we got here, and now contained two beds, a dresser, a small table and chairs, and a gas stove. The floor was packed dirt. My few boxes sat on the bed, and I had just started unpacking them when Irene walked in. She took one look at my face, and silently took me in her ample arms.

"You're going to be okay, sweetie," she said as I sobbed. "I'm here, and we'll be company for each other. Our life's not so bad. You'll get used to it—I did. At least we don't have to worry about Ervil here."

I nodded and wiped my eyes; then, pulling away, I sat down. "I don't know how you stand it," I whispered, my chin quivering. "How have you stood it this long, and what's the point of it all? Oh, Irene, maybe you're cut out for this, but I'm not. I can't bear to have my children here, living like this on dirt floors. Forrest isn't even walking yet. What's he supposed to do, crawl in the mud?"

She pursed her lips and was silent. Then sighing, she pulled out a chair and sat. "Look, we can either make the best of the situation, or choose to be miserable," she said quietly. "I don't know what the Lord has in mind for us. But I love Verlan and intend to support him in this. I know it's hard! I don't understand it all, either, and I'm not convinced that this will ever be a gathering place. But Verlan's the best we've got for a leader right now, and we need to make his life easier, not harder. So let's find the good things about Nicaragua, and not worry about the little inconveniences. Okay?"

Feeling chastised, I dried my eyes and reluctantly nodded. Life was what you made it, and no one knew that better than I. There had to be some positive things about this place—I just had to quit acting like a big baby and find them.

The following morning Verlan held Sunday school in the barn. In spite of the rain, he sat by the open door so he could see to read the New Testament's Book of Acts to us. Even the children all sat patiently as he droned on, then Lucy went to the piano and we gathered around and sang hymns until we were all hoarse.

The children and I went to our shack after lunch for a nap. Verlan dropped by to lie down for half an hour, then he and the boys went to the garden to pull weeds while the sun was out. By four o'clock it was raining again and it continued until dark. After supper, Irene came over for a game of Scrabble. She'd made fudge and we played and snacked until bedtime.

The following morning Irene took me to the creek to do laundry. It was easier than I thought it would be; we waded in to the large rocks Verlan had placed in the creek, and with a plastic tub held between us for the clean clothes, we fished the soaking ones out of the sunken reed basket. We used the big rocks for a scrub-board, and once the plastic tub was full of scrubbed clothes, we pulled it back to the bank and wrung the clothes. Then we hauled them up the hill and hung them on the barbed-wire fence. The trick was to keep an eye on the clouds. Just before it started to rain, we would have to retrieve the still damp clothes from the fence, take them inside, and lay them on the bed to wait until the sun came out again. Then we would re-hang them. Sometimes it took two or three times to get them dry—but that was all we could do, Irene said.

Verlan had built a large, wood-fed, brick kiln in the back yard for bread baking which worked quite well. He and the boys were in the process today of building an outdoor, wood-fed stove, for cooking beans and the like.

As Irene and I did laundry, Lucy did the cooking and watched the babies, and Charlotte taught school to Verlan's children. One room of Charlotte's house was the schoolroom, complete with blackboard and primers. Seven-year-old Melanie had become her new student.

We had a corral of goats, two milk-cows and a young bull, and a dozen good laying hens. One corner of the barn held fifty-gallon barrels filled with beans and wheat and corn, and we had several five-gallon tins of oil and honey. With the coming vegetables, Verlan's Nicaragua families were set for awhile.

Verlan stayed for two weeks, clearing ground and planting more gardens. In a large, open area, he placed poles and strung clotheslines, planning to eventually build a rain cover over them. He organized the boys and older girls to do the garden-work, and put Lucy in charge of this project. Irene and I were left with the bulk of the cooking and laundry to do.

Verlan promised to be back in three months, before my fifth child was born. On the morning he left, the whole family stood outside in the rain. We waved until he was out of sight.

Chapter 39

L ife in Nicaragua became a series of rain-scattered days, followed by lengthy black nights where, surrounded by my four children, I sought escape in slumber. But the moist air dampened my bed covers, and small, kicking feet scattered bits of dried mud across my sheets. Sleep eluded me. I awoke each morning worn out and loathing the task of facing another day.

During my daily chores, my plagued thoughts reviewed restlessly the lifestyle Verlan had chosen for us. I tried to reconcile myself to accepting this foreign land, with its strange, half-naked natives and harsh existence. But to settle in for good seemed senseless. I abhorred the thought of raising my children in an environment where they would have little contact with the outside world. They would doubtless grow up to be shy, backward men and women, who would have little choice but to either marry the natives or leave their mother and return to civilization to seek a better life. Either way was unacceptable to me.

As the weeks in Nicaragua slowly turned into months, I desperately yearned for Colonia LeBaron and my own dear relatives. But even more than that, I couldn't deny my growing desire for a husband of my very own, someone to live with, who would be a loving, caring father for my children and a real friend to me throughout my days. My restless body ached for a man's gentle touch.

Deep inside, I had known from my first day in Nicaragua that I would never stay and make it my home. With each passing day my resolve to return to Colonia LeBaron deepened, and soon I was secretly biding my time until Verlan returned and my baby was born. What I would do with my life once I was back home, I wasn't certain. Though I cherished Verlan's wives and adored his many children, Verlan himself had become a driven, exasperating stranger. My desire and longing for him had withered completely.

Irene became my daily companion. We spent our free time reading books together and playing Scrabble and Canasta, and lightly joking about how wonderful it would be to have a man around. Irene ruled the kitchen and cooking areas in the barn, and cheerfully washed mountains of laundry in the creek. I tried to be of help to her, but my small children were demanding and my pregnancy was advanced and kept me uncomfortable most of the time.

One sunny day Irene and I went for a long hike. We started up the hilly, winding dirt road, which was thickly bordered on either side by coffee bushes growing amidst the trees. Our destination was the tiny country store on the main "highway," set among a handful of shacks, which held a few grocery items, including sodas. I'd determined that the bite and fizz of a Coke was long overdue and Irene heartily agreed.

As we waded through the second creek, two long-skirted native women and several young children traipsed toward us. I tried not to stare at the exposed, dangling, brown breasts of these shy peasants, or at the bare display of the male, pre-teen's uncovered genitals. Though I'd seen this style before on our journey here, now it was directly in front of me, and I felt myself redden with discomfort. I hastily moved on.

Not Irene though. She greeted the women and stopped to chat awhile, and since I didn't yet comprehend much of the dialect, I rested on the creek bank and waited patiently for the chatter to cease.

Finally Irene joined me and we trudged on. "Oh, Susan, I wish you understood them better," she exclaimed. "They're such sweet, happy people! They don't live very far from us, just a short walk to the West, through the jungle. The younger woman invited me to come over for coffee tomorrow. You want to?"

Having been ages since I'd tasted coffee, I was desperate for something to break the monotony. "Sure, I'll go with you," I agreed.

We finally reached the store, purchased two sodas and two American candy bars—which cost a small fortune—and started the long walk back home. Once we reached the creek bank, we sat down to have our treat.

As we rested, I carefully broached the subject foremost in my mind. Irene listened, then finally admitted to me her own despondence. "You're not the only one, Susan," she confessed. "I hate it here too. I'm sick of being a pioneer, and I'm sure it'll be ages before Verlan can build us decent homes. I'm so tired of his long absences! He promised me that he would be spending most of his time here! But he still has a church to run—and Beverly and Ester will never come to Nicaragua. So even if he eventually moves Lillie and Elizabeth down, he'll still have to travel back and forth. Seven days' drive each way." She shook her head, popped the last bite of her candy bar into her mouth, and disgustedly threw the wadded wrapper into the creek.

"Nicaragua was a dumb idea, Irene," I said quietly. "I wanted us to get away today, because I need to tell you in private that I won't be staying. The minute Verlan returns I'm going to ask him to take me back home. Please don't be mad."

She stared at me, her blue eyes suddenly wary. "Well, he won't get here until right before your baby's due! You've only been here a few months, for heaven's sake! Can't you at least give it a year?"

I took a sip of my soda and stared into the smoothly flowing water beneath my feet. Irene thought I was being a spoiled baby, and that my main problem was homesickness and the lack of decent living accommodations. But it went much deeper than that, and I could no longer hold my tongue.

"Has it ever occurred to you that Verlan, himself, never stays for very long in any of these remote dumps he moves us to? He comes for a short visit, and receives the very best each of us have to offer. We make special food, and wait on him hand and foot, and wash his clothes in the creek—he's never had to stand in the cold water and rub his own knuckles raw on those rocks! And he has a willing wife to snuggle up to every night he's home. How do you think he'd feel if he were the one sleeping alone, knowing that you, or me, was next door with another man? I just wonder how long he'd stand for it. And then within a week or so he's off, to see another batch of wives, where they also give him the very best they have to offer. Have you ever thought about these things?"

Irene sighed. "Of course I've thought about it. Millions of times. But, Susan, that's just the way things are—and we have to accept it. Verlan has his own crosses to bear, don't think he doesn't! He has our huge family to support, and all the problems of the church on his shoulders, not to mention trying to keep so many wives happy! How would you like those challenges?"

"I wouldn't!" I flared. "But he doesn't support his families, his big boys do that for him. And he's brought most of his other problems upon himself! He didn't have to marry so many women; he's done that because he's greedy and he's never satisfied! Oh, he moans around about how he wants to make us happy, and he always says he plans to spend more time with us, but then he turns around and marries more women! Now, I'm sorry, Irene, but that's just plain selfish and stupid, and I can't go along with it."

She was staring hard at me, her blue eyes flashing fiery missiles in my direction. "So, what are you telling me? Are you saying you're leaving here or leaving Verlan?"

I fidgeted, my hands trembling as I held onto my soda bottle. "I don't know," I finally moaned. "I don't know what I'm doing! But I've been studying the scriptures for a long time now, trying to come to grips with things, and they just don't make sense. One book says one thing, and the others say something else. The *Doctrine and Covenants* says that if women don't accept all the wives their husband takes, they'll be destroyed. But the *Book of Mormon* in the second chapter of Jacob says polygamy is wickedness and an abomination in the sight of God. He warns all men against it. He calls it, "committing whoredoms," and He says for men not to lead women astray and not to break their tender hearts."

Irene was silent, her wild, red hair sticking out around her face as she stared at the stream. I continued my tirade. "I've also found several places in the New Testament where it says elders in God's Church should be the husbands of but one wife. First Peter, chapter seven, says that a man's wife, wife—not wives—is his partner, and she inherits with him the gift of life. So, which do we believe, that one place in the *Doctrine and Covenants* that commands Joseph Smith's wife Emma to accept polygamy or be destroyed, or all the other places, in all the other scriptures, that condemns it?"

Irene jumped up and started walking. I followed her, noting her stiff back and quick, angry steps. "You can interpret the scriptures any way you like," she shot at me when I caught up to her. "Keep searching and twisting, and you can make them say anything you want. You've been looking for a way out, and you think you've found one! But you're just being rebellious, Susan! You've lost your faith, and if you continue with this you'll be giving up your eternal blessings. Joseph Smith's revelation is what you should believe, and Joel's testimony, and you should stop feeling sorry for yourself!"

We continued our swift march home in bristling silence. Irene led the way across the stream and up the little hill, and she entered the barn without another word. I walked around to my own little shack, where Lucy's daughter had taken my children. I thanked her and sent her home, then threw myself on my bed next to my napping babies and quietly sobbed myself to sleep.

"Hallo!" Irene called out to the native woman when we walked into the clearing around her ragged-looking bamboo hut, built against a low, rock cliff. The woman immediately appeared at the doorway, a tiny, naked boy clutching her skirt. Two other children scurried outside to stare at us. One was a skinny boy of seven or eight who was naked from the waist down. The other child was a small girl with a ragged dress on, whose black hair was a mass of snarls around her thin face. The woman was grinning widely at us; the gap of her missing tooth was partially covered by her brown hand. She immediately waved us inside the gloomy interior of her hut, and had us sit on large rocks. These primitive seats circled the larger, flat-surfaced rock that was her table.

I gingerly sat and peered around me. The children were standing in the sunlit doorway, and seemed reluctant to come inside. They stared at us, their eyes huge and round and unblinking, and I smiled and motioned for them to join us but they ignored me. Soon they moved away, out into the yard.

The back of the hut appeared to be a large indentation in the cliff face—sort of a shallow cave, which added enough room to the hut's interior for the family's harvested corn. I stared in wonder at the dried and shucked ears of their food supply. The ears had been stacked, row on top of perfectly neat, criss-crossed row, and woven into a solid, flat-surfaced rectangle about four feet high. On top of this display of workmanship were several empty gunny sacks. The rope stitching had been ripped out of these, and now the opened, rough sacks were the family's covers against the chilly night air. This shocking fact became apparent when the woman laid her naked toddler down on the queen-mattress-sized, lumpy bed of corn, and covered him up with a sack.

As the woman jabbered to Irene, she ground coffee beans between two rocks, poured them into a container of water, and set the concoction to boil over her open fire spit. I tore my eyes away from the family "bed" and examined the rest of her smoky hut. Not a stick of actual furniture was here, only the rock "table and chairs" and the corn "bed," the fire spit, and odds and ends against one wall. I had seen poverty before in some of the Mexicans' houses around Colonia LeBaron, but nothing compared to this. Yet our hostess was so bubbly and full of laughter, and although I didn't understand much of what she was talking about, I was certain she loved life and considered herself blessed.

She poured the coffee into actual, glass cups, and handed us each one. I didn't see any sugar, and I wanted to ask for some, but Irene read my eyes and shook her head. I carefully sipped.

The brew was thick, and so stout I couldn't help but make a face—not like any coffee I'd ever tasted. But I continued to sip at it, hoping the boiled water had killed any germs. I glanced again at the boy on the corn, and wondered how often he peed in the bed.

I tried hard to follow the conversation but finally gave up. The dialect was foreign to me, and delivered at an incredible speed. Irene, too, was having difficulty with some of it but was enjoying herself anyway. We finished our coffee, then Irene stood up and announced that the woman was now coming to our house for a visit.

The native children stayed behind and stared after us as Irene led the way. The woman's bare feet padded softly on the trail, her breasts swinging a bit as she walked. I wondered what our kids would think of her and I hoped they were still in class up at Charlotte's house. Lucy was watching our smaller kids, but they were old enough to notice a half-naked woman. Well, they'd probably seen bare breasts before, and if they hadn't they might as well get used to it.

The peasant woman followed Irene into the barn, with me right on her heels. Suddenly she came to a startled halt.

"Aaay!" she exclaimed. Her eyes darting in all directions, she slowly walked on in and stopped next to Irene's double bed.

Sit down, Irene motioned to her; then Irene sat down herself. The woman stared at the bed and touched it with her palm. She gently pushed in, her eyes widened with amazement. She pushed at the mattress again, and finally turned and sat, then bounced up and down, her face ecstatic with joy.

She rattled off excited questions to Irene, who laughed and answered her. Suddenly the woman's eyes lit up even brighter. "Oooh," she exclaimed, pointing at the dirt floor next to the bed.

Puzzled, Irene and I both stared. A lavender-colored, cardboard Kotex box, its sides decorated with the picture of a big white rose, sat at Irene's bedside. The top had been cut out, and Irene was using the empty box for a trash container.

"Ooh, so beautiful!" the woman gasped, picking it up. She examined the box and ran her fingers tenderly over the white flower. Enthralled, she jabbered away.

Irene's eyes met mine. We both fought startled grins. Then Irene gently took the box from the woman's hands and hurried with it to the kitchen, where she emptied the trash into the stove. She hastened back, the box outstretched.

"Would you like to have it?" she offered.

"Ooh, no, no." The woman shrank back, her arguments becoming weaker as Irene insisted. Finally she accepted Irene's gift and clutched it tightly as we showed her through the rest of the house.

She touched the soft, blond hair of our babies, and stood at the piano while I played her a tune. She examined our cook stove and our log table, her eyes moving excitedly about. She stayed for an hour and drank a glass of milk and ate fresh wheat bread and honey. Lucy wrapped up a loaf of bread for her to take home. Irene and I selected several items from our kids' clothing, and put them in a sack for her. She seemed excited about all her loot, but nothing impressed her as much as Irene's first gift. With her beautiful Kotex box safely under one arm and her sack of goods clutched in her other hand, our neighbor lady finally went home to her children.

Hammers pounded in my ears, and I did my best to ignore the noise as I mashed potatoes for supper. Lucy worked next to me, chopping vegetables for a salad. She dashed outside for a moment to check on the beef roast in the outdoor oven, then she came in again and finished the salad. The special family dinner that Verlan had ordered was almost ready, and we worked silently, the air between us thick with tension.

Never before had Lucy been irritated with me, at least that I knew of. But she was today, and I didn't blame her. The nails being hammered into my new house out back gave her every reason.

Verlan had been home for the past three days, and after I'd had my say to him and informed him that he was to take me home immediately, his answer to my troubled state of mind was to build me a house before Lucy and Irene got one. Hence, I'd become an outcast among the wives, and according to Irene, a "spoiled rotten" one, at that. According to Irene's scathing accusation, our husband's pampering me left little doubt, at least in her mind, that "Susan is obviously Verlan's favorite wife."

The potatoes squashed through the long-handled masher, already creamy and perfectly smooth, but I couldn't let them go yet. I mashed harder, stirred and mashed some more, crushing my anger into the bottom of the pan. Finally I pushed the pan away, grabbed Forrest out of the highchair, and stormed out the door.

I didn't want to fight with Lucy. She wasn't good at fighting back, at least not out loud. Oh, how had I ever gotten myself into this mess? I didn't want a new house–all I wanted was to go home!

I wandered around the yard, looking for my other children. Melanie, Jeannette, and even James were busy with Irene and Lucy's kids, down by the creek making mud pies. With Forrest in tow, I waddled down, and I scolded one and all for playing so close to the creek. Jeannette's mouth had mud around it, and I snapped, "Quit eating the pies, dammit, Jeannette! They're just for play!"

Then I made all the children come up to get ready for supper, and I puffed my way back up the hill, with kids running all around me. I was out of breath before I reached the barn, and my huge stomach felt hard as a basketball. Only two and a half weeks before you're due, I chided myself. You shouldn't be walking up and down this hill. Well, Irene had spent most of the afternoon up at Charlotte's house holding a powwow with her, and someone had to be in charge of the children. The subject under discussion between my two sister-wives was doubtless my own selfishness...

Somehow I had to find a way to get through to Verlan. I couldn't bear the thought of giving birth here in this horrid jungle, so far away from a doctor. Having my other children here was bad enough—poor little Jeannette had a huge boil on her neck—but having a newborn living in these conditions was unthinkable! And I couldn't imagine washing out diapers for two children in the creek. Forrest wasn't even close to being potty trained yet.

My face flamed again at the memory of Irene's angry words to Verlan two days ago. As he and Lucy were driving out of the yard, making the rush trip to Matagalpa to buy the lumber for my house, she'd shouted, "So that's it, huh! The squeaky wheel gets the grease! Whatever it takes to keep your favorite little wife happy!"

"Irene, just stop it! Get control of yourself!" Verlan roared back. Shaking his head, he floored the gas petal and the truck bounced on down the hill.

I stared at Irene's red face, my fists clenched. "I don't even want the damn house, Irene!" I yelled. "Who would want a stupid house here in the jungle? Not me; you're welcome to it! I told Verlan to build you one instead, but he wouldn't listen to me."

Her eyes narrowed. "Yeah, right," she sneered. "Do you think I'm stupid? I know what you're doing and how you're manipulating him. He's so afraid you'll leave him that he can't concentrate on the rest of us! That's all I've heard out of his mouth since he's been home! 'I've got to spend more time with Susan! How can I make Susan happy?'" she mimicked sarcastically. She shook her head, turned on her heel and marched back toward Charlotte's.

Irene, being forced into alliance with her archenemy Charlotte, over me. I stared at her retreating back, my hands shaking with anger. This was all so unbelievable; so sad. What was even sadder was the fact that for the past three days, Verlan had been treating me with more tenderness and passion and respect than ever before. After my angry showdown with him, I'd insisted that I wanted to go home immediately. He'd hardly even argued with me. Instead, he spent part of Charlotte's night with me in my shack.

"Please, just love me, Susan," he'd whispered. "Just be patient and have faith in me. Oh, I'm sick that you've been so unhappy! I'm so sorry! I'll do anything I can to make it up to you, anything you ask. But just give Nicaragua a chance. I promise I'll be here as much, just as much as I can. Please say you'll stay!"

"Verlan, I hate it here and I want to go home! I need my family around me—"

He buried his face in my neck and sighed, "I adore you, Susan. I know that once you have your own place here, you'll see that it's not so bad, and you'll start to feel at home. Please, just be patient and give me a chance."

I finally insisted that he go, before Charlotte came looking for him, but he refused to leave until I promised that I would try to love him again. He cried when I finally agreed to try, and he begged me to let him stay the night. I had to push him out the door.

I was still in bed the next morning when Verlan stopped by again. "I've thought all night long about you, my love," he whispered as he sat beside me on the bed. "I've decided to build your house while I'm here. I want you settled in before the baby's born, so I'll need to get started right away. I'm going to move heaven and earth to make you happy, Susan."

I sat up, pushing my hair out of my eyes. "Can't you understand, Verlan? I don't want a house," I said impatiently. "I just want to go back to Colonia LeBaron. Now."

He patted me and stood up. "Remember that you promised to love me and be patient with me. Just let me get you into your own little house. We'll fix it up real nice, and you'll see that Nicaragua is a wonderful place to live. We'll enjoy life together in this beautiful countryside. You'll see." He dashed out, waving my angry protests away.

And now Irene refused to speak to me, and although Lucy spoke, she wouldn't look at me. Charlotte still treated me civilly, but then, she already had her own house.

Verlan and his older boys worked steadily from first light until it was too dark to see, and the wood house out back had sprung up at an incredible pace. I couldn't bear to look at it, and I'd spent most of my time for the past two days holed up in my shack.

I couldn't fathom how Verlan was able to ignore all the tension. He was acting as if everything was just fine, and he'd ordered this special family meal to celebrate his homecoming. Except for working with frenzy on the new house, and hollering even more than usual at the big boys to stop fooling around and keep busy, he'd taken Irene's haranguing, and Lucy's aloofness, right in stride.

I washed up my kids, and we walked to the barn for supper. Charlotte and her family had already arrived, and everyone was seated and waiting on us for the prayer. I sat my older children down on the floor with the younger ones, then I put Forrest into the highchair, and I hurried to the end of the table and squeezed onto the bench.

"Susan, Sweetheart, come sit here beside me. I saved you a seat," Verlan called over the din caused by twenty-seven children. He patted the empty spot next to him.

"No, no. I'm fine right here," my face flamed with instant exasperation and embarrassment. Irene groaned her annoyance, and Charlotte hastily slipped off her end of the bench and busied herself at the stove.

Verlan stood up and strode toward me. "Okay," he said cheerfully. "Then I'll just have to come over by you. Kaylen, trade me places, would you?"

As the boy stood to obey, Irene jumped up and shouted at Verlan. "I've got a great idea! Why don't you two lovebirds just take your food over to Susan's new house, where you can have a romantic little dinner without having to be disturbed by the rest of us! Go ahead, we won't care!"

The din around us became instant silence. The children stared at their father, then at Irene, then at me. "Okay, Irene, that'll be about enough," Verlan snapped. "You're making a scene. Now, sit down and behave yourself, and let's have prayer. Why don't you say it; maybe it'll make you feel better."

"No, I'll say it," I said swiftly. I stood up and bowed my head. "Heavenly Father," I loudly began before I could get an argument, "Thank you for this food, and for our many blessings. Please, dear Lord—be with each of us here. Help us to be friends and treat each other with respect. Please, bless each child in this family and each adult. Thank you, Lord, that Verlan can be here with us, and please, please help him to finish Irene's new house swiftly, so that he can take my children and me back to Colonia LeBaron before my baby's born. If he does this, we won't be forced to hitchhike. This I pray, in the name of Jesus Christ. Amen."

The children began to eat. Charlotte sat down again, and without a word, the food was passed around the table. Verlan didn't look at me, but I could sense his angry resignation. The special dinner of roast beef, mashed potatoes and gravy, salad and biscuits was consumed mostly in silence. There was no pie for dessert, since that was Irene's specialty, and she'd been too mad to help cook. But as she and I cleared the dishes after the meal, her damp eyes, penitent demeanor, and soft touch on my arm, assured me that she loved me and that she was sorry.

A s Verlan skillfully drove the narrow, winding roads back through the mountainous terrain of Central America, my bold, persistent questioning of our church's doctrinal beliefs had him upset and defensive, and finally he admitted that he had no real, solid answers for me. He became evasive, and hesitant, and was insistent that we had to have faith in Joel's teachings, regardless of the conflict in scripture about polygamy. Would I please just stop worrying about things I didn't understand? I should be willing to trust his judgment, and know that we were on the only true path to the Celestial Kingdom.

"Well, what about the fact that we have no living prophet now that Joel's gone? Doesn't this worry you? Because it sure worries me, and it would even more if I were in your shoes!" I snapped.

"Sure, I have questions. But I trust that the Lord's in control, and when the time is right someone will step forward. Meanwhile, you're worrying about things that you don't need to worry about. There's no other answer out there, Susan. Surely you agree with me that the L.D.S. church is off track, and I'm entirely confident that most of the basic Christian churches are just a money-making sham. We alone have the fullness of the gospel! So we just need to practice faith and endurance, and be willing to sacrifice."

I finally gave up and stopped heckling him. He didn't know what to say to me, and I was beginning to feel guilty for being so disagreeable. In Verlan's eyes I was treading upon the brink of apostasy, and the only thread of hope for my sad state was to bind me tightly with his love and forbearance.

As the seven days and nights of border crossings and fussing children, gas stations, and potty stops wore on, he showed unaccustomed patience with the kids and constant concern for my needs. He knew what a chance he was taking by traveling such a great distance with an imminently due, pregnant wife, and he was frantic that he might have to deliver the baby himself en route. This had been his major argument against my unreasonable demand to leave immediately for the colony.

"In the first place, it won't happen," I'd assured him. "And in the second place, I'd rather have my baby in back of this pickup with you in attendance, than in that damp, muddy, fly-infested house you threw together, with your angry wives playing mid-wife." I hadn't really meant it, but he'd seemed impressed.

In spite of my firm resolve while in Nicaragua to keep my emotional distance from Verlan, he'd been so considerate the whole trip, and so anxious to please me, that once again I'd found myself sucked into the bottomless quicksand of loving him. I became captivated by his desperation to keep me—and in spite of my shaken beliefs, my parched soul shamelessly sopped up the tenderness and attention he offered. For the first time in our marriage I felt as though we were a real family, and I realized the closeness and dependency that monogamous couples took for granted.

The cooler temperatures of the Northern Mexico States began to replace the tropical climates of Yucatan and Jalisco. At last, the lights of Chihuahua City loomed on the horizon and were soon far behind us. Finally the sleepy little pueblo of my childhood, surrounded by hills covered in frozen cactus and mesquite bushes, came into view, just as I remembered it from pre-Ervilite times. There were no guards at the entrances, no watchful men on horseback patrolling the streets. Bundled children ran skipping and playing on their way to school, and women sauntered to Jensen's little grocery store for their mail and supplies as though they hadn't a single care.

Verlan drove us directly to my sister Fara's adobe house where she gleefully welcomed us and insisted she had plenty of room, and we should stay for as long as we needed to. She bustled around making us breakfast and catching me up with her life. She'd remarried while I was away—she was now the second wife to a young convert from Yakima, Washington. He was presently in the states working. Although she was dealing with an extremely jealous first wife, Fara insisted that she was happy and truly in love.

Verlan's immediate plan for the day was to locate a vacant home for me to move to, and to help me get settled once again before the baby came. He would stay in Colonia LeBaron with us for a month or more, he'd assured me, so that he could attend to my needs and be at the birth. I felt certain that he also planned to work on strengthening the frayed cord of my faith.

Helen Leany, the first widow Verlan married, had become disillusioned with his gadabout lifestyle over the past year and had finally left the family. But Elizabeth was here. Verlan needed to spend some time with her, and he also had plenty of church matters to deal with. He would be only too happy to settle down with us for awhile and get some rest.

But Verlan hadn't reckoned with Ervil in mind. Sigfried Widmar came looking for Verlan the moment he heard we were in town. He stomped into Fara's living room and announced he had disturbing news. One of Ervil's "soldiers," a giant of a man named Dean Vest who had apparently attempted to defect from Ervil's organization had just been found murdered in San Diego. Strong evidence pointed to Ervil's wife, Vonda, because police had found blood spatters on her shoes and clothes. Sigfried was heading immediately for San Diego, and needed Verlan to accompany him.

"I've got to go," Verlan whispered to me as Sigfried dashed out again. "Honey, you know that I can hardly bear to leave you, but I have no choice! Getting Vonda just may give us a real break where Ervil is concerned! I'll be back to you as soon as I can. Hopefully before the baby's born."

I knew he would never be back in time. Feeling numb with resignation, I stood on Fara's porch and watched him drive away. He would stop in to see Elizabeth and his mother for a few minutes, and then he would be on the highway again with Sigfried. I glanced at my watch. We'd been in the colony for exactly two hours. Just long enough to unpack my things from Verlan's truck, stretch our cramped legs, and get a bite to eat. Verlan had driven all night and he was exhausted. I hoped he would sleep while Sigfried drove to San Diego.

I shivered against the chilly February wind and wiped my wet cheeks on my jacket sleeve. I felt angry with myself for crying. After all, I was used to this. Underneath the veneer of security Verlan's presence had offered me the past week, I'd known that it was only temporary. His assertion of devotion to me was only a thin bandage for my battered heart. Life with Verlan would never be any different—there were too many things to come between us. My competitors for his time were his wives, the Church, and Ervil, each a justified reason to leave me.

But now Verlan, too, had a rival. His contender for my allegiance was my ever-growing lack of trust in our doctrine. I wasn't able to "just have faith". The conflicting passages I'd found tormented my conscience, and I was certain that other issues would come to light once I continued my studies. What to do with this anguishing knowledge was the question.

A noise behind me pulled me out of my reverie. Fara had joined me on the porch, and she hugged me tight in an effort to console me. "Don't worry, Sue," her gray eyes were soft with sympathy. "I'll be here, even if he doesn't make it back in time. Mom's here and Mona's here, and we'll celebrate your return from the wilds with a party! Do you have any idea how surprised and happy everyone will be to see you?"

Taking a shaky breath, I mentally shoved my despondency to the side. I couldn't bear to deal with it all right now. For now, I needed to see the rest of my family and prepare for my baby's birth.

During our long trip together, Verlan had told me what had been happening with Ervil. Charlotte's mother, a woman named Rhea Kunz, had narrowly escaped an attempted kidnapping. Mrs. Kunz was a prominent member of a fundamentalist church in Salt Lake, and the sister of its leader. The police were convinced a kidnapping would have resulted in her death. That the Ervilites were the perpetrators was a certainty, since this group of fundamentalists had received some of Ervil's threatening pamphlets. Next was the disappearance of a Utah man named Robert Simons, a self-styled polygamist from Grantsville. His family was claiming that one of Ervil's henchmen had lured him from his home. Simons, also targeted by Ervil's pamphlets, hadn't been seen for over three weeks. Nothing could be proven, but it was believed he was dead.

Numerous leading fundamentalists throughout Utah had received more written threats signed by Ervil's group. These peace-loving people were again put under highest alert. Ervil's blood-atonement warnings had escalated, and Verlan felt compelled to respond to Ervil with open letters of his own.

Would it never stop? How many people would Ervil kill to satisfy his blood-thirsty, power-crazed mind? Somewhere in California, my Chynoweth relatives—along with all the other Ervilites—were hiding from the law, and plotting with their leader to commit even more atrocities in the name of God.

One thing I hadn't taken into consideration before leaving Nicaragua was that Colonia LeBaron was still a target. With my stubborn decision to leave the jungle, I'd brought my children back to possible danger. It amazed me that the colony members were going on about their business as though everything was fine. Well, as I'd realized before, we couldn't hide forever. In spite of Ervil and his Lambs of God, life had to go on.

My labor began on our fourth evening back from the South. My mother and Jay's second wife, Karen, and Doris the midwife, and her teenage sister all arrived for the birth. Fara's living room couch made down into a bed, and we had everything ready. Fara bought sodas, popped corn, and made caramels, and we all sat around the kitchen table, giggling and playing Scrabble while we timed the contractions. Just before midnight, I got down to the serious business of delivering a baby. I moved to the couch.

Forrest woke up with a howl and wandered into the living room just as the baby was crowning. None of the women could stand to leave the room at this exciting time, so my sixteen-month old son became a fascinated member of the birthing party. He was among the first to welcome his new brother.

Never had a birth gone so smoothly for me. This had been a fun, relaxing way to have a baby! Fara and Mom pampered me and tended my children, and within three days I felt almost normal. Memories of the nightmare ordeal after Forrest was born flashed through my mind, and I shuddered and thanked God and my family for this new experience.

I'd been exhausted from the long trip and so frantic to prepare for a new baby, that I hadn't made the rounds to see my friends. Jay and Carmela had been by to see us, as had Rose Ann and her children, and Mona and her two little boys. And Grandma LeBaron stopped by to meet her new grandson. Surprisingly, she didn't inquire about my quick return from Nicaragua as everyone else had—doubtless Verlan had filled her in on my reasons. She didn't approach the subject, and I gathered she was avoiding an uncomfortable discussion.

I'd explained to no one the real reason why I'd left Nicaragua. I'd only said that I felt the kids and I would be better off living in the colony. They'd accepted this without question. I knew from my discussions with Irene and Verlan that I would get no sympathy for my scriptural discoveries. My family would consider me a faithless apostate, and our relationship would change. I couldn't bear the thought.

The children and I plunged back into colony life. I entered Melanie in second grade and James in kindergarten. We attended church on Sunday and visited friends, and I shared a baby-sitter with Fara for the Saturday night dance.

Fara told me that Debbie Bateman was living back in the colony, in the basement of an old, unfinished house. Excited, I bundled up my three week-old baby and hurried over to see her. I hadn't talked to Debbie since that day in Los Molinos when she'd still been married to Ervil, and I was anxious to see for myself if she'd adjusted.

Two years had passed since she'd become Ritchie Stubbs' third wife—Ritchie, Lane's half-brother, and the handsome husband of one of my childhood friends. I gingerly descended the cement steps and knocked on Debbie's door, which swung wide open. Her upturned hazel eyes and delighted smile welcomed me.

"Oh, Susan!" she squealed. "I heard you were here! Oh, wow, I'm so glad you came to see me!" Pulling me into the dark interior of her house, she took the baby from my arms and cooed over him a minute, then handing him back, she said, "This is just so awesome! Give me just a sec, Suze, while I take care of these kids. Come on in and sit down!"

My eyes had slowly adjusted to the poor light of her basement, and I looked around in dismay. Debbie was hugely pregnant. She wore a faded muumuu, and her bare feet were rough and splayed. Her four children sat at a table littered with bread crumbs and dirty dishes. They quietly ate their beans. The basement was scantily furnished, with unpainted cement walls and bare, cement floors, and so cold I couldn't imagine how Debbie could stand to be barefoot.

I sat on the tattered couch and waited—my anger just under the surface. How had this happened to Debbie Bateman, my spirited, fun-loving, gum-chewing friend from Southern California! She'd had the courage to leave Ervil, and that was wonderful. But to come to this? This was almost as bad a life as that poor little native woman in Nicaragua!

I closed my eyes and mentally fought for control of my tongue. I always wanted to rescue people—I couldn't help it, I couldn't bear to see other people suffering! But I couldn't let Debbie see my rage at her husband for not providing better—it wasn't my business.

"Would you like something, maybe a cup of mint tea?" Debbie offered when she joined me. She appeared anxious to play the hostess, and genuinely pleased that I was here, yet obviously I'd caught her at a bad time.

"No, really, I'm just fine," I assured. "It's just been so long, and I wanted to see how you're doing. How's everything with you, and how's Ritchie?"

Everything was good, she told me, her eyes evasive. Her baby was due in a week, and her mom was coming to help her. Ritchie was keeping busy with farming.

"It's been forever since I've seen Ritchie," I murmured. "Is he around?"

"No, not tonight," she said quietly. I nodded, wanting to change the subject, but Debbie blurted, "He's gone to ask Laura out to the movies."

"Laura! Laura LeBaron?!" I gasped. Verlan and Charlotte's twenty-year old, single daughter had been in town for the past few days. Verlan's three oldest girls, Rhea, Laura, and Donna hadn't gone to Nicaragua. They each had taken jobs in California. Laura had become a lovely girl with a lithe, long-legged body, and soft brown hair and eyes. She was visiting from San Diego and staying with Grandma LeBaron. She'd stopped by to see the kids and me a couple of times. Several of the brethren were relentlessly pursuing her, but as yet she'd shown no real interest in anyone.

I stared at Debbie, with her bare feet and rag of a dress, and I lost my head. "Ritchie's trying to court Laura?" I hissed. "Look at you, all big and pregnant and living like this, and your husband's out chasing the prettiest girl in town! This is the sickest thing I've ever heard!"

Debbie's face turned white. She struggled to her feet and snapped back, "Well, what about your own husband! How many wives has he got? Something like, ten or so, isn't it? And he's still after more. How do you feel about his courting Priscilla? He needs another wife like he needs another hole in the head."

We stared into each other's eyes, my own face slowly blanching with shock. "What!" I finally gasped. "What did you say? Verlan's–courting Priscilla?"

Images of the prophet Joel's beautiful young widow flashed in front of me. Priscilla, the exquisite girl I'd spoken to at the airport while we waited for Joel's body to arrive from Ensenada. Priscilla, Ritchie's sister, Joel's widow, Verlan's new conquest?

Debbie sat back down again, her shoulders slumping. "You didn't know, did you?" she said softly. "I'm so sorry, Sue. That was so rotten of me. You shouldn't have found out like this. Oh, Lord, I'm so sorry."

I dropped onto the couch, hugged my baby tightly and slowly rocked him. I swayed back and forth with Verlan's tiny, sleeping son; my frozen lips locked in a kiss against his soft forehead.

Debbie talked quietly to me, but I didn't really hear her. My thoughts were dazed, yet running swiftly over my married life.

My first lonely months: living with Lucy in Ensenada, Verlan's courtship of Lillie–Beverly's coldness and subsequent friendship–Charlotte's distaste of the child I'd been–Irene's sweetness–Ervil–and my heartache over the Chynoweths. Verlan's constant absence–My first house, that horrid trailer that was just as bad as this place of Debbie's–The poverty. My guitar–Lillie. Kim. Helen and Elizabeth. Nicaragua and the dirt floors and flies.

As I finally left Debbie, I choked out my own apology. I hadn't meant to be rude–I really hadn't. I'd just been so upset . . . I'd spoken my furious thoughts out loud . . . With my baby clutched tightly against me, I hurried back through the cold, semi-darkness to Fara's.

My brain still whirled with the news. I hadn't questioned Debbie's knowledge of Verlan and Priscilla's courtship. She'd know what she was talking about–Priscilla was her husband's sister. Besides, I'd always been aware of Verlan's admiration for Priscilla. It showed in his eyes each time he was around her.

My anger was harsh and deeper than what I'd felt about Lillie. But now, it wasn't directed so much at Verlan or even at Priscilla. They were both victims of the same powerful, deceptive indoctrination that my own mind no longer tolerated. My anger was mostly at myself for being weak, for being a victim of my own heart and insecurity. Somehow I had to free myself from the hold Verlan and my other loved ones had on me.

How long had I suspected that this church I belonged to was based on principles that were, in so many ways, unchristian? Since Los Molinos, when I'd finally understood women were considered mindless baggage—and if submissive, we would be admitted to heaven on our husband's coattails. That had been the beginning. Since then, I'd come to realize that not just the women were leaning on the arm of flesh, but our men also. Joel's teachings had become more important to Verlan and the others, than Christ's. And in many ways they weren't the same teachings at all.

Polygamy was the key to the door of disaster in this church. The task of living polygamy so overwhelmed us all, that the very reason for the Church's existence—our solemn duty to share the precious gospel of salvation with the world before it was too late—was lost in the confusion.

Admittedly, I didn't understand all the ramifications. But I did know that if this huge part of our doctrine was in error, then we were in serious trouble. Why couldn't Verlan see this? He was an intelligent man—how could he be so blind? Was the thrill of always having a new woman on the horizon, the blind spot? Was the feeling of power, of being a god over his own little kingdom here on earth, too large a sacrifice to make for truth?

I'd been so blind! Why had it taken Debbie's appalling living circumstances to open my eyes wide to what our men were doing! Verlan's wives lived no better! Verlan himself ignored the dreadful squalor of his families' conditions, and chased after women with wantonness that was truly sinful. And he did it while hiding behind the skirt of religious purity.

Laura's face crept into my imagination—Laura, Charlotte's innocent daughter, who soon would choose a polygamous husband and inevitably join the ranks of heartbroken, abandoned, abused, plural wives.

I shuddered, my steps racing up the gentle incline to Fara's. My own little children would not be raised this way! My daughters would never go through this heartache, nor would my sons be taught that they could control and abuse women's emotions. Somehow I would get them away from this, where they would be free to search for the truth, and would never be subjected to the empty promises, and resulting degradation of polygamy.

Chapter 41

My baby son Lance was six weeks old when Verlan returned from San Diego. Beverly and her children were with him. She planned to move in with her parents temporarily, since she refused to stay any longer in Los Molinos.

"She wants to live close to her folks," Verlan sighed, looking at me with a strange, accusing glint in his eye. I ignored the silent implication. I could read his mind—he was blaming me for starting something in his family, something that was getting out of control.

Verlan's stop in Colonia LeBaron was brief. He was on his way back to Nicaragua. He'd received urgent letters from the wives there, demanding that they be returned to civilization immediately. My husband's demeanor seemed cowed and resigned, and he'd taken little notice of my own reserve toward him.

Nothing was going right, he complained. Ervil's wife, Vonda, had been released for lack of evidence in the murder of Dean Vest. More members of our church had "bailed out," the primary one being Bruce Wakeham, one of Verlan's two main counselors. And now, this demand by his three wives in Nicaragua! It would take several trips to get all three families relocated, and he "didn't have a clue where to take them." They wanted to come to Colonia LeBaron, but he had no homes available for them.

"I have found you a little house, though," he said, brightening a bit. "Harv Stubbs has sold me that little place on the corner, down by Stubbsville. You can move in while I'm gone, and we'll fix it up and get you some furniture when I get back. There's no outhouse, but I'll have someone get right on it and build you one."

I bit my tongue and nodded. I couldn't stay with Fara forever, and as yet I still had no concrete scheme for leaving Colonia LeBaron. I didn't dare reveal my ultimate plans to leave him and the church. The pressure on me would be enormous, and Verlan would never willingly allow me to take his children.

"I have a question for you," I coldly changed the subject. "It's been called to my attention that you're courting another woman. Is this true?"

Verlan stared at me, his face becoming grave, "Who told you this?"

I sighed, "What does that matter? Is it true or not?"

"The only thing you could possibly be talking about is that Priscilla's asked me to be her spiritual head," he said slowly. "Now, Susan, that's all there is to it. You know the rule of the Church; I've explained it to you. Single women need to be under the authority and guidance of a man of the priesthood. She's chosen me to be the one. Don't make a big deal out of it, please!"

"That's the silliest thing I've ever heard!" I snapped scornfully. "Why would she want you? You don't even have the time to "guide" your own wives! Why would any woman ask you to be her spiritual head! Don't insult my intelligence, Verlan; there's more to this Priscilla thing than you're telling me."

"I don't want to talk about this," he countered swiftly. "You're not being rational, and I don't like being called on the carpet this way. I've told you to trust me, and you may as well decide to do it. Look, I'm here to spend some time with you! Can't we enjoy each other's company for awhile?" He reached out to touch me, and I pushed his hands away.

"If I were you, I wouldn't want to be judged, either," I retorted. I closed my eyes and leaned my head against the cupboard. Enough of this, I thought. What Verlan did with Priscilla would never affect me—not as it did his other families.

He lounged against Fara's kitchen counter, pursed his lips and tiredly shook his head. He still couldn't fathom why his having other women should upset me. He was doing the right thing by taking care of his brother's widow; what could be my problem?

My voice softening a bit, I continued, "Verlan, I love you. I do, and I always will no matter what happens. But I don't agree with the way you live your life or with the way you treat your wives. I hope some day that you realize that women have rights, too. We have the right to be loved and cared for. We have the right to expect our husbands to be real daddies for our children. And we should also be respected and allowed to have an opinion about the actions of our husband that affect our own lives. I just hope that some day you truly realize this."

His aqua-colored eyes stared into mine, absorbing my every word. The house became silent. The morning sun poured warmth through the window, its rays reflecting against the metal snaps on Verlan's Western shirt. Outside, I could vaguely hear the soft voices of the children as they played in Fara's sandbox.

Verlan's hand slid along the counter to where my hand rested against the sink. He lifted it to his lips. "Do you have any idea how much I love you?" he whispered. "Oh, Susan, my little charm. God knows that sometimes I'd just like to run away with you. Just you! We'd live a normal life, where I didn't have to deal with all the pressures of the church and everyone else. I'd make you so happy! We'd have our beautiful children, and each other . . . we wouldn't need anyone else."

"You'd be bored stiff in a week," I retorted. "If you didn't have your harem and the church to keep you busy, you wouldn't know what to do with yourself. You'd end up driving me crazy."

"No, I wouldn't. I'd find plenty of things to do! I'd learn to golf, for one thing. I've always thought that looked like fun."

He leaned over and kissed me, soft and deep. Forsaking his usual chaste smack, his kiss deepened and searched. Tears instantly filled my eyes, my heart and soul ached with sorrow as I returned his kiss. Verlan didn't know it but he was kissing me for the last time, and my breath came in harsh gasps when I finally pulled away.

He grabbed my hand again and urged me toward the bedroom, his eyes desperate with sudden desire. "No! No, I can't," I moaned, my own traitorous longing for him weakening my will. "I can't." I yanked my hand free and shoved it behind my back. Then I moved away from him, my grief apparent in my eyes.

"Why?" He growled.

My frozen brain searched for an excuse—Fara—my period—the children. They would all work.

I shook my head, my face contorted with anguish. "I just can't," I sobbed. "Please go away! Please!"

Verlan silently nodded. He stepped past me. Hesitating at the door, he looked back. "Send for me when you want me," he muttered. The screen door latched softly behind him.

I stood motionless, my tears falling silently, my heart bursting with misery. Into my shattered thoughts my dream of long ago crept—the dream I'd considered a personal revelation from God, the one I'd been taught to expect from childhood. In my dream Verlan had come. He had rescued me from evil. He'd kissed me, and Grandma had assured me this meant he was the one I should marry. The reality was, I had married Verlan and we had five wonderful children. He'd saved me from marrying Ervil and becoming part of Ervil's madness. The other reality was, Verlan lived with a certain madness of his own, one that I could no longer agree with. As of now, that part of my life was over.

Dad's yellow Toyota pickup sped swiftly past the sandy, cactus-covered landscape, moving ever closer to the United States border and New Mexico. The little truck, with its camper shell on its back, bumped over the rough roads and swayed around the turns. I grasped the side of the mattress and softly cursed my father's driving.

Six-year old James looked at me and grinned, showing off the gap of his missing front teeth. "You said a bad word," he announced.

"You're right, I did. Oops." I smiled at him, then used my feet to hold the suitcases from sliding at us as we turned into another curve.

Forrest and Lance both slept—one curled on either side of me. Melanie and Jeannette were in the cab with Grandpa. James leaned against the camper shell, his long legs reaching the end of the mattress. He stared out the open window, the breeze blowing his shaggy blond hair about his face. Blue-green eyes snapped with excitement—he was going to visit his uncles from the states!

My heart still fluttered, but it no longer pounded with fear. We were far away from the colony now, and no one could stop us. Verlan was somewhere in California—probably San Diego—and he wasn't aware of our escape. No one, including my father, knew that we would never return.

Dad had been so sweet and happy for the company when I'd asked if the kids and I could ride along on his trip to Utah. We needed a vacation, I'd told him, just a little break. I hated lying to him but I knew I had no choice. He would never have agreed to take us otherwise.

I'd packed two suitcases and a cardboard box. Then I'd wandered nervously around the little house Verlan had procured for me. I was actually doing it. I was leaving.

I glanced regretfully at my brand new, beautiful, oak cabinets in the kitchen. They'd just been delivered yesterday from the carpenter in Casas and remained empty. They were the most beautiful things I'd ever had, and I was leaving them. Well, they were one of my few regrets. Verlan would eventually give them to someone else. Maybe Priscilla would get them. She and Verlan planned to be married soon.

I turned to stretch my legs, but James had all the space. He obligingly scooted a bit, and I blew him a kiss. He grinned and continued his excited study of the desert. I buried my face in the pillow and closed my eyes, my worried thoughts scurrying.

It was November 1976. We would be arriving unannounced on Thanksgiving Day. What would my brothers say when I arrived with five children? I was asking so much of them! Yet from the hints they had made in the past, I knew they would take us in. They would help me get on my feet and show me how to survive. I would get a job, and perhaps go to school—I would manage . . . I relaxed and slept.

The snow in Cedar City, Utah was two feet deep as my father pulled into Perry's driveway. I shivered with nervous excitement as Dad and I bundled the children and trudged to the front door. Dad wasted no time on niceties. He turned the doorknob and marched the six of us inside.

"Hallo, anybody home?" he boomed. Perry, Darlene, and their two blond girls and little boy jumped up from the dining room table. Grinning, they raced to us, shouting excited questions while hugging us at the same time. Coats and snow-covered shoes were removed. We were herded into the brightly-lit kitchen, where Dad placed calls to Dale and Ross, my two brothers who lived on the outskirts of town.

"How long can you stay?" Perry asked, his eyes twinkling with excitement as he served up Thanksgiving leftovers. He placed them in front of my wide-eyed children who crowded around his table. Darlene poured foamy glasses of milk and passed them around, then she took Lance from my arms and fed him mashed potatoes and gravy.

Dad was still on the phone and the kids were occupied with their supper. I took Perry's arm and led him toward a back bedroom. I closed the door and stared into his blue eyes, my legs shaking, my own eyes filling with tears as I tried to speak.

"Talk to me, Sis," he prodded gently.

But I didn't know how to begin, and I crumbled against him. He rocked me, his arms strong and sure as he waited for me to get control. "I don't want to go back!" I finally moaned against his chest.

His grasp tightened around me. He kissed my wet cheek, then he whispered, "Oh, Suze, you've come to the right place. You can all stay right here. We have plenty of room. There's a whole, separate apartment in the basement, with a bathroom and kitchen and everything you'll need. We'll help you!"

I couldn't speak; I only nodded. I glanced about, and finally settled for wiping my nose on the arm of my sweater. Perry went for Kleenex, then sat me on the bed. "Does Dad know?" he asked.

"He has no idea, and I'm scared to tell him," I wailed. "I tricked him into bringing us. He thinks we wanted a vacation!"

Perry waved that away. "He won't be a problem. Susan, are you sure this is what you want? Are you actually ready to leave Verlan? Are you sure?"

"I'm sure," I whispered.

"Then let's tell Dad. Let's get it over with."

I bowed my head, closed my eyes and nodded.

When I looked up, Dad stood over me. "What's going on?" he asked softly, his bright blue gaze searching my swollen face. I glanced at Perry and he nodded reassuringly.

"I'm not going back with you, Dad," I said, my voice surprisingly strong. "I'm leaving Verlan. Please don't be mad."

His eyes narrowed. "Does Verlan know about this?" he growled.

I shook my head and blew my nose. "I didn't dare tell him until we were gone. He wouldn't have let us go."

"I see." He rocked on the balls of his feet, then snapped, "Well, go and call him. Tonight. I don't agree with some of that man's ways, but I won't have him think that I'm a party to this underhanded business."

God, give me strength, just give me strength, my mind chanted. Please be with me. I walked to the kitchen phone, dialed information for Ossmen Jones' San Diego number. I asked Sister Jones to locate Verlan. It was an emergency, and he should call me immediately at my brother Perry's.

Darlene and I bedded the kids down while I waited. Twenty minutes later the phone rang. Darlene motioned to me, I picked it up, and Verlan's frenzied voice came on the line. "What's wrong? What are you doing in Utah?"

My own voice was devoid of emotion. "I'm here because I'm leaving you. I'm never going back, Verlan. Please don't try to stop me; it's over. Just know that my dad wasn't aware of my plans when he brought us here, so don't blame him. I'm sorry to do it this way."

"Susan, you know I can't let this happen!" His voice was frantic. "I understand that you're upset, but I'll make it up to you! You know I will. Now, just have a good visit with your family, and I'll be there to pick you and the kids up on Saturday."

"NO!" I shouted in alarm. "Don't come here! You'd be wasting your time. I will not go back. Just accept it and leave us alone."

"I'll be there on Saturday." The phone clicked in my ear.

Dad left on business to Salt Lake, and we spent the next two days settling into Perry's basement. Ross, Dale and their families had come over and offered their moral support, bringing household goods, toys, and clothing for the children. Baskets of food found their way onto Darlene's counter, my sisters-in-law determined to help in every way. I felt numb with gratitude.

My children unquestioningly accepted the change of residence. They loved the attention lavished by their relatives, and Melanie and James started babbling excitedly about attending school on Monday with their cousins.

My stomach rolled with nervousness as Saturday dawned. Verlan arrived late in the afternoon, and with heart pounding, I hastened outside to converse with him. I refused to invite him in. I didn't want my brother's family subjected to the row I knew would occur.

Be strong! I told myself as I followed him to his pickup. Don't show any weakness or he'll never let you go. Just don't look at him.

Verlan started the engine and turned the heater on. Then he turned to me and reached for my hand, but I yanked it back. "Don't! You shouldn't have come," I said coldly. "We won't be going back, and you've wasted a trip clear up here."

"Susan, I've been thinking and praying ever since we talked on the phone about how I can keep you with me all the time. That's what we need, darling, to spend time together, and I think I've come up with a way to make it happen. Will you listen?" he pleaded. His eyes were red-rimmed and threatening to flow over.

"No!" I snapped. "I told you it's over. Go back and marry your beautiful Priscilla. You won't have me in the way now."

He bowed his head and wiped his cheeks. "I won't marry her if you'll come home."

"Oh, Verlan," I sighed. "She's not the problem. I'm the problem. I don't love you anymore, and I don't believe polygamy's right, and I won't raise my kids that way. Just go home."

He was silent. His shoulders seemed thinner; the skin on his neck more wrinkled than I remembered. His grip on the steering wheel whitened his knuckles. He cleared his throat and whispered, "I will divorce Charlotte and marry you legally. That way I can take you with me always. Just come back to me."

I eyed him sharply. "Now, I'll just bet Charlotte would go for that!" I shook my head. "No, Verlan, forget it. Besides, I don't believe in the church anymore. I don't know what I do believe in, but it's not the church. I'll find my place some day but it won't be with you. Go home."

He stared at me, his sad, blue-green eyes slowly turning angry. "Fine then," he snapped coldly. "Have it your way. I give up. You can have your freedom, but I'm taking the kids back with me. They are my kids, and I won't have them raised in the States. Go pack their things."

I gaped at him. "Are you out of your mind?" I exploded. "They are MY children! I gave birth to most of them alone, while you were away. I raised them and cared for them, without a bit of help from you. They hardly know you! You didn't even support them; your boys did. So don't threaten me. With one phone call I can have you arrested, and don't you forget it! Goodbye, Verlan, go back to your families. They need you, you know."

I opened the door, slammed it closed, and dashed into the house, my whole body shaking with anger and fear. Perry waited in the kitchen, and I threw myself into his arms. "He says he's taking my kids," I sobbed. "I told him I'd call the police! I can do that if I need to, can't I? He can't take them, can he?"

"Shh, shh. No, honey, he doesn't have a legal leg to stand on, and he knows it. Don't worry, he can't take them."

I peeked out the window to where Verlan still sat slumped in his pickup. As I watched him, my anger toward him slowly receded. He looked so alone. So sad! Suddenly I knew that his threat to take the children had been nothing more than an act of desperation—just as his offer to divorce Charlotte had been. Anything to keep me.

"I'll tell him that he can come in and see the kids for a few minutes, then he has to leave," Perry suggested.

I nodded and wiped my cheeks. "Let him know that Lance is asleep, and, will you stay with them until he's gone? I don't want to see him again. I'll stay up here in the bedroom."

I threw a final glance out the window, then I hurried to the room where my baby was sleeping. Verlan wouldn't bother with seeing him. He'd never wasted much time with the smaller children. I sat on the bed and softly caressed Lance's blond hair. My heart ached, oh, so badly!

I could hear the men descend the stairs into the basement where the children were watching television. Verlan's voice occasionally carried to me as they visited. He must have agreed to leave when he was through, or Perry would have come and told me.

I sighed, propped myself up on two pillows beside my baby, and stared at the dark ceiling. "Well, Lord, I've finally done it," I whispered. "My past is almost history, and I'm counting on you to guide my future. I'll need lots of help, Lord, to find a place of my own and a job somewhere so that we won't be a burden on my brothers. I don't know what you have in store for the kids and me, but I'm certain you'll lead me to a fine man someday, someone who will love us, and who will be a real daddy for my kids. We'll raise them to be open-minded, to value freedom, to search for truth and knowledge, and to love you."

Outside, an engine purred to life. Jumping up, I pulled the curtain and looked out the window. Snow was beginning to swirl under the porch light, and Verlan's truck was backing out of the driveway. Its headlights glared yellow against the icy cement. He turned onto the street and within moments his red taillights were out of sight. He was gone, back to his busy world of chasing dreams, keeping a dying church together, hiding from Ervil, and visiting his scattered families.

The huge lump in my throat choked me, and I began to sob. Some part of me would always love him. He was a good man in his own way, sincere in his driven, yet blinded, search for the pathway to heaven. I would always believe that the quandary polygamy created, along with the concocted justifications for it, had sidetracked him and the others from the plain and simple truths that Jesus offered; truths that were lost in all the confusion.

My heavy thoughts turned to the women that I'd shared so much with. Verlan's wives would have mixed feelings about my leaving the family. Most of them would be sad, especially Lillie and Irene—and perhaps even Charlotte, who had sacrificed so much more than the rest of us for Verlan's sake. She had shared the husband of her youth over and over again. She'd left her children to help support Verlan's families. She'd done things that I'd never have been willing to do, because in her heart, she was serving God.

I would always care about Verlan's families. They held a piece of my heart, and would forever. Maybe one day, a few of them would find their way out of the whirlpool that sucked them under. That would always be my prayer, for them, and for my own Ray family still in Mexico. Sweet Heavenly Father—let it be so.

Epilogue

I left Verlan and Colonia LeBaron in November of 1976. The children and I lived in Perry's basement in Cedar City for the first few months; then we moved into an apartment of our own. Melanie and James had immediately started school, as had I. I also maintained a job; first as a waitress, then as a telephone operator. Once I achieved my high school diploma, I signed up at the local college.

Life was difficult. My emotions were raw, my courage teetering, and my self esteem bottomed out. I quickly found that being a single woman with five children in the United States was completely different from being a so-called married woman, whose husband was just away, in Mexico. Loneliness plagued me, as did the effort to try to fit into a world so different from the one I was used to. Each potential friend I met had her own husband, and only one or two children; and here I was saddled down to a houseful of rambunctious kids—not exactly the family you wanted to invite over for dinner and Scrabble. Although my brothers included us in the important holidays, and an occasional Sunday meal, they were busy with their own livelihoods and families.

Out of necessity, I'd signed up for welfare. Although I was trying, the money I earned wasn't, as yet, enough to meet our needs. Of course, Verlan couldn't afford to send me anything. He stopped in to see us on a fairly frequent basis, more often—it seemed to me—than he had when we were married. Each time he came, he did his best to woo me into going home. I stubbornly declined. He reminded me on more than one occasion that I had to give our separation six months before I could consider myself divorced. I icily reminded him that we were never legally married in the first place, so we didn't need a legal divorce. I wanted a real husband, and someday I would have one.

After a few months I met a promising young man, a returned Mormon missionary. Bill seemed so perfect; fun-loving, musical, handsome, and best of all, he adored my children! Within weeks, we were inseparable. God was finally smiling on me, and I was filled with happiness and optimism for our future. On one of Verlan's visits to the children, I introduced him to Bill. He was reluctantly impressed. He told me that since I wouldn't allow him to be in our lives, then he would give Bill and me his blessing.

Within a few months, to my horror I realized that I was pregnant. Bill was

411

literally blown away. He immediately decided that he wasn't ready for a wife and six children, and without a backward glance, he walked out of my life.

Oh, how could I have allowed this to happen? My mind and soul spun in desperate self-loathing. What kind of shameless person was I, to wander into such immoral sin? How could I face my loved ones with the consequences of it? A baby out of wedlock, with no father! Oh, what should I do? But, my brothers were wonderful. They hugged me and assured me that I was okay. They would help me through this new twist in my life. In spite of their reassurances, I wandered around in a stupor for days. No snake crawling on the earth felt lower than I did.

Suddenly Verlan was pounding on my front door. Once again, he'd stopped in to reason with me and to persuade me to come home. I used my new situation as ammunition. Coldly, I blasted him with the fact that he should just give up. He wouldn't even want me now; I was expecting another man's child! But his reaction surprised me. He pleaded that if I would just return to him, the baby I carried would become his in every way. No one else would ever have to know my shameful secret.

In abject desperation, I toyed with his offer. Not only had Bill left my heart shattered, but he'd made me face the glum realization that in all probability, I was destined to remain single for many long, lonely years. It would doubtless take an act of God for any man to accept me as his bride, knowing he would also become an instant father to six young children. I had spun quite the unrealistic dream for myself.

Verlan needed to leave immediately for Colonia LeBaron, and he convinced me to bring the kids and go along. The trip would do me good, he argued. It would give me time to think about what would be best for everyone concerned. Still in a daze and feeling totally hopeless, I agreed to go along, and also to consider returning to him. But before we were even halfway to Mexico, I realized this was not a solution I could live with. Being around Verlan again, with his fanaticisms and unrealistic dreams for a dying church, reminded me of why I'd left him in the first place. At the end of my first day back in the colony, I told him I wouldn't stay.

Immediately, the Church Priesthood called me into a court hearing, where my membership was revoked on grounds of adultery. Although the process was humiliating, I was more than ready to be officially released. I wanted no part of a people whose polygamous, self-righteous men sat in stern judgment on the wayward wife of their leader, for loving one man and giving herself to

412

that one person. It was true; I hadn't been legally married to Bill. No judge had signed a marriage certificate for us. But I'd felt more married to him than I'd ever felt with Verlan.

That night, the kids and I returned to Utah. I determined to hold my head high, pick up the ragged pieces of my life, and stop feeling sorry for myself. My children needed me. Seven months later, with my sister-in-law Bobett holding my hand, my beautiful new son was born.

My desire for a husband of my own became a reality in 1979. Dennis was from Southern California, of Christian faith, and he took a timid, scared, twenty-five year old woman with a house-full of young children and made us his own. He patiently patched my frayed heart and restored my faith in men. Between us we added one more, fine son to the family. Dennis became "Dad" to all seven of my children.

Idaho has been good for us and a wonderful place to call home! Several of my children graduated from school with honors. They have all grown into successful, caring people, and most have little ones of their own. Each one loves God and serves Him in his or her individual way. We lead an active, laughter-packed life, most of us in a small town in Southern Idaho. We frequently get together for an on-going family reunion. Although my boys are successful businessmen, they love to play. They spend much of their free time on the golf course, and all are avid sportsmen. My girls are both busily climbing corporate ladders. In fact, Melanie became Verlan's only child to earn a bachelor's degree. She went on to become a Certified Public Accountant.

As for myself, I've come to an understanding with God. I love him more than ever, and I know he loves me just as much as any man he ever created. I thank him daily for saving me, and for blessing me with my wonderful family. I also thank him for the experience I had being in Mexico. It's made me into the happy, grateful person I am today, who recognizes her blessings and who doesn't take them for granted. I've even enjoyed the strange assortment of jobs I've worked at through the years. Mostly I've enjoyed being a wife, mother, and grandmother.

For many years after leaving Mexico, I was plagued with reoccurring nightmares. I would wake up every week or so with the gut-wrenching knowledge that I'd just had another one. In these dreams, Verlan and his many wives grasped at me, argued with me, pulled at me. Ervil haunted me. My Chynoweth cousins beckoned me. But just this past year, since completing this book, the nightmares have finally, thankfully, become a thing of the past.

You will want to know what happened to the people I wrote about. First of all, of my own Ray family: My mother and father are both gone now. Dad stayed in Mexico with Maria and her children until his death in 1995. He is buried close to Colonia LeBaron. My dear mother left the colony a few years after I did. She stayed with Grandma Susie until Grandma's death. Mom passed away in 1998, and is buried as she wished, near her childhood home, in Panguitch, Utah.

Rose Ann, Jay, Fara and Mona are still in Mexico. They cling to their faith in fundamentalist Mormonism and polygamy, though the church itself has splintered several times. Each group still waits for a new "prophet" to step forward and claim "The Keys."

Verlan officiated as the president of the Church of the Firstborn until his own death from a "suspicious" auto accident in August 1981. Of his ten wives, only six remained with him until his death; Beverly, Ester, Helen and I had left him. He fathered fifty-seven children.

Irene and most of her family, along with many of Charlotte's, Lucy's, and Beverly's children, have since left Mexico and the church. Most of these are now of the Christian faith, Irene included. They are spread across the United States and live normal, fulfilling lives. Irene married Hector Spencer a few years after Verlan died. At the time of this publication, she and Hector are still in good health and fully enjoying being grandparents to Irene's remarkably large posterity.

My Chynoweth relatives remained with Ervil's Church of the Lamb of God for several years. Mark, Duane and Rena, along with Victor Chynoweth, their older brother, all became "hit men" for Ervil. They assisted in several blood atonement murders and in various other crimes.

In Ervil's immediate family, and killed by his own order, were two women. First was his pregnant, teenage daughter, Rebecca LeBaron Chynoweth. Becky, a plural wife to my cousin Victor, was rebellious and causing Ervil headaches. Her slain body was loaded into the trunk of her father's car and carted to the desert for burial. This happened in 1977. Ervil's wife, Lorna Chynoweth LeBaron, disappeared in 1982. Her body was never found, but according to the confession of one of Ervil's men, she too, was ordered killed by Ervil. Her own sons allegedly "blood atoned" her.

The most notorious murder masterminded by Ervil was that of Dr. Rulon C. Allred, a naturopathic physician and leader of a fundamentalist church in

Murray, Utah. My teenage cousin, Rena, along with a daughter of Ervil's wife, Anna Mae, walked into Dr. Allred's office and shot him in cold blood. Though tried for Allred's murder, Rena was found not guilty by lack of evidence. Later in her own published book, *The Blood Covenant*, she confessed that indeed, at the bequest of Ervil, she had committed this crime.

While attending Dr. Allred's funeral, Verlan's own life was placed in jeopardy. Ervil's main purpose for assassinating Allred was to bring Verlan out to the funeral where he could become a target. The planned attempt on his life was foiled because of the huge number of people milling about at the funeral. The Ervilites made numerous attempts on Verlan's life. Many of the Church of the Firstborn believe that Verlan's demise from a "car accident" was in actuality the result of a successful murder attempt by the Ervilites.

Ervil's wife, Vonda, was brought to justice for the murder of Dean Vest. She is still serving her sentence in Southern California.

Ervil himself was finally captured, tried and convicted for masterminding Dr. Allred's murder. He was sentenced to life, but died in the Utah State Penitentiary of a heart attack three days before Verlan's death in August 1981.

During Ervil's stay in the Penitentiary, he spent much of his time penning a lengthy epistle to his followers, which he called *The Book of New Covenants*. Shortly before his death, one of his visiting henchmen smuggled it out of the prison. Along with detailed instructions for the carrying on of his "Work," it contained a hit list which Ervil's faithful followers were commanded to fulfill. The hit list contained the names of Dan Jordan, Eddie Marston, Mark and Duane Chynoweth, and a number of other people Ervil had become disillusioned with and whom he felt needed to be "atoned."

Ervil's teenage children, many of them Lorna's, took the reins of leadership. Thus began their sacred charge: to honor their deceased father's wishes by eliminating the faithless scoundrels named on his list. As the "work" was accomplished, a bloody power struggle between Ervil's children resulted in many of their own murders. Lorna's son Aaron LeBaron became the leader for a time, but he was ultimately captured and imprisoned for the murders of the Chynoweth brothers. Mark and Duane were shot dead in Houston, Texas in 1988, for defecting from Ervil's organization. Also murdered at that time was a small daughter of Duane's. Anna Mae's son Eddie Marston was simultaneously shot for his defection, in a suburb of Dallas.

Police found the body of Robert Simons, the Utah self-styled polygamist, after an informant told them where he was buried.

Dan Jordan, Joel LeBaron's killer, was shot to death in 1987 for leaving the cult.

Naomi Zarate Chynoweth's body was never found. She is believed to be buried somewhere in the desert below Ensenada.

I don't know where Aunt Thelma is. The last I heard, she's still alive. Her children, including many of her grandchildren, were lost to the evil of Ervil LeBaron.

My uncle Bud Chynoweth defected with his two youngest wives and moved to the Yucatan, where he died several years later.

Rena Chynoweth's current whereabouts are unknown. She and her new family went into hiding after the murders of her brothers and Eddie Marston.

Grandma LeBaron died shortly after I left Mexico.

Those from my book who still live in Colonia LeBaron are:

My childhood friend, Francisca Widmar Stubbs, currently married to Lane's brother, Shawn Stubbs.

Debbie Bateman Stubbs, wife of Ritchie Stubbs.

Lane and Estela Stubbs.

Lillie, my former sisterwife, now married to my brother Jay.

Verlan's widows, Charlotte, Elizabeth, Beverly (now re-married), Ester (now re-married), and Priscilla (now re-married).

My sister Ramona and her husband, Joel, Jr.

Lillie's mother, and Joel LeBaron's widow, Jeannine.

Joel LeBaron's widows, Gaye, Magdalena, and Isabel.

My sister, RoseAnn Stubbs, and her husband, Harv.

Verlan's brother, Alma LeBaron.

Verlan's counselors, Sigfried Widmar and Ossmen Jones.

My brother Jay and four of his wives live in the jungles of Yucatan, where they have started a new colony. My sister Fara and her family, and also my sister-wife, Lucy, also reside in the new jungle colony, as does Verlan's brother, Floren LeBaron.

Colonia LeBaron and the re-built Los Molinos, still stand today.

Other books about the LeBarons include:

Verlan's own self-published book, *The LeBaron Story*. The book covers the history of the LeBaron family, detailing how and why the Church of the Firstborn of the Fullness of Times began. It covers a timeline of the church's growth and of the dissension between its prophet, Joel and its patriarch, Ervil. It culminates in Joel's murder and Ervil's insane, power-grasping trip down the path of numerous blood atonement killings. Ultimately it relates how the U.S. legal system prosecuted Ervil and several of his followers. Verlan's book was published in 1981 shortly before his death.

Prophet of Blood, by Ben Bradlee, Jr. and Dale Van Atta, published by Putnam Publishing Group in 1982, reveals the known details of the Ervil LeBaron saga, up to the time of its publication.

The Blood Covenant, by Rena Chynoweth with Dean M. Shapiro, published in 1990 by Diamond Books, picks up the story, and details Rena's involvement with Ervil LeBaron, her traumatic years as his child-bride, and her confession to the slaying, at Ervil's bequest, of rival fundamentalist leader, Dr. Rulon C. Allred. This book follows the saga to its conclusion with the arrest, conviction and imprisonment of the last of the blood atonement murderers.

The Four O'clock Murders, authored by Scott Anderson and published by Doubleday in 1993, focuses on the continued slayings by the Lambs of God, primarily, the murders of the Chynoweth men in Houston.

A CBS TV movie starring Brian Dennehy, *Prophet of Evil: The Ervil LeBaron Story*, produced by Jud Taylor, aired in 1993.

Rulon C. Allred's daughter, Dorothy Allred Solomon, is the author of two books on polygamy that touch lightly on the LeBaron saga. *In My Father's House*, published by Franklin Watts, Inc. in 1984, and *Predators, Prey and Other Kinfolk*, published in 2003 by W.W. Norton.

*Photo
Album*

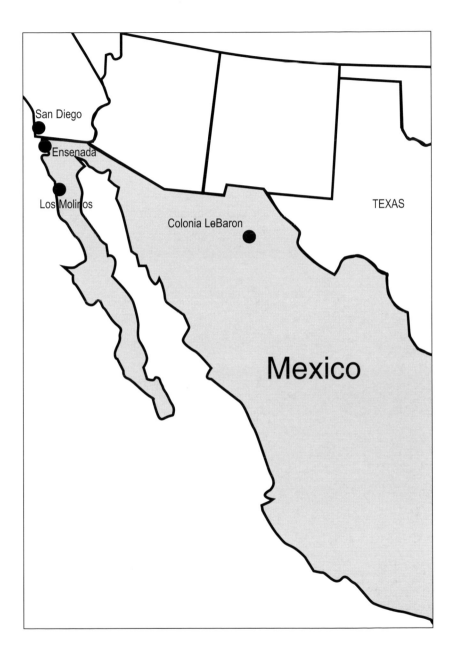

Map showing points of interest in the story. As I recall, it took about two hours to drive from San Diego to Ensenada.

Colonia LeBaron, August 2004.

Susan at about age 25.

Verlan LeBaron as President of the Twelve Apostles, taken shortly before our marriage in 1968.

Family photo taken in 1977 after our divorce. Standing: Susan, Verlan.
Second row: Jeannette, Forrest, Lance, Melanie, James.

Left: Joel LeBaron about age 45. Right: Ervil LeBaron around age 42.

Joel and Dad, with church house in the background, about 1968.

Ervil and children by his first wife, Delfina, in approximately 1960.

Some of the church priesthood leadership at Conference, about 1967. Back Row (left to right): Raul Rios, Tom Liddiard, Ervil LeBaron, Brother Hunter, Sigfried Widmar, Harv Stubbs. Front row: Howard Wakeham, Daniel Jordan, Joe Parson, Hector Spencer, Delfino Paisono.

Some of my family in 1960. Back row, standing: Ross, Jay. Front row: Fara, Mom, Dad, Ramona, Judy, Baby Randy, Susan.

My family about 1986. Back row: Perry, Dale, Ross, Jay. Second row: Rose Ann, Judy, Susan, Fara, Ramona. Front row: Mathel and Vern Ray.

Dad's second family at Colonia LeBaron. Back row: Linda, Mario, Thelma, Olivia, Ariel. Middle row: Adam, Ema, Maria, Vern. Front row: Mark, Albert.

Left: Mom in front of our house, November 1971. Right: Jay and Carmela.

Verlan's family two years before I joined the family. Back row: Lucy, Charlotte, Verlan, Irene, Beverly, Ester.

Maud "Grandma" LeBaron.

Verlan, Susan, Melanie, James and Jeannette in 1974

Top: Irene, 1968. Bottom: Lillie and Susan, about 1980.

Verlan and Lucy, April 1981, four months before his death.

About half of Verlan's boys.

431

All of Verlan's daughters on a cruise together, 2003.

Verlan's family at his funeral services, August 1981.

Top: *Cover from Joel LeBaron's funeral service.* Bottom: *A handwritten note from Joel LeBaron to Ervil challenging some of Ervil's doctrine.*

434